Augmented Realit
Developers

Build practical augmented reality applications with Unity,
ARCore, ARKit, and Vuforia

Jonathan Linowes
Krystian Babilinski

BIRMINGHAM - MUMBAI

Augmented Reality for Developers

First published: October 2017

Production reference: 1051017

Published by Packt Publishing Ltd.
Livery Place
35 Livery Street
Birmingham
B3 2PB, UK.
ISBN: 978-1-78728-643-6

www.packtpub.com

Credits

Authors
Jonathan Linowes
Krystian Babilinski

Reviewers
Micheal Lanham

Commissioning Editor
Amarabha Banerjee

Acquisition Editor
Reshma Raman

Content Development Editor
Anurag Ghogre

Technical Editor
Jash Bavishi

Copy Editor
Safis Editing

Project Coordinator
Ulhas Kambali

Proofreader
Safis Editing

Indexer
Rekha Nair

Graphics
Abhinash Sahu

Production Coordinator
Melwyn Dsa

About the Authors

Jonathan Linowes is principal at Parkerhill Reality Labs, an immersive media Indie studio. He is a veritable 3D graphics enthusiast, Unity developer, successful entrepreneur, and teacher. He has a fine arts degree from Syracuse University and a master's degree from the MIT Media Lab. He has founded several successful startups and held technical leadership positions at major corporations, including Autodesk Inc. He is the author of other books and videos by Packt, including *Unity Virtual Reality Projects* (2015) and *Cardboard VR Projects for Android* (2016).

>   *Special thanks to Lisa and our kids for augmenting my life and keeping my real-reality real.*

Krystian Babilinski is an experienced Unity developer with extensive knowledge in 3D design. He has been developing professional AR/VR applications since 2015. He led Babilin Applications, a Unity Design group that promotes open source development and engages with the the Unity community. Krystian now leads the development at Parkerhill Reality Labs, which recently published Power Solitaire VR, a multiplatform VR game.

About the Reviewer

Micheal Lanham is a solutions architect with petroWEB and currently resides in Calgary, Alberta, in Canada. In his current role, he develops integrated GIS applications with advanced ML and spatial search capabilities. He has worked as a professional and amateur game developer; he has been building desktop and mobile games for over 15 years. In 2007, Micheal was introduced to Unity 3D and has been an avid developer, consultant, and manager of multiple Unity games and graphic projects ever since.

Micheal had previously written *Augmented Reality Game Development* and *Game Audio Development with Unity 5.x*, also published by Packt in 2017.

www.PacktPub.com

For support files and downloads related to your book, please visit www.PacktPub.com.

Did you know that Packt offers eBook versions of every book published, with PDF and ePub files available? You can upgrade to the eBook version at www.PacktPub.com and as a print book customer, you are entitled to a discount on the eBook copy. Get in touch with us at service@packtpub.com for more details.

At www.PacktPub.com, you can also read a collection of free technical articles, sign up for a range of free newsletters and receive exclusive discounts and offers on Packt books and eBooks.

https://www.packtpub.com/mapt

Get the most in-demand software skills with Mapt. Mapt gives you full access to all Packt books and video courses, as well as industry-leading tools to help you plan your personal development and advance your career.

Why subscribe?

- Fully searchable across every book published by Packt
- Copy and paste, print, and bookmark content
- On demand and accessible via a web browser

Customer Feedback

Thanks for purchasing this Packt book. At Packt, quality is at the heart of our editorial process. To help us improve, please leave us an honest review on this book's Amazon page at `https://www.amazon.com/dp/1787286436`.

If you'd like to join our team of regular reviewers, you can email us at `customerreviews@packtpub.com`. We award our regular reviewers with free eBooks and videos in exchange for their valuable feedback. Help us be relentless in improving our products!

Table of Contents

Preface

Augmented Reality has been said to be the next major computing platform. This book shows you how to build exciting AR applications with Unity 3D and the leading AR toolkits for a spectrum of mobile and wearable devices.

The book opens with an introduction to augmented reality, including the markets, technologies, and development tools. You will begin with setting up your development machine for Android, iOS, and/or Windows development, and learn the basics of using Unity and the Vuforia AR platform as well as the open source ARToolKit, Microsoft Mixed Reality toolkit, Google ARCore, and Apple's ARKit!

You will then focus on building AR applications, exploring a variety of recognition targeting methods. You will go through full projects illustrating key business sectors, including marketing, education, industrial training, and gaming.

Throughout the book, we introduce major concepts in AR development, best practices in user experience, and important software design patterns that every professional and aspiring software developer should use.

It was quite a challenge to construct the book in a way that (hopefully) retains its usefulness and relevancy for years to come. There is an ever-increasing number of platforms, toolkits, and AR-capable devices emerging each year. There are solid general-purpose toolkits such as Vuforia and the open-source ARToolkit, which support both Android and iOS devices. There is the beta Microsoft HoloLens and its Mixed Reality Toolkit for Unity. We had nearly completed writing this book when Apple announced its debut into the market with ARKit, and Google ARCore, so we took the time to integrate ARKit and ARCore into our chapter projects too.

By the end of this book, you will gain the necessary knowledge to make quality content appropriate for a range of AR devices, platforms, and intended uses.

What this book covers

Chapter 1, *Augment Your World*, will introduce you to augmented reality and how it works, including a range of best practices, devices, and practical applications.

Chapter 2, *Setting Up Your System*, walks you through installing Unity, Vuforia, ARToolkit, and other software needed to develop AR projects on Windows or Mac development machines. It also includes a brief tutorial on how to use Unity.

Chapter 3, *Building Your App*, continues from Chapter 2, *Setting Up Your System*, to ensure that your system is set up to build and run AR on your preferred target devices, including Android, iOS, and Windows Mixed Reality (HoloLens).

Chapter 4, *Augmented Business Cards*, takes you through the building of an app that augments your business card. Using a drone photography company as the example, we make its business card come to life with a flying drone in AR.

Chapter 5, *AR Solar System*, demonstrates the application of AR for science and education. We build an animated model of the solar system using actual NASA scale, orbits, and texture data.

Chapter 6, *How to Change a Flat Tire*, dives into the Unity user interface (UI) development and also explores the software design pattern, while building a how-to instruction manual. The result is a regular mobile app using text, image, and video media. This is part 1 of the project.

Chapter 7, *Augmenting the Instruction Manual*, takes the mobile app developed in the previous chapter and augments it, adding 3D AR graphics as a new media type. This project demonstrates how AR need not be the central feature of an app but simply another kind of media.

Chapter 8, *Room Decoration with AR*, demonstrates the application of AR for design, architecture, and retail visualization. In this project, you can decorate your walls with framed photos, with a world-space toolbar to add, remove, resize, position, and change the pictures and frames.

Chapter 9, *Poke the Ball Game*, demonstrates the development of a fun ballgame that you can play on your real-world coffee table or desk using virtual balls and game court. You shoot the ball at the goal, aim to win, and keep score.

Each project can be built using a selection of AR toolkits and hardware devices, including Vuforia or the open source ARToolkit for Android or iOS. We also show how to build the same projects to target iOS with Apple ARKit, Google ARCore, and HoloLens with the Microsoft Mixed Reality Toolkit.

What you need for this book

Requirements will depend on what you are using for a development machine, preferred AR toolkit, and target device. We assume you are developing on a Windows 10 PC or on a macOS. You will need a device to run your AR apps, whether that be an Android smartphone or tablet, an iOS iPhone or iPad, or Microsoft HoloLens.

All the software required for this book are described and explained in Chapter 2, *Setting Up Your System*, and Chapter 3, *Building Your App*, which include web links to download what you may need. Please refer to Chapter 3, *Building Your App*, to understand the specific combinations of development OS, AR toolkit SDK, and target devices supported.

Who this book is for

The ideal target audience for this book is developers who have some experience in mobile development, either Android or iOS. Some broad web development experience would also be beneficial.

Conventions

In this book, you will find a number of text styles that distinguish between different kinds of information. Here are some examples of these styles and an explanation of their meaning.

Code words in text, database table names, folder names, filenames, file extensions, pathnames, dummy URLs, user input, and Twitter handles are shown as follows: "We can include other contexts through the use of the include directive."

A block of code is set as follows:

```
[default]
exten => s,1,Dial(Zap/1|30)
exten => s,2,Voicemail(u100)
exten => s,102,Voicemail(b100)
exten => i,1,Voicemail(s0)
```

When we wish to draw your attention to a particular part of a code block, the relevant lines or items are set in bold:

```
[default]
exten => s,1,Dial(Zap/1|30)
exten => s,2,Voicemail(u100)
exten => s,102,Voicemail(b100)
exten => i,1,Voicemail(s0)
```

Any command-line input or output is written as follows:

```
# cp /usr/src/asterisk-addons/configs/cdr_mysql.conf.sample
    /etc/asterisk/cdr_mysql.conf
```

New terms and **important words** are shown in bold. Words that you see on the screen, for example, in menus or dialog boxes, appear in the text like this: "Clicking the **Next** button moves you to the next screen."

 Warnings or important notes appear in a box like this.

 Tips and tricks appear like this.

Reader feedback

Feedback from our readers is always welcome. Let us know what you think about this book—what you liked or disliked. Reader feedback is important for us as it helps us develop titles that you will really get the most out of.

To send us general feedback, simply e-mail feedback@packtpub.com, and mention the book's title in the subject of your message.

If there is a topic that you have expertise in and you are interested in either writing or contributing to a book, see our author guide at www.packtpub.com/authors.

Customer support

Now that you are the proud owner of a Packt book, we have a number of things to help you to get the most from your purchase.

Downloading the example code

The completed projects are available on GitHub in an account dedicated to this book: https://github.com/arunitybook. We encourage our readers to submit improvements, issues, and pull requests via GitHub. As AR toolkits and platforms change frequently, we aim to keep the repositories up to date with the help of the community.

You can download the example code files for this book from your account at `http://www.packtpub.com`. If you purchased this book elsewhere, you can visit `http://www.packtpub.com/support` and register to have the files emailed directly to you. You can download the code files by following these steps:

1. Log in or register to our website using your email address and password.
2. Hover the mouse pointer on the **SUPPORT** tab at the top.
3. Click on **Code Downloads & Errata**.
4. Enter the name of the book in the **Search** box.
5. Select the book for which you're looking to download the code files.
6. Choose from the drop-down menu where you purchased this book from.
7. Click on **Code Download**.

Once the file is downloaded, please make sure that you unzip or extract the folder using the latest version of:

- WinRAR / 7-Zip for Windows
- Zipeg / iZip / UnRarX for Mac
- 7-Zip / PeaZip for Linux

The code bundle for the book is also hosted on GitHub at `https://github.com/PacktPublishing/Augmented-Reality-for-Developers`. We also have other code bundles from our rich catalog of books and videos available at `https://github.com/PacktPublishing/`. Check them out!

Downloading the color images of this book

We also provide you with a PDF file that has color images of the screenshots/diagrams used in this book. The color images will help you better understand the changes in the output. You can download this file from `https://www.packtpub.com/sites/default/files/downloads/AugmentedRealityforDevelopers_ColorImages.pdf`.

Errata

Although we have taken every care to ensure the accuracy of our content, mistakes do happen. If you find a mistake in one of our books-maybe a mistake in the text or the code-we would be grateful if you could report this to us. By doing so, you can save other readers from frustration and help us improve subsequent versions of this book. If you find any errata, please report them by visiting `http://www.packtpub.com/submit-errata`, selecting your book, clicking on the **Errata Submission Form** link, and entering the details of your errata. Once your errata are verified, your submission will be accepted and the errata will be uploaded to our website or added to any list of existing errata under the Errata section of that title. To view the previously submitted errata, go to `https://www.packtpub.com/books/content/support` and enter the name of the book in the search field. The required information will appear under the **Errata** section.

Piracy

Piracy of copyrighted material on the internet is an ongoing problem across all media. At Packt, we take the protection of our copyright and licenses very seriously. If you come across any illegal copies of our works in any form on the internet, please provide us with the location address or website name immediately so that we can pursue a remedy. Please contact us at `copyright@packtpub.com` with a link to the suspected pirated material. We appreciate your help in protecting our authors and our ability to bring you valuable content.

Questions

If you have a problem with any aspect of this book, you can contact us at `questions@packtpub.com`, and we will do our best to address the problem.

1
Augment Your World

We're at the dawn of a whole new computing platform, preceded by personal computers, the internet, and mobile device revolutions. **Augmented reality (AR)** is the future, today!

Let's help invent this future where your daily world is augmented by digital information, assistants, communication, and entertainment. As it emerges, there is a booming need for developers and other skilled makers to design and build these applications.

This book aims to educate you about the underlying AR technologies, best practices, and steps for making AR apps, using some of the most powerful and popular 3D development tools available, including Unity with Vuforia, Apple ARKit, Google ARCore, Microsoft HoloLens, and the open source ARToolkit. We will guide you through the making of quality content appropriate to a variety of AR devices and platforms and their intended uses.

In this first chapter, we introduce you to AR and talk about how it works and how it can be used. We will explore some of the key concepts and technical achievements that define the state of the art today. We then show examples of effective AR applications, and introduce the devices, platforms, and development tools that will be covered throughout this book.

Welcome to the future!

We will cover the following topics in this chapter:

- Augmented reality versus virtual reality
- How AR works
- Types of markers
- Technical issues with augmented reality
- Applications of augmented reality
- The focus of this book

What is augmented reality?

Simply put, AR is the combination of digital data and real-world human sensory input in real-time that is apparently attached (registered) to the physical space.

AR is most often associated with visual augmentation, where computer graphics are combined with actual world imagery. Using a mobile device, such as a smartphone or tablet, AR combines graphics with video. We refer to this as *handheld video see-through*. The following is an image of the *Pokémon Go* game that brought AR to the general public in 2016:

AR is not really new; it has been explored in research labs, military, and other industries since the 1990's. Software toolkits for desktop PCs have been available as both open source and propriety platforms since the late 1990's. The proliferation of smartphones and tablets has accelerated the industrial and consumer interest in AR. And certainly, opportunities for handheld AR have not yet reached their full potential, with Apple only recently entering the fray with its release of ARKit for iOS in June 2017 and Google's release of ARCore SDK for Android in August 2017.

Much of today's interest and excitement for AR is moving toward wearable eyewear AR with optical see-through tracking. These sophisticated devices, such as Microsoft HoloLens and Metavision's Meta headsets, and yet-to-be-revealed (as of this writing) devices from Magic Leap and others use depth sensors to scan and model your environment and then register computer graphics to the real-world space. The following is a depiction of a HoloLens device used in a classroom:

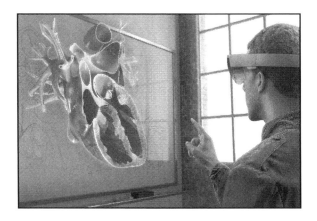

However, AR doesn't necessarily need to be visual. Consider a blind person using computer-generated auditory feedback to help guide them through natural obstacles. Even for a sighted person, a system like that which augments the perception of your real-world surroundings with auditory assistance is very useful. Inversely, consider a deaf person using an AR device who listens and visually displays the sounds and words going on around them.

Also, consider tactic displays as augmented reality for touch. A simple example is, the Apple Watch with a mapping app that will *tap* you on your wrist with haptic vibrations to remind you it's time to turn at the next intersection. Bionics is another example of this. It's not hard to consider the current advances in prosthetics for amputees as AR for the body, augmenting kinesthesia perception of body position and movement.

Then, there's this idea of augmenting spatial cognition and way finding. In 2004, researcher *Udo Wachter* built and wore a belt on his waist, lined with haptic vibrators (buzzers) attached every few inches. The buzzer facing north at any given moment would vibrate, letting him constantly know what direction he was facing. Udo's sense of direction improved dramatically over a period of weeks (https://www.wired.com/2007/04/esp/):

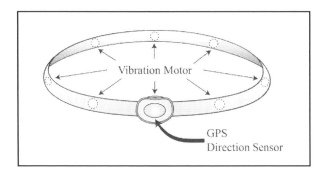

Can AR apply to smell or taste? I don't really know, but researchers have been exploring these possibilities as well.

> *What is real? How do you define "real"? If you're talking about what you can feel, what you can smell, and what you can taste and see, then "real" is simply electrical signals interpreted by your brain. ~ "Morpheus in The Matrix (1999)"*

OK, this may be getting weird and very science fictiony. (Have you read *Ready Player One* and *Snow Crash*?) But let's play along a little bit more before we get into the crux of this specific book.

According to the Merriam-Webster dictionary (`https://www.merriam-webster.com`), the word *augment* is defined as, *to make greater, more numerous, larger, or more intense*. And *reality* is defined as, *the quality or state of being real*. Take a moment to reflect on this. You will realize that *augmented reality*, at its core, is about taking what is real and making it greater, more intense, and more useful.

Apart from this literal definition, augmented reality is a technology and, more importantly, a new medium whose purpose is to improve human experiences, whether they be directed tasks, learning, communication, or entertainment. We use the word *real* a lot when talking about AR: *real-world, real-time, realism, really cool*!

As human flesh and blood, we experience the real world through our senses: eyes, ears, nose, tongue, and skin. Through the miracle of life and consciousness, our brains integrate these different types of input, giving us vivid living experiences. Using human ingenuity and invention, we have built increasingly powerful and intelligent machines (computers) that can also sense the real world, however humbly. These computers crunch data much faster and more reliably than us. AR is the technology where we allow machines to present to us a data-processed representation of the world to enhance our knowledge and understanding.

In this way, AR uses a lot of **artificial intelligence** (**AI**) technologies. One way AR crosses with AI is in the area of computer vision. Computer vision is seen as a part of AI because it utilizes techniques for pattern recognition and computer learning. AR uses computer vision to recognize targets in your field of view, whether specific coded markers, **natural feature tracking** (**NFT**), or other techniques to recognize objects or text. Once your app recognizes a target and establishes its location and orientation in the real world, it can generate computer graphics that aligns with those real-world transforms, overlaid on top of the real-world imagery.

However, augmented reality is not just the combining of computer data with human senses. There's more to it than that. In his acclaimed 1997 research report, *A Survey of augmented reality* (`http://www.cs.unc.edu/~azuma/ARpresence.pdf`), `Ronald Azuma proposed AR meet the following characteristics:`

- Combines real and virtual
- Interactive in real time
- Registered in 3D

AR is experienced in real time, not pre-recorded. Cinematic special effects, for example, that combine real action with computer graphics do not count as AR.

Also, the computer-generated display must be registered to the real 3D world. 2D overlays do not count as AR. By this definition, various head-up displays, such as in Iron Man or even Google Glass, are not AR. In AR, the app is aware of its 3D surroundings and graphics are registered to that space. From the user's point of view, AR graphics could actually be real objects physically sharing the space around them.

Throughout this book, we will emphasize these three characteristics of AR. Later in this chapter, we will explore the technologies that enable this fantastic combination of real and virtual, real-time interactions, and registration in 3D.

As wonderful as this AR future may seem, before moving on, it would be remiss not to highlight the alternative possible dystopian future of augmented reality! If you haven't seen it yet, we strongly recommend watching the *Hyper-Reality* video produced by artist Keiichi Matsuda (`https://vimeo.com/166807261`). This depiction of an incredible, frightening, yet very possible potential future infected with AR, as the artist explains, *presents a provocative and kaleidoscopic new vision of the future, where physical and virtual realities have merged, and the city is saturated in media*. But let's not worry about that right now. A screenshot of the video is as follows:

Augmented reality versus virtual reality

Virtual reality (VR) is a sister technology of AR. As described, AR augments your current experience in the real world by adding digital data to it. In contrast, VR magically, yet convincingly, transports you to a different (computer-generated) world. VR is intended to be a totally immersive experience in which you are no longer in the current environment. The sense of *presence* and *immersion* are critical for VR's success.

AR does not carry that burden of creating an entire world. For AR, it is sufficient for computer-generated graphics to be added to your existing world space. Although, as we'll see, that is not an easy accomplishment either and in some ways is much more difficult than VR. They have much in common, but AR and VR have contrasting technical challenges, market opportunities, and useful applications.

 Although financial market projections change from month to month, analysts consistently agree that the combined VR/AR market will be huge, as much as $120 billion by 2021 (`http://www.digi-capital.com/news/2017/01/after-mixed-year-mobile-ar-to-drive-108-billion-vrar-market-by-2021`) with AR representing over 75 percent of that. This is in no way a rebuff of VR; its market will continue to be very big and growing, but it is projected to be dwarfed by AR.

Since VR is so immersive, its applications are inherently limited. As a user, the decision to put on a VR headset and enter into a VR experience is, well, a commitment. Seriously! You are deciding to *move yourself* from where you are now and to a different place.

AR, however, brings virtual stuff *to you*. You physically stay where you are and augment that reality. This is a safer, less engaging, and more subtle transaction. It carries a lower barrier for market adoption and user acceptance.

VR headsets visually block off the real world. This is very intentional. No external light should seep into the view. In VR, everything you see is designed and produced by the application developer to create the VR experience. The technology design and development implications of this requirement are immense. A fundamental problem with VR is motion to photon latency. When you move your head, the VR image must update quickly, within 11 milliseconds for 90 frames per second, or you risk experiencing motion sickness. There are multiple theories why this happens (see
`https://en.wikipedia.org/wiki/Virtual_reality_sickness`).

In AR, latency is much less of a problem because most of the visual field is the real world, either a video or optical see-through. You're less likely to experience vertigo when most of what you see is real world. Generally, there's a lot less graphics to render and less physics to calculate in each AR frame.

VR also imposes huge demands on your device's CPU and GPU processors to generate the 3D view for both left and right eyes. VR generates graphics for the entire scene as well as physics, animations, audio, and other processing requirements. Not as much rendering power is required by AR.

On the other hand, AR has an extra burden not borne by VR. AR must register its graphics with the real world. This can be quite complicated, computationally. When based on video processing, AR must engage image processing pattern recognition in real time to find and follow the target markers. More complex devices use depth sensors to build and track a scanned model of your physical space in real time (**Simultaneous Localization and Mapping**, or **SLAM**). As we'll see, there are a number of ways AR applications manage this complexity, using simple target shapes or clever image recognition and matching algorithms with predefined natural images. Should this be: Custom depth sensing hardware and semiconductors are used to calculate a 3D mesh of the user's environment in real time, along with geolocation sensors. This, in turn, is used to register the position and orientation computer graphics superimposed on the real-world visuals.

VR headsets ordinarily include headphones that, like the visual display, preferably block outside sounds in the real world so you can be fully immersed in the virtual one using spatial audio. In contrast, AR headsets provide open-back headphones or small speakers (instead of headphones) that allow the mix of real-world sounds with the spatial audio coming from the virtual scene.

Because of these inherent differences between AR and VR, the applications of these technologies can be quite different. In our opinion, a lot of applications presently being explored for VR will eventually find their home in AR instead. Even in cases where it's ambiguous whether the application could either augment the real world versus transport the user to a virtual space, the advantage of AR not isolating you from the real world will be key to the acceptance of these applications. Gaming will be prevalent with both AR and VR, albeit the games will be different. Cinematic storytelling and experiences that require immersive presence will continue to thrive in VR. But all other applications of 3D computer simulations may find their home in the AR market.

For developers, a key difference between VR and AR, especially when considering head-mounted wearable devices, is that VR is presently available in the form of consumer devices, such as Oculus Rift, HTC Vive, PlayStation VR, and Google Daydream, with millions of devices already in consumers' hands. Wearable AR devices are still in Beta release and quite expensive. That makes VR business opportunities more realistic and measurable. As a result, AR is largely confined to handheld (phone or tablet-based) apps for consumers, or if you delve into wearables, it's an internal corporate project, experimental project, or speculative product R&D.

How AR works

We've discussed what augmented reality is, but how does it work? As we said earlier, AR requires that we combine the real environment with a computer-generated virtual environment. The graphics are registered to the real 3D world. And, this must be done in real time.

There are a number of ways to accomplish this. In this book, we will consider just two. The first is the most common and accessible method: using a handheld mobile device such as a smartphone or tablet. Its camera captures the environment, and the computer graphics are rendered on the device's screen.

A second technique, using wearable AR smartglasses, is just emerging in commercial devices, such as Microsoft HoloLens and Metavision's Meta 2. This is an optical see-through of the real world, with computer graphics shown on a wearable near-eye display.

Handheld mobile AR

Using a handheld mobile device, such as a smartphone or tablet, augmented reality uses the device's camera to capture the video of the real world and combine it with virtual objects.

As illustrated in the following image, running an AR app on a mobile device, you simply point its camera to a target in the real world and the app will recognize the target and render a 3D computer graphic registered to the target's position and orientation. This is *handheld mobile video see-through* augmented reality:

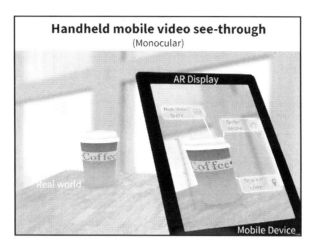

We use the words *handheld* and *mobile* because we're using a handheld mobile device. We use *video see-through* because we're using the device's camera to capture reality, which will be combined with computer graphics. The AR video image is displayed on the device's flat screen.

Mobile devices have features important for AR, including the following:

- Untethered and battery-powered
- Flat panel graphic display touchscreen input
- Rear-facing camera
- CPU (main processor), GPU (graphics processor), and memory
- Motion sensors, namely accelerometer for detecting linear motion and gyroscope for rotational motion
- GPS and/or other position sensors for geolocation and wireless and/or Wi-Fi data connection to the internet

Let's chat about each of these. First of all, mobile devices are... mobile.... Yeah, I know you get that. No wires. But what this really means is that like you, mobile devices are free to roam the real world. They are not tethered to a PC or other console. This is natural for AR because AR experiences take place in the real world, while moving around in the real world.

Mobile devices sport a flat panel color graphic display with excellent resolution and pixel density sufficient for handheld viewing distances. And, of course, the killer feature that helped catapult the iPhone revolution is the multitouch input sensor on the display that is used for interacting with the displayed images with your fingers.

A rear-facing camera is used to capture video from the real world and display it in real time on the screen. This video data is digital, so your AR app can modify it and combine virtual graphics in real time as well. This is a monocular image, captured from a single camera and thus a single viewpoint. Correspondingly, the computer graphics use a single viewpoint to render the virtual objects that go with it.

Today's mobile devices are quite powerful computers, including CPU (main processor) and GPU (graphics processor), both of which are critical for AR to recognize targets in the video, process sensor, and user input, and render the combined video on the screen. We continue to see these requirements and push hardware manufacturers to try ever harder to deliver higher performance.

Built-in sensors that measure motion, orientation, and other conditions are also key to the success of mobile AR. An accelerometer is used for detecting linear motion along three axes and a gyroscope for detecting rotational motion around the three axes. Using real-time data from the sensors, the software can estimate the device's position and orientation in real 3D space at any given time. This data is used to determine the specific view the device's camera is capturing and uses this 3D transformation to register the computer-generated graphics in 3D space as well.

In addition, GPS sensor can be used for applications that need to map where they are on the globe, for example, the use of AR to annotate a street view or mountain range or find a rogue Pokémon.

Last but not least, mobile devices are enabled with wireless communication and/or Wi-Fi connections to the internet. Many AR apps require an internet connection, especially when a database of recognition targets or metadata needs to be accessed online.

Optical eyewear AR

In contrast to handheld mobiles, AR devices worn like eyeglasses or futuristic visors, such as Microsoft HoloLens and Metavision Meta, may be referred to as *optical see-through eyewear* augmented reality devices, or simply, *smartglasses*. As illustrated in the following image, they do not use video to capture and render the real world. Instead, you look directly through the visor and the computer graphics are optically merged with the scene:

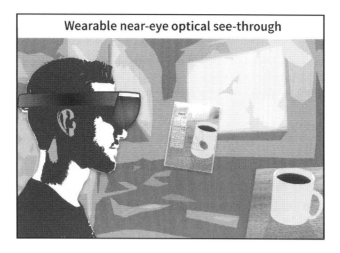

Wearable near-eye optical see-through

The display technologies used to implement optical see-through AR vary from vendor to vendor, but the principles are similar. The glass that you look through while wearing the device is not a basic lens material that might be prescribed by your optometrist. It uses a *combiner* lens much like a beam splitter, with an angled surface that redirects a projected image coming from the side toward your eye.

An optical see-through display will mix the light from the real world with the virtual objects. Thus, brighter graphics are more visible and effective; darker areas may get lost. Black pixels are transparent. For similar reasons, these devices do not work great in brightly lit environments. You don't need a very dark room but dim lighting is more effective.

We can refer to these displays as *binocular*. You look through the visor with both eyes. Like VR headsets, there will be two separate views generated, one for each eye to account for parallax and enhance the perception of 3D. In real life, each eye sees a slightly different view in front, offset by the inter-pupillary distance between your eyes. The augmented computer graphics must also be drawn separately for each eye with similar offset viewpoints.

One such device is Microsoft HoloLens, a standalone mobile unit; Metavision Meta 2 can be tethered to a PC using its processing resources. Wearable AR headsets are packed with hardware, yet they must be in a form factor that is lightweight and ergonomic so they can be comfortably worn as you move around. The headsets typically include the following:

- Lens optics, with a specific field of view
- Forward-facing camera
- Depth sensors for positional tracking and hand recognition

- Accelerometer and gyroscope for linear and rotational motion detection and near-ear audio speakers
- Microphone

Furthermore, as a standalone device, you could say that HoloLens is like wearing a laptop wrapped around your head--hopefully, not for the weight but the processing capacity! It runs Windows 10 and must handle all the spatial and graphics processing itself. To assist, Microsoft developed a custom chip called **holographic processing unit** (**HPU**) to complement the CPU and GPU.

Instead of headphones, wearable AR headsets often include near-ear speakers that don't block out environmental sounds. While handheld AR could also emit audio, it would come from the phone's speaker or the headphones you may have inserted into your ears. In either case, the audio would not be registered with the graphics. With wearable near-eye visual augmentation, it's safe to assume that your ears are close to your eyes. This enables the use of spatial audio for more convincing and immersive AR experiences.

Target-based AR

The following image illustrates a more traditional target-based AR. The device camera captures a frame of video. The software analyzes the frame looking for a familiar target, such as a pre-programmed marker, using a technique called **photogrammetry**. As part of target detection, its deformation (for example, size and skew) is analyzed to determine its distance, position, and orientation relative to the camera in a three-dimensional space.

From that, the camera pose (position and orientation) in 3D space is determined. These values are then used in the computer graphics calculations to render virtual objects. Finally, the rendered graphics are merged with the video frame and displayed to the user:

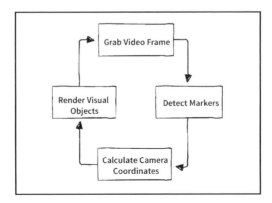

iOS and Android phones typically have a refresh rate of 60Hz. This means the image on your screen is updated 60 times a second, or 1.67 milliseconds per frame. A lot of work goes into this quick update. Also, much effort has been invested in optimizing the software to minimize any wasted calculations, eliminate redundancy, and other tricks that improve performance without negatively impacting user experience. For example, once a target has been recognized, the software will try to simply track and follow as it appears to move from one frame to the next rather than re-recognizing the target from scratch each time.

To interact with virtual objects on your mobile screen, the input processing required is a lot like any mobile app or game. As illustrated in the following image, the app detects a touch event on the screen. Then, it determines which object you intended to tap by mathematically casting a ray from the screen's XY position into 3D space, using the current camera pose. If the ray intersects a detectable object, the app may respond to the tap (for example, move or modify the geometry). The next time the frame is updated, these changes will be rendered on the screen:

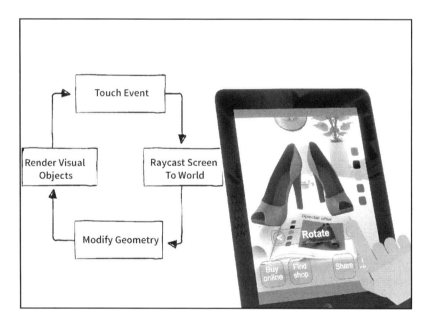

A distinguishing characteristic of handheld mobile AR is that you experience it from an arm's length viewpoint. Holding the device out in front of you, you look through its screen like a portal to the augmented real world. The field of view is defined by the size of the device screen and how close you're holding it to your face. And it's not entirely a hands-free experience because unless you're using a tripod or something to hold the device, you're using one or two hands to hold the device at all times.

Snapchat's popular augmented reality selfies go even further. Using the phone's front-facing camera, the app analyzes your face using complex AI pattern matching algorithms to identify significant points, or nodes, that correspond to the features of your face--eyes, nose, lips, chin, and so on. It then constructs a 3D mesh, like a mask of your face. Using that, it can apply alternative graphics that match up with your facial features and even morph and distort your actual face for play and entertainment. See this video for a detailed explanation from Snapchat's Vox engineers: `https://www.youtube.com/watch?v=Pc2aJxnmzh0`. The ability to do all of this in real time is remarkably fun and serious business:

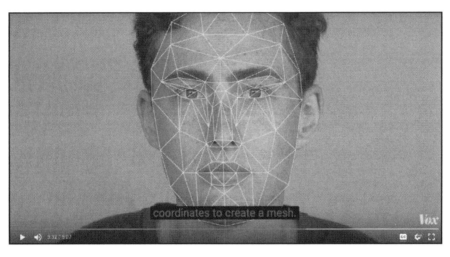

Perhaps, by the time you are reading this book, there will be mobile devices with built-in depth sensors, including Google Project Tango and Intel RealSense technologies, capable of scanning the environment and building a 3D spatial map mesh that could be used for more advanced tracking and interactions. We will explain these capabilities in the next topic and explore them in this book in the context of wearable AR headsets, but they may apply to new mobile devices too.

3D spatial mapping

Handheld mobile AR described in the previous topic is mostly about augmenting 2D video with regard to the phone camera's location in 3D space. Optical wearable AR devices are completely about 3D data. Yes, like mobile AR, wearable AR devices can do target-based tracking using its built-in camera. But wait, there's more, much more!

These devices include depth sensors that scan your environment and construct a *spatial map* (3D mesh) of your environment. With this, you can register objects to specific surfaces without the need for special markers or a database of target images for tracking.

A depth sensor measures the distance of solid surfaces from you, using an **infrared** (**IR**) camera and projector. It projects IR dots into the environment (not visible to the naked eye) in a pattern that is then read by its IR camera and analyzed by the software (and/or hardware). On nearer objects, the dot pattern spread is different than further ones; depth is calculated using this displacement. Analysis is not performed on just a single snapshot but across multiple frames over time to provide more accuracy, so the spatial model can be continuously refined and updated.

A visible light camera may also be used in conjunction with the depth sensor data to further improve the spatial map. Using photogrammetry techniques, visible features in the scene are identified as a set of points (nodes) and tracked across multiple video frames. The 3D position of each node is calculated using triangulation.

From this, we get a good 3D mesh representation of the space, including the ability to discern separate objects that may occlude (be in front of) other objects. Other sensors locate the user's actual head in the real world, providing the user's own position and view of the scene. This technique is called SLAM. Originally developed for robotics applications, the 2002 seminal paper on this topic by Andrew Davison, University of Oxford, can be found at https://www.doc.ic.ac.uk/~ajd/Publications/davison_cml2002.pdf.

A cool thing about present day implementations of SLAP is how the data is continuously updated in response to real time sensor readings in your device.

> *"As the HoloLens gathers new data about the environment, and as changes to the environment occur, spatial surfaces will appear, disappear and change."*
> (`https://developer.microsoft.com/en-us/windows/holographic/spatial_mapping`)

The following illustration shows what occurs during each update frame. The device uses current readings from its sensors to maintain the spatial map and calculate the virtual camera pose. This camera transformation is then used to render views of the virtual objects registered to the mesh. The scene is rendered twice, for the left and right eye views. The computer graphics are displayed on the head-mounted visor glass and will be visible to the user as if it were really there--virtual objects sharing space with real world physical objects:

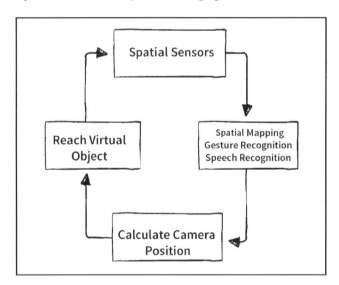

That said, spatial mapping is not limited to devices with depth sensing cameras. Using clever photogrammetry techniques, much can be accomplished in software alone. The Apple iOS ARKit, for example, uses just the video camera of the mobile device, processing each frame together with its various positional and motion sensors to fuse the data into a 3D point cloud representation of the environment. Google ARCore works similarly. The Vuforia SDK has a similar tool, albeit more limited, called Smart Terrain.

Developing AR with spatial mapping

Spatial mapping is the representation of all of the information the app has from its sensors about the real world. It is used to render virtual AR world objects. Specifically, spatial mapping is used to do the following:

- Help virtual objects or characters navigate around the room
- Have virtual objects occlude a real object or be occluded by a real object to interact with something, such as bouncing off the floor
- Place a virtual object onto a real object
- Show the user a visualization of the room they are in

In video game development, a *level designer's* job is to create the fantasy world stage, including terrains, buildings, passageways, obstacles, and so on. The Unity game development platform has great tools to constrain the navigation of objects and characters within the physical constraints of the level. Game developers, for example, add simplified geometry, or *navmesh*, derived from a detailed level design; it is used to constrain the movement of characters within a scene. In many ways, the AR spatial map acts like a navmesh for your virtual AR objects.

A spatial map, while just a mesh, is 3D and does represent the surfaces of solid objects, not just walls and floors but furniture. When your virtual object moves behind a real object, the map can be used to occlude virtual objects with real-world objects when it's rendered on the display. Normally, occlusion is not possible without a spatial map.

When a spatial map has collider properties, it can be used to interact with virtual objects, letting them bump into or bounce off real-world surfaces.

Lastly, a spatial map could be used to transform physical objects directly. For example, since we know where the walls are, we can paint them a different color in AR.

This can get pretty complicated. A spatial map is just a triangular mesh. How can your application code determine physical objects from that? It's difficult but not an unsolvable problem. In fact, the HoloLens toolkit, for example, includes a *spatialUnderstanding* module that analyzes the spatial map and does higher level identification, such as identification of floor, ceiling, and walls, using techniques such as ray casting, topology queries, and shape queries.

Spatial mapping can encompass a whole lot of data that could overwhelm the processing resources of your device and deliver an underwhelming user experience. HoloLens, for example, mitigates this by letting you subdivide your physical space into what they call **spatial surface observers**, which in turn contain a set of spatial surfaces. An observer is a bounding volume that defines a region of space with mapping data as one or more surfaces. A surface is a triangle 3D mesh in real-world 3D space. Organizing and partitioning space reduces the dataset needed to be tracked, analyzed, and rendered for a given interaction.

For more information on spatial mapping with HoloLens and Unity, refer to `https://developer.microsoft.com/en-us/windows/mixed-reality/spatial_mapping` and `https://developer.microsoft.com/en-us/windows/mixed-reality/spatial_mapping_in_unity`.

Input for wearable AR

Ordinarily AR eyewear devices neither use a game controller or clicker nor positionally tracked hand controllers. Instead, you use your hands. Hand gesture recognition is another challenging AI problem for computer vision and image processing.

In conjunction with tracking, where the user is looking (gaze), gestures are used to trigger events such as select, grab, and move. Assuming the device does not support eye tracking (moving your eyes without moving your head), the gaze reticle is normally at the center of your gaze. You must move your head to point to the object of interest that you want to interact with:

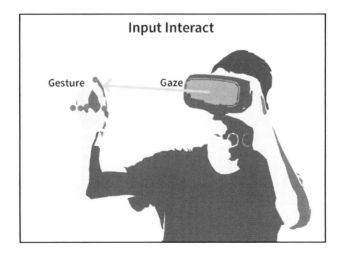

More advanced interactions could be enabled with true hand tracking, where the user's gaze is not necessarily used to identify the object to interact; however, you can reach out and *touch* the virtual objects and use your fingers to push, grab, or move elements in the scene. Voice command input is being increasingly used in conjunction with true hand tracking, instead of hand gestures.

Other AR display techniques

In addition to handheld video see-through and wearable optical see-through, there are other AR display techniques as well.

A monocular headset shows a single image in one eye, allowing the other eye to view the real world unaugmented. It tends to be lightweight and used more as a **heads-up display (HUD)**, as if information were projected on the front of a helmet rather than registered to the 3D world. An example of this is Google Glass. While the technology can be useful in some applications, we are not considering it in this book.

Wearable *video see-through* uses a **head-mounted display (HMD)** with a camera and combines real-world video with virtual graphics on its near-eye display. This may be possible on VR headsets such as HTC Vive and Samsung GearVR, with camera passthrough enabled, but it has a few problems. First, these VR devices do not have depth sensors to scan the environment, preventing the registration of graphics with the real 3D world.

The camera on such devices is monoscopic, yet the VR display is stereoscopic. Both the eyes see the same image, or what is called *bi-ocular*. This will cause issues in correctly rendering the graphics and registering to the real world.

Another problem is that the device's camera is offset from your actual eyes in front by an inch or more. The viewpoint of the camera is not the same as your eyes; the graphics would need to be registered accordingly.

For these reasons, wearable video see-through AR presently can look pretty weird, feel uncomfortable, and generally not work very well. But if you have one of these devices, feel free to try the projects in this book on it and see how it works. Also, we can expect new devices to come on the market soon which will position themselves as combined VR + AR and hopefully solve these issues, perhaps with dual stereo cameras, optical correction, or other solutions.

Types of AR targets

As we've seen and discussed, the essence of AR is that your device recognizes objects in the real world and renders the computer graphics registered to the same 3D space, providing the illusion that the virtual objects are in the same physical space with you.

Since augmented reality was first invented decades ago, the types of targets the software can recognize has progressed from very simple markers for images and natural feature tracking to full spatial map meshes. There are many AR development toolkits available; some of them are more capable than others of supporting a range of targets.

The following is a survey of various target types. We will go into more detail in later chapters, as we use different targets in different projects.

Marker

The most basic target is a simple marker with a wide border. The advantage of marker targets is they're readily recognized by the software with very little processing overhead and minimize the risk of the app not working, for example, due to inconsistent ambient lighting or other environmental conditions. The following is the *Hiro* marker used in example projects in ARToolkit:

Coded Markers

Taking simple markers to the next level, areas within the border can be reserved for 2D barcode patterns. This way, a single family of markers can be reused to pop up many different virtual objects by changing the encoded pattern. For example, a children's book may have an AR pop up on each page, using the same marker shape, but the bar code directs the app to show only the objects relevant to that page in the book.

The following is a set of very simple coded markers from ARToolkit:

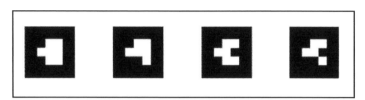

Vuforia includes a powerful marker system called VuMark that makes it very easy to create branded markers, as illustrated in the following image. As you can see, while the marker styles vary for specific marketing purposes, they share common characteristics, including a reserved area within an outer border for the 2D code:

Images

The ability to recognize and track arbitrary images is a tremendous boost to AR applications as it avoids the requirement of creating and distributing custom markers paired with specific apps. Image tracking falls into the category of **natural feature tracking** (**NFT**). There are characteristics that make a good target image, including having a well-defined border (preferably eight percent of the image width), irregular asymmetrical patterns, and good contrast. When an image is incorporated in your AR app, it's first analyzed and a feature map (2D node mesh) is stored and used to match real-world image captures, say, in frames of video from your phone.

Multi-targets

It is worth noting that apps may be set up to see not just one marker in view but multiple markers. With multitargets, you can have virtual objects pop up for each marker in the scene simultaneously.

Similarly, markers can be printed and folded or pasted on geometric objects, such as product labels or toys. The following is an example cereal box target:

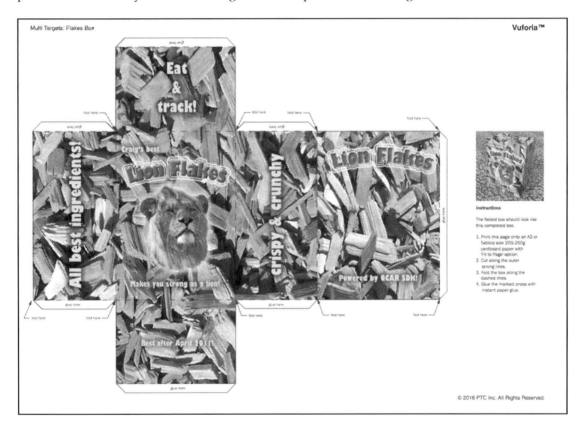

Text recognition

If a marker can include a 2D bar code, then why not just read text? Some AR SDKs allow you to configure your app (train) to read text in specified fonts. Vuforia goes further with a word list library and the ability to add your own words.

Simple shapes

Your AR app can be configured to recognize basic shapes such as a cuboid or cylinder with specific relative dimensions. Its not just the shape but its measurements that may distinguish one target from another: Rubik's Cube versus a shoe box, for example. A cuboid may have width, height, and length. A cylinder may have a length and different top and bottom diameters (for example, a cone). In Vuforia's implementation of basic shapes, the texture patterns on the shaped object are not considered, just anything with a similar shape will match. But when you point your app to a real-world object with that shape, it should have enough textured surface for good edge detection; a solid white cube would not be easily recognized.

Object recognition

The ability to recognize and track complex 3D objects is similar but goes beyond 2D image recognition. While planar images are appropriate for flat surfaces, books or simple product packaging, you may need object recognition for toys or consumer products *without their packaging*. Vuforia, for example, offers Vuforia Object Scanner to create object data files that can be used in your app for targets. The following is an example of a toy car being scanned by Vuforia Object Scanner:

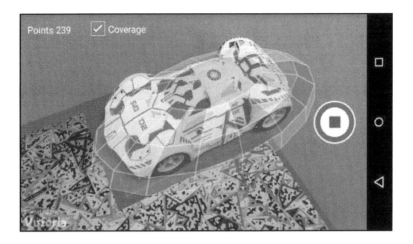

Spatial maps

Earlier, we introduced spatial maps and dynamic spatial location via SLAM. SDKs that support spatial maps may implement their own solutions and/or expose access to a device's own support. For example, the HoloLens SDK Unity package supports its native spatial maps, of course. Vuforia's spatial maps (called *Smart Terrain*) does not use depth sensing like HoloLens; rather, it uses visible light camera to construct the environment mesh using photogrammetry. Apple ARKit and Google ARCore also map your environment using the camera video fused with other sensor data.

Geolocation

A bit of an outlier, but worth mentioning, AR apps can also use just the device's GPS sensor to identify its location in the environment and use that information to annotate what is in view. I use the word *annotate* because GPS tracking is not as accurate as any of the techniques we have mentioned, so it wouldn't work for close-up views of objects. But it can work just fine, say, standing atop a mountain and holding your phone up to see the names of other peaks within the view or walking down a street to look up Yelp! reviews of restaurants within range. You can even use it for locating and capturing Pokémon.

As an introduction to developing for augmented reality, this book focuses on all kinds of target tracking. This way, each of our projects can be built using either handheld or eyewear AR devices. Where a project's user experience can be enhanced on a more advanced device or technique, we'll try to include suggestions and instructions for supporting that too.

Technical issues in relation to augmented reality

In this section, we do a brief survey of some of the tricky issues that AR researchers have struggled with in the past, and present and are likely to struggle with in the future.

Field of view

In a theatre, on a computer screen, in a handheld mobile device, or in an AR headset, the angle from one edge of the view area to the opposite is commonly referred to as the angle of view or **field of view** (FOV). For example, a typical movie theatre screen is about 54 degrees; an IMAX theatre screen is 70 degrees. The human eye has about 160 degrees horizontal (monocular) or 200 degrees combined binocular FOV. The HTC Vive VR headset has about 100 degrees. Note that sometimes FOV is reported as separate horizontal and vertical; other times, it's a (better-sounding) diagonal measure.

Although not commonly discussed this way, when you hold a mobile device in front of you, it does have a field of view that is measured by the size of the screen and how far away you're holding it. So, an arm's length, about 18 inches away, is just 10 degrees or so. This is why you often see people preferring a large screen tablet for mobile AR rather than a phone.

When it comes to wearables, the expectations are greater. The Microsoft HoloLens FOV is only about 35 degrees, equivalent to holding your smartphone about 6 to 8 inches in front of your face or using a 15-inch computer monitor on your desk. Fortunately, despite the limitation, users report that you get used to it and learn to move your head instead of your eyes to discover and follow objects of interest in AR. Metavision Meta 2 does better; it's FOV is 90 degrees (diagonal).

The following image illustrates the effect of FOV when you wear a HoloLens device (image by Adam Dachis/NextReality):

Visual perception

The rendered image needs to satisfy the expectations of our visual perceptions to the extent that the goal of AR is to display virtual objects so they could realistically seem to reside in our physical environment. If the AR is just an overlay or annotation of the real world, then this may not be as important.

When rendering objects for 3D view, the views from the left and right eyes are offset slightly, based on your interpupillary distance (distance between the eyes), called parallax. This is not a problem and is handled in every VR and wearable AR device, but it's still worth mentioning.

Virtual AR objects coexisting in the real world that are in front of real objects should hide the objects behind them. That's easy; just draw the object on top. The opposite is not as simple. When the virtual object is behind a real-world one, say your virtual pet runs under a table or behind a sofa, it should be partially or completely hidden. This requires a spatial map of the environment; its mesh is used to occlude the computer graphics when rendering the scene.

An even more difficult problem comes up with photorealistic rendering of virtual objects. Ideally, you'd want the lighting on the object to match the lighting in the room itself. Suppose in the real world, the only light is a lamp in the corner of the room, but your AR object is lit from the opposite side. That would be conspicuously inconsistent and artificial. Apple ARKit and Google ARCore address this issue by capturing the ambient light color, intensity, and direction and then adjusting the virtual scene lighting accordingly, even offering the ability to calculate shadows from your virtual objects. This provides a more realistic render of your objects in the real world.

Focus

Photographers have known about depth of field since the beginning of photography. When a lens is focused on an object, things more in the foreground or further away may be out of focus; that range is called the **depth of field**. The iris in your eye is a lens too, and it adjusts to focus on near versus far objects, called accommodation. We can actually feel our iris changing its focus, and this oculomotor cue of stretching and relaxing also contributes to our depth perception.

However, using near-eye displays (in VR as well as AR), all the rendered objects are in focus, regardless of their distance perceived via parallax. Furthermore, the angle between your eyes changes when you're focused on something close up versus something further away, called **vergence**. So, we get mixed signals, focus (*accommodation*) on one distance and vergence at another. This results in what is called an **accommodation-vergence conflict**. This disparity can become tiring, at best, and inhibits the illusion of realism. This is a problem with both wearable AR and VR devices.

Potential solutions may emerge using eye tracking to adjust the rendered image according to your vergence. There is also the promise of advanced light-field technology that more accurately merges computer-generated graphics with real-world light patterns (see Magic Leap at `https://www.magicleap.com`).

Resolution and refresh rate

No discussion of AR displays would be complete without mentioning pixels, those tiny colored dots that make up the image on the display screen. The more, the better. It is measured in terms of resolution. What's more important, perhaps, is *pixel density*, pixels per inch, as well as the *color depth*. Higher density displays produce a crisper image. Greater color depth, such as HDR displays (high dynamic range), provides more bits per pixel so there could be a more natural and linear range of brightness.

We also talk about motion-to-photon latency. This is the time it takes for the AR device to detect changes in the location and orientation and have that represented on the screen. A lagged latency is not just unrealistic and feels sloppy, it can result in motion sickness, especially in wearable displays. Depending on the device, the screen may refresh in cycles of 60 frames per second or more. All the sensor readings, analysis, geometry, and graphics rendering must be performed with that tiny timeframe or the user will experience latency.

Ergonomics

Finally, the look and feel and comfort of devices is critical to their market acceptance and usefulness in practical situations. Handheld devices continue to get thinner and more lightweight. That's awesome, provided they continue to be important for AR.

Most of us agree that eventually all of this will move into wearable eyewear. Unless you're in an industrial hardhat environment, we all look forward to the day when AR eyewear becomes as lightweight and comfortable as a pair of sunglasses. Then, we'll wish for AR contact lenses (then, retinal implants?).

In 2009, Rolf Hainich described the ultimate display in his book *The End of Hardware: Augmented Reality and Beyond* as follows:

> *a nonintrusive, comfortable, high-resolution, wide-FOV, near-eye display with high dynamic range and perfect tracking.*

Applications of augmented reality

Why augmented reality? In today's world, we are flooded with vast amounts of information through 24/7 media, internet connectivity, and mobile devices. The problem is not whether we have enough information, but that we have too much. The challenge is how to filter, process, and use valuable information and ignore redundant, irrelevant, and incorrect information. This is explained by Schmalsteig and Hollerer in their book, *Augmented Reality, Principles, and Practice* (Addison Wesley, 2016):

> *"augmented reality holds the promise of creating direct, automatic, and actionable links between the physical world and electronic information. It provides a simple and immediate user interface to an electronically enhanced physical world. The immense potential of augmented reality as a paradigm-shifting user interface metaphor becomes apparent when we review the most recent few milestones in human-computer interaction: the emergence of the World Wide Web, the social web, and the mobile device revolution." - Augmented Reality, Principles and Practice, Schmalstieg & Mollerer*

What kinds of applications can benefit from this? Well, just about every human endeavor that presently uses digital information of any kind. Here are a few examples that we will further illustrate as actual projects throughout this book.

Business marketing

AR markers printed on product packaging with a companion app could provide additional details about the product, testimonials, or marketing media to augment the product. AR business cards are a way to show off how cool you are. See `Chapter 4`, *Augmented Business Cards*, for more details. Just as you may see QR codes in advertising today to take you to a website, AR markers in advertising may be a thing in the near future.

Education

For years, AR has been used in children's books to bring stories to life. Older students studying more serious subjects may find more augmentation of their educational textbooks and media resources, bringing more immersive and interactive content to the curriculum. In `Chapter 5`, *AR Solar System*, we will build a sample educational project, a simulation of our Solar System.

Industrial training

AR-based how-to-fix-it apps have been demonstrated to improve technical training and reduce mistakes. How many reams of paper training manuals have already been digitized? But seriously, just converting them into PDFs or web pages is only a little bit better.

Instructional videos go a bit further. With AR, we can have the benefits of more interactive 3D graphics, personal coaching, and hands-on tutorials. In `Chapter 7`, *Augmenting the Instruction Manual*, we will illustrate techniques for building an industrial training in AR, showing you how to change a tire on your car.

Retail

Have you seen the video of a woman standing in front of an smart mirror trying on clothes, interacting with the system using hand gestures? For example, see Oak Labs at `http://www.oaklabs.is/`. The Wayfair online furniture store uses AR to help you visualize new furniture in your home before you purchase (`https://www.wayfair.com`). In `Chapter 8`, *Room Decoration with AR*, we will build a little app that will let you decorate your room with framed photos.

Gaming

Can you say Pokémon? Of course, there's more to AR gaming than that, but let's give credit where it's due. Ninantic did bring AR in to popular culture with it. We won't describe all the possibilities of AR-based gaming. But, in `Chapter 9`, *Poke The Ball Game*, we will build a little AR ball game.

Others

In engineering and other design disciplines, 3D artists and CAD engineers still build stuff in a 3D on 2D screen with a mouse. When is that going to change? It's time to get your hands into the virtual world and make things happen.

Music, cinema, storytelling, journalism, and so on will all benefit from the popular adoption of augmented reality. The possibilities are as infinite as the human imagination.

The focus of this book

This book is for developers who are interested in learning and gaining real hands-on experience by building AR applications. We do not assume you have knowledge of the Unity game engine, C# language, 3D graphics, or previous experience with VR or AR development; although, any prior experience from novice to seasoned expert will be helpful.

Our focus will be on visual augmented reality. We will include some audio, which can be very important to complete an AR experience, but not other senses.

Mobile devices are natural platforms for AR, both mobile phones and tablets, and Android and iOS. We refer to this as handheld AR with video see-through tracking. All the projects in the book can be built and run on mobile devices, including iPhone, iPad, and Android phones and tablets.

Much of today's interest and excitement about AR is the wearable eyewear AR with optical see-through tracking, such as Microsoft HoloLens. Most of the projects in this book can also be built and run on eyewear AR devices. Cases where changes are required in the user interface and interactivity, for example, will be called out.

There is a risk in trying to cover such a wide range of target devices and platforms in one book. We will do our best to separate any device-specific dependencies in our step-by-step tutorial instructions and make it easy for you to follow the instructions relevant to your setup and skip those that do not pertain to you.

We've included topics regarding setting up your Windows or Mac development machine to build AR applications (sorry, Linux not included) and uploading the app onto your device.

For app development, we use the Unity 3D game development platform (`https://unity3d.com/`), which provides a powerful graphics engine and full-featured editor that you can drive using C# language programming. There are many sources that review and discuss the virtues and benefits of using Unity. Suffice to say, Unity includes native support for photorealistic rendering of computer graphics, humanoid and object animations, physics and collision, user interface and input event systems, and more. With Unity, you can create a project and then build it for any number of supported target platforms, including Windows, Android, iOS, as well as many other popular consoles and mobile devices.

For our AR toolkit, we will teach you how to use the popular and professional Vuforia AR SDK (`https://www.vuforia.com/`). AR development requires some sophisticated software algorithms and device management, much of which is handled quite elegantly by Vuforia. It was first published in 2008 by Daniel Wagner in a paper titled *Robust and unobtrusive marker tracking on mobile phones*, then it grew into the award-winning Vuforia by Qualcomm and was later acquired by PTC in 2015. Today, Vuforia supports a wide range of devices, from handheld mobiles to wearable eyewear, such as HoloLens. As we will see throughout this book, the SDK supports many types of tracking targets, including markers, images, objects, and surfaces; therefore, it can be used for many diverse applications. They also provide tools and cloud-based infrastructure for managing your AR assets.

Vuforia requires you have a license key in each of your apps. At the time of writing this, licenses are free for the first 1,000 downloads of your app; although, it displays a watermark in the corner of the display. Paid licenses start at $499 per app.

An alternative to Vuforia is the free and open source ARToolkit SDK (`http://artoolkit.org/`). ARToolkit was perhaps the first open source AR SDK and certainly the one that lasted the longest; it was first demonstrated in 1999 and released as open source in 2001. ARToolkit is now owned by DAQRI (`https://daqri.com/`), a leading industrial AR device and platform manufacturer.

As of this writing, the current ARToolkit 5 version is focused on marker and image-based targeting, and it is more limited than Vuforia. (ARToolkit version 6 is in Beta and it promises exciting new features and an internal architecture, but it is not covered in this book.) It does not support as wide a range of devices as Vuforia out of the box. However, since it is open source and has a sizable community, there are plugins available for just about any device (provided you're willing to tinker with it). The Unity package for ARToolkit does not necessarily support all the features of the native SDK.

Apple's ARKit for iOS (`https://developer.apple.com/arkit/`) is also in Beta and requires iOS 11 (also in Beta as of this writing). ARKit works on any iPhone and iPad using an Apple A9 or A10 processor. Unity provides an asset package that simplifies how to use ARKit and provides example scenes (`https://bitbucket.org/Unity-Technologies/unity-arkit-plugin`).

We are pleased to provide an introduction to Google ARCore (`https://developers.google.com/ar/`) in this book, but only an introduction. ARCore is brand new and at the time of writing this, it is in early preview only. The documentation and demo scene they provide is very bare-bones. The setup will likely be different when Unity supports ARCore in the final release. Things such as installing a preview of AR services APK will change. The list of supported Android devices is very short. Please refer to the the GitHub repository for this book for new implementation notes and code using Google ARCore for Android: `https://github.com/ARUnityBook/`. The principles are very similar to ARKit, but the Unity SDK and components are different.

Microsoft HoloLens is a Windows 10 MR (mixed reality) device. See `https://www.microsoft.com/en-us/hololens/developers` for more information. Using its companion, MixedRealityTooklit (formerly, HoloToolkit) components (`https://github.com/Microsoft/MixedRealityToolkit`) facilitates development using this fascinating AR device.

AR technology is moving ahead quickly. We really want you to learn the concepts and principles behind AR and its best practices, apart from specific SDK and devices.

The following table sorts out the various combinations of platforms, devices, and tools that will be covered in this book:

Target device	Dev platform	Dev engine	AR SDK
Android mobile	Windows	Unity	Vuforia
Android mobile	Windows	Unity	ARToolkit
Android mobile	Windows	Unity	Google ARCore
iOS mobile	macOS	Unity	Vuforia
iOS mobile	macOS	Unity	Apple ARKit
HoloLens	Windows	Unity	Vuforia
HoloLens	Windows	Unity	MixedRealityToolkit

Summary

In this chapter, we introduced you to augmented reality, trying to define and describe what AR is, and what it is not, including comparing AR to its sister technology, namely virtual reality. Then, we described how AR works by separating handheld mobile AR from optical eyewear AR devices. In both cases, we described the typical features of such devices and why they're necessary for AR applications. Traditionally, AR is accomplished using video see-through and preprogrammed targets, such as markers or images. Wearable eyewear AR and emerging mobile devices use 3D spatial maps to model the environment and combine virtual objects more realistically because they can do things such as occlusion and physics between the real-world map and virtual objects. We then reviewed the many types of targets, including coded markers, images, and complex objects, and summarized many of the technical issues with AR, including field of view, visual perception, and display resolution. Finally, we looked at some real applications of AR, including those illustrated with projects in this book.

In the next chapter, we get to work. Our first step will be to install Unity and the major AR development toolkits--Vuforia, ARToolkit, Apple ARKit, Google ARCore, and Microsoft MixedRealityToolkit--on your development machine, either Windows or macOS. Let's get to it!

2
Setting Up Your System

Over the next two chapters, we are going to help set up your computer for augmented reality development. This chapter will focus on getting your Windows or macOS system ready for Unity development and installing various AR tool kits. The next chapter will focus on how to build and deploy project builds to specific AR devices. Also, we will use this opportunity to introduce you to the Unity development platform, including a little tour of the editor user interface and other key features of Unity.

If you are an experienced developer and are already using Unity, then you may be able to just skim through sections of this chapter, or even skip them altogether. Choose the topics that are relevant to you and your environment.

In this chapter we will cover the following topics:

- Installing and using Unity
- Using cameras in AR
- Installing and using Vuforia
- Installing and using ARToolkit

The installation of the Microsoft MixedRealityToolkit (aka HoloToolkit) for HoloLens development, Google ARCore, and the Apple ARKit for iOS development are covered in Chapter 3, *Building Your App*.

If you are only interested in developing for Microsoft HoloLens, we still recommend you install the Vuforia library because some of the projects in this book use Vuforia's support for HoloLens, rather than the Microsoft MixedRealityToolkit.

Likewise, if you are only interested in developing for Apple iOS devices, we still recommend you install the Vuforia library as some of the projects in this book use Vuforia's support for iOS, rather than the Apple ARKit.

Okay, let's go!

Installing Unity

All of the projects in this book will be built using the Unity 3D game engine. Unity is a powerful, cross-platform 3D environment with a user-friendly development editor. It consists of an amalgamation of various modules for managing and rendering 3D objects, lighting, physics, animations, audio, and more. It is also widely used for developing 2D games; however, the only 2D-specific features we will use in a project are the screen-space **user interface (UI)**. Each of the Unity modules has a programmer interface, or API, with a rich set of classes and functions, so the entire system can be accessed through scripts written in the C# programming language.

Unity provides a range of subscription and licensing options. For more details, see `https://store.unity.com/`. The basic Personal version is free to download and use, and is great for AR development. In fact, the Personal version has all the same features of the paid versions! You need to go to a paid version only if your product revenue exceeds $100K or if you want to use Unity's suite of additional online services for professional developers.

Requirements

There are a number of prerequisites to get started. You should have a Mac or PC with enough resources to install and run Unity. Details of the current system requirements for Unity can be found on their website (`https://unity3d.com/unity/system-requirements`), including the supported operating system version, the graphics card or built-in GPU, sufficient disk space, and necessary RAM memory.

For AR development, it is also recommended that you have a webcam attached to your PC for testing your projects within the Unity editor, even if the PC is not the target platform for your app, and a color printer for printing hard copies of target images.

There may be additional minimum requirements for your development system dictated by the target device. For HoloLens builds, Windows 10 is required. For iOS builds (iPhone and iPad), a Mac is required.

Download and install

Much of the following installation instructions can also be found directly in Unity online documentation (`https://docs.unity3d.com/Manual/InstallingUnity.html`). Although they have not changed much over the years, you should consult the site's current details.

Whether installing on Windows or macOS, the steps are similar:

1. Go to `https://store.unity.com/` and select the plan you wish to subscribe to, such as the free Personal:

2. This will download the download assistant installer specific to your operating system (Windows or macOS). It is a small executable about 1 MB in size. Install the current Unity version (as of writing, this is Unity 2017.1):

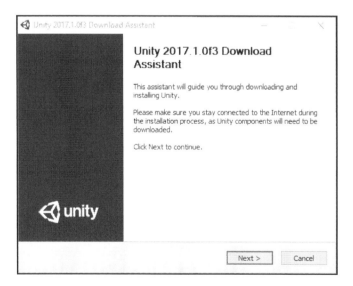

3. When it opens, accept the license agreement.

4. Then you can select which components of the Unity Editor you want to download and install, as shown here:

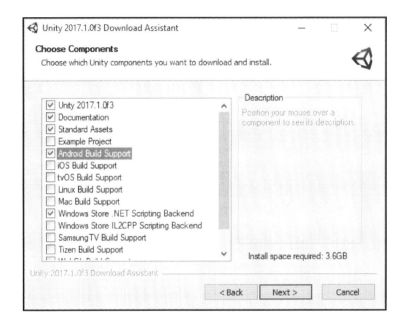

In addition to Unity itself and other default components, be sure to select the support components required for each of your target build devices:

- If you plan to build for an Android device, choose **Android Build Support**
- If you plan to build for an iOS device, choose **iOS Build Support**
- If you plan to build for a HoloLens, choose **Windows Store .NET Scripting Backend**

Unity also supports a newer, more performant Windows Store IL2CPP scripting backend. As of writing, it is still experimental. If you want to try it, we recommend you still also install the .NET backend so you can switch back and forth in your build settings.

5. You are then prompted to select the download and install locations of the program files. Note that this does not need to be on your Windows C: drive, and since it can be quite large, I often install it onto a secondary drive where more space is available:

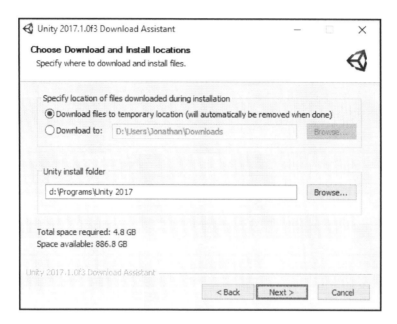

6. The components will begin downloading. Depending on your internet connection, you may need to get a cup of coffee or go out for a long run through the woods.

When the installation is complete, you will have the option to launch Unity. Click Finish. Congratulations!

When you first launch Unity, you may be prompted to **Sign into your Unity ID**. If you do not yet have an account, choose the option to create one. Having an account gives you access to many developer services, some free, including the discussion forums. Or you may *skip* this step to get to the welcome screen.

Introduction to Unity

When opening Unity, you are given the choices to start a new project, open an existing project, or watch a getting started video, as shown here:

To get started, let's create a new 3D project. Name it AR_is_Awesome or whatever you'd like as shown ahead:

Fill in the name for your project and verify that the folder location is what you want. Ensure that **3D** is selected. There is no need to select any extra asset packages at this time. Click on **Create Project**.

Exploring the Unity Editor

Your new project opens in the Unity Editor, as shown here in its default layout:

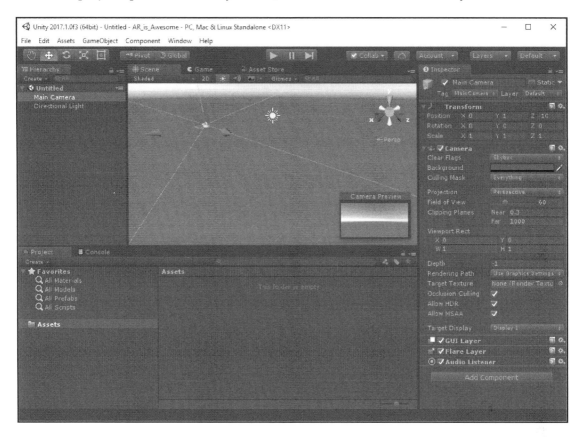

The Unity Editor consists of a number of non-overlapping windows, or panels, that may be subdivided into panes. Here's a brief explanation of each of the panels shown in the preceding default layout image:

- The graphical **Scene** panel in the upper-middle is where you can visually compose the 3D space of the current scene, including the placement of objects.
- Occupying the same panel, on a hidden tab, is the **Game** view, which shows the actual game camera view. When in *Play* Mode, your game runs in this panel.
- A third tab takes you to the Unity Asset store where you can find a plethora of free and purchased content from the Unity community, including scripts, artwork, and editor extensions.

- In the upper-left is the **Hierarchy** panel, which provides a tree-view of all the objects in the current scene.
- At the bottom is the **Project** panel. It contains all the reusable resources for the project, including ones imported, as well as those you'll create along the way.
- Occupying the same panel, on a hidden tab, is the **Console** panel, which shows messages from Unity, including warnings and errors from code scripts.
- On the right is the **Inspector** panel, which contains the properties of the object currently selected (objects are selected by clicking on them, whether in the **Scene**, **Hierarchy**, or **Project** panel). The **Inspector** has separate panes for each component of the object.
- Along the top is the Main Menu bar (on a macOS this will be on the top of your screen, not on top of the Unity window), and a Toolbar area with various controls that we'll use later on, including the Play (triangle icon) button that starts Play Mode.

In the preceding screenshot, the **Main Camera** is presently selected in the **Scene** panel, and it's Edit Mode is for the position transform, as indicated by the arrows icon in the Toolbar (shown in the following image), and by the axes gizmo centered on the camera in the Scene panel. Also, because the **Main Camera** is selected, a convenient **Camera Preview** window is inset in the **Scene** panel:

If any of these panels or tabs are not visible in your Unity Editor, use the Window dropdown from the Main Menu to find all the panel windows available to you. The editor interface is very configurable. Each panel can be rearranged, resized, and tabbed, for example, by grabbing one of the panel tabs and dragging it. *Go ahead and try it!* To the top-right is a layout selector that lets you choose between various default layouts or save your own preferences.

Most of the Unity screenshots in this book show the Unity Pro skin. If you are using the Personal edition, your editor will be a lighter gray. Also, we often arrange the window panes in a custom layout that we prefer, to maximize productivity and keep relevant information together for screen captures.

Objects and hierarchy

As shown in the preceding screenshot, the default empty Unity scene consists of a main camera and a single directional light. These are listed in the **Hierarchy** panel, and depicted in the **Scene** view panel. Your **Scene** panel also shows a perspective view of an infinite reference ground plane grid, like a piece of graph paper with nothing on it. The grid spans across the *x* (red) and *z* (blue) axes. The *y* axis (green) is up.

 An easy way to remember the Gizmo axis colors is: R-G-B correspond to x-y-z

The **Inspector** panel shows the details of the currently selected item. Try the following in your Unity editor:

1. Select the **Directional Light** with your mouse, either from the **Hierarchy** list or within the scene itself.
2. Look at the **Inspector** panel for each of the properties and components associated with the object, including its transform.

An object's transform specifies its position, rotation, and scale in the 3D world space. For example, a position (0, 3, 0) is 3 units above (*y* direction) the center of the ground plane (**X**=0, **Z**=0). A rotation of (50, 330, 0) means that it's rotated 50 degrees around the *x* axis and 330 degrees around the *y* axis. As you'll see, you can change an object's transforms numerically here, or directly with the mouse in the **Scene** panel.

Similarly, if you click the **Main Camera**, it may be located at position (0, 1, -10) with no rotation. That is, it's pointed straight ahead, towards the positive *z* direction.

When you select the **Main Camera**, as shown in the preceding editor screen capture, a **Camera Preview** inset is added to the **Scene** panel, which shows the view that the camera presently sees (if the **Game** tab is open, you'll see the same view there too). Presently the view is empty and the reference grid is not rendered, but a foggy horizon is discernible, with the grey ground plane below and the blue default ambient skybox above.

Scene editing

To introduce you to using Unity, we'll make a simple 3D scene with a couple of objects. This is not augmented reality specifically, but don't worry, we'll get to that soon.

Adding a cube

Let's now add an object to the scene: a unit-sized cube:

1. Within the **Hierarchy** panel, use the **Create** menu and choose **3D Object | Cube**. (The same selection can also be found in the Main Menu bar **GameObject** dropdown).

   A default white cube is added to the scene, centered on the ground plane at position (0, 0, 0), with no rotation and a scale of one, as you can see in the **Inspector** panel. This is an object's reset transform setting.

    The **Reset Transform** values are position (0, 0, 0), rotation (0, 0, 0), and scale (1, 1, 1).

2. If for some reason your cube has other transform values, you can set new values in the **Inspector** panel, or locate the small gear icon in the upper-right of the **Inspector Transform** component. Click it and select **Reset**. Its local center is the center of the cube.

   This cube has dimensions of one unit on each side. This can be an arbitrary unit that you can choose depending on your application's scale, whether meters, inches, or even miles. But as we'll see later, when you are using physics, it is best to define that one unit in Unity corresponds to one meter in world coordinates.

Your scene may look like this:

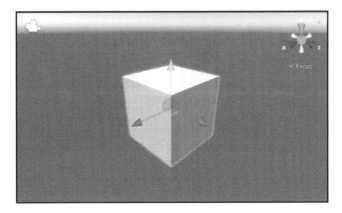

Adding a plane

Now let's add a ground plane object into the scene:

1. Within the **Hierarchy** panel **Create** menu (or main **GameObject** menu), choose **3D Object | Plane**.

   A default white plane is added to the scene, resting centered on the ground plane at position (0, 0, 0) (if not, select **Reset** from the **Inspector Transform** gear icon).

    At a scale of (1, 1, 1), Unity's plane object actually measures 10 by 10 units in X and Z. In other words, the plane's own size is 10 x 10 and its transform scale is 1.

   The cube is centered at position (0, 0, 0), just like the plane. But maybe it doesn't look like it to you. The **Scene** panel may be showing a perspective projection that renders 3D scenes onto a 2D image. The perspective distortion makes the cube appear not to be centered on the plane, but it is. Count the grid lines on either side of the cube! But as we'll see, when viewed in AR, the perspective is the same as the video camera image (or actual optical see-through view); it won't look distorted at all:

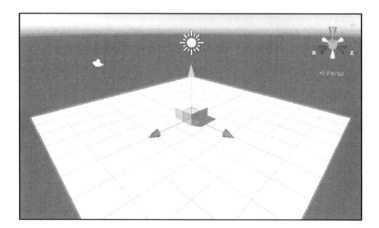

The cube is submerged in the plane because its local origin is at its geometric center-it measures 1 by 1 by 1, and its middle point is (0.5, 0.5, 0.5). This might sound obvious, but it is possible for the origin of a model to not be its geometric center (such as one of its corners). The transform position is the world space location of the object's local origin:

2. Move the cube onto the surface of the plane-in the **Inspector** panel; set its **Y Position** to 0.5: **Position** (0, 0.5, 0), as shown in the following screenshot:

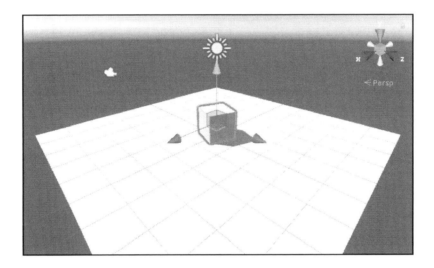

3. Now let's rotate the cube a little around the y axis. Enter 20 into its **Y Rotation: Rotation** (0, 20, 0).

Note the direction it rotates in. That's 20 degrees clockwise. Using your left hand, give a *thumbs-up* gesture-see the direction your fingers are pointing? Unity uses a *left-handed* coordinate system (there is no standard for coordinate system-handedness; some software uses left-handedness, while others use right-handedness, as illustrated in the following image):

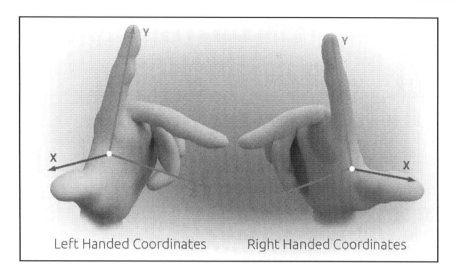

Left Handed Coordinates   Right Handed Coordinates

By Primalshell - Own work, CC BY-SA 3.0, https://commons.wikimedia.org/w/index.php?curid=27531327

 Unity uses a left-handed coordinate system-when the y axis is up and x is horizontal, then z positive is pointing away from you.

It is also worth noting the angle in which the cube is lit, its shading, and the direction of its shadow. This is determined by the directional light in the scene.

4. Click on **Directional Light** in the **Hierarchy**, and in the **Inspector** under **Transform**, you can see its rotational orientation about the X, Y, and/or Z axes, in degrees.

We moved and rotated the cube numerically in the **Inspector** panel, but you can also change it by direct manipulation with your mouse in the **Scene** panel. Note in the preceding image that the active gizmo is for positioning, using the three arrows for each the x, y, and z axis. To move the object, click the tip of one of the arrows, which will constrain movement along that axis.

The transform gizmos that are available from the Unity docs are illustrated in the following screenshot, for (left to right) *position, rotation, scale,* and *rect transform* (rect transform is commonly used for positioning 2D elements, such as screen space UI elements). For more information, visit

`http://docs.unity3d.com/Manual/PositioningGameObjects.html.`

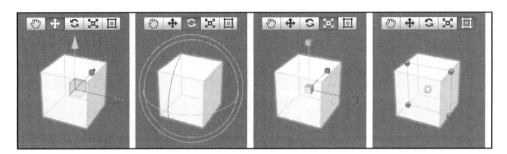

 A **gizmo** is a graphical control that lets you manipulate the parameters of an object or view. Gizmos have grab points or *handles* that you can click and drag with the mouse.

Adding a material

To add some color to the cube, we can give a quick introduction to *materials*. Materials define how a surface should be rendered, including references to colorings and the textures used (a **texture** is an image file that gets painted on the object surface, not unlike wallpaper or package labeling, used for simulating details and making objects more realistic). For now, let's just add a touch of color to our white cube, technically referred to as **albedo**. Follow these steps:

1. In the **Project** panel, select the top-level **Assets** folder, and select **Create | Folder**. Rename it `Materials`.
2. With the **Materials** folder selected, select **Create | Material**, and rename it `Red`.
3. In the **Inspector** panel, click the white rectangle to the right of **Albedo**, which opens the **Color** panel. Choose a nice red.
4. Select and drag the **Red** material from the **Project** panel into the **Scene** and drop it onto the cube. It should now look red.

Your scene should now look something like this:

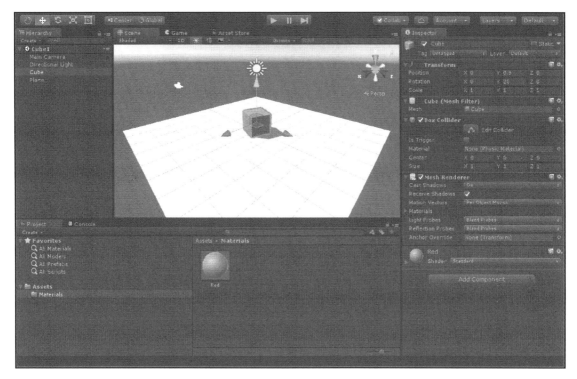

We will talk a lot more about materials in other projects in this book.

Saving the scene

Let's save our work.

1. From the Main Menu bar, select **File | Save Scene** and name it `Cube1`.

    Note that, in the **Project** panel, the new **Scene** object was saved in the top-level **Assets** folder.

2. Click **File | Save Project** for good measure.

Changing the Scene view

At any time, you can change the Scene view in a number of ways, depending on whether you have a 3-button, 2-button, track pad, or a Mac with only one button. Read up on it in the Unity manual (`http://docs.unity3d.com/Manual/SceneViewNavigation.html`) to find what works for you.

In general, combinations of left/right mouse clicks with the *Shift/Ctrl/Alt* keys will let you:

- Drag the camera around
- Orbit the camera around the current pivot point
- Zoom in and out
- *Alt* + right-click the mouse to swing the current eye orbit up, down, left, or right
- When the hand tool is selected (upper-left icon bar), the right mouse button moves the eye (the mouse middle-click does a similar move)

In the upper-right of the **Scene** panel, you have the **Scene** view gizmo, which depicts the current scene view's orientation. It may indicate, for example, a perspective view with X extending back to the left and Z extending back to the right:

You can change the view to look directly along any of the three axes by clicking on the corresponding colored cone. Clicking the small cube in the center (or the text beneath the gizmo) changes between a perspective view and an orthographic (nondistorted) view. Note that this only affects your Scene Editor view, not the perspective that your app camera will render when it's running:

That covers some of the basics of using the Unity Editor to create and transform objects in the **Scene**.

Also, as you will see, objects can be grouped together by dragging one object onto another object in the **Hierarchy** tree, creating a parent-child relationship between them. Moving, rotating, and scaling the parent will transform the target object and all its child objects together as a group.

Explore the **GameObject** menu from the Main Menu to see the many kinds of things you can add to your scene.

Game development

In addition to creating, arranging, and rendering objects in the scene hierarchy, the Unity engine offers much more functionality that is needed for games and augmented reality applications. We will introduce some of these now.

Material textures, lighting, and shaders

Previously, we introduced the use of Materials that can be attached to objects to determine how they look when rendered in the scene.

An object can have a relatively simple 3D *mesh*-a set of points connected into triangles that define the outward-facing surface shape of the object. Mapping an Albedo *texture* onto the mesh surface gives the impression of it having much more detail than the mesh itself provides. This is a critical technique for making detailed shapes with less than a hundred triangles, for example, instead of hundreds of thousands, and saving the amount of processing needed by orders of magnitude.

Shaders are the code that runs in the GPU to render objects using their materials, textures, and lighting properties. Unity's standard shader is quite advanced and optimized. In addition to an Albedo texture, you can specify **Normal Map**, **Height Map**, and **Occlusion Map**, which further allow more realistic-looking surface and **physically based shading** (**PBS**), in addition to reflective *Metallic* properties. The following is an example material for a realistic wooden table:

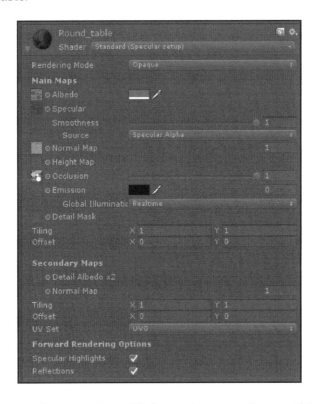

Unity also allows you to place a variety of light sources anywhere within your scene, including *Directional* lights, *Point* lights, *Spotlights,* and *Area* lights. Lights can vary in intensity, hue, and other properties. Lights can also cast shadows.

Depending on your application, these nice material and lighting features may or may not be very important in augmented reality. For example, if you're building a technical training manual and your AR art style is more illustrative, then simple flat shading may be sufficient. On the other hand, if you're objective is to render objects that look like they're occupying the room with you and belong there, you may want to make them look as realistic as possible. Unfortunately, there is a lot of rendering performance overhead using soft shadows and shadow cascades, so these are best to be avoided on mobile devices and the HoloLens.

As mentioned in Chapter 1, *Augment Your World*, a current challenge in AR is trying to match the lighting and shading of virtual objects with the actual lighting situation in real life. The Apple ARKit, for example, provides a component we can add to the light source in the scene to adjust its parameters when trying to match the lighting conditions of the real-world room.

Animation

Animation can be defined as the moving and changing of objects over time. A simple animation may be moving an object a little bit along a specific trajectory with each frame (direction vector) with a fixed velocity (units per second). In Unity, animation can be implemented by writing simple C# scripts that update an object's transform with each frame Update().

More complex animations can be defined using the **Animation** panel to draw curves for how object properties change over time. In the following example, the animation moves a ball linearly along the y axis while letting it wobble back and forth a small amount in the other two directions:

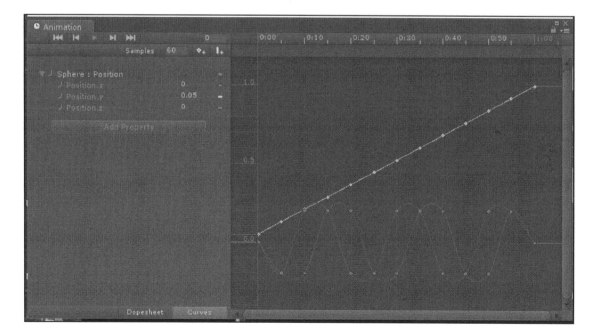

Unity also provides a third, even more advanced tool, known as the **Animator Controller**. This allows you to program more complex animation sequences that respond to specific events and object states. Animator controllers are state machines that determine which animations are currently being played, and blend the animations seamlessly. They can be programmed using a graphic, flow-chart-like visual programming interface, depicted here (source `https://docs.unity3d.com/Manual/class-AnimatorController.html`):

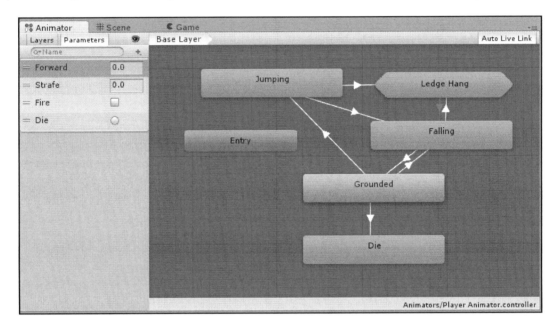

Physics

Other than programmed animations, Unity objects can be set up to move and interact on their own, using physics properties. When an object is assigned a *Rigid Body*, it can have *Mass* and *Drag* (resistance), and respond to *Gravity*. Once set in motion, Unity's physics engine will automatically calculate the object's next move and update it with each frame.

Separately, objects can be given a *Collider* mesh that defines the shape and bounds of itself used to calculate if and when the objects hit other objects. This may be as simple as a table standing steadfast on the floor (gravity), or a projectile in flight hitting its target. Objects can also be given a *Physic Material* that defines how it responds, such as landing like a brick or bouncing like a ball.

Furthermore, you can program how your Unity project responds to collision events, and then initiate other effects, animations, sounds, and so on. So when a projectile hits its target, you can play awesome *Audio* sounds, show amazing *Particle* effects and control other objects that are used in the application. We'll get to play with some of these features in the projects in this book.

Additional features

Unity also provides great support for audio in your application. Augmented reality apps are much more effective and immersive when sound accompanies what you see on the screen. There is a rich trove of audio clips on the Asset Store and elsewhere on the internet that you can use in your projects.

Everything in Unity can be scripted. Several programming languages are supported, but we recommend C# (C-Sharp) and use that in this book. If you are completely new to programming, there are some good tutorials on using C# in Unity on the Unity site (`https://unity3d.com/learn/tutorials/topics/scripting`). Even so, no worries: we'll ease you into it when it's needed, beginning with the project in `Chapter 5`, *AR Solar System*.

So that's a quick intro to Unity. We'll dive in deeper in the coming chapters. In addition to materials, physics, and audio, there are lots more features. For example, you can further organize your objects using *Tags*, *Layers*, and prebuilt *Prefabs*. Please explore the Unity Manual (`https://docs.unity3d.com/Manual/index.html`) and scripting API documentation (`https://docs.unity3d.com/ScriptReference/index.html`). If you're like me, you'll live there for a long time to come!

Using Cameras in AR

One more object we haven't discussed yet that is essential for any Unity application is the *Camera*. Unity developers may often add a Main Camera to their project scene and not give it much more thought. But in AR, the camera is especially important.

Cameras are devices that capture and display the virtual world for the player. For rendering computer graphics, the camera's **Pose** (**position and rotation transform**), its rectangular **Viewport** and **Field of View** (**FOV**) together define how much of the scene is visible and rendered on the screen. The camera Pose is where the camera is pointing. The Viewport is like a rectangular window that we're looking through; anything outside the Viewport is clipped and not drawn. The Field of View defines the viewing angle. In regular video games, developers enjoy the option to modify any of these options to give the cinematic camera effects they want to emulate on the screen.

But for augmented reality, the constraints on these parameters are dictated by the physical device running the app. The perspective view must match that of the real world, as seen through the user's device video camera or their own eyes' view through wearable glasses (for video see-through or optical see-through AR devices, respectively). The Viewport will correspond to the device's camera view or FOV of eyewear.

 The Camera prefabs provided with your AR SDK will usually have the Unity Camera properties you need already set up for you.

Fortunately, most of the default settings of the Camera object or camera prefabs provided with your AR SDK are good. The following screenshot shows the **Inspector** pane of a **Camera** with the Vuforia prefab:

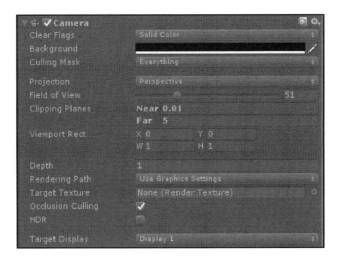

In Unity, when a new frame is rendered in the frame buffer memory, it is cleared to a *skybox* image (like a nice blue sky with clouds or a 360-degree image), or a solid color. For AR, we want the background to be transparent and with the only objects rendered on each frame being those that are visible, without any background skybox or anything else. Specifically, in our AR view, any pixel in the frame buffer without a color (that is, black) will be transparent. On optical see-through devices, you'll look through the glasses when there are no colored pixels. On video see-through devices, the camera view frame will be visible as the background. Therefore, in our Camera, we set the **Clear Flags** to **Solid Color**, and the **Background** color to black (0, 0, 0).

The following **Hierarchy** shows the Vuforia **AR Camera** prefab. It contains a **Camera** as already described. Then there's a **BackgroundPlane** that is a child of the **Camera**. The video image is painted on this plane when the scene is rendered:

AR cameras for AR SDK also have special scripts, or *Components*, attached that implement the interface with the underlying toolkit SDK algorithms and device drivers. The specifics vary from one toolkit to the next. Sometimes you'll be instructed to review and modify the parameters in these components to configure the behavior of your AR application.

In newer versions of Unity, AR cameras are being introduced with native support in Unity. At the time of writing this, the only built-in AR camera is for Microsoft HoloLens. In this case, you may not need any special AR components on the Camera object. Instead, we'll use Player Settings to enable Virtual Reality Supported and choose the Windows mixed-reality holographic SDK. We will explain these steps in detail in the next chapter. Stay posted for built-in support for other AR devices as they become available directly from Unity.

Although Unity presently provides built-in support for HoloLens, at the time of writing this, we cannot preview Play mode without a HoloLens device connected or the emulator installed. Similarly, the Apple ARKit offers a remote control feature for Play mode when an iOS device is connected. Other SDKs (Vuforia and ARToolkit) do support Play mode previews in the **Game** panel of the editor with only a standard webcam attached to your PC, as we'll see in the next topics. Therefore, in most cases, your PC should have a working webcam attached. On Windows, you can see it in the Windows **Start Menu | Device Manager | Imaging devices | your device name**.

 To verify that your webcam is attached and working properly, on Windows, run the Windows Camera app, or another app that uses the camera. On a macOS, you can use the macOS Photo Booth app.

In the rest of this chapter we help you add an AR SDK to your Unity projects. We consider two general toolkits, which both have Unity interface packages: Vuforia and ARToolkit.

Getting and using Vuforia

Now that you have Unity up and running on your development machine, the next step is to get the AR SDK imported into your Unity project. This section describes the Vuforia toolkit. If you do not want to use Vuforia, you can skip to the next section on getting and using ARToolkit.

Vuforia with Unity supports building AR applications for various platforms, including:

- Android smartphones and tablets, using Windows or macOS
- iOS iPhones and iPads, using macOS only
- Windows 10 devices, including HoloLens, via UWP-Universal Windows Platform

The current list of devices supported can be found at `https://www.vuforia.com/Devices`.

In deciding to use Vuforia, please be aware of its licensing terms and pricing policy. This is commercial software. It is free to download and develop in your projects, but there are usage and distribution limitations in the free version (for example, up to 1,000 cloud recognition images per month), and your app will display a Vuforia logo watermark in the corner of the screen. For larger volume distribution of your app, you will need to pay a license fee. At the time of writing this, this is $499 one-time fee per app, or $99 monthly for apps that use cloud-based storage and recognition.

To begin, open a project in Unity. As described in detail earlier in this chapter, if you want to start a new project, take the following steps:

1. Open Unity and click **New** on the startup dialog box.
2. Give the project a name and location.
3. Ensure **3D** is selected and click **Create Project**.

Or, if you already have Unity open, you can add a new scene to an existing project by going to the Main Menu, and clicking **File** | **New Scene** (or pressing *Ctrl + N* on Windows or *Command + N* on macOS).

Installing Vuforia

The first step to installing Vuforia is to go to their website, `https://www.vuforia.com/`, and log into the Dev Portal. If you don't have an account, you will need to register first to download and use the toolkit.

Downloading the Vuforia Unity package

From the **Downloads SDK** tab, choose the link to **Download for Unity** and agree to the software license. This will begin the download of the Unity package, named something like `vuforia-unity-x-x-x.unitypackage`. The **Downloads** page for Vuforia 6.2 is shown in the following screenshot:

Other toolkits are also available for native development on platforms, including Android, iOS, and UWP. You do not need to download these.

Once downloaded, you should copy it into a memorable place outside your current Unity project. We're going to import it now, but you might want to import it again into other projects as well.

Next, while on the **Downloads** page, click the **Samples** tab and download the **Core Features** samples using its **Download for Unity** link. This will begin the download of a .zip file, named something like vuforia-samples-core-unity-x-x-x.zip. This file contains additional component scripts and other useful files, including a bunch of sample targets that we may use in various projects in this book. Unzip and copy the files into a memorable place outside your current Unity projects for later use. It should include two more Unity project files: imageTargets-x-x-x.unitypackage and VuforiaSamples-x-x-x.unitypackage.

There's other optional stuff too. If you are using an optical eyewear device, you may want to download the **Digital Eyewear** samples .zip file. In addition, there are **Advanced Topics** samples, **Best Practices** samples, and **Vuforia Web Services** samples downloads. The **Tools** tab provides more downloads for additional tools, including the VuMark Designer, that help you create your own custom-branded encoded markers. Object Scanner is an Android APK that allows you to create a target by scanning an object with an Android device. Calibration Assistant is used to create custom calibration settings for optical see-through devices for separate users. We will be using some of these in later projects, but we won't download them until you need them. Information on using these samples, tools, and much more can be found in the documentation library at https://library.vuforia.com/.

Importing the Vuforia Assets package

Now that the Vuforia package is downloaded, we can import it into our Unity project.

These steps may be very familiar, since they're commonly used any time you import a third-party package into Unity, but we'll walk through it in detail this one time:

1. In Unity, go to the Main Menu and click **Assets | Import Package | Custom Package**, and find your Vuforia .unitypackage file:

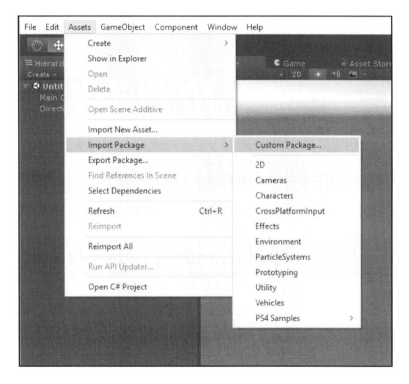

This will open the Unity import dialog with the list of files contained in the package.

2. We might as well select all of them (the default), and then click **Import**:

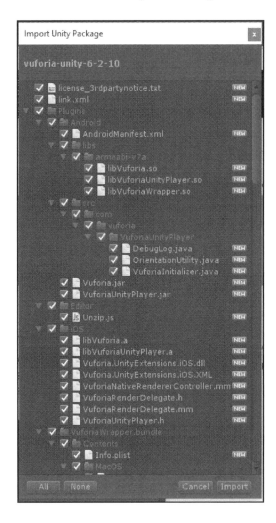

If the package files are slightly older than your current version of Unity, you may then get an import warning that the scripts need to be updated. Go ahead to complete the import:

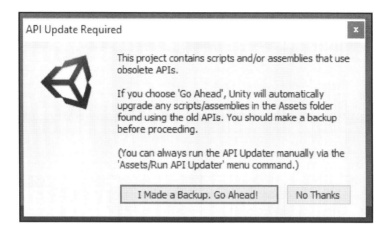

The Vuforia package is now imported into your Unity project. Look in the **Project** panel. You will see several new folders, including `Plugins`, `Resources`, and `Vuforia` as shown in the following screenshot:

The `Plugins` folder is where Unity keeps platform-specific binary and API code files. It now contains Vuforia's low-level API libraries and related files for Windows, iOS, Android, and other supported platforms.

The `Resources` file contains a special file named `VuforiaConfiguration`, and, as the name implies, this file maintains the project's Vuforia configuration parameters. This file will be included in the project build and is read at runtime by your AR app. We'll use many of these parameters throughout this book.

The `Vuforia` folder contains many Unity assets that may be useful in your project, including `Materials`, `Prefabs`, `Scripts`, `Shaders`, and `Textures`. We'll be exploring these further in our projects.

VuforiaConfiguration setup

Before you can start developing any project with Vuforia, we must make sure our application has a license key.

Go into the `Assets/Resources` folder in your Unity Editor, click on the `VuforiaConfiguration` file, and look at the **Inspector** panel. An image of its default settings is shown in the following screenshot. We must make sure the **App License Key** is filled in.

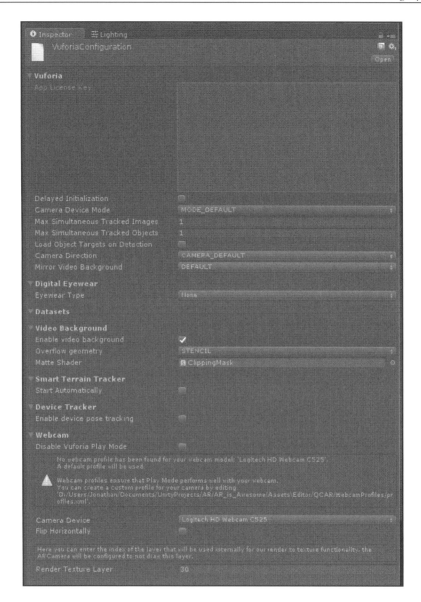

License key

To obtain a license key, head on over to the Vuforia website, and go into the Dev Portal (`https://developer.vuforia.com/`). Be sure you're logged in and click on the **Develop** tab and the **License Manager** subtab, as shown ahead:

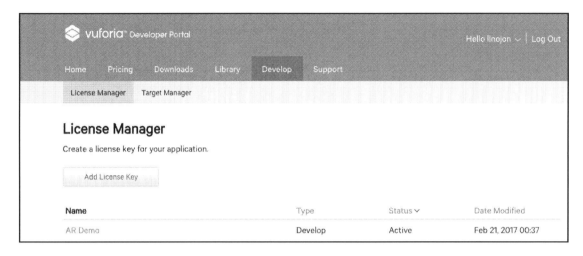

To create a new key, click on the **Add License Key** button. You are prompted to select the **Project Type**-choose **Development**. Then you are prompted to enter an app name (such as `AR Demo`). After you confirm the license key on the next screen, you're sent back to the **License Manager** dashboard.

Once you have a license key that you want to use, click on it in the **License Manager** dashboard. The encrypted key will be in a text box, as shown in the following screenshot. Select all the text and copy it to your clipboard. From this screen, the **Usage** tab lets you review the cloud usage details of your key and its associated app:

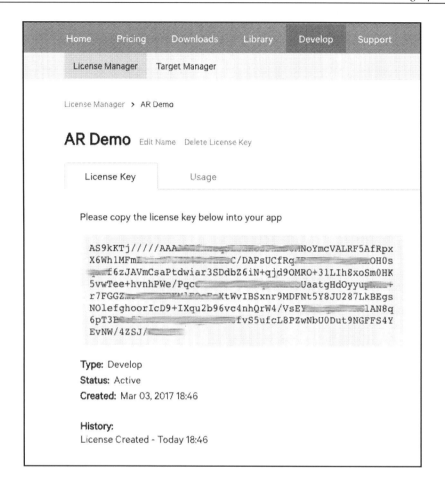

Now back in Unity, click in the **App License Key** field in the **VuforiaConfiguration Inspector** and paste your key. Done!

Create one key to use across all your learning, demo, and experimentation projects. Vuforia doesn't care if you reuse a key in multiple apps as long as its usage analytics don't exceed the license. But once you're developing a real, specific application, then go and get a unique license key for that project.

Webcam

If you want to test your applications from the Unity Editor using your PC's webcam (and you do), it needs to be configured too. Towards the bottom of the **Inspector**, under the **Webcam** heading is the **Camera Device** selector. As shown in the following screenshot, you can see we have a **Logitech HD Webcam C525** device installed and configured. Ensure your preferred camera is set up:

Building a quick demo with Vuforia

Let's try it out! As a quick validation check, we'll do a couple of very simple things and it'll be fun!

We'll assume you have started with a new Unity Scene and imported the Vuforia Asset package. As we did previously, at a minimum you need to set the app license key, and be sure your webcam camera is selected (as explained previously).

Adding AR Camera prefab to the Scene

The first step is to replace the default **Main Camera** with Vuforia's **AR Camera** prefab:

1. In the **Hierarchy** panel, delete the **Main Camera** (select it and press the *Delete* key or right-click **Delete**).
2. In the **Project** panel in the `Assets/Vuforia` folder, there's a `Prefabs/` folder-click on that.
3. Select the prefab named **AR Camera** and drag it into the **Hierarchy** list.

When you press **Play** (the play icon on the toolbar at the top-center of Unity), you should see the feed from your selected web camera in the **Game** panel. This allows us to debug the AR application within the Unity Editor.

If you do not see the video feed, double check that the VuforiaConfiguration's **Webcam Camera Device** is set to your webcam, and/or that the camera is working properly (in Windows, it can be found in **Device Manager** | **Imaging Devices**).

We also want add the **CameraSettings** component to the camera. For some reason, the Vuforia **AR Camera** prefab does not use autofocus by default. For some platforms, such as Android, this is really needed:

1. Select **AR Camera** in **Hierarchy**
2. In **Inspector** choose **Add Component** and search for **Camera Settings** (or navigate to **Scripts | Camera Settings**)
3. Select the component to add it to the camera object.

Adding a target image

Now we can start creating the AR application. First, let's decide what to use for an image target and tell the application about it. In later chapters, you will get to choose your own picture or another target, but for now we will use one of the samples that Vuforia provides.

If you haven't done so already, please download the **Core Features** samples from the Dev Portal (`https://developer.vuforia.com/downloads/samples`) and unzip it. Then do the following:

1. Import the package, named, for example, `VuforiaSamples-x-x-x.unitypackage` into your app (via the Main Menu, clicking on **Assets | Import Package | Custom Package...**).

   There's a lot of stuff in that package, including an image target database. We're going to use one of those images right now-the one named `stones_scaled.jpg`.

    Keep in mind that AR mixes the real world with the virtual world. When developing, you not only need a digital copy of your target image, but you also need a printed hardcopy to test out your app.

   In your operating system (Windows or macOS), among the files installed with the samples package, is a printable copy of the `stones` image as a PDF file. Navigate to the `Assets/Editor/Vuforia/ForPrint/` folder.

2. Open the `target_stones_USLetter.pdf` (or `target_stones_A4.pdf`) file, and print it.

It looks like this:

Back in Unity:

1. In the **Project** panel, navigate to `Assets | Vuforia | Prefabs` and select and drag the **ImageTarget** prefab into the **Hierarchy**.
2. Look in the **Inspector** panel. Under the **Image Target Behavior** component, for **Type**, select **Predefined**.
3. Then for **Database**, select **StonesAndChips**.
4. For **Image Target**, select **stones**.

It should now look like this:

Note the width and height dimensions of the image in the component properties: *0.247 x 0.1729*. That is the actual size of the printed image in meters (*9.75 x 6.5* inches).

You should now be able to see the Image Target in your Scene view panel. If you cannot, it may be out of view. A quick way to find a specific object in the **Scene** view is to double-click on the object in the **Hierarchy** (alternatively, select the object in the **Hierarchy**, mouse over to the **Scene** panel, and press *F* on the keyboard). As described earlier in the chapter, you can further modify the **Scene** view using the 3-axis gizmo in the upper-right corner, or using the right-mouse, or middle-mouse buttons (on Windows). Here's what mine looks like now:

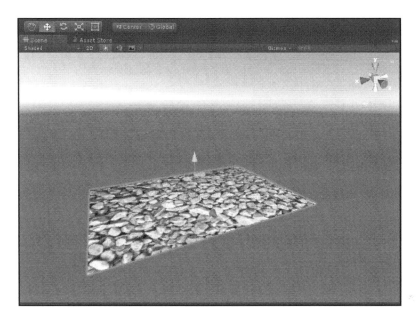

We also need to tell Vuforia and Unity that we're going to use one of the image databases:

1. From the Main Menu, click **Vuforia | Configuration**.
2. In **Inspector**, check the **Load StonesAndChips Database** checkbox.
3. Then check its **Activate** checkbox, as shown here (macOS):

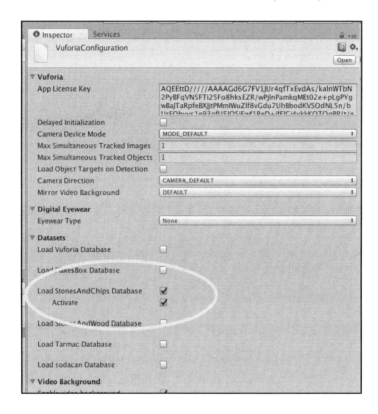

Adding a cube

Now we'll add an object to the scene, just a simple cube:

1. In the **Hierarchy**, select **Create**, then **3D Object | Cube** (or from the Main Menu, choose **GameObject | 3D Object | Cube**). This will create a unit-sized cube, one meter on all sides.
2. Obviously, that's much too big for our target, which is closer to 0.2 units in size. So, over in the **Inspector**, in the **Transform** component, modify the **Scale** to something more manageable, like (0.05, 0.05, 0.05).

Also, the cube appears submerged into the image. Let's move it up so it's sitting on the target instead:

3. You can do this by selecting and dragging the yellow (vertical) arrow, or in the **Inspector**, changing the **Transform Position** to (0, 0.03, 0) as follows:

Finally, we need to parent the object under the **ImageTarget**.

4. In the **Hierarchy**, select and drag the **Cube** so that it is a child of the **ImageTarget**, like so:

Note that the order in which we changed the scene is significant. We first scaled and positioned the cube, then parented it under the **ImageTarget**. At this point, the cube's transform values have changed in the **Inspector**, although the object looks unchanged on the screen. Why? Because the cube transform has *local* values relative to its parent transform. Unity makes the adjustment for us when you move things in the **Hierarchy**! So, we had a cube size of 0.05 and the **TargetImage** object size of 0.25; now as a child object, the cube's *local* size changed to 0.2, but its *world* size is still 0.05 (0.2 times 0.25 equals 0.05).

If you don't completely get this, don't worry; you'll get used to it, and usually the hard numbers are less important than how things look on the screen. The **Scene** should now look something like this:

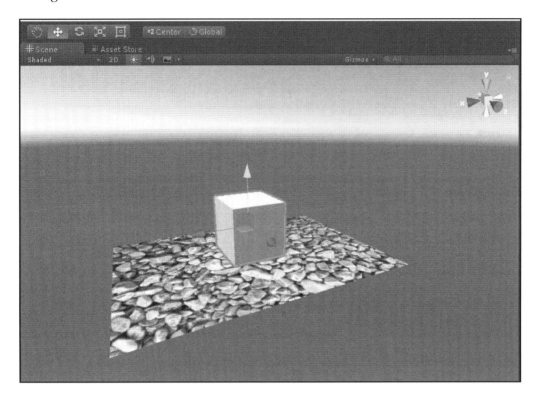

Save the Scene and project:

1. From the Main Menu, click **File | Save Scene**.
2. Then **File | Save Project**.

Now we're ready to see it work. Press **Play** again in the Unity toolbar. Point your webcam at the stones image. Our cube should appear. Woot!!!

The following image shows me pointing my webcam at the target pebbles image, with Unity running the scene on the monitor in the back. In the **Game** panel, you can see the video feed from the webcam, with the cube added to it, in all its augmented reality glory!

If you also want to try another SDK, ARToolkit, you can follow the next topic, or move on to the next chapter.

Getting and using ARToolkit

This section describes the ARToolkit SDK for augmented reality development (http://artoolkit.org/). If you don't want to use ARToolkit, you can skip this section.

ARToolkit is an open source software project. It is free to use both for the development and the distribution of your apps that use it. Unlike Vuforia, there are no license fees. As an open source project, the source code is available to anyone who wants to use it, read it, and even extend it. ARToolkit is owned by DAQRI, a prominent AR industry leader, and is free to use under a LGPL v3.0 license (see http://archive.artoolkit.org/artoolkit-licensing).

If you distribute an app built with ARToolkit, it needs to include an acknowledgement and license notice, for example, in an about box. ARToolkit has the distinction of being perhaps the first and continuously supported open source AR SDK since 1999.

ARToolkit compares favorably to Vuforia, provided your needs fit within the scope of its features. However, Vuforia supports more target types, and if you need one of those, such as shape recognition, ARToolkit may not be a fit. Vuforia may seem to have a more polished developer experience, partly because of their easy-to-use, cloud-based services. On the other hand, ARToolkit offers more direct access to low-level tools and parameters that may be important to your application. Some people will want and need this extra level of control. Also, since it's open source, you can go in and see how it works, make custom changes, and write your own extensions to suit your requirements. Its GitHub repositories can be found at `https://github.com/artoolkit`.

At the time of this writing, ARToolkit is transitioning from Version 5 to the new Version 6 (Beta). This book covers V5.3.2, at `https://archive.artoolkit.org/` versus `https://artoolkit.org/`

ARToolkit with Unity supports building AR applications for various platforms, including:

- Android smartphones and tablets, using Windows or macOS
- iOS iPhones and iPads, using macOS only
- Windows and macOS desktop

To begin, open a project in Unity. As described in detail earlier in this chapter, if you want to start a new project, do the following:

1. Open Unity and click **New** on the startup dialog box. Give the project a name and location, ensure **3D** is selected, and click **Create Project**.
2. Or, if you already have Unity open, you can add a new scene to an existing project by going to the Main Menu, and clicking **File** | **New Scene** (or pressing *Ctrl + N* on Windows or *Command + N* on macOS).

Installing ARToolkit

To install ARToolkit, begin by going to the website and downloading the Unity package (`https://archive.artoolkit.org/download-artoolkit-sdk`). The file may be named something like `ARUnity5-x.x.x.unitypackage`:

Using Unity?

The latest ARToolKit for Unity package includes a full project and examples source, plus binaries for plugins and utilities. Plugins and utilities sources are in the ARToolKit packages.

Latest Version: 5.3.2

⬇ **DOWNLOAD UNITY PACKAGE**

DOWNLOAD ADDITIONAL UNITY TOOLS ▼

Once downloaded, you should copy it into a memorable place outside your current Unity project. We're going to import it now, but you might also want to import it again into other projects.

Next, download the `Additional Unity Tools` zip file, which includes, among other things, utilities required to generate an image target. Choose the download for Windows or macOS that is appropriate for you. The file may be named `ARUnity5-x.x.x-tools-win.zip` or `ARUnity5-x.x.x-tools-osx.tar.gz`. Unzip it and move the resulting folder to a memorable place. On Windows, you might choose to put it into `C:\Program Files`. It contains a bunch of subfolders, including the `bin/` directory which contains executable utilities that you will need in future chapters, including target creation and camera calibration tools. Documentation on using these tools, and all that's included with ARToolkit, can be found online at `https://archive.artoolkit.org/documentation/`.

The `tools` folder also includes a `doc/` directory with some sample images, including one that we're going to use now, named `gibraltar.jpg`. Please print a hardcopy of this image. When developing, you not only need a digital copy of your target image, but you need a printed hardcopy as well, to test out your app:

Importing the ARToolkit Assets package

Now that the ARToolkit package is downloaded we can import it into our Unity project. In Unity, do the following:

1. Go to the Main Menu
2. Click on **Assets** | **Import Package** | **Custom Package...**, find your ARToolkit Unity package file
3. Import the files into your project.

These steps may be very familiar since they're common any time you import a third-party package into Unity and were detailed previously for Vuforia (please refer to the previous instructions, if you wish).

 Some versions of the ARToolkit Unity package for macOS, including 5.3.2, erroneously include Unity system files that should not be imported. In the Import Unity Package dialog, be sure to tick the checkboxes of only `ARToolKit5-Unity`, `Plugins`, and `StreamingAssets`, and not any other Unity folders, as shown here.

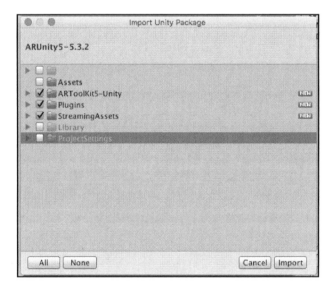

The ARToolkit package is now imported into your Unity project. Look at the **Project** panel. You will see several new folders, including `ARToolkit5-Unity`, `Plugins`, and `StreamingAssets`:

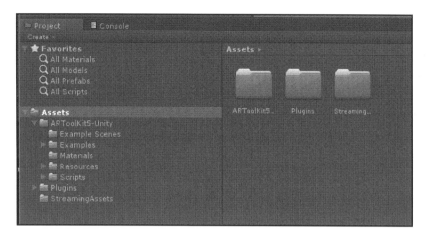

The `Plugins` folder is where Unity keeps platform-specific binary and API code files. It now contains ARToolkit's low-level API libraries and related files for Windows, iOS, Android, and other supported platforms.

Note the `ARWrapper bundle` folder in Plugins. It is an intermediary layer of code between the Unity SDK and lower-level API, an important feature of the ARToolkit device-independent architecture. We will learn to deal with this in Visual Studio in the next chapter.

The `StreamingAssets` folder is where Unity expects to find media files that may be used by the app at runtime. For ARToolkit, this is where you'll copy target data you've prepared for your application. It now contains some example files used by the example scenes.

The `ARToolkit5` folder contains many Unity assets that may be useful in your project, including `Materials`, `Scripts`, `Shaders`, and `Examples`. We'll explore these further in our projects.

ARToolkit Scene setup

We're now ready to try it out! There are several steps to setting up your scene for ARToolkit.

First, we'll set up the Unity Scene. Rather than using prefabs, we construct each of the game objects we need, but it's not difficult. These steps are required for any new AR Scene, including:

- AR controller-For initialization
- AR origin-By default is (0, 0, 0)
- AR tracked object-Defines the marker and tracked space
- AR camera-Allows the AR content to be rendered

Adding the AR Controller

Every scene requires an AR controller object with toolkit components used to drive the app. The AR controller manages initialization, setup, and features, such as the video stream projection from the phone.:

1. In your Unity project, in the **Hierarchy** panel, select **Create | Create Empty** (or, in the Main Menu, **GameObject | Create Empty**).
2. Then, over in the **Inspector** panel, rename it to `ARController`.
3. Click **Add Component**, find **Scripts** in the list, and add the **AR Controller** component to this object.

   This object will be the base of all the interactions with ARToolkit. A fully expanded view of this component is shown here:

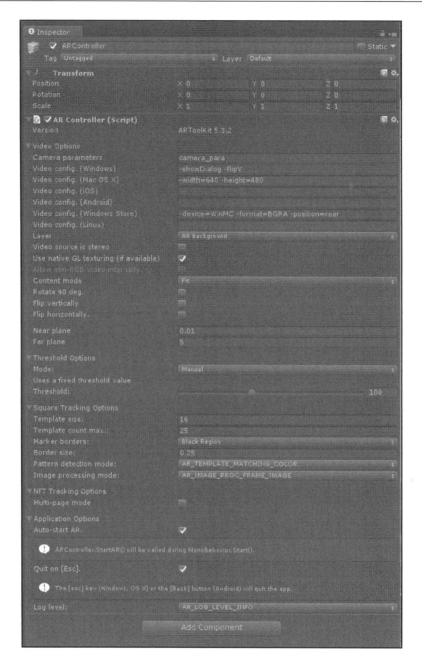

Almost all of these options can be ignored for now and left at their default value.

Make note of the **Video Options Layer** setting (we're referring to the **Layer** parameter within the **AR Controller (Script) Video Options**, not the object's **Layer** at the top of the **Inspector**).

When you imported the package, it should have automatically added layers named **AR background**, **AR background 2**, and **AR foreground**.

4. Click the **Layer** selection to make sure they're there, and add them, if necessary, to the layers list and to the **AR Controller** component **Layer** option:

Adding the AR Root origin

The rest of the AR objects we add will be parented under an object named ARRoot. This object will serve as the origin of our AR scene:

1. Create another empty **GameObject** in the **Hierarchy** and name it ARRoot. Be sure that its **Transform Position** is (0, 0, 0).

2. The AR**Root** object, and any of its child objects, should reside on the **AR Background 2** layer. In **Inspector**, set its **Layer** to **AR Background 2** (this is the object's layer set at top of the **Inspector**).

3. Then, use **Add Component** to add the script **AR Origin**.

Quickly locate the scripts and components you want in the Add Component dialog by typing the first couple of letters of the name in the search field, such as AR for ARToolkit components.

Adding an AR camera

Next, we need an AR camera. We can use the default **Main Camera** already in the scene, but it must be parented by ARRoot.

1. Select **Main Camera** from the **Hierarchy** and drag it to make it a child of **ARRoot**.
2. Reset the Main Camera's **position** to (0, 0, 0) if necessary (**Transform gear-icon | Reset**).
3. We want this camera only to be working with objects in **Root**. Therefore, set its **Culling Mask** to **AR Background 2** so that it matches the layer that **Root** is in (select **Culling Mask | Nothing**, then **Culling Mast | AR Background 2**).
4. Then, use **Add Component** to add the **AR Camera** component to the camera.

 You can readily reset the **Transform Values** by using the gear icon in the upper right of the **Transform** pane and selecting **Reset**.

The **Hierarchy** should now look like this:

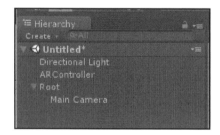

At this point we can test it. When you press **Play** (the play-icon on the toolbar at the top-center of Unity), you should see the feed from your web camera in the **Game** panel. This allows you to debug the AR application within the Unity editor.

 On Windows systems, immediately after pressing Play, you may be presented with a **Properties** dialog that lets you choose your webcam device (if you have more than one) and its properties. This dialog is part of the ARToolkit and is launched because, in your AR Controller, the Video Config (Windows) property includes the directive -show Dialog.

You can exert a great deal of control over the physical camera options via this component. Using C# scripts you can write. You can also use the separate `calib_camera` camera calibration utility included with the ARToolkit tools. See more at `https://archive.artoolkit.org/documentation/doku.php?id=2_Configuration:config_camera_calibration`.

Troubleshooting

If you encounter an error like `DllNotFoundException: [...]/Assets/Plugins/ARWrapper.dll` locate the DLL file(s) in the projects `Assets/Plugins/x86_64` path (if running 64 bit Unity on Windows, for instance), and make sure that Editor is one of the Include Platforms specified. We have heard of cases where developers never got it to work when using Play from the Unity Editor, but could still successfully build and run to their Android device just the same.

Saving the Scene

Let's save our work.

1. From the Main Menu bar, select **File | Save Scene** and name it `Test1`.

    Note that, in the **Project** panel, the new **Scene** object was saved in the top-level `Assets` folder.

2. Also click **File | Save Project** for good measure.

Building a quick demo with ARToolkit

With the basics of our scene built, we can now add a target and an object for the AR project. When the app runs, if the camera sees and recognizes the target in real life, the virtual object will be added to the combined view on your screen.

Identifying the AR Marker

We need to tell the AR Controller what target data to use for tracking. For this little demo, we will use the example `gibraltar.jpg` image we printed earlier. The data for this image is already included in the ARToolkit assets that we imported at the start, and is located in the `Assets/StreamingAssets` folder.

Add an ARMarker component to the ARController:

1. In the **Hierarchy**, select your **ARController**, then select a script named **ARMarker**.

    Now we need to set the ARMarker parameters:

2. We need to give it a tag name, say `gibraltar`, and enter that text into the **Marker Tag** field.
3. For **Type**, select **NFT** as the target type, because we're going to be tracking an image.
4. Then, for **NFT Dataset Name**, enter `gibraltar`. This is actually the name of the dataset found in the `StreamingAssets` folder and, conveniently, is the same as our image!

The controller's **ARMarker** pane should now look like this (the actual UID may vary):

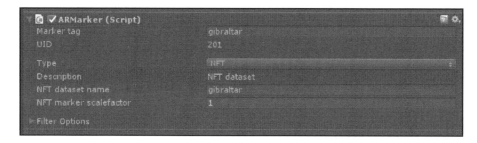

 NFT is an acronym for natural feature tracking (introduced in `Chapter 1`, *Augment Your World*), a fancy way of saying an image, usually a `.jpg` or `.png` file, that has sufficient irregular detail so that the software can track it as it moves from one video frame to another.

Adding an AR Tracked Object

We now need to actually add the target to the scene as a new **GameObject** under **Root**:

1. In the **Hierarchy**, select **Root**, right-click, then **Create Empty** (and make sure the new empty **GameObject** is a child of **Root**).
2. In **Inspector**, rename it `GibraltarTarget`.
3. Ensure its **Transform** is reset (**position** at 0, 0, 0).

4. **Add Component** named **AR Tracked Object**.
5. In the **AR Tracked Object** component **Marker Tag** field, give it the tag we used earlier in the **AR Controller**, `gibraltar`.

If you spelled everything correctly (yeah I know; gibraltar is tough!), your tracked object should have been found in the database and the component will look like this (the actual UID may vary):

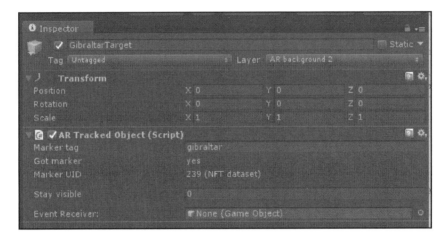

Adding a cube

Now we'll add an object to the **Scene**, just a simple cube:

1. In the **Hierarchy**, select the **GibraltarTarget**, right-click **3D Object | Cube** (or, from the Main Menu, choose **GameObject | 3D Object | Cube** and make it the child of the **target object**).

   This will create a unit-sized cube, one meter on all sides. Obviously, that's much too big for our target, which is closer to 0.2 units sized. So, over in the Inspector, in the **Transform** component, modify the **Scale** to something more manageable right now, such as (0.05, 0.05, 0.05).

You may need to adjust your view in the **Scene view** panel, but when you do, you can see that our target object appears along with the cube, as shown here:

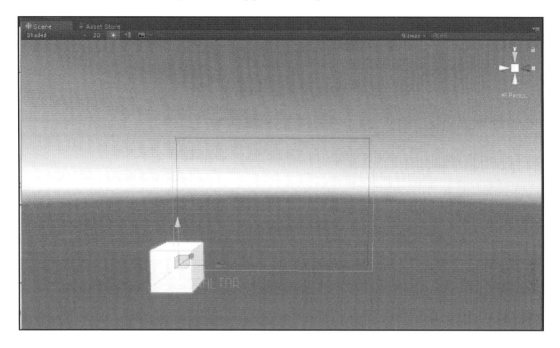

 As described earlier in this chapter, in the topic, Changing the Scene view, to change the Scene view, use the right mouse and/or middle mouse buttons on Windows, and other controls. Also see the Unity Manual at `http://docs.unity3d.com/Manual/SceneViewNavigation.html`.

It's somewhat awkward to have the target standing vertically, when, in real life you might expect it to be lying horizontally (that is, flat):

2. Select **Root** in the **Hierarchy** and, in **Inspector**, change its **Rotation-X** to 90 degrees.

3. We can also move the cube so that it's positioned in the center of the target, more or less.

After adjusting the position of the cube in my scene to **Position** (0.12, 0.076, -0.037), it looks like this:

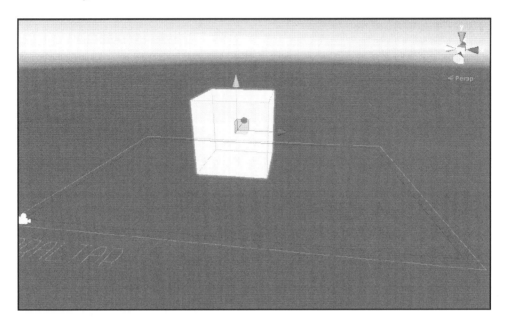

One last thing: double check that the objects under **ARRoot** are all on the **AR background 2** layer.

4. If you select **ARRoot** and, in **Inspector**, set its layer again, Unity will prompt you to change all of its children's layers as well. Do it.

Now we're ready to see it work. Press **Play** again in the Unity toolbar. Point your webcam at the printed Gibraltar image. Our cube should appear. Woot again!!!

If the app seems slow when you press Play from the Editor, this could be due to a lot of messages being printed to the console window. That can be adjusted in the **AR Controller** by setting the **Log Level** to **Debug** or just **Error**.

The following image shows me pointing my webcam at the target Gibraltar image, with Unity running the scene on the monitor in the background. In the **Game** panel, you can see the video feed from the webcam, with the cube added to it, in all its augmented reality awesomeness!

Summary

In this chapter, we got our development system set up and ready to do augmented reality development, whether that be a Windows PC or a macOS. First, we installed Unity, which will be the game engine platform for all the projects in this book, including optional components that you will need, depending on your target build AR device. Then we presented a short introduction to using Unity, emphasizing the key features that you'll need to get started.

Then we introduced two AR SDKs that we use in this book. Vuforia is a professional toolkit that has many features and is easy to use, but carries a license fee for commercial products. We also looked at ARToolkit, an open source project, perhaps less capable than Vuforia but more transparent and extendable. For each SDK, we walked you through the installation and then built a simple demo AR application.

However, that's only half the setup battle. In the next chapter, we show you how to set up your system to build and deploy your projects onto various target devices that can run your AR app, including Android, iOS, and/or HoloLens.

3
Building Your App

In the previous chapter, we started with the process of setting up our system for AR development, installing the Unity 3D engine and one or more AR development kits. In this chapter, we will complete the setup process by installing and using additional tools in order to build an app for various target devices, be it Android or iOS mobile devices (phone or tablet), macOS, Windows 10 desktop, or Microsoft Mixed Reality.

In the first topic of this chapter, we will cover general procedures for building from Unity. After that, you can skip to the topic(s) you need, among the following:

- Building and running from Unity and targeting desktops
- Targeting Android
- Targeting iOS
- Targeting Microsoft MR Holographic

We apologize for how technical this can get, but it's a necessary evil. Think of it as an initiation rite. Everyone must go through it, at least once. Fortunately, once your machine is set up for target builds, you may not have to do it ever again. Well, that is, until you change machines or after you have a major upgrade.

Identifying your platform and toolkits

The following table shows which AR SDK and development platform you can use for various target platforms for your AR app, as of the time of writing this book:

Target AR Platform	AR SDK	Development Platform	
		Windows 10	Mac OS X
Android	Vuforia	Yes	Yes
Android	ARToolkit	Yes	Yes
Android	ARCore	Yes	Yes
iOS	Vuforia	no	Yes
iOS	ARToolkit	no	Yes
iOS	Apple ARKit	no	Yes
OS X Desktop	Vuforia	no	no
OS X Desktop	ARToolkit	no	Yes
Windows Desktop	Vuforia	(as UWP)	no
Windows Desktop	ARToolkit	Yes	no
Windows HoloLens	Vuforia	Yes	no
Windows HoloLens	MixedRealityToolkit	Yes	no

Naturally, this and many of the installation details in this chapter are subject to change. Refer to the SDK online documentation for the most up-to-date details:

- For Vuforia, refer to `https://www.vuforia.com/`
- For ARToolKit, refer to `https://artoolkit.org/`

- For Apple ARKit, refer to `https://developer.apple.com/arkit/`
- For Google ARCore, refer to `https://developers.google.com/ar/`
- For Microsoft MixedRealityToolkit (HoloToolkit), refer to `https://unity3d.com/partners/microsoft/hololens`

 At the time of writing this, the Microsoft platform is transitioning its strategic branding from Holographics and HoloToolkit to Mixed Reality, MR, and the Mixed Reality Toolkit.

Building and running from Unity

In the previous chapter, we saw how to create a new project in Unity; import an AR SDK package, such as Vuforia or ARToolkit, into the project; and build a scene with a camera, target image recognition, and virtual object (cube). To summarize, a Unity AR-ready scene, such as the demo scene we built in the previous chapter, should contain the following:

- A camera with SDK-specific AR components attached
- A game object representing an image target, with an SDK-specific component identifying the image to use and where to find it
- Game objects to render when the target is recognized at runtime, parented by the target, and registered to the target's position in the 3D space
- The scene hierarchy, arranged according to the requirements of the specific SDK, including additional SDK-specific components

We tested our demo scene by running it in the Unity editor and using the webcam attached to the PC to capture the target and show the augmented view. You can readily make fresh changes, fixes, and improvements, and test it again. This is an iterative process as per which we develop apps.

Now we want to test it on the actual target device. We will build the app as a separate executable that runs outside of Unity.

We will configure **Build Settings** for your target platform. If your platform is a desktop PC or macOS, like the one you're developing with, there's not a lot of extra work. We'll do a build like that now. You can follow along even if it's not your actual target, just for fun.

To build your project, perform the following steps:

1. Go to **File** | **Build Settings**; this will open the **Build Settings** dialog box, as shown next:

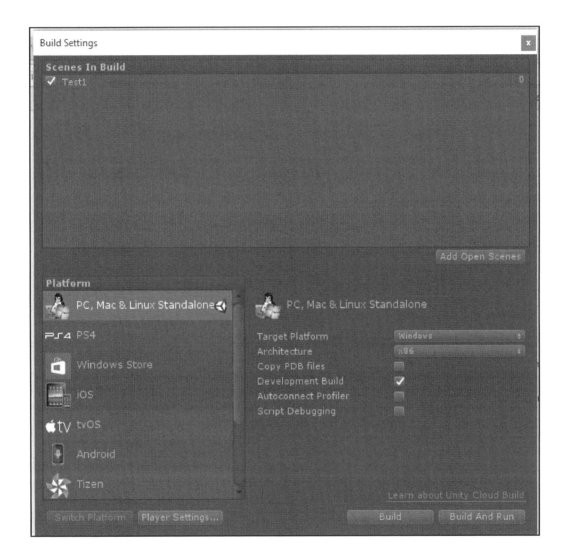

At the top of the dialog is the **Scenes In Build** list. This should contain the name of the scene you want to include in this build with its checkbox checked. A quick way to add the current scene that is presently open in Editor is using the **Add Open Scenes** button.

2. Click on the **Add Open Scenes** button.

In the preceding case, I had a scene named Test1, which we built earlier. Remove or uncheck all the scenes from the list, except the one you want to build.

Working with Unity, it is often convenient to save your work or experiments in a new scene. You can end up with multiple scenes in your project. When you go to build, be sure to double-check that **Scenes In Build** refers to the actual scene you want to build.

As shown in the preceding screenshot, in the **Platform** list, you can see that **PC, Mac & Linux Standalone** is presently selected, among the other platforms available. (Your list of platforms may vary depending on your Unity version, the components you installed with Unity, and perhaps your authorization licenses.)

Using Vuforia, you cannot build a macOS desktop app. For a Windows 10 desktop with Vuforia, you must switch to the Windows Store platform to build a UWP version of the app.

If you plan to install for Android or another platform, see the following sections of this chapter.

Vuforia does not support desktop apps, only devices with *embedded cameras*. For Apple products, this means only iPhones and iPads. For Windows, if you want to build it to run on a Windows desktop, you must build for **Universal Windows Platform** (**UWP**).

In Unity, you do this by changing platforms from standalone to Windows Store, as follows:

1. In the **Platform** list, select **Windows Store** and click on **Switch Platform**.
2. If it asks you to verify anything, just say **OK**.
3. Also, choose **SDK** (on the right-hand side) as **Universal 10**, as shown in the next screenshot. (If grayed out, you may need to install the missing platform support using the Unity download installer that installed Unity originally on your machine.)
4. You can leave **Target device** as **Any device** or specify **PC**.

The following screenshot shows **Build Settings** for Vuforia on a Windows desktop:

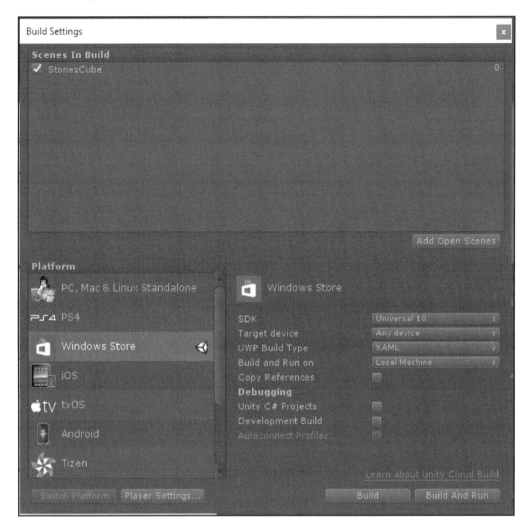

Finally, although we won't go there this time, it's worth pointing out the **Player Settings...** button; it opens the player settings parameters in the inspector. We do not need to change these now, but eventually we will.

5. To build the executable, click on **Build And Run**.

6. You will be prompted for a name and location of the build files. We recommend that you create a new folder in your project root named `Build` and specify the file or subfolder name under that, as needed.

   If the build encounters errors, well, that's a normal part of getting things going. We can't see your screen right now, so I recommend you check Google for answers. Additionally, there's a great community of users at the Unity Answers forum (`http://answers.unity3d.com/`).

7. Once the build completes successfully, because we also chose **Build And Run**, it will start running. You will see an initial Unity run dialog, as shown in the next screenshot. I often check the **Windowed** checkbox before clicking on **Play!**

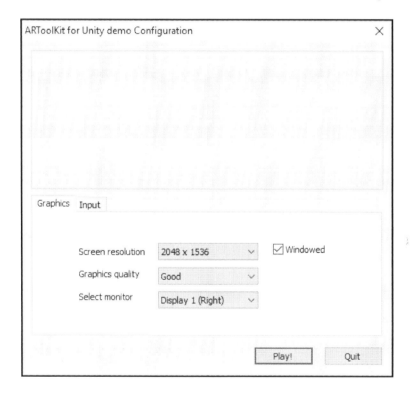

8. Depending on the AR SDK configuration, you may receive additional prompts before you launch the app itself. The property sheet dialog ahead is for ARToolkit. Unless you want to toy with property values, just accept the defaults and click on **OK**. (The directive to pop up this dialog is an option you can control from your scene's AR controller video options.)

If all goes well, you will have a standalone build of your AR app running.

9. Hold your image target in view of the webcam and the computer graphics should appear.

The next sections will cover additional tools and SDK that need to be installed for each of the other target platforms. Jump to the topic section(s) you want.

Targeting Android

This section will help you set up Android development from Unity on your Windows PC or macOS. The requirements are not specific to augmented reality; these are the same steps required by anyone building any Android app from Unity. The process is also well-documented elsewhere, including the Unity documentation at `https://docs.unity3d.com/Manual/android-sdksetup.html`.

The steps include the following:

- Install **Java Development Kit (JDK)**
- Install Android SDK
- Install USB device drivers and debugging
- Configure the Unity external tools
- Configure the Unity player settings for Android

OK, let's get going.

Installing Java Development Kit (JDK)

You may already have Java installed on your machine. You can check by opening a terminal window and running the `java -version` command, as shown next (macOS):

```
[[15:40][jonathan@Jonathans-iMac:~]$ java -version
java version "1.8.0_121"
Java(TM) SE Runtime Environment (build 1.8.0_121-b13)
Java HotSpot(TM) 64-Bit Server VM (build 25.121-b13, mixed mode)
[15:40][jonathan@Jonathans-iMac:~]$
```

You can see that this machine is running Java version 1.8.0, or more commonly, JDK 8 (the `1.` prefix is unspoken). You should have the current version. If you do not have Java or need to upgrade, browse to the Java SE Downloads web page, `http://www.oracle.com/technetwork/java/javase/downloads/index.html`, and get it.

Look for the **Java Platform (JDK)** button icon, as shown in the following image; it will take you to the **Downloads** page:

Choose the package for your system. For example, for a macOS, choose **Mac OS X**; for Windows, choose **Windows x64**. After the file is downloaded, open it and follow the installation instructions.

Make a note of the installation directory for later reference.

Once installed, open a fresh terminal window and run `java -version` once more to verify.

About your JDK location

Whether you have just installed the JDK or it was already there, make a note of its location on your disk. You will need to tell Unity about this in a later step.

On Windows, the path is probably something like `C:\Program Files\Java\jdk1.8.0_111\bin`.

If you can't find it, open Windows Explorer, navigate to the `Program Files` folder, look for `Java`, and drill down until you see its `bin` directory, as shown in the following screenshot:

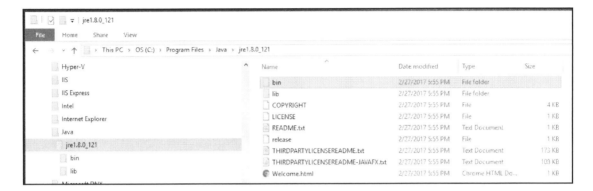

On macOS, the path is probably something like this: `/Library/Java/JavaVirtualMachines/jdk1.8.0_121.jdk/Contents/Home`

If you can't find it, from a terminal window, run `/usr/libexec/java_home`.

The output of this command is shown in the following screenshot:

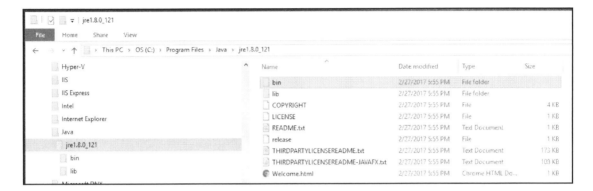

Installing an Android SDK

You also need to install an Android SDK. Specifically, you need *Android SDK Manager*. This is available by itself as a command-line tool or part of the full Android Studio **integrated development environment** (**IDE**). If you can afford the disk space, I recommend you to install Android Studio, as it provides a nice graphical interface for SDK Manager.

Installing via Android Studio

To install the Android Studio IDE, go to
`https://developer.android.com/studio/install.html` and click on **Download Android Studio**. When the download is done, open it and follow the installation instructions given:

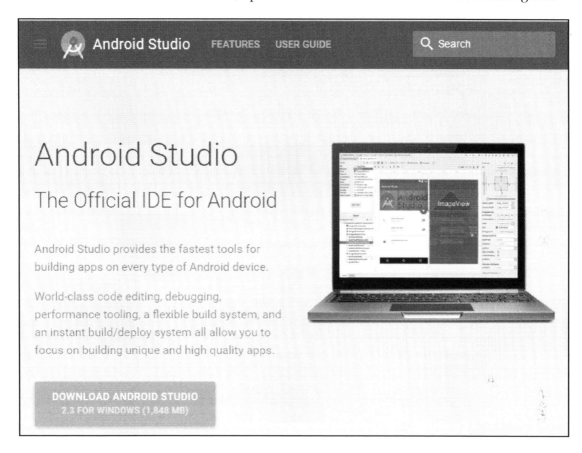

You will be prompted for the locations of the Android Studio IDE and the SDK. You can accept the default locations or change them. Make a note of the SDK path location; you will need to give Unity this information at a later step.

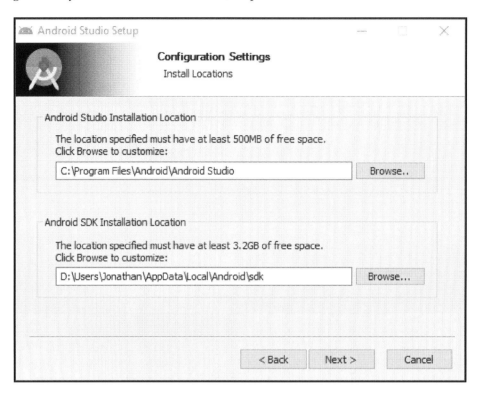

Personally, I have more room on my D: drive, so I will install the app to D:\Programs\Android\Android Studio. And, I like to keep the SDK near the Android Studio program files. It's easier to find that way again, so I changed **Android SDK Installation Location** to D:\Programs\Android\sdk.

Installing via command-line tools

Unity really only needs command-line tools to build projects for Android. If you prefer, you can install just that package and save on disk space. Scroll to the section named **Get just the command line tools** at the bottom of the downloads page. Select the package for your platform.

Get just the command line tools

If you do not need Android Studio, you can download the basic Android command line tools below. You can use the included sdkmanager to download other SDK packages.

These tools are included in Android Studio.

Platform	SDK tools package	Size	SHA-1 checksum
Windows	tools_r25.2.3-windows.zip	292 MB (306,745,639 bytes)	b965decb234ed793eb9574bad8791c50ca574173
Mac	tools_r25.2.3-macosx.zip	191 MB (200,496,727 bytes)	0e88c0bdb8f8ee85cce248580173e033a1bbc9cb
Linux	tools_r25.2.3-linux.zip	264 MB (277,861,433 bytes)	aafe7f28ac51549784efc2f3bdfc620be8a08213

See the SDK tools release notes.

This is a `.zip` file; uncompress it to a folder and remember its location. As mentioned earlier, on Windows, I like to use `D:\Programs\Android\sdk`. This will contain a `tools` subfolder.

The ZIP file only has the tools, not the actual SDK. Use `sdkmanager` to download the packages you'll need. See `https://developer.android.com/studio/command-line/sdkmanager.html` for details.

To list the installed and available packages, run `sdkmanager --list`. You can install multiple packages by listing them in quotes, delimited with a semicolon, as follows:

```
sdkmanager "platforms;android-25"
```

As of this writing, the minimum Android API levels are as follows (check the current documentation for changes):

- Vuforia: API Level 22 (Android 5.1 Lollipop)
- ARToolkit: API Level 15 (Android 4.0.3 IceCreamSandwich)

About your Android SDK root path location

If you already have Android installed or if you have forgotten where the SDK is installed, you can find the root path by opening the SDK Manager GUI. While Android Studio is open, navigate to **Tools** | **Android** | **SDK Manager**. You can find the path at the top:

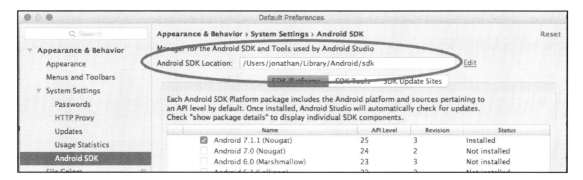

On Windows, the path is probably something like `C:\Program Files\Android\sdk`.

On macOS, the path is probably something like `/Users/Yourname/Library/Android/sdk`.

Installing USB device, debugging and connection

The next step is to enable USB debugging on your Android device. This is part of **Developer Options** in your Android settings. But, **Developer options** may not be visible and has to be enabled:

1. Find the **Build number** property by navigating to **Settings** | **About** on the device. Depending on your device, you may even need to drill down another level or two (such as **Settings** | **About** | **Software Information** | **More** | **Build number).**

2. Now, for the magic incantation, tap on the build number seven times. It'll count down until **Developer Options** is enabled and then appear as another choice in the Settings pane.

3. Go to **Settings** | **Developer**, find **USB debugging**, and enable it.

The following screenshot shows an Android device with USB debugging enabled:

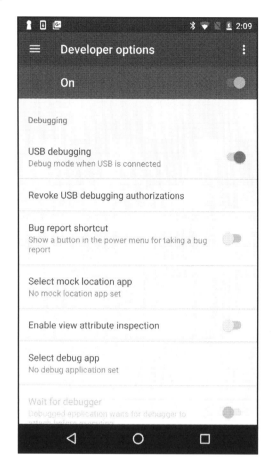

4. Now, connect the device to your development machine via a USB cable.

The Android device may automatically be recognized. If you are prompted to update the drivers, you can do this through Windows Device Manager.

On Windows, if the device is not recognized, you may need to download **Google USB Driver**. You can do this through SDK Manager, under the SDK Tools tab. For more information, go to
`https://developer.android.com/studio/run/win-usb.html`. The following screenshot, for example, shows the SDK Manager's **SDK Tools** tab with **Google USB Driver** selected:

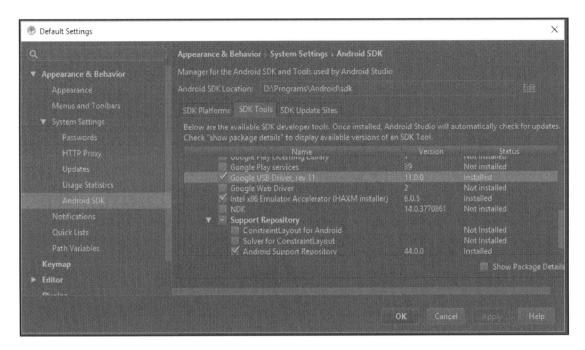

Great job so far!

Configuring Unity's external tools

Armed with all the stuff we need and the paths to the tools we installed, you can now go back to Unity. We need to tell Unity where to find all of the Java and Android stuff. Alternatively, if you skip this step, then Unity will prompt you for the folders when building the app. In Unity, do the following:

1. On Windows, navigate to **Edit | Preferences**, then select the **External Tools** tab on the left-hand side. On macOS, it's under **Unity | Preferences**.
2. In the **Android SDK** text slot, paste the path of your Android SDK.
3. In the **Java JDK** text slot, paste the path of your Java JDK.

Unity Preferences with my SDK and JDK are shown in the following screenshot:

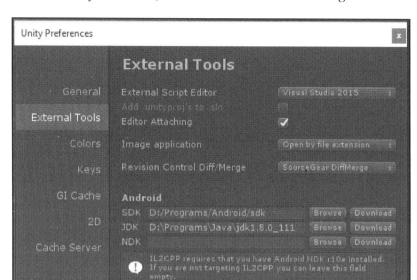

Configuring a Unity platform and player for Android

We will now configure your Unity project to build for Android, as discussed in the following list. First, ensure *Android* is your target platform in **Build Settings**:

1. In Unity, navigate to **File | Build Settings** and examine the **Platform** pane.
2. If **Android** is not presently selected, select it now and click on **Switch Platform**.

It may take a while to reimport assets and convert them into Android-compatible formats. The **Build Settings** box is shown in the following screenshot:

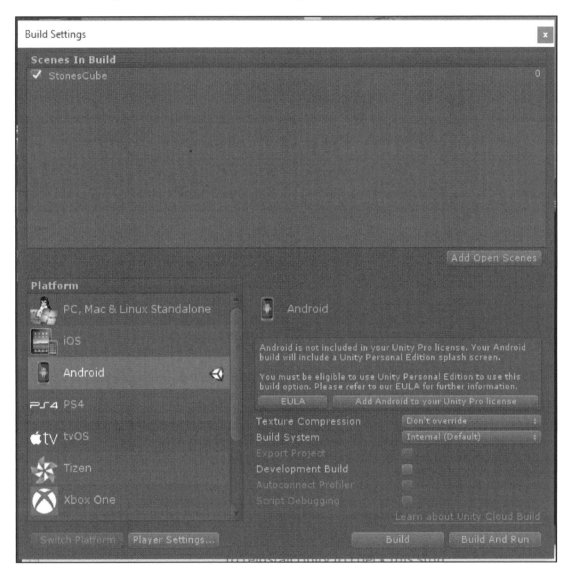

Unity provides a great deal of support for Android, including configuration and optimization for runtime features and the capabilities of mobile devices. These options can be found in **Player Settings...**. We only need to set a couple of them now. The minimum requirements to build our demo project include **Bundle Identifier** and **Minimum API Level**:

1. If you have the **Build Settings** window open, click on the **Player Settings...** button. Alternatively, you can get there from the main menu by navigating to **Edit | Project Settings... | Player**.
2. Look across at the **Inspector** panel, which now contains the player settings.
3. Find the **Other Settings** group of parameters and click on the header bar (if it's not already opened) to find the **Identification** variables, as shown in the following screenshot:

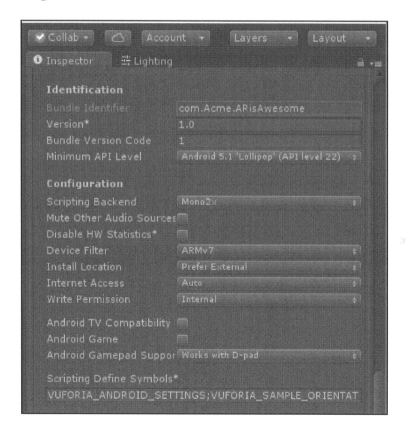

Set **Bundle Identifier** to a unique name for your product; it must resemble a traditional Java package name. An ID is required for all Android apps. Typically, it is in the `com.CompanyName.ProductName` format. It must be unique on the target device, and eventually, unique in the Google Play Store. You can choose whatever name you want.

4. Note that we also specified **Minimum API Level**. We selected **Android 5.1 Lollipop (API Level 22)** since we're using Vuforia, and as stated earlier in this chapter, this is presently its minimum Android version.

Again, there are many other options in **Player Settings...**, but we can use their defaults for now.

Building and running

Alright! We should be good to go, as follows:

1. Be sure your device is connected and turned on, and you have granted access to the PC.
2. In **Build Settings**, click on the **Build And Run** button to begin building. You will be prompted for a name and location for the build files.

We recommend that you create a new folder in your project root named `Build` and specify the file or subfolder name under that, as needed.

 On macOS, your `library` folder may be hidden. When prompted for the SDK Root path, you can press *Command+Shift+G* and type `~/Library`, then locate `~/Library/Android/sdk`.

If all goes well, Unity will create an `Android.apk` file and upload it to your device. You now have a running AR app that you can show off to your friends and family!

Troubleshooting

Here are some suggestions for common errors you may encounter when trying to build for an Android device from Unity.

Android SDK path error

If you encounter an error like the one shown in the following screenshot, it may be because the Android SDK root path is not configured properly or something is missing. In some releases of Android Studio, the `tools` folder is incomplete. Try downloading the command-line tools separately (refer to the *Via command line tools* section shown earlier), and remove and replace the `sdk/tools/` folder with the updated one.

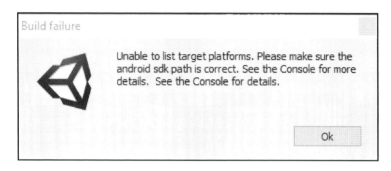

Plugins colliding error

If you encounter an error concerning **Plugins colliding with each other**, particularly using ARToolkit and its `libARWrapper` file, this is because there are several files in your `Plugins` folder with the same name that are getting linked to the build. Keep the version in `Plugins/Android`, but in the other folders, namely `x86` and `x86_64`, select the offending file. In **Inspector**, ensure that the **Android** platform is not checked, as shown in the following screenshot:

For other errors, Google is your friend.

Using Google ARCore for Unity

In August 2017, Google announced a new Android core SDK for augmented reality, called *ARCore*. Presumably, it directly derives from the Google project *Tango*. Tango is Google's augmented reality platform that has been in development, a beta release, for several years and is beginning to emerge in mobile devices equipped with depth sensing cameras. ARCore, on the other hand, does not require any specialized hardware other than a phone or tablet with an ordinary camera and a fast processor (such as Google Pixel or Samsung Galaxy S8 phones). For current supported devices, see `https://developers.google.com/ar/discover/#supported_devices`. Much like Apple's ARKit (as described later in this chapter), it is being rapidly adopted and promises to be a leading platform for augmented reality.

 We are pleased to provide an introduction to Google ARCore in this book, but only an introduction. ARCore is brand new, and at the time of writing this, it is in preview release only. The documentation and demo scene they provide is very bare-bones. And, the setup will likely be different when Unity supports ARCore in the final release. Things such as installing the preview of AR Services APK will change. Refer to the GitHub repository for this book for new implementation notes and code using Google ARCore for Android: `https://github.com/ARUnityBook/`. The principles are very similar to ARKit, but the Unity SDK and components are different.

For some of your projects, you can use Google ARCore for Android instead of a general-purpose toolkit, such as Vuforia or ARToolkit. While Vuforia, for example, is best a target-based AR, ARCore is especially good at anchoring virtual objects in real-world 3D space and recognizing surfaces in the real world. In that sense, it shares similar use cases with Microsoft HoloLens and Apple ARKit.

At the time of this writing, ARCore requires Android SDK version 7.0 (API Level 24) and a supported device. The system requirements, API, and SDK are subject to change.

The arcore-unity-sdk project from Google provides a thin wrapper around the native ARCore SDK. Note that `arcore-unity-sdk` is an open source project hosted on GitHub at `https://github.com/google-ar/arcore-unity-sdk`. It provides Unity scripts, components, and prefabs that you can use. It also includes several example scenes.

To install `arcore-unity-sdk`, perform the following steps:

1. Be sure you are using a compatible version of Unity (at time of this writing, Unity 2017.2 Beta 9 or later is required).

2. Download the SDK `Unitypackage` file, using the link provided on the **Getting Started** page at `https://developers.google.com/ar/develop/unity/getting-started`

3. Import the asset package into your Unity project (from the Unity main menu, choose **Assets | Import Package | Custom Package...** and then find the selected `unitypackage` file on your system).

4. Then, press **Import**.

Review the folders and files installed in your `Assets` folder. The `Assets/GoogleARCore` folder contains the HelloAR example scene along with various supporting subfolders. The ARCore plugin's actual assets reside in the `Assets/GoogleARCore/SDK/` folder.

The project's `Asset` folders are shown in the following screenshot, with `SDK/Scripts/` selected:

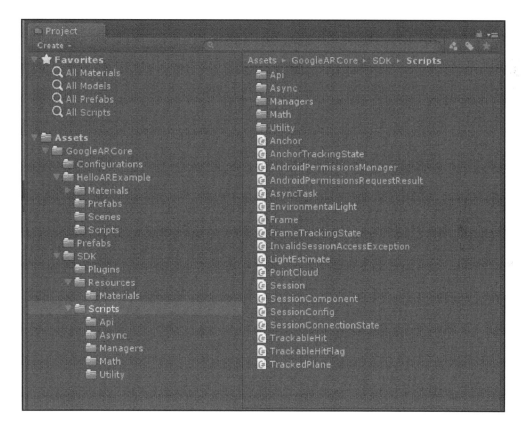

Once installed, you can try ARCore by opening one of the example scenes. The `HelloAR` scene is a basic scene with an example Android robot. It demonstrates all of the basic functionality of ARCore. Open the scene as follows:

1. In the **Project** window, navigate to
   `Assets/GoogleARCore/HelloARExample/Scenes/`.
2. Double-click on **HelloAR**.

You will notice that the **Hierarchy** scene contains the following objects that are basic to any ARKit scenes:

1. First is **ARCore Device**; it contains a child **First Person Camera** object. It includes **Tracked Pose Driver**, a component for tracking the camera pose in 3D space, and **Session Component** for managing the AR session connections.
2. Then we have **Environmental Light**; this automatically adjusts the lighting settings for the scene to be in line with those estimated by ARCore from the real world.

The `HelloAR` hierarchy is shown in the following screenshot:

The other objects are examples specific to this demo application scene. Although subject to change as the plugin matures, the current scene includes the following:

- **ExampleController** handles camera tracking, horizontal plane detection, plane visualization, and hit detections.
- **PointCloud** visualizes the point cloud as ARCore detects 3D nodes in the spatial mesh construction of the real-world space.
- **Canvas and Event System** are ordinary Unity objects for handling **user interface (UI)**.

In preparation of building the scene, perform the following steps:

1. From the main menu, navigate to **File | Build Settings**.
2. Select **Add Open Scenes** and/or uncheck all the scenes in **Scenes in Build**, except **HelloAR.**
3. In the **Platform** pane, ensure **Android** is selected and click on **Switch Platform**, if needed.

The **Build Settings** box is shown in the following screenshot:

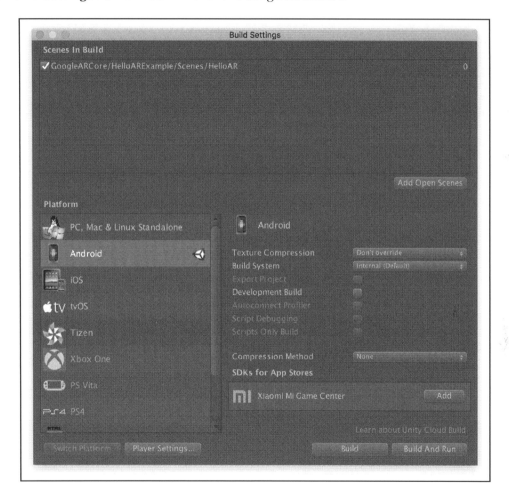

There are build and player settings you should consider. If you load ARKit into a new Unity project, these settings (or similar) may already be set up. Let's take a look at the following steps:

1. Click on **Player Settings....**
2. In **Inspector**, under **Other Settings**, uncheck the **Multithreaded Rendering** checkbox.
3. Enter a valid **Bundle Identifier** (in the form of `com.company.product`) as described previously.
4. For **Mininum API Level**, choose **Android 7.0 or higher**.
5. For **Target API Level**, choose **Android 7.0 or 7.1**.
6. In **XR Setting**, check the **Tango Supported** checkbox.

At the time of this writing, there is no emulator for running and testing ARCore apps from within Unity and no remote option to let you use the play mode from Unity to test your app without the need to build and run each time. This is obviously subject to change and will hopefully be resolved by the time you are reading this, as *time keeps on moving, into the future.*

Targeting iOS

This section will help you set up your macOS for iOS development from Unity for iPhones and iPads. The requirements are not specific to augmented reality; these are the same steps required by anyone building any iOS app from Unity. The process is also well-documented elsewhere, including the Unity documentation at `https://docs.unity3d.com/Manual/iphone-GettingStarted.html`.

The downside of Apple's closed ecosystem is you must use macOS as your development machine to develop for iOS. That's just the way it is. The upside is that the setup process is very straightforward.

The steps include the following:

1. Having an Apple ID.
2. Installing Xcode.
3. Configuring Unity Player Settings for iOS.
4. Building and running.

Okay, let's take a bite of this apple.

Having an Apple ID

To develop for iOS, you need a Macintosh computer and an Apple ID to log in to the App Store. This will permit you to build iOS apps that run on your personal device.

We also recommend that you have an Apple Developer account. It costs $99 USD per year but is your admission ticket to the tools and services, including the setup provisioning profiles needed to share and test your app on other devices. You can find out more about the Apple Developer Program at `https://developer.apple.com/programs/`.

Installing Xcode

Xcode is the all-in-one toolkit for developing for any Apple device. It is free to download from the Mac App Store: `https://itunes.apple.com/gb/app/xcode/id497799835?mt=12`. Beware, it is quite big (over 4.5 GB as of this writing), but *ya gotta do what ya gotta do*. Download it, open the downloaded `.dmg` file, and follow the installation instructions.

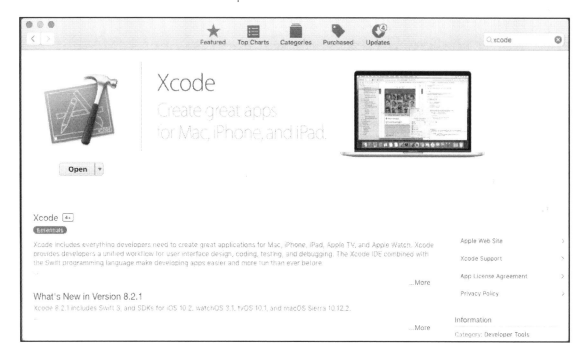

Configuring the Unity player settings for iOS

We will now configure your Unity project to build for iOS. First, ensure *iOS* is your target platform in **Build Settings**.

1. In Unity, navigate to **File | Build Settings** and examine the **Platform** pane. If **iOS** is not presently selected, select it now and press **Switch Platform**, as shown in the following screenshot. It may take a while to reimport the assets to convert them into iOS-compatible formats.

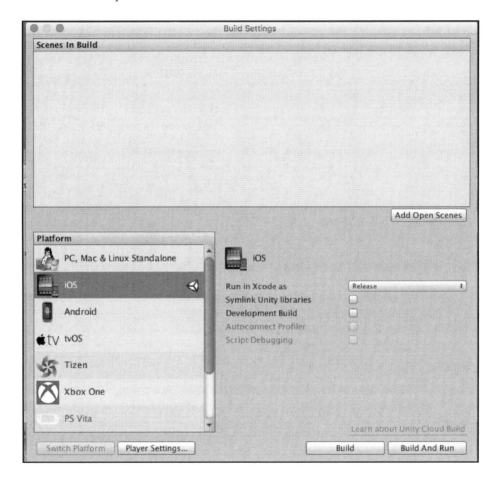

Unity provides a great deal of support for iOS, including configuration and optimization for runtime features and the capabilities of mobile devices. These options can be found in player settings. We only need to set a couple of them now, which is the minimum that is required to build our demo project.

2. If you have the **Build Settings** window open, press the **Player Settings...** button. Alternatively, you can get there by navigating to **Edit | Project Settings | Player**. Look across at the **Inspector** panel, which now contains the player settings.

3. Find the **Other Settings** group of parameters and click on the header bar (if it's not already opened) to find the **Identification** variables, as shown here:

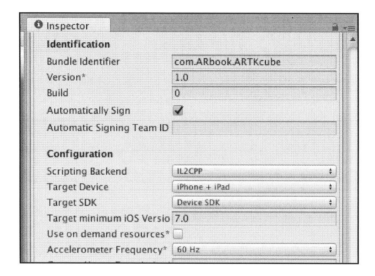

4. Set **Bundle Identifier** to a unique name for your product that resembles a traditional Java package name. An ID is required for all iOS apps. Typically, it is in the `com.CompanyName.ProductName` format. It must be unique on the target device, and eventually, unique in the App Store. You can choose whatever name you want.

5. In the **Configuration** section, fill in **Camera Usage Description** with something like `Augmented Reality` to ask the user permission to use the camera:

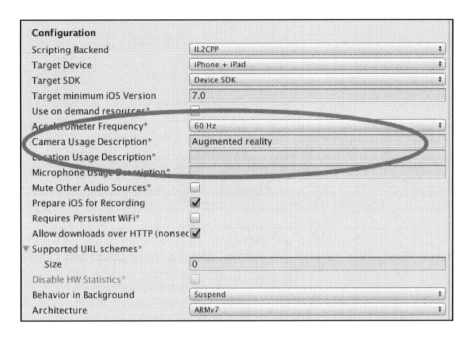

Again, there are many other options in the player settings, but we can use their defaults for now.

ARToolkit player settings

If you are using the open source ARToolkit, you may need additional player setting requirements. Also, refer to their documentation for additional suggested settings, which is available at `https://archive.artoolkit.org/documentation/doku.php?id=6_Unity:unity_on_ios`.

For the **Architecture** option, choose **ARMv7** as its library does not support Bitcode (at the time of this writing).

Building and running

Xcode consists of an IDE that hosts your Xcode projects. When you build for iOS from Unity, it doesn't actually build an iOS executable. Rather, Unity builds an `Xcode-ready` project folder that you then open in Xcode to complete the compile, build, and deploy process in order to run the app on your device. Let's go:

1. Be sure your device is turned on, connected, and you have granted access to the Mac.
2. In **Build Settings**, click on the **Build And Run** button to begin building.
3. You will be prompted for a name and location for the build files. We recommend that you create a new folder in your project root named `Build` and specify the file or subfolder name under that, as needed.

If all goes well, Unity will create an Xcode project and open it in Xcode. It will attempt to build the app, and if successful, upload it to your device. You now have a running AR app on your device that you can show off to your friends and family.

Troubleshooting

Here are some suggestions for common errors you may encounter when trying to build for an iOS device from Unity and Xcode.

Plugins colliding error

If you encounter an error concerning **Plugins colliding with each other**, particularly using ARToolkit and its `libARWrapper` file, this is because there are several files in your `Plugins` folder with the same name that are getting linked to the build. Keep the version in `Plugins/iOS`, but in the other folders, namely `x86` and `x86_64`, select the offending file.

In **Inspector**, ensure that the **iOS** platform is not checked, as shown in the following screenshot:

Recommended project settings warning

If it fails within Xcode, you might see some errors and warnings, as shown in the following screenshot:

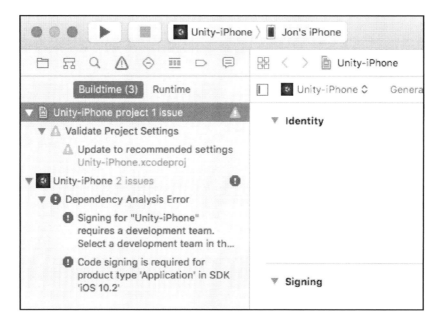

If you click on **Update to recommended settings**, a dialog will appear with a list of suggested changes. Click on the **Perform Changes** button.

Requires development team error

If you click on the **Signing for "Unity-iPhone" requires a development team** error, a hint will appear instructing you to select a development team in the project editor. To correct this, perform the following steps:

1. Click on the project name at the root of the error tree on the left-hand side (in the preceding case, that's **Unity-iPhone**).

2. Then, in the main area toolbar, select your project name in the leftmost **Targets** list (as shown in the following screenshot, that (also) is **Unity-iPhone**):

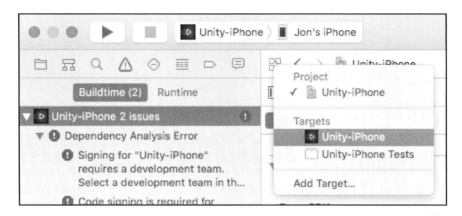

3. Select the **General** tab, then look to the **Signing** section and choose a team from the select list, as shown here:

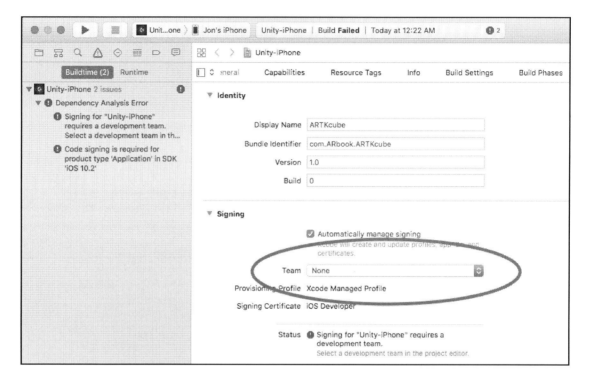

4. If you do not yet have a team in the list, you probably have not yet configured your Apple ID with Xcode. In that case, first go to **Preferences | Accounts** and add an Apple ID by tapping on the plus sign.

Now, once again, try to build by pressing the **Play** icon in the upper-left corner of Xcode (hint: the **Play** button's tooltip will say "Build and then run the current scheme").

Linker failed error

If you receive a linker error, **Linker command failed**, with a reason that a library does not contain bitcode (as may be the case with ARToolkit's `libARWrapper.a` file), try disabling Bitcode using the following steps:

1. Click on the project name at the root of the error tree on the left-hand side (in the preceding case, that's **Unity-iPhone**).
2. Then, in the main area toolbar, select your project name in the leftmost **Targets** list, which (also) is **Unity-iPhone**.
3. Select the **Build Settings** tab, then look to the **Build Options** section and the **Enable Bitcode** option. Set it to **No**:

No video feed on the iOS device

If the Unity app loads but the screen is blank, that could be due to a number of causes. Double-check to see that you've granted permissions to use the camera by filling in **Camera Usage Description**.

With ARToolkit, users have also reported that you should enable **Allow non-RGB video internally** in the AR Controller component (and try disabling **Use native GL texturing**):

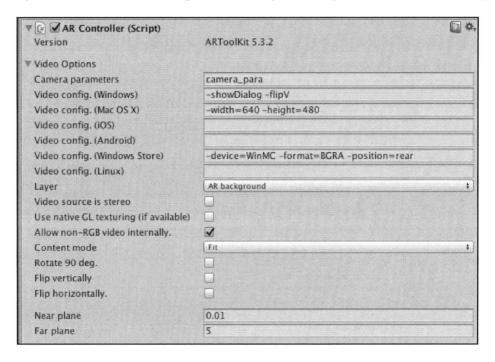

For other errors, Google is your friend.

Using Apple ARKit for Unity

In June 2017, at the **Worldwide Developers Conference** (**WWDC17**), Apple announced their first plunge into augmented reality with the introduction of **ARKit**, a new framework on iOS for creating AR experiences for iPhone and iPad. Although new, it is being rapidly adopted and promises to be a leading platform for augmented reality, albeit limited to Apple devices and not for image target or marker-based applications.

For some of your projects, you can use the Apple ARKit for iOS instead of a general-purpose toolkit, such as Vuforia or ARToolkit. While Vuforia, for example, is best a target-based AR, ARKit is especially good at anchoring virtual objects in real-world 3D space and recognizing surfaces in the real world. In that sense, it shares similar use cases with Microsoft HoloLens.

Like any iOS development, developing with ARKit requires using a macOS computer and a current version of the Xcode development environment.

 At the time of this writing, ARKit is in beta version and requires iOS 11. This means that it is available to developers and limited to specific iOS devices. It also means that the system requirements, API, and SDK are subject to change. Based on past experiences, our expectation is that by the time it is released and you read this, the interface to ARKit will not be very different from the version we are working with, but there is that possibility.

The `Unity-ARKit-Plugin` project, maintained by Unity Technologies, provides a thin wrapper around the native ARKit SDK. It provides Unity scripts, components, and prefabs you can use. It also includes several example scenes.

`Unity-ARKit-Plugin` is an open source project hosted on Bitbucket at `https://bitbucket.org/Unity-Technologies/unity-arkit-plugin`. If you want the latest and greatest version, go there. But, there is also an Asset Store package, which is regularly kept up to date, and we recommend using it.

To install `Unity-ARKit-Plugin`, perform the following steps:

1. In Unity, if the Asset Store tab is not visible, go to **Window** | **Asset Store**.
2. Enter `ARKit` in the search box to find the current package.
3. Select **Download**, then click on **Import** to import it into your project.

Review the folders and files installed in your `Assets` folder. The `Assets/UnityARKitPlugin` folder contains the example scenes along with various supporting subfolders. The ARKit plugin's actual assets reside in the `Assets/UnityARKitPlugin/Plugsin/iOS/UnityARKit/` folder.

The project's `Asset` folders are shown in the following screenshot:

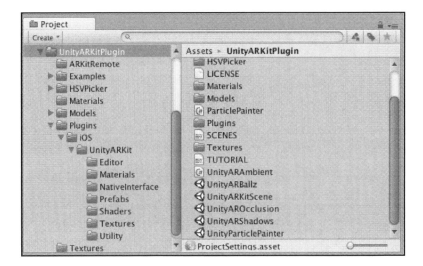

Once installed, you can try ARKit by opening one of the example scenes. The `UnityARKitScene` scene is a basic scene with a simple cube. It demonstrates all of the basic functionality of ARKit. Open the scene as follows:

1. In the **Project** window, navigate to `Assets/UnityARKitPlugin/`.
2. Double-click on **UnityARKitScene**.

You will notice that the **Hierarchy** scene contains the following objects that are basic to any ARKit scenes:

- **Main Camera**, parented by an empty **CameraParent** object, has a **UnityARVideo** component for rendering live video feed and handling device orientation.
- **ARCameraManager**, with the **UnityARCameraManager** component, interfaces the camera with the native ARKit SDK, including the current camera pose transform.
- **Directional Light**, with an optional **UnityARAmbient** component, will adjust the scene lighting based on the ARKit's detection of ambient lighting conditions in the real world.
- **GeneratePlanes**, with the **UnityARGeneratePlane** component, will generate Unity objects in the scene for planes detected by ARKit. You can supply prefabs to render, for example, occlusion of objects or shadows of your virtual objects in the real world.

The `UnityARKitScene` hierarchy is shown in the following screenshot:

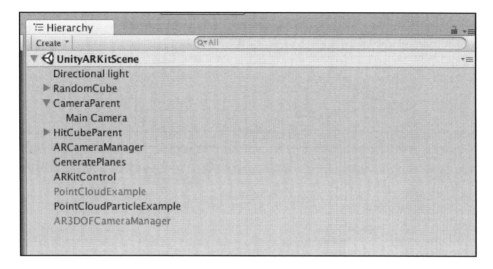

The other objects are examples specific to this demo application scene. Although subject to change as the plugin matures, the current scene includes the following:

- **RandomCube**: This is a cube with a checkboard pattern rendered one meter in front of you when the app starts.
- **HitCube** (parented by **HitCubeParent**) with **UnityARHitTestExample**: This is an example of using screen touch input to place cubes in the AR scene.
- **PointCloudParticleExample**: This along with **PointCloudParticleExample** renders ARKit's current scanning results as fuzzy particles. As ARKit scans your environment, it generates a point cloud of key points in 3D space on depth surfaces it has detected.
- **ARKitControl**: This along with the **ARKitControl** component provides a simple GUI for controlling the AR session with buttons for start, stop, and other options.

In preparation of building the scene, perform the following steps:

1. From the main menu, navigate to **File | Build Settings**.
2. Select **Add Open Scenes** and/or uncheck all the scenes in **Scenes in Build**, except **UnityARKitScene**.
3. In the **Platform** pane, ensure **iOS** is selected and click on **Switch Platform**, if needed.

The **Build Settings** box is shown in the following screenshot:

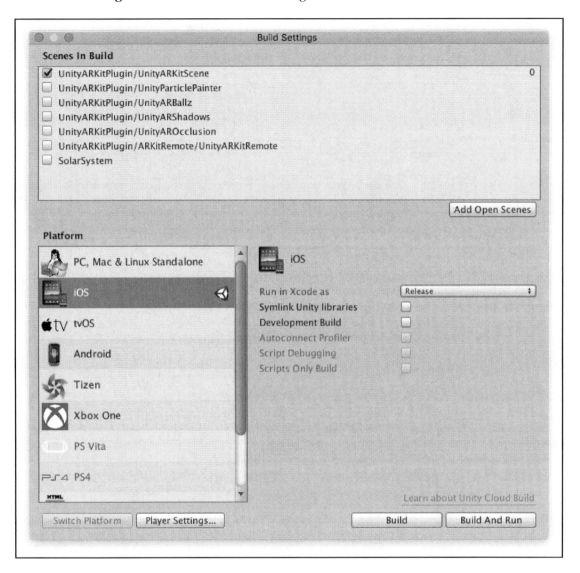

There are build and player settings you should consider. If you load ARKit into a new Unity project, these settings (or similar) may already be set up. Let's take a look at the following steps:

1. Click on **Player Settings....**
2. In **Inspector**, uncheck the **Auto Graphics API** checkbox and click on **Metal Graphics API**.
3. Enter a valid **Bundle Identifier** (in the form of `com.company.product`), as described previously.
4. Fill in **Camera Usage Description**, as described earlier (such as `augmented reality`).
5. Optionally, for a better user experience, check the **Use Animated Autorotation** and **Render Extra Frame on Pause** checkboxes.

We can also optimize the quality settings. The default **High** settings are closest to what are used in the ARKit example projects; so, if you're starting a new project, you can start as follows:

1. Go to **Edit | Project Settings | Quality**.
2. In the **Levels** table, select the **High** row.
3. For **Shadows**, click on **Hard Shadows Only**.
4. For **Shadows Projection**, click on **Close Fit**.
5. Set **Shadow Distance** to 20.
6. For **Shadowmask Mode**, select **Shadowmask**.
7. Set **Shadow Near Plane Offset** to 2.

8. Now, in the **Levels** column for iOS, at the bottom, select the down triangle and choose **High** as the default quality setting, as shown in the following screenshot:

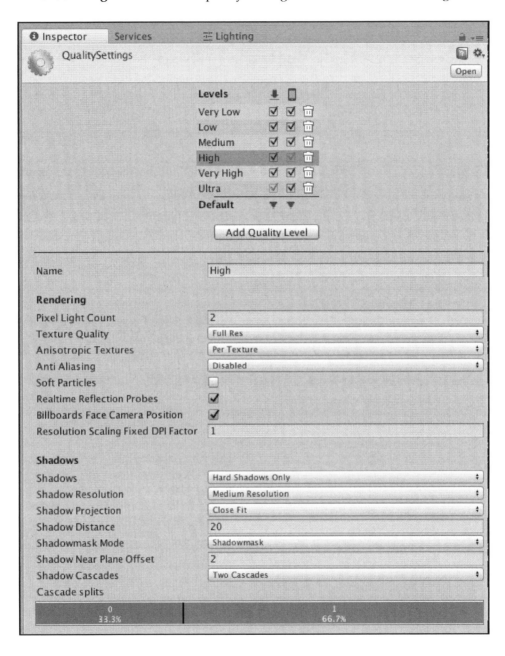

When you're ready, go ahead and click on **Build And Run**. As described earlier, like any iOS app, Unity will generate Xcode project files and launch into Xcode, which in turn will do the heavy lifting of compiling and building the actual iOS code.

At the present time, there is no emulator for running and testing ARKit apps from within Unity. However, there is a remote option that lets you use play mode from Unity to test your app without the need to build and run it each time. With the remote app running on your attached device, the Unity project can access the video and sensor data on the device and behave as if it's running on the device, but it plays in the **Unity Editor Game** window. This remote app comes as a scene in the ARKit package we just installed and can be found at `Assets/UnityARKitPlugin/ARKitRemote/UnityARKitRemote.unity`. To use it, add another game object to your scene with the **ARKitRemoteConnection** component added. Instructions are included in the `readme` file in that folder. For more information, refer to `https://blogs.unity3d.com/2017/08/03/introducing-the-unity-arkit-remote/`.

Targeting Microsoft HoloLens

This section will help you set up your Windows PC for Windows Mixed Reality holographic development with Unity.

In addition to Android and iOS, a third important emerging target platform for augmented reality is Microsoft Mixed Reality. Microsoft uses the term "*Mixed Reality*" to encompass their combined strategy for augmented reality and virtual reality. These technologies do have a lot in common, and especially at the system and software architecture level, Microsoft has decided to mix these realities under one API banner. Microsoft's AR device is HoloLens, presently in Beta. And their mixed reality support specifically is often referred to as **holographics**.

Windows 10 brings us UWP, which provides a common platform for any device that runs Windows 10, including desktops, game consoles (Xbox), mobile devices, VR headsets, and HoloLens. It includes a common set of core APIs guaranteed across devices. And, Windows Store provides a unified distribution channel for your apps. This is not just for Microsoft-manufactured hardware. UWP is and will continue to be supported by products from Microsoft industry partners, including HP, Acer, and all.

While Microsoft UWP holographic refers to a class of mixed reality devices, this book will focus on the HoloLens device and may use the terms interchangeably.

We will now walk you through the setup steps. But given that this is a new platform, things are subject to change. Here are some first-source references that will also help you get started and keep you up to date:

- Microsoft Mixed Reality overview at `https://developer.microsoft.com/en-us/windows/mixed-reality`

- Microsoft Mixed Reality Unity development overview at `https://developer.microsoft.com/en-us/windows/mixed-reality/unity_development_overview`

- Unity Windows Holographic Getting Started at `https://docs.unity3d.com/Manual/windowsholographic.html`

- Vuforia development for HoloLens at `https://library.vuforia.com/articles/Training/Developing-Vuforia-Apps-for-HoloLens`

- Microsoft HoloToolkit Getting Started (renamed from HoloToolkit-Unity) at `https://github.com/Microsoft/MixedRealityToolkit-Unity/blob/master/GettingStarted.md`

- Get started with Visual Studio at `https://www.visualstudio.com/vs/getting-started/`

- Microsoft Holograms 101E, introduction with Emulator, at `https://developer.microsoft.com/en-us/windows/mixed-reality/holograms_101e`

There are minimum requirements and software versions that you will need, as shown in the following list. Again, this will certainly change in time:

- 64-bit Windows 10 (not the *Home* edition)
- Visual Studio 2015 Update 3 or later, Visual Studio 2017 preferred
- Vuforia 6.1 or later
- Unity 5.5.1 or later, Unity 2017 preferred
- Hololens Emulator (recommended even if you have a physical device)
- Holographic Remoting Player (recommended, installed on a HoloLens device); refer to `https://developer.microsoft.com/en-us/windows/mixed-reality/holographic_remoting_player`

The major steps for setting up your development machine for HoloLens development include:

1. Having a Microsoft developer account.
2. Enabling Windows 10 Hyper-V.
3. Installing Visual Studio.
4. Installing HoloLens Emulator.
5. Setting up HoloLens for development.
6. Configuring Unity project settings.
7. Configuring Unity player settings.
8. Vuforia settings for HoloLens.
9. Building and running.

OK, time to fire up the hologram and head over to *Alderaan*.

Having a Microsoft developer account

The first step is to make sure you have a Microsoft developer account. It costs just $19 USD per year ($99 USD for company accounts). A developer account is not required, but it is certainly recommended. You will need a personal Microsoft account to associate with your developer account. It gives you access to the tools and services to submit apps and provide access to the Dev Center portal. You can find out more about the Microsoft developer program at `https://developer.microsoft.com/en-us/store/register/faq`.

Enabling Windows 10 Hyper-V

Developing for HoloLens requires that you are developing on a machine with Windows 10. It should be a 64-bit version and must be *Windows 10 Pro, Enterprise*, or *Education* editions, *not* Windows 10 *Home*. If you have the Home edition, you can upgrade to Pro via the Windows Store for $99; search for **Windows 10 Pro**.

You must enable **Hyper-V** (**hypervisor**) on your system to use the HoloLens emulator. Hyper-V allows you to run virtual machines on your host PC. After all, HoloLens is a separate computer unto itself, running Windows 10. When we run a HoloLens emulator, we are basically firing up a virtual machine in our computer that is pretending to be a HoloLens device.

To enable Hyper-V, follow the following steps:

1. Go to Windows **Control Panel** | **Programs** | **Programs and Features** | **Turn Windows Features on or off**.
2. Ensure that **Hyper-V** is selected.

Good!

Installing Visual Studio

When you install Unity, you have the option to install Microsoft Visual Studio Tools for Unity as the default script editor. However, this is not a full version of Visual Studio.

Visual Studio is a powerful IDE for all kinds of projects. When we build for UWP from Unity, we will actually build a Visual Studio-ready project folder that you can then open in VS to complete the compile, build, and deploy process in order to run the app on your device.

At a minimum, you will need Visual Studio 2015, Update 3, with the following components (see `https://developer.microsoft.com/en-us/windows/holographic/install_the_tools`):

- Windows 10 SDK (10.0.10586)
- Tools 1.4

Visual Studio comes in three editions, namely *Community*, *Professional*, and *Enterprise*; any of these are sufficient for us. The Community version is free and can be downloaded from `https://www.visualstudio.com/vs/`.

Once the installer is downloaded, open it to choose which components to install. As shown in the following image, under the **Workloads** tab, we have selected the following:

- **Universal Windows Platform development**
- **Game development with Unity**

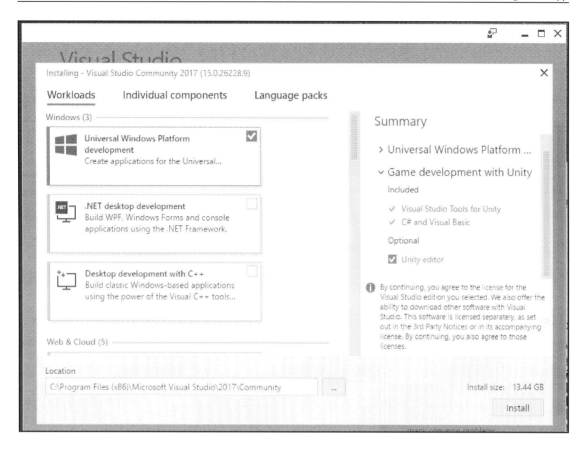

Also, select the **Game development with Unity** options, as follows:

Under the **Individual Components** tab, in addition to the default Windows 10 SDK, ensure the one named **Windows 10 SDK (10.0.10586)** is marked, as shown here:

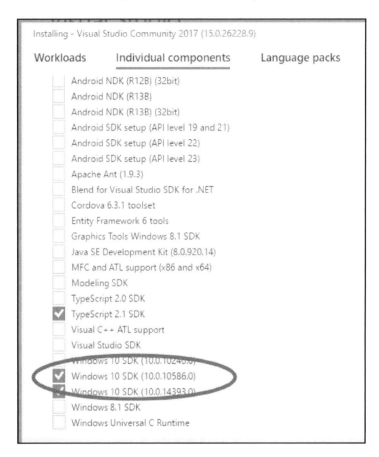

Begin the download and install it.

 It is risky for us, as authors, to embalm such details in a book. The specific SDK version is likely to change by the time you read this. But we think it is worthwhile to cover the details of the installation and setup process and let you infer how it differs for you, rather than leave it out altogether.

If you already had Visual Studio installed (minimum VS 2015, Update 3) or if you ever want to verify you have the required components, you can check as follows:

1. Go to Windows **Control Panel | Programs | Programs and Features**
2. Locate the Visual Studio you have installed (for example, **Microsoft Visual Studio Community 2015 with Updates**), then right-click and choose **Change**, as shown here:

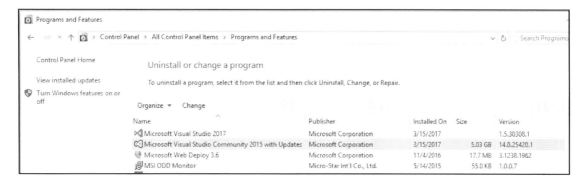

3. In the next dialog box, click on **Modify**.
4. Check any missing features and update your installation, as shown here:

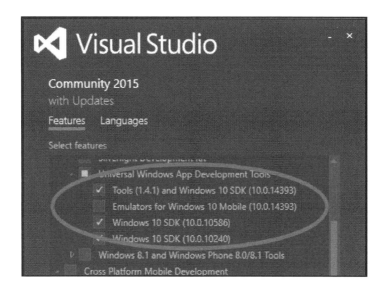

Installing the HoloLens emulator

The HoloLens emulator lets you simulate a physical HoloLens device while developing apps. It is not technically required, especially if you have a physical device on hand throughout your development cycle. Even so, devices get borrowed, moved around, or otherwise become unavailable, so it's wise to have a *plan B*:

1. From the **Install the tools** page (`https://developer.microsoft.com/en-us/windows/holographic/install_the _tools`), use the **HoloLens Emulator** link to download its installer.

2. Open it and follow the instructions to install the emulator, as shown here:

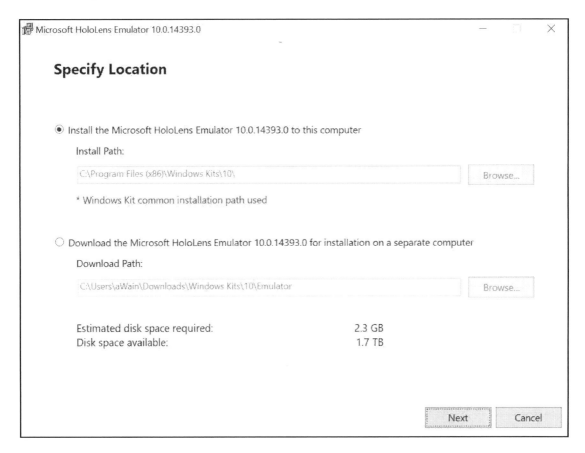

3. Accept the privacy and license agreements, then install it.
4. When it's complete, you should see a welcome message. Click on the **Close** button.

5. You should reboot your computer after installing the emulator.

 Usage documentation of the HoloLens emulator can be found at `https://developer.microsoft.com/en-us/windows/holographic/using_the_hololens_emulator`.

The next time you're in Unity, the emulator will be available, as we'll see when we start building our AR projects with HoloLens.

Setting up and pairing the HoloLens device for development

Your physical HoloLens device needs to be set up for development. If it hasn't been set up yet, follow these instructions from the video on the **Install the tools** page. You will only need to pair each device once, per development machine.

First, you'll need to have the Windows Device Portal set up on your HoloLens device. It lets you configure and manage your device remotely over Wi-Fi or USB. According to the documentation, the Device Portal *is a web server on your HoloLens that you can connect to from a web browser on your PC*. It includes tools to help manage your HoloLens and debug and optimize your apps. See the **Using the Windows Device Portal** page at `https://developer.microsoft.com/en-us/windows/holographic/using_the_windows_device_portal`.

To enable Device Portal in the HoloLens device, perform these steps:

1. Perform the *bloom* gesture to launch the main menu.
2. Gaze at the **Settings** tile and tap on **gesture**.
3. Perform a second tap gesture to place the app in your environment. The *Settings* app will launch after your place it.
4. Select the **Update** menu item.
5. Select the **For developers** menu item.
6. Enable **Developer Mode**.
7. Scroll down and enable **Device Portal** and Enable **remote device management**.

The Device Portal with remote management enabled, is shown ahead:

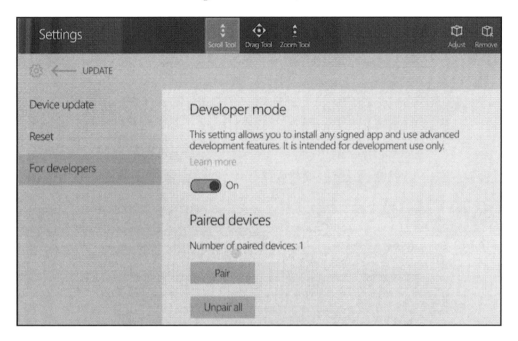

To pair your device, connect it to your PC via USB. Go to the online device portal to request a PIN, as shown here:

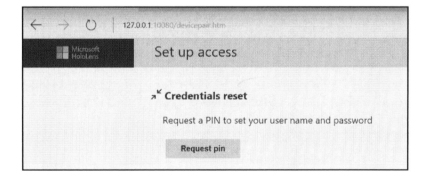

Looking through the HoloLens device, you will see the unique PIN for the device. Now go back to the device portal and enter the PIN along with the username and password. Pair the HoloLens device with the development PC by entering the username and password you just entered, as follows:

The window with the pairing number on the device should present a **Done** button when the device is paired. Use a zooming (*Tap*) gesture on this button to continue: press your thumb and forefinger together with a closed hand, then extend your thumb and forefinger.

You're now ready to start developing on HoloLens.

Configuring Unity's external tools

We can now go to Unity. First, we should make sure Unity knows we're using Visual Studio as shown in the steps ahead:

1. Go to **Edit | Preferences**.
2. In the **External Tools** tab, make sure **Visual Studio** is selected as your **External Script Editor**, like so:

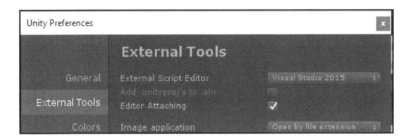

Configuring the Unity platform and player for the UWP holographic

Now we will configure our Unity project to build for Windows UWP holographic.

Build settings

First, ensure Windows Store is your target platform in **Build Settings**. That's what it's called when we're building for UWP:

1. In Unity, navigate to **File | Build Settings** and examine the **Platform** pane.
2. If **Windows Store** is not presently selected, select it now and press **Switch Platform**.

On the right-hand side of the dialog are options for the Windows Store platform. Choose the following:

1. **SDK: Universal 10**
2. **UWP Build Type: D3D**
3. **Unity C# Projects** (check this box)

Quality settings

Unity's project quality settings provide preconfigured groups of settings that let you tune your app for different target platforms, managing the trade-offs between performance and rendering quality. Typically, for desktop platforms, you will go for high quality because it has the processing power. For mobile platforms, you'll favor speed at the expense of quality.

For other mobile platforms, the quality settings will most likely be tailored for lower performance processors and conservation of battery life. In particular, soft shadows and shadow cascades are too expensive to use on HoloLens and should be avoided. UWP builds may not have this setting by default. Change the Quality settings as follows:

1. Navigate to **Edit | Project Settings | Quality**.
2. In **Inspector**, you'll see a table with rows for different quality levels.
3. Find the column for Windows Store (**Windows-icon**).
4. At the bottom of the column, click on **down-triangle** and select **Fastest** for the default quality level, as shown here:

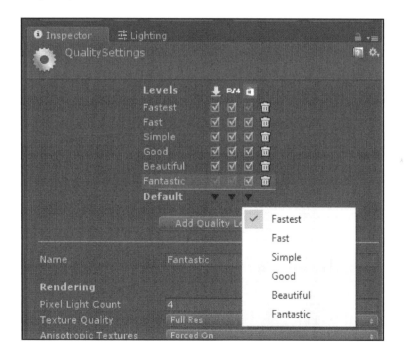

For more details and additional performance suggestions, see Microsoft's **Performance recommendations for Unity** at
`https://developer.microsoft.com/en-us/windows/mixed-reality/performance_recomme` `ndations_for_unity`.

Player settings - capabilities

Unity provides a great deal of support for UWP, including configuration of device capabilities. We need to enable a bunch of them for HoloLens as shown ahead:

1. If you have the **Build Settings** window open, press the **Player Settings...** button. Or, you can get there from **Edit** | **Project Settings** | **Player**.
2. Look across at the **Inspector** panel, which now contains the player settings.
3. Find the **Publishing Settings** group of parameters and click on the header bar (if it's not already opened) to find the **Capabilities** pane. Ensure all the following items are enabled (checked):
   - **InternetClient** - for Vuforia's cloud target database
   - **PicturesLibrary** - for PhotoCapture camera frame functionality
   - **MusicLibrary** - for VideoCapture audio recording
   - **VideosLibrary** - for VideoCapture video recording
   - **WebCam** - required for PhotoCapture and VideoCapture
   - **Microphone** - required for voice recognition
   - **SpatialPerception** - required for spatial mapping

Player settings - other settings

HoloLens uses Unity's built-in virtual reality support for stereoscopic rendering, among other things as shown ahead:

1. In **Player Settings...**, find the **Other Settings** group and click on the header bar.
2. Check the **Virtual Reality Supported** checkbox.
3. You should see **Windows Holographic** in the list of **Virtual Reality SDKs** (or, **Windows Mixed Reality**, depending on your version of Unity).

4. If not, click on + to add it:

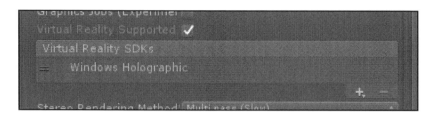

Projects that use MixedRealityToolkit can skip to the Building and running section. Projects that are using Vuforia with HoloLens, such as the one we begin in the next chapter, will also need to configure Vuforia.

Vuforia settings for HoloLens

If we're using Vuforia, we will need to tell it that we're using a HoloLens device. This includes binding the HoloLens camera and enabling extended tracking. For more details, see the **Developing Vuforia Apps for HoloLens** documentation at
`https://library.vuforia.com/articles/Training/Developing-Vuforia-Apps-for-HoloL ens`.

Enabling extended tracking

We will explain extended tracking in `Chapter 4`, *Augmented Business Cards*. So, for now, let's just turn it on as shown ahead because HoloLens needs it.

1. In Unity, in **Hierarchy**, select the **Image Target** object.
2. Then, in **Inspector**, in the **Image Target Behavior** component, check the checkbox to **Enable Extended Tracking**.

Adding HoloLensCamera to the Scene

To configure Vuforia to use the HoloLens camera, there are a few things to do. First, we will add a HoloLens camera to the scene, then we'll bind it to the AR Camera as shown ahead. Refer to the **Camera in Unity** documentation from Microsoft at
`https://developer.microsoft.com/en-us/windows/holographic/camera_in_unity`.

1. Select **GameObject | Camera**.
2. In **Inspector**, rename it to **HoloLensCamera**.

3. Set **Clear Flags** to **Solid Color.**
4. Set **Background** to black (0,0,0,0).
5. The HoloLens docs recommend setting **Clipping Planes | Near** to 0.85 and that may be a best practice for comfort, but I find it constraining working in my small office.
6. Reset its **Transform Position** to (0,0,0).

The resulting camera settings are shown in the following image:

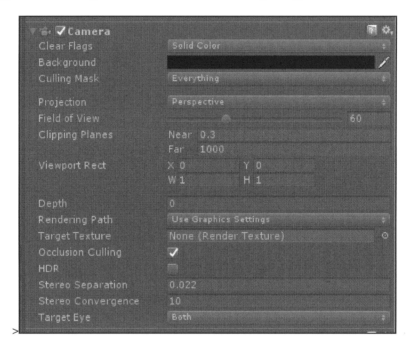

 For HoloLens, it will be easier to lay out your app if you imagine the starting position of the user as (X: 0, Y: 0, Z: 0). You'll want to adjust your target and virtual objects' positions accordingly, say, 2 meters in front of you, (0, 0, 2).

Binding the HoloLens Camera

Set up the scene for stereo rendering in the Vuforia configuration. To do this, perform the following steps:

1. From the main menu, go to **Vuforia | Configuration.**
2. In **Inspector**, set **Eyewear Type** to **Optical See-Through.**
3. Set **See Through Config** to **HoloLens.**

The configuration is shown as follows:

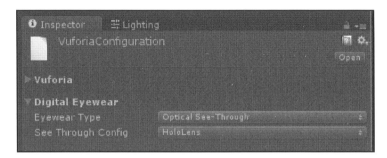

Now, bind the AR Camera to use the HoloLens camera as follows:

1. In **Hierarchy**, select the **AR Camera** object.
2. Drag **HoloLensCamera** from the **Hierarchy** onto the **Central Anchor Point** slot in the **Vuforia Behavior** component.

The resulting **ARCamera** component is shown as follows:

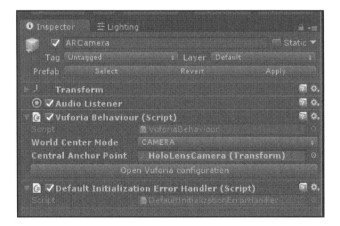

Building and running

Wow! That was fun, wasn't it? Now we're ready to build a Visual Studio project:

1. In Unity, use the **File | Build Settings** window and press **Build.**
2. Specify a folder to put the project files. As mentioned in `Chapter 2`, *Setting Up Your System*, I'd like to make a folder named `Build` and then make a subfolder for this build; let's call it `hololens-cube`.
3. Now open the project in Visual Studio.
4. An easy way is to navigate to the `Build` folder in **File Explorer** and look for the `.sln` file for the project (`.sln` is for the Microsoft *solution* file). Double-click it to open the project in Visual Studio.

We have a few settings to set here too:

1. Change the solution configuration selector from **Debug** to **Release.**
2. Set the target to **x86.**
3. Set **Device** to your target device. In the following example, we selected **HoloLens Emulator 10.0.14393.0.**
4. If using a physical HoloLens device, select **Remote Machine** and you will be prompted to enter the IP of the device to run on; select **Universal (Unencrypted Protocol) for Authentication Mode**.

The Visual Studio settings are as follows:

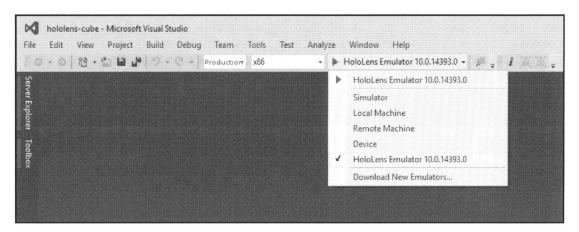

5. Finally, select **Debug | Start Debugging**.

The following image is of the emulator open next to Visual Studio that is launching the app:

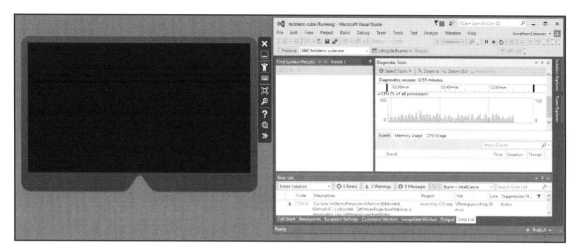

Holographic emulation within Unity

Unity developers are accustomed to the *Play* mode within the Unity editor, which allows you to run your project without having to build and install it on the target device after every change. Holographic emulation within the Unity editor allows you to work in a similar iterative process with HoloLens.

There are two modes, namely **Remote to Device** and **Simulate in Editor**:

- The **Remote To Device** mode requires you to have a connection to a physical HoloLens device. The app behaves like it's running on the device, but the graphics are displayed in Unity. The device's sensors are used as input to the **Game** window.
- In the **Simulate In Editor** mode, your app runs on a simulated Holographic device, directly in the editor with no connection to a real-world device. You use a game controller to control the virtual human player.

To enable holographic emulation, follow these steps:

1. From the main menu, choose **Window | Holographic Emulation.**
2. Choose **Emulation Mode**, either **Simulate in Editor** or **Remote to Device.**

The pane is as follows:

For more information, including other Holographic emulation options, see the Unity manual page on **Holographic Emulation** at
`https://docs.unity3d.com/Manual/windowsholographic-emulation.html.`

MixedRealityToolkit for Unity

For some of our projects, you will also need MixedRealityToolkit for Unity (formerly called HoloToolkit) from Microsoft. This is a package of additional utility scripts that facilitate HoloLens development in Unity. It can be found at `https://github.com/Microsoft/MixedRealityToolkit-Unity.`

Download the latest version from the `Releases` folder (`https://github.com/Microsoft/MixedRealityToolkit-Unity/releases`) and keep it where you can find it again when you need it.

Learn more about these awesome components at `https://github.com/Microsoft/MixedRealityToolkit-Unity/wiki.`

Summary

In this chapter, we went through a lot of work to make your development system capable of building for any device you may want to target to run your augmented reality applications. There are many possible combinations, depending on whether you're developing on a Windows PC or a macOS; using Vuforia or the ARToolkit SDK or Apple ARKit or Google ARCore; targeting Android, iOS, Windows desktop, Mac desktop, or Windows Mixed Reality for HoloLens. We covered just about all of them.

For Android, we installed the Java JDK and Android SDK. For iOS, we installed Xcode. For HoloLens, we installed Visual Studio. For each of these cases, we went over the Unity build, project, and player settings.

Now we're ready to have some fun! In the coming chapters, we will work through some exciting and interesting different projects that demonstrate different ways to apply and implement AR. We will learn how to use Unity and many of the principles and practices of 3D graphics and augmented reality. Let's do it!

4
Augmented Business Cards

Alright! Your system should now be set up for AR development-- in `Chapter 2`, *Setting Up Your System*, we installed Unity and AR development kits, and in `Chapter 3`, *Building Your App*, we installed the tools required to build your target device. You now get to build your first full AR project!

In this chapter, we will create an AR app that demonstrates a use of augmented reality in business and marketing. Using your own business card (or any other suitable image) we'll show how to make an app that will augment your professional image and impress your clients and business partners. We may even throw in a couple other fun ideas too!

Technically the project is a good introduction to the basics of creating an AR app. Although there are a lot of similar tutorials on YouTube and elsewhere, we will help you get started with AR using Unity and talk you through some of principles behind each of the components as we use them in the project.

In this chapter, you will learn about:

- Planning your AR development
- Creating a new Unity AR project
- Selecting and preparing target images
- Adding objects in scale in real and virtual space
- Animating objects in Unity
- Building and running your app

Some of these topics were introduced in earlier chapters. Here is a chance to review those steps and put it all together.

Please refer to the the GitHub repository for this book for completed projects for each platform `https://github.com/ARUnityBook/`

Planning your AR development

To be an effective AR developer you should gain an understanding of some of the core principles behind AR technology, and dig down into the details of how to control specific options in the SDKs. And that's what we're here to help you do. These powerful development tools enable you to focus on the implementation of your application and user experience instead of the hardcore mathematics, pattern recognition, and other challenges that go into augmented reality technology.

In addition to deciding your development platform, SDK, and target AR device, there are other steps you should consider to plan and implement your project, common to most all AR projects, including the following:

1. Decide which target technique will be used, such as markers, images, objects, spatial map. Select and prepare the actual targets, such as a suitable image.
2. Choose and prepare the computer graphic assets that will be used to augment the live scene.
3. Create the Unity project and new scene.
4. Add an AR camera to the scene.
5. Insert a placeholder for the AR target and assign its properties to the specific target image.
6. Insert the assets into the scene that should appear when the target is recognized.
7. Test by playing the scene in the Unity editor.
8. Build and run the project to test on your target AR device.

Project objective

I have a friend who runs a drone photography business called *PurpleFinch PhotoDrone*. As a favor, I offered to make an AR app that recognizes his business card and displays a flying drone. Once the app is opened, the user will be able to look at (point the camera) the company's business card, and a virtual drone will appear and fly around. It'll be a cool little promotional thing he can share with clients and friends. The following is a screenshot of his website:

You can follow along with this specific project (the assets are available for download from the publisher's download site for this book). Or feel free to do something that is closer to home for you, using your own assets. We will walk you through the entire process.

AR targets

The plan for this project is to use a business card or other image related to your business as the target. Actually, as we will explain, the size and image of a business card could be a problem. AR best practices recommend larger and detailed images work best. But this is what I want to do, because it's so cool! And it still can work pretty well. So, we will also use this as a teaching moment to explore what works better or worse and why. The card looks like the following image:

A .jpg image of the card is included with this chapter's asset pack. If you are doing this for another business, scan or take a photo of the card you want to use, you will need a copy in .jpg or .png file format.

For best results, a target image for AR should not be too small or too large. A business card is about as small as you can get. See the following discussion for best practices in choosing a good target image. If you need an even smaller target then consider using a specially designed *marker*. We will discuss markers in a later chapter.

Graphic assets

When the target is recognized our app should display an object related to your business. Your choices may vary, and we'll discuss easy ways to find and import 3D models for use in your app.

For PurpleFinch, we are going to show a drone quadcopter, and let it fly around a bit. It's in the Unity package we named `SimpleDrone.unitypackage`, as depicted in the following image:

The drone comes with scripts to animate the rotors. We will also animate the model to take off and land on the business card.

Obtaining 3D models

The objects you choose for your business may be different from our drone. If you're good at 3D modeling you can make your own. If not, fortunately (amazingly) there are tons of objects available on the Unity Asset Store, some free, some at a price. There are also many 3D model sharing sites, including the following:

- Sketchfab

    https://sketchfab.com

  Turbosquid

    http://www.turbosquid.com/

- Blendswap

    http://www.blendswap.com/

- And others

Models found in the Asset Store are ready to be used in Unity. Models from other sources may require some manual adjustment and/or format conversion. Unity lets you import models in FBX or OBJ format. You can also import proprietary formats such as MAX (3D Studio Max) or BLEND (Blender) provided you have that application installed on your system. But we recommend you convert proprietary files to FBX (or OBJ) before import, so everyone on your team does not need the 3D creation application to be present. Likewise, you yourself could need to open the Unity project on another machine that is not your primary development one.

Simplifying high poly models

If you obtain a model with thousands or even millions of faces it should be simplified before import into Unity because that is unnecessarily too large. Especially for AR applications on mobile devices, you do not want (or need) such complex models.

 Blender is a free and open source 3D creation tool. We use it for editing 3D models and animations. It also provides a full suite of additional features including simulation, rendering, and even game creation. `https://www.blender.org/`.

We cannot go into much detail here, but briefly, for example, using Blender you can simplify a model as follows:

1. If necessary, download and install Blender from `https://www.blender.org/` website.
2. Open Blender and delete the default objects (press on keyboard *A*, then *A* again, then *X* to delete).
3. Import the model (**File | Import | file type**), locate your model and press **Import.**
4. If needed, scale the model so it's a manageable size on the screen (move mouse into the viewport, press *S*, and slide the mouse to scale, right-click when satisfied).
5. Ensure you're in Object Mode (see bottom toolbar), and in the **Inspector** on the right, find the **wrench-icon** to access the modifiers.
6. Click **Add Modifier** and choose **Decimate** (see the following screenshot).
7. The current number of faces in the mesh is shown in the **Modifier** pane. In the **Ratio** input field enter a number, such as `0.1` to reduce the faces to one-tenth. Press **Apply.**
8. Export the model as `.fbx` (**File | Export | FBX**).

In addition, there are several packages that let you simplify models directly in the Unity editor, such as **Simple LOD** (`https://www.assetstore.unity3d.com/en/#!/content/ 25366`). The caveat there is that the model still needs to be of a reasonable size to import, in the first place; otherwise, Unity will get bogged down. Simple LOD is intended to let you generate a series of simpler meshes at multiple **levels of detail** (**LOD**) for optimization and use, depending on the object distance from the in-scene camera.

Target device and development tools

Having defined the project's objective, target image, and objects, we also should know by now which development platform, version of Unity, AR SDK, and the target device(s) that we are using. This chapter includes instructions for the following combinations:

Target AR Platform	AR SDK	Development Platform
Android	Vuforia	Windows 10
iOS	Vuforia	macOS
HoloLens	Vuforia	Windows 10
Android	ARToolkit	Windows 10

In the interest of clarity, this chapter first walks you through the entire project as if developing with Vuforia for Android devices. At the end of the chapter we will work through the steps for the other development scenarios: iOS, HoloLens, and ARToolkit.

Setting up the project (Vuforia)

To begin implementation, we create a new project in Unity and get it ready for AR. You may already know the drill, but we'll step you through it quickly. If you require more detail, please refer to the relevant topics in `Chapter 2`, *Setting Up Your System*, and `Chapter 3`, *Building Your App*.

Let's create a new project and import the Vuforia package:

1. First, open Unity and create a new 3D project. I will call mine `BusinessCard`.

2. Import the Vuforia package. From the Unity main menu, choose **Assets | Import Package | Custom Package...** and then find and select the `Vuforia.unitypackage` file on your system (if you need to download the package please refer to the instructions in `Chapter 2`, *Setting Up Your System*).

3. Then press **Import**.

   This will create several new folders in your Project `Assets` including `Plugins`, `Resources`, and a main `Vuforia` folder that contains a bunch of other subfolders.

   Also, import the Vuforia samples package.

4. Again, choose **Assets | Import Package | Custom Package** and then find and select the `VuforiaSamples-x-x-x.unitypackage` file on your system (at the time of writing the filename is `VuforiaSamples-6-2-10`).

   Set the app license key: we now need to give the application your license key.

5. As shown in `Chapter 2`, *Setting Up Your System* go to the Vuforia website Developer Portal's License Manager, `https://developer.vuforia.com/targetmanager/licenseManager/licenseListing`. (You must be logged in to access this link).

6. Create a new license key, or choose an existing one. I like to keep one key that I reuse for random AR projects and only create a dedicated key for specific apps that I plan to publish.

7. Click the key name to open it.

8. Copy the license key codes from the textbox on the screen.

Back in Unity:

1. From the Unity main menu choose **Vuforia | Configuration**.

2. In the **Inspector**, paste your license key into the **App License Key** area.

3. Also in the **VuforiaConfiguration Inspector** pane, double-check that your **Webcam Camera Device** is selected.

Add the AR camera to the scene: we will replace the default **Main Camera** with Vuforia's **ARCamera** prefab.

1. Delete the **Main Camera** object from the **Hierarchy**.

2. Then locate the **ARCamera** prefab in the Project `Assets/Vuforia/Prefabs` folder, select, and drag it into the **Hierarchy** list.

3. Add the camera settings component to the camera to enable auto-focus. While **ARCamera** is selected in the **Hierarchy**, choose **Add Component** in **Inspector** and find **Scripts | Camera Settings**.

4. Let's save our work so far. Choose from main menu **File | Save Scene As** and give it a name, such as `BusinessCard` and save it into the `Assets` folder.

5. Also save the project, **File | Save Project**.

At this point, if you press the **Play** button in the Unity editor, you should see the video feed from the webcam camera. This will allow you to debug AR applications inside the Unity editor.

Adding the image target

We can start creating the AR application. As we saw in `Chapter 2`, *Setting Up Your System*, we can use the Vuforia cloud service to generate and maintain the database of our target image(s) and then download it for import into Unity, using the following steps.

Adding ImageTarget prefab to the scene

The first part of that is requiring an image target in the scene:

1. In the Project `Assets/Vuforia/Prefabs` folder there's a prefab named `ImageTarget`. Drag that into the **Hierarchy**.

2. In the **Inspector**, in the **Image Target Behavior** component, locate the **Type** parameter. It may say **No Targets Defined**. Press the button to do the creation.

That will open your internet browser to the **Vuforia Target Manager** web page. This will allow us to use their software to create the target database.

Creating the target database

Let's create a new database for the business card:

1. Press **Add Database** and name it `BusinessCard`.
2. We will plan to store the image with the app on the device, so define the database as **Device** type.
3. In the **Target Manager | BusinessCard** you can see the (empty) list of targets.
4. Press **Add Target** to add an image target.
5. We're adding a **Single Image** type, click **Browse** to choose the image file to upload.
6. Specify the real-world width of the image in meters. Ours is 3.5 inches, or 0.09 meters.
7. Then upload.

We selected the **Device** type option, which means the image database will be bundled with your app and reside on the device. But suppose you wanted to be able to expand the app to handle more or different images after the app is built and distributed. With Vuforia you also have the option to keep the database in the Vuforia cloud. This would require the app to have internet access at runtime, to retrieve the target data (or data updates) when you open the app. This could be slower than having the data built into the app. But having the database on the cloud could be a powerful solution.

The **Add Target** page is shown as follows:

Note that Vuforia requires the image to be either `.jpg` or `.png`, and 24-bit or 8-bit (grayscale). Often `.png` files are RGBA, with alpha channel, and this will be rejected when you try to upload. A `.jpg` never has an alpha channel, it must be RGB or grayscale. In Vuforia, the maximum image file size is 2.25 MB.

In the following screenshot, you can see we have uploaded the card image to the database. Notice it is high contrast line art so it gets an excellent five-star feature recognition rating:

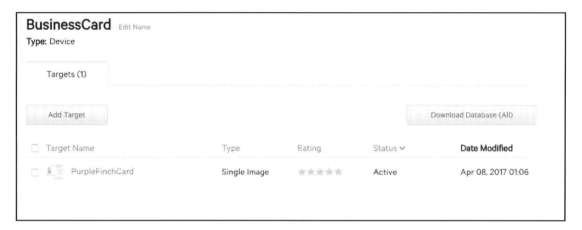

We can now download the database to use in Unity:

1. Press **Download Database.**
2. Select **Unity Editor** and press **Download.**

Our downloaded file is aptly named `BusinessCard.unitypackage`. And now we can import it into Unity.

Importing database into Unity

In Unity, to import the database we follow the steps shown ahead:

1. From the main menu go to **Assets | Import Package | Custom Package...**
2. Select the database file we just downloaded.
3. Click **Import**.

Once imported, it creates a folder named `StreamingAssets`. This is where all the database information will be held for the rest of our imported tracking points, whether it be images, objects, or any of the other tracking targets that Vuforia supports.

With the **ImageTarget** selected in the **Hierarchy**, look to the **Inspector** and in the **Image Target Behavior** component, for the Database parameter select your database, **BusinessCard**. It will default to the first target (which is fine since our database has only one target!)

Activating and running

Lastly, we must activate the database:

1. Go into the `VuforiaConfiguration` file (main menu **Vuforia | Configuration**).
2. In **Inspector Datasets** check the **Load BusinessCard** checkbox (or whatever you named your database), and then mark it as **Activate**.
3. Now with the image data set up, let's do a quick test of our work. In the **Hierarchy**, create a cube (for example, **GameObject | 3D Object | Cube**).

Our business card measures less than 0.1 meters, and our cube is 1.0 meters in size. That's too big.

1. Change its **Transform Scale** to something like (0.05, 0.05, 0.05) and its **Position** to (0, 0.025, 0).
2. And in **Hierarchy**, move the cube so it is a child of the **ImageTarget**.

Press **Play**, point the webcam at the business card and the cube should appear.

Enable extended tracking or not?

Vuforia offers a powerful feature enabled with a simple checkbox -- **extended tracking**. Ordinarily your AR app will detect a target and show the associated virtual objects. When the target exits the view of the camera then the app forgets the target and the virtual object stops being rendered. Sometimes this is exactly what you want. Sometimes it is not.

For example, suppose the virtual object is much taller than the user's phone can capture in one frame. You'll want to pan the phone camera to examine the entire shape. You will want to continue viewing the object even when the target is out of view. Extended tracking allows the user to move the phone around and still preserve the tracking.

In our project, we are planning to animate the drone so it takes off and flies around above the business card. We may need to pan the camera to watch it fly. Also, without extended tracking, if the drone was flying and then tracking is reset, the animation will start back at its beginning position. Hence, we want extended tracking:

1. To enable **extended tracking,** in the **Image Target Behavior**, click the **Enable Extended Tracking** checkbox. This will allow the user to then move around the environment and not lose tracking.

2. The **ImageTarget** must also be marked as **Static** in the scene: check the **Static** checkbox in the upper right of the **Inspector**.

With extended tracking enabled, we can move the camera around and not lose tracking. But it assumes the target does not move in real life. Plan to leave the business card on a table when running your app.

What makes a good image target?

What makes a good image target and how will we know that it will track well? We can identify characteristics of the physical target and the image on it.

The target itself should have a matt finish to avoid reflections and specular highlights that might confuse the recognition software when it's processing the video feed at runtime.

It also should be rigid so it won't be distorted or morphed when the camera is viewing it. Thus, a card or paper board won't be able to bend or crease as easily as a regular piece of paper. The tracking will be more consistent.

The image should have a border so it can be readily distinguished from the background. The recommendation is this border should be roughly 8% of the image size. The border can be just white around the perimeter. Or it can be part of a texture. But just keep in mind that 8% from the border will not be taking that pattern into account.

Given these requirements, or shall we say guidelines, an ordinary business card is marginally acceptable as an image target. Your standard business card is probably not five inches wide! You can choose to redesign your cards, or try it anyway, deal with it, and hope for the best. In the case of PurpleFinch we'll take the second approach!

Another issue is size of the target. The real-life image target must be large enough in the camera's view to provide an adequate number of pixels for its recognition algorithms to work. A rough formula is the image width should be one-tenth the distance from the camera. For example, given a table top about four feet away (50 inches), the image should be at least five inches wide (that is 120 cm distance and 12 cm wide).

The following figure shows the relationship between target physical size, distance of device camera, and size on the screen sufficient for the recognition algorithms to work properly:

In this project, when running the app, we will expect the user to be holding their mobile device in one hand and point it at the business card on a table, close up. So, a business card 3.5 inches wide held about 18 inches away provides plenty of scale to make this work (9 cm and 45 cm).

When a target is smaller, there are other solutions than moving the camera up close. Instead of arbitrary images, you can use highly recognizable special markers. Markers can even be encoded with QR-code-like graphic coding so a given marker design might be used and recognized for dozens of separate virtual objects. We will get into marker techniques in a later chapter.

The image on the target also needs to meet certain criteria to be recognized correctly. It should be detailed, non-symmetric, and non-repetitive. Be cognizant that the AR software needs to graph features in the image that will be recognized in the video feed. If the patterns in the image do not have sufficient detail, it will not be recognized. If the image looks the same from various angles, the software will be confused as to how it is oriented.

The image should also have good contrast. When an image is line art, like our business card, this is not an issue. Most of the area will be a solid background color (white in our case) and that contrasts well with the printed text and icon art.

But when the image is a photograph it requires what is technically referred to as **natural feature tracking** (**NFT**). In this case, the image must have good contrast. Let's see what that means.

Vuforia uses a grayscale version of your target image to discover identifiable features. So, think about the image's gray values rather than contrasting colors.

Image editing software such as Gimp and Photoshop provide a histogram tool that lets you see the distribution of pixel values across the grayscale spectrum from black to white. You will want to use a *linear* histogram rather than a *logarithmic* one. A linear histogram represents how a camera will see the image, whereas the logarithm histogram represents how our eyes would see it.

The following examples, taken from the Vuforia documentation (`https://library.vuforia.com/content/vuforia-library/en/articles/Solution/Optimizing-Target-Detection-and-Tracking-Stability.html`), illustrates how you can use the histogram to help assess that the pebbles image provides an excellent contrast, whereas the leaves do not. The first example is not a good image target because it is low contrast across a concentrated grayscale spectrum:

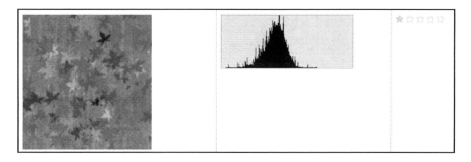

The next example is a very good target with a good grayscale range and even contrast:

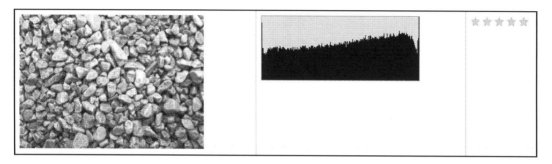

Images with high contrast will have distributed uneven histogram graphs. The image will appear *spikey* and not too smooth. And it will have values spread across the entire grayscale rather than concentrated in narrow values.

Even so, our PurpleFinch business card miserably fails the histogram test. But that's OK because it is line-art, not NFT. That is good too. As shown previously, it actually received five-stars in feature detection rating!

In summary, for best results a target image should have the following characteristics:

- Matt finish
- Rigid card
- Adequate border (about 8%)
- Size in proportion to expected camera distance (1/10)
- Detailed, non-repetitive, non-symmetric image
- Good contrast (line art, or distributed uneven histogram)

Let's move ahead with our project.

Adding objects

We're now ready to add virtual objects to the scene. For this project, we want to augment the business card with a flying drone quadcopter.

In AR, when the camera recognizes a target, we want the associated objects to appear and augment the scene. This association is defined by making the virtual objects a child of the target in the **Hierarchy**.

First, we'll remove the cube and then add the drone:

1. If you added a cube under **ImageTarget** you can delete it now (right-click **Delete**).

   Assuming you have the `SimpleDrone.unitypackage` file provided with the file downloads for this book from the publisher, you can import it now in Unity.

2. From main menu choose **Assets | Import Package | Custom Package**, locate the `SimpleDrone` package file and select **Import.**

   This will create a folder in your `Assets` with sub-folders for Animation, Materials, Mesh, and Prefabs, as shown in the following screenshot:

3. In the `Prefab` folder, select the **SimpleDrone** prefab and drag it into the **Hierarchy**, as a child of **ImageTarget**.

   Ensure the object is a child of **ImageTarget**, as shown in the following screenshot:

   Our drone model is life sized; we need to shrink it down (we will now discuss scale).

4. With the **SimpleDrone** selected, change the scene edit gizmo to **Scale**.

5. In the **Scene** pane, click the small cube in the center of the scale gizmo and drag the mouse to shrink the model.

The model shown in the following screenshot is at Scale (0.1, 0.1, 0.1), and slightly above the card (**Position Y** = 0.06), which visually works.

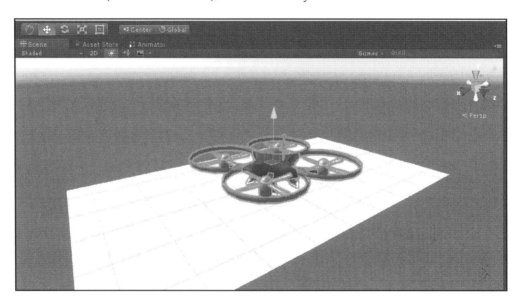

Save the scene and then press **Play**. When you point your camera at the business card, the object should appear. And the blades should be spinning. We will explore how that works later in this chapter.

Building and running

We can now build and run the app on our target device-- an Android phone. Follow these steps. If you want more detail and explanation, please refer back to the relevant sections of chapter 3, *Building Your App*:

1. First, be sure to save the scene (**File | Save Scenes**) and project (**File | Save Project**).

2. In **Build Settings** (**File | Build Settings**) make sure the scene is the only one listed in **Scenes In Build** (press **Add Open Scenes**).

3. In **Build Settings Platform**, make sure **Android** is the target platform (select **Android** and press **Switch Platform**).

4. Now go to **Player Settings** (press **Player Settings** in **Build Settings**, or main menu **Edit | Project Settings | Player**) and look at the **Inspector** on the right for the settings for Android.

5. Under **Other Settings**. the **Package Name** must be set to a unique identifier, in the format com.Company.ProductName such as com.PurpleFinch.BusinessCard.

6. For **Minimum API Level**, select **Android 5.1 Lollipop** (API level 22 or whichever is the current minimum for Vuforia).

7. Once more, save the project.

Now make sure your phone is connected via USB and unlocked. Then press **Build And Run**. As mentioned in Chapter 3, *Building Your App*, we recommend you make a folder named Build and save your executable build files there. We can name it BusinessCard.apk.

The following is an image of me holding the business card in one hand (steadily!) and phone in the other, with the drone augmenting the card on the screen:

Understanding scale

Let's talk about scale. So far in our discussion we have encountered issues of size and units in several separate situations. Specifically, we are concerned with real-life space, AR device camera views, AR targets, virtual space, and the Unity transform hierarchy. And they are all related.

Real-life scale

Most of us live in the real world, normally (ha ha!). That's the place where things can be measured objectively. With standard units of measurement, we can write specifications and have conversations that are shared, consistent, and repeatable. Standards of measurement are important. And this is good, because human perception is not so reliable. Depending on the context, an object 1 meter long may appear subjectively to be larger or smaller than its actual size until it's measured.

A meter in length is the same whenever and wherever it is used. A caveat is, we must refer to the same units of measurement when sharing numbers. In September 1999, NASA lost its Mars Climate Orbiter spacecraft because one team used English units (for example, inches, feet, and pounds) while another used metric used for key spacecraft operations! (`https://mars.nasa.gov/msp98/news/mco990930.html`). Let's try to avoid such catastrophes in our augmented realities too.

Things appear to get smaller with distance. As humans we're quite used to this and size plays an important role in understanding the world around us, including perception of depth. This can be objectively measured too. Using an optical lens, or even a pinhole camera, a scene can be projected onto a flat surface, and then the size of objects in the scene can be measured. A large tree in the distance will measure smaller than a child standing close by. And as Renaissance artists discovered, objects and spatial relationships can be depicted on a flat surface using *perspective* where lines (edges) of object converge towards a single central vanishing point.

When augmenting reality with computer graphics, we need to take all this into account. With handheld video see-through AR, we're capturing and augmenting one frame at a time. The image recognition algorithm in the AR SDK tries to match patterns in the frame with target images in its database. Viewed face-on is easier, both the real-life target and stored image have square corners.

But when the real-life target is viewed at an angle, the algorithm must account for perspective and depth. It then determines the relative position of the camera. This is used to position the pose of the virtual camera and render the virtual objects together with the captured real-life video frame, onto the display, as depicted in the following diagram:

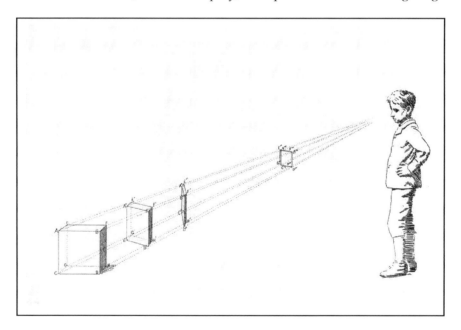

source https://commons.wikimedia.org/wiki/File:Eakins_Perspective_Study_Of_Boy_Viewing_Object.jpg *Creative Commons.*

It gets even more complex with wearable optical see-through AR devices. Infrared and optical sensors measure the 3D space, depth, and object size, building a spatial map. This is represented as a mesh correlating to surfaces in the environment. The computer does the math to calculate the actual size and distance of these surfaces in the environment. Augmenting these scenes, we can attach virtual objects to 3D locations in 3D space.

The takeaway point here is that developing for augmented reality entails real-life objects in real-world 3D space. And virtual 3D objects mapped to scale into that 3D space. If it's new to you, thinking in 3D may take some time and getting used to.

More typically, we think in two dimensions. I travel roads that are north-south or east-west. Sure, we can go up and down too, especially using elevators, drones, or starships, but that is not so conventional thinking. As Spock noted in the Star Trek movie The Wrath of Khan, *He's intelligent but not experienced. His pattern indicates two-dimensional thinking.* (https://www.youtube.com/watch?v=RbTUTNenvCY). When developing for AR we need experience in three-dimensional thinking.

Virtual scale and Unity

Using a computer graphic engine, such as Unity and other 3D design applications, we work on 3D objects defined by x, y, z coordinates in a virtual three-dimensional space. There are many ways to digitally represent objects. Unity prefers a set of points connected to form a mesh of triangular faces. These faces are rendered with texture maps, lighting, and shaders to provide ever increasing degrees of realism and simulation of physical properties.

The default unit in Unity is meters. This is somewhat arbitrary. Your application can choose to allow one unit to be another measure, such as inches or kilometers. But unless really needed, it is recommended to stick with the 1 meter units (other parts of Unity assume this and may be affected by an altered scale, for example, the physics engine calculations of mass and velocity). As stated earlier, the most important thing is to be consistent.

Every object has a **Transform** component that defines how its geometry may be positioned, rotated, or scaled relative to its default shape. Thus, the reset or *identity* transform is **Position** (0, 0, 0), **Rotation** (0, 0, 0), and a **Scale** of (1, 1, 1). To make it twice the length, make the **Scale X** value 2.0. To rotate it around to see its backside, make its **Rotation Y** value 180 degrees.

Objects can be grouped and parented under another object, forming a hierarchy of objects. Thus, the **Hierarchy** pane in the Editor shows all the objects in your current scene arranged in a tree. For example, the **SimpleDrone** we used in our project contains two child groups, **Drone_Body** and **Drone_Rig**. The body consists of its **Arms**, **Body**, **Rotor_1**, and so on.

The **SimpleDrone** hierarchy is shown in the following screenshot:

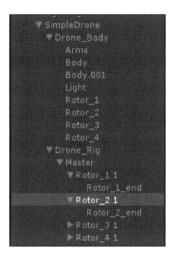

If the **Transform** of the parent object, **SimpleDrone** is changed, all its children objects are moved along with it, as you would expect. Earlier we resized the drone by scaling the **SimpleDrone**, all its child objects scaled with it. Later we will animate the drone, moving it up and around over time by changing its **Transform Position**. In contrast, the rotors spin independently relative to their own *local* axis of rotation. The drone model with one of its rotors selected is shown as follows:

Target scale and object scale

If you recall, when we added the business card image to the Vuforia database it asked us to specify the real-world width of the object. We say it's 3.5 inches, but first we converted it into meters and entered 0.09 meters for the width. Then, when we used the image on the **ImageTarget**, it has the actual size in the scene.

The camera's position relative to the target is calculated at runtime by tracking the target. To track the target continuously we need to keep in mind the target's size and its distance from the device's camera. You can estimate the minimum size for a target by dividing the camera-to-target distance by 10. For instance, a 10 cm wide target would be detectable up to about 1 meter (10 cm x 10). In this example, we are using a business card (0.09 m), which is usually viewed at arm's length (0.81 m). Although this calculation doesn't consider lighting conditions, we can feel confident that our business card image is trackable.

We also want to make sure that our image has enough detail to be tracked at the calculated distance. To do this, we should take into account the image target resolution or **dots per inch** (**dpi**). Vuforia's target extracts the correct resolution automatically and recommends images that are 320 pixels.

In contrast, ARtoolkit is not so automated. It asks you to define the range of the extracted resolutions. This calculation depends on camera resolution. If you are using a variety of HD video feed, you might want to use 20 dpi as the minimum and the image target's dpi as a maximum. Since this might lead to excess data, you can also use the *NFT Utilities for ARToolkit* (found under the path: `[downloaded ARToolkit Utilities root directory]/bin`).

When we added our drone to the scene, we made it a child of **ImageTarget**. By default, objects under **ImageTarget** are disabled and not rendered. But at runtime when the AR software recognizes the target specified in **ImageTarget**, all its children are enabled and become visible.

How big should we make the drone or any other virtual object you want to augment your scene? One way to think about it is how big would it be in real life? If you want the drone to rest on the business card like a big bug, then envision a big bug on the card and measure it! Conversely, if you wanted to represent a real drone flying actual size in your room, you would make sure the drone model is scaled to actual size in Unity (for that scenario, you will probably use a bigger target image than a business card, or a different target type altogether).

Animating the drone

Creating and managing animations with Unity can be simple, or very complicated. There are several pieces that work together, including:

- **Animator component**: It is attached to objects that you want to animate
- **Animator Controller**: It is a state machine that says what animations to use and when
- **Animation clips**: It describes how specific parameter values change over time

The Animator component is attached to an object in the scene and is used to assign animation to it. It requires a reference to an Animator Controller that defines which animation clips to use, and controls how to transition between the clips. Animators are used for simple objects like our drone, as well as for complex humanoid avatars.

An Animator Controller is a state machine that determines which animations are going to be played.

How do the blades spin?

In fact, our **SimpleDrone** already has an Animator component that makes its blades spin. This animation was imported with the original model (for example, from Blender), contained in its `.fbx` file. Let's explore how it is assembled:

1. Select the **SimpleDrone** in the **Hierarchy** and look at its **Inspector** (or the **Prefab** in the Project `Assets/SimpleDrone/Prefab` folder), you can see the component's **Animator Controller** is called `RotorSpin`, as shown in the following screenshot:

2. Double-click the **RotorSpin** controller and it will open in the **Animator** window (the window can be docked by dragging its tab). As shown in the following screenshot, we can see the states in the controller:

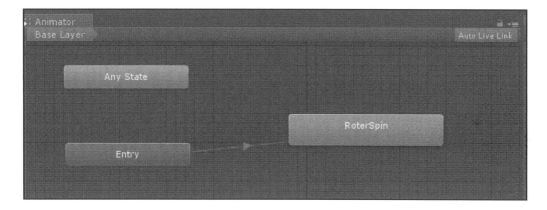

3. Click the **RotorSpin** state, you can see (in the **Inspector**) which animation the state is mapped to (in its **Motion** parameter).

4. Click the **Motion** parameter, your **Project** window will go to where the animation is located. The following screenshot shows that our **RotorSpin** animation is a child (second from the bottom) of the **QuadDrone** mesh:

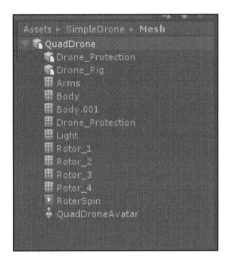

5. Select the **QuadDrone** mesh, then you can see the animation parameters in the **Import Settings' Animation** tab, as shown in the following screenshot:

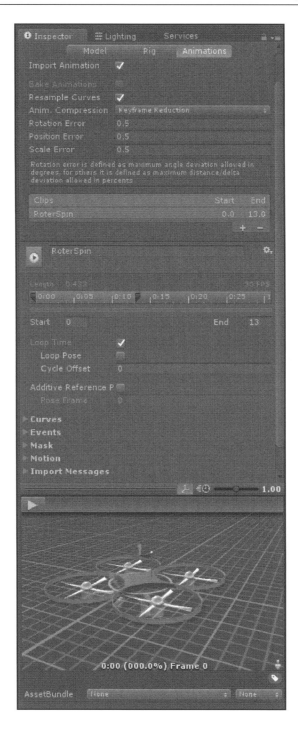

Since we want the rotors to spin continuously, the **Loop Time** checkbox is checked (if it's not, please check it now and press **Apply**). You can even preview the model animation by pressing the **Preview Play** at the bottom of the **Inspector**.

Now drilling down even deeper, if you want to see the **RotorSpin** animation clip itself:

1. Select the **RotorSpin** animation file (child of **QuadDrone**).
2. And then open the **Animation** window (main menu **Windows | Animation**, the window can be docked by dragging its tab).

It may default to the keyframe **Dopesheet** view. In the following screenshot, we switched to the **Curves** view and selected the **Rotor_1 1** under `Drone_Rig/Master/`. You can see that the rotor is directed to rotate not just at a constant rate, but in an oscillating pattern that cleverly simulates a strobing pattern you might observe on fast rotating blades.

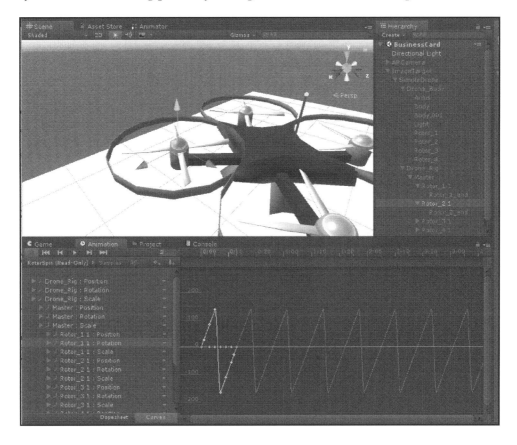

Thus, we've seen that the drone rotor blade animation is an *Animator* component of the **SimpleDrone** object, which references the **RotorSpin** *Animation Controller* (state machine graphic). That animator in turn references an imported *animation*, which we first examined in the FBX file *Import Settings*. And then we found the actual **RotorSpin** *Animation clip*, and viewed its dopesheet and curves in the **Animation** window.

Now let's go make one ourselves.

Adding an Idle animation

Our objective is to make the drone take off, fly around, and then land. And repeat. This will entail two animation clips.

To simplify our explanation let's first put the **SimpleDrone** into a parent **FlyingDrone** object and animate that:

1. In the **Hierarchy**, create an **Empty Object** under **ImageTarget** and rename it FlyingDrone.
2. Move the **SimpleDrone** to be a child of **FlyingDrone**.
3. With **FlyingDrone** selected, **Add Component Animator**.

Now we can begin creating the first Animation clip for the drone representing its resting state.

1. Open the **Animation** tab (add it if needed via **Window | Animation**). It will be empty, and will helpfully say **To begin animating FlyingDrone, create an Animation Clip**.

 In this step, we're using the **Animation** window, not the **Animator** one-- that's different!

2. Click the **Create** button.
3. A file dialog opens, navigate to a place you want to put your animations (for example, a folder named SimpleDrone/Animation) and give it the name Idle.

In the **Animation** window, we're presented with a timeline where our keyframes will be positioned. The `Idle` animation is extremely simple, it does nothing but sit there for two seconds! (At a later time, you could enhance it to maybe bounce or shake a little).

1. Click **Add Property.**
2. Then in **Transform**, select **Position**, as shown in the following screenshot:

By default, two keyframes are created, at 0 seconds and at 60 seconds. Because we want the drone to stay on the ground for a couple of seconds, we make sure that all the keyframes have the same position. **Position** (0, 0, 0). The **Samples** field specifies how many frames are required to make up one second. Since we want two seconds, we can change the number down to 30.

1. Enter 30 into the **Samples** field.
2. Use the mouse scroller to zoom out of the *Dopesheet* timeline and see the full two seconds, like the **Animation** window shown in the following screenshot:

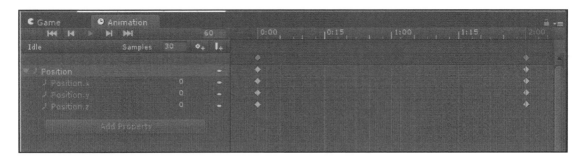

3. To make sure the animation does not loop, navigate to the **Idle** animation in Project `Assets`, select it, and make sure **Loop Time** is unchecked.

Adding a fly animation

Next, we will make our second animation, the flying animation. With **FlyingDrone** selected in **Hierarchy**:

1. In the **Animation** window, in the upper left there is a clip selected. It presently has the name of the current clip, `Idle`. Select it and choose **Create New Clip...**

2. Name the animation `Fly`.

    This time the animation is going to be more complicated and we're going to use the record feature in Unity.

3. Press the red circle in the upper left of the **Animation** window to begin recording.

While recording, all the properties that are animated will highlight red in the editor. New keyframes will appear on the frame (red vertical timeline) you select.

This will be a simple animation and we can reduce the number of samples that it has. Let's reduce it down to 10 samples, so every 10 frames will equal one second.

1. Enter `10` in the **Samples** field.

    The drone will start (and end) at its origin starting position (0,0,0).

2. **Position** the timeline at frame `0`.
3. Select the **FlyingDrone** (in **Hierarchy**) and make sure its **Position** in **Inspector** is (`0`, `0`, `0`).

We want the drone to fly up and reach its desired height in one second. We don't want the drone to fly too far up because we want to make sure the image continues to be tracked with the device camera.

1. Set the red timeline at the one-second mark.
2. In the **Scene** view, make sure the position gizmo is selected (showing red, green, blue axis arrows for moving the object).
3. And move the **Y** position to the flying height you want.

The resulting **Animation** set at the one-second timeline is shown in the following screenshot:

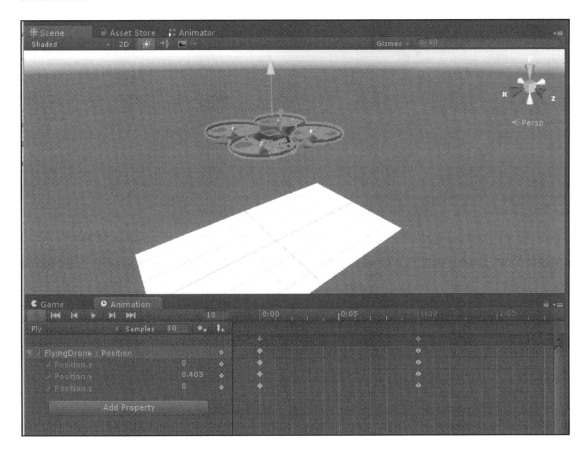

Next, we want it to fly in a small circle. To make this easier, change the **Scene** view to top-down as follows:

1. Click the **Y**-cone in the upper-right of the **Scene** window.
2. Change the view to orthographic.

The modified **Scene** view should now look something like this:

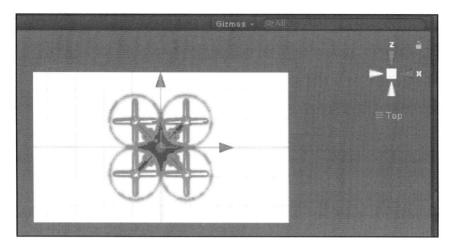

Starting at the two-second mark, we will add keyframes every 20 frames, changing the drone position to the center of each edge, sequentially in a circle. Use the following steps to create the flying animation we desire:

1. Zoom out the timeline so we can see about five additional seconds.
2. Set the red timeline to two seconds (frame 20).
3. Move the drone along the *x* axis so it's positioned at the middle of the left edge.
4. Set the red timeline to four seconds (or type 40 in the frames field).
5. Move the drone to the middle of the bottom edge.
6. Set to six seconds (frame 60).
7. Move the drone to the middle of the right edge.
8. Set to eight seconds (frame 80).
9. Move the drone to the middle of the top edge.
10. Set to nine seconds (frame 90).
11. Move the drone to the center of the card.
12. Set to 10 seconds (frame 100).
13. In **Inspector**, set the Position back to (0, 0, 0).

The **Animation dopesheet** now looks like this:

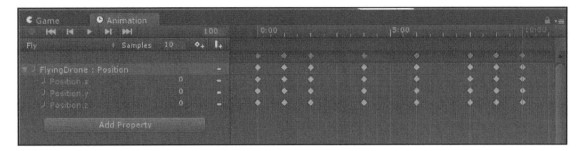

1. Press the red circle **Record** button again to stop recording.
2. Adjust the **Scene** view so it's perspective again and change the viewing angle (for example, *Alt*+left-mouse click).
3. Then press the **preview play** button to preview the animation.

So now the drone flies in a diamond shaped pattern. We could fix this by adding more keyframes. But we will smooth it out using curves.

4. Select the **Curves** view of the **Animation** from the bottom left of the window.

You may be familiar with curve editing from other applications. Each node point has handles to adjust the incoming and outgoing slope of the curve as it passes through that node. You can play around with the curves to make the transitions appear smoother, in each of the X and Z positions along the circle, and the Y position as the drone goes up and down.

If you need to refine a curve you can add extra keyframes by right-clicking on the curve where you want to insert a new node. For example, in the take-off Y position curve shown in the following screenshot, we added some ease-in ease-out smoothing and acceleration for good effect:

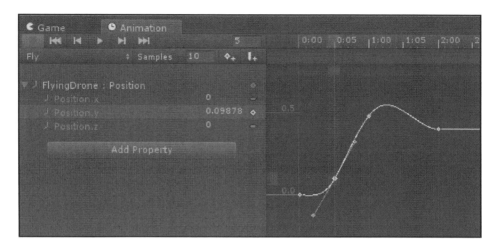

5. To make sure the animation does not loop, navigate to the `Fly` animation in Project `Assets`, select it, and make sure **Loop Time** is unchecked.

Connecting the clips in the Animator Controller

Now we need to add the clips to the **FlyingDrone** Animator Controller and transition between them:

1. In **Hierarchy**, select the **FlyingDrone**, and double-click the **FlyingDrone** Animator Controller in the Animator component.

   The Controller now shows the two animation states, with Idle as the default entry state. We now want to connect it to the **Fly** animation. And when **Fly** is done, it should transition back to Idle.

2. Right-click on the **Idle** state, select **Make Transition**, and drag it onto the **Fly** state.

   You can preview a transition by clicking on the transition line. Then in **Hierarchy**, drag the **FlyingDrone** onto the preview area in **Inspector**.

3. Right-click the **Fly** state, select **Make Transition**, and drag it back onto **Idle.**

Now the animation tree will play in a loop.

You can watch the animation states change when playing your game in the Unity Play mode when the **Animator** window is visible.

Playing, building and running

That should do it. Save the scene and save the project. Press **Play** and point your webcam at the business card. You should see the drone appear and fly about as you directed in your animation clips.

Finally, press **Build and Run**, and then compile and build an executable to try it on your target device. Hooray!

Building for iOS devices

Follow this section if you want to build this project for iOS devices including iPhone and iPad using the Vuforia SDK. This is mostly a step-by-step walk-through. If you want a better explanation, please refer back to the previous corresponding section.

As explained in previous chapters, you must use a Mac to develop for iOS devices. In Chapter 2, *Setting Up Your System*, we installed Unity on your machine and downloaded the Vuforia unity packages. In Chapter 3, *Building Your App*, we installed Xcode. Your system should now be ready for AR development with Unity and Vuforia on a Mac to build and run on iOS.

If you have been following the chapter and have already developed the Unity scene, you can skip to the 9.X *Build Settings* section. We'll step through it again now, quickly.

Setting up the project

Let's jump right in:

1. Create a new 3D project in Unity, named `BusinessCard`.
2. Import the **Vuforia** asset package using **Assets | Import Package | Custom Package...**.
3. Import the **VuforiaSamples** asset package also using **Assets | Import Package | Custom Package...**.

4. Set the app license key in **Vuforia | Configuration** obtained from the Vuforia Dev Portal.
5. Delete the **Main Camera** from the **Hierarchy**.
6. Drag the **ARCamera** prefab from Project **Assets** into the **Hierarchy**.
7. Add the **Camera Settings** component to the camera to enable auto-focus.
8. Save your work: **File | Save Scene As and File | Save Project.**

Adding the image target

We will now add the image target to the project and import the image database:

1. In your web browser Browse to the Vuforia Dev Portal (`https://developer.vuforia.com/`).
2. Create a target database, and give it a name like `BusinessCard` and **Type: Device**.
3. Click **Add Target** to add a **Type: Single Image**, specify a file (`PurpleFinchCard.png`), a width (in meters) (`0.09`), and **Add** it to the database.
4. Download the database using **Download Database**, be sure to select **Unity Editor** as type.

Back in Unity:

1. Drag the **ImageTarget** prefab into the **Hierarchy**.
2. Import the downloaded database package using **Assets | Import Package | Custom Package....**
3. Select **ImageTarget** in **Hierarchy**, and in **Inspector** select your **Database** (`BusinessCard`).
4. Check the **Enable Extended Tracking** checkbox.
5. Check the **Static** checkbox in the upper-right of **Inspector** for **ImageTarget**.
6. Go to the **Vuforia | Configuration** and in **Inspector Datasets**, check the **Load BusinessCard** checkbox (or your db name), and then mark it as **Activate.**

Adding objects

We now can add the drone to the project:

1. Import the **SimpleDrone** package using **Assets | Import Package | Custom Package.**
2. Drag the **SimpleDrone** prefab into the **Hierarchy**, and make it a child of **ImageTarget**.
3. Select the drone and set the scene gizmo to **Scale**, or enter the **Transform Scale** to (0.1, 0.1, 0.0) and move it to resting on the card (**Position Y** = 0.06).

You should also add the animations to make the drone fly. We won't repeat the details here, please refer to the previous section.

Build settings

We will now set up the project to build for an iOS device:

1. First, be sure to save the scene (**File | Save Scenes**) and project (**File | Save Project**). If prompted for a scene name choose what you want, such as PurpleFinch.
2. Go into **File | Build Settings** and make sure the scene is the only one listed in **Scenes In Build** (press **Add Open Scenes**).
3. In **Build Settings Platform**, make sure **iOS** is the target platform (select **iOS** and press **Switch Platform**).
4. Now go to **Player Settings** and look at the **Inspector** on the right.
5. Under **Other Settings** the **Package Name** must be set to a unique identifier, in the format com.Company.ProductName such as com.PurpleFinch.BusinessCard.
6. In the **Configuration** section, fill in the **Camera Usage Description** with something like augmented reality to ask the user permission to use the camera.
7. Again, **Save Scene** and **Save Project**.

Building and running

Let's now build and run the app on the iOS device. Ensure your device is connected to the Mac via USB, turned on, unlocked, and you have granted permission for the Mac to access it.

Press **Build and Run** to begin building. We recommend you create a new folder in your project root named `Build` and specify the file or subfolder name under that, as needed.

Please refer to the iOS section of `Chapter 3`, *Building Your App*, for any troubleshooting at this point. Briefly you may need to address some of the following:

1. **Plugins colliding error**: Find the offending plugins (for example, X86 and X86_64) and disable them for iOS.
2. **Recommended project settings warning**: Accept the recommended settings.
3. **Requires development team error**: Be sure to set your team in **General** tab, **Signing** section of options.
4. **Linker failed error**: Try disabling Bitcode in **Build Options**.

The app should now be running on your iOS device!

Building and running using Apple ARKit

Presently, ARKit does not support image target recognition to trigger augmented graphics the way Vuforia does. Rather, ARKit is great at anchoring objects to 3D locations in space. So that would really be off topic from the theme of the chapter, which is specifically to recognize and augment a business card. Still, it may be fun to try our drone model using the Apple ARKit if you have a compatible device.

The simplest approach is to start a new Unity project, import the ARKit package, and add the drone to the **UnityARKitScene** scene. Please refer to the ARKit topic in `Chapter 3`, *Building Your App* for additional details. Take the following steps:

1. On your Mac, create a new Unity project, named `DroneDemo`.
2. From **Window | Asset Store**, **Download** and **Import** the Apple **ARKit** package.
3. Open the scene **UnityARKitScene** via **File | Open Scene.**
4. In the scene **Hierarchy**, **Create Empty** game object child of **HitCubeParent** named `Flying Drone`.

5. **Add Component** named `UnityARHitTestExample` to **FlyingDrone**, and drag **HitCubeParent** onto its **Hit Transform** slot.

6. Disable the **HitCube** object to hide it.

7. Import the **SimpleDrone** package using **Assets | Import Package | Custom Package.**

8. Drag the **SimpleDrone** prefab into the **Hierarchy**, and make it a child of **FlyingDrone**.

9. Assuming you also want the drone to fly around, follow the instructions earlier in the chapter for *Animating the Drone*.

The resulting **Hierarchy** looks like this:

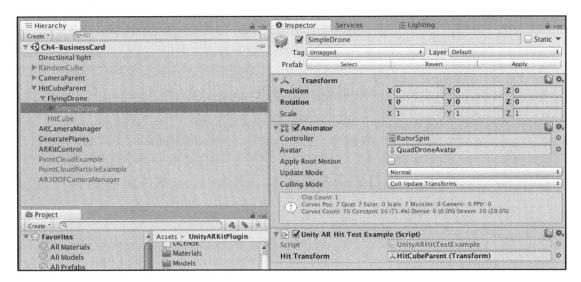

Now just **Build and Run** this scene, and then build it from Xcode to enjoy your augmented drone. The following is a screen capture of our drone flying around my kitchen:

Building for Google ARCore

Please refer to the GitHub repository for this book for the implementation notes and code using Google ARCore for Android: `https://github.com/ARUnityBook/`. The principles are very similar to ARKit but the Unity SDK and components are different.

Building for HoloLens

Follow this section if you want to build this project for Microsoft Windows 10 UWP (Universal Windows Platform), for mixed reality devices including HoloLens, using the Vuforia SDK. This is mostly a step-by-step walk-through. If you want a better explanation please refer back to the previous corresponding section.

As explained in previous chapters, you must use a Windows 10 PC. In Chapter 2, *Setting Up Your System*, we installed Unity on your machine and downloaded the Vuforia unity packages. In Chapter 3, *Building Your App*, we verified you have a supported version of Windows and installed Visual Studio (with necessary Windows 10 SDK), and optionally the HoloLens emulator. Unity should be set up to use Visual Studio as the External Script Editor. So now your system should be ready for AR development with Unity and Vuforia on Windows 10 for HoloLens.

Setting up the project

Let's jump right in:

1. Create a new 3D project in Unity, named `BusinessCard`.
2. Import the **Vuforia** asset package using **Assets | Import Package | Custom Package....**
3. Import the **VuforiaSamples** asset package also using **Assets | Import Package | Custom Package....**
4. Set the app license key in **Vuforia | Configuration** obtained from the Vuforia Dev Portal.
5. Delete the **Main Camera** from the **Hierarchy**.
6. Drag the **ARCamera** prefab from Project **Assets** into the **Hierarchy**.
7. Add the **Camera Settings** component to the camera to enable auto-focus.
8. Save your work: **File | Save Scene As** and **File | Save Project.**
9. Bind HoloLens camera to Vuforia.
10. Select **GameObject | Camera,** rename it `HoloLensCamera`.
11. Set **Clear Flags** to **Solid Color.**
12. Set **Background** to black (0,0,0).
13. Go to **Vuforia | Configuration.**
14. In **Inspector**, set **Select Eyewear Type** to **Optical See-Through.**
15. Set **See Through Config** to **HoloLens.**
16. In **Hierarchy**, select the **AR Camera** object.
17. Drag the **HoloLensCamera** from **Hierarchy** onto the **Central Anchor Point** slot in the **Vuforia Behavior** component.

Adding the image target

We will now add the image target to the project and import the image database:

1. In your web browser, go to the Vuforia Dev Portal (`https://developer.vuforia.com/`).
2. Create a target database, give it a name like `BusinessCard` and **Type: Device.**

3. Click **Add Target** to add a **Type: Single Image**, specify a file (`PurpleFinchCard.png`), a width (in meters) (`0.09`), and **Add** it to the database.

4. Download the database using **Download Database**, be sure to select **Unity Editor** as type.

Back in Unity:

1. Drag the **ImageTarget** prefab into the **Hierarchy**.

2. Import the downloaded database package using **Assets | Import Package | Custom Package.**

3. Select **ImageTarget** in **Hierarchy**, and in **Inspector** select your **Database** (`BusinessCard`).

4. Check the **Enable Extended Tracking** checkbox.

5. Check the **Static** checkbox in the upper-right of **Inspector** for **ImageTarget**.

6. Go to the **Vuforia | Configuration** and in **Inspector** Datasets, check the **Load BusinessCard** checkbox (or your db name) and then mark it as **Activate.**

Adding objects

We now can add the drone to the project:

1. Import the **SimpleDrone** package using **Assets | Import Package | Custom Package.**

2. Drag the **SimpleDrone** prefab into the **Hierarchy**, and make it a child of **ImageTarget**.

3. Select the drone and set the scene gizmo to **Scale**, or enter the **Transform Scale** to (`0.1, 0.1, 0.0`) and move it to resting on the card (**Position Y** = `0.06`).

You should also add the animations to make the drone fly. We won't repeat the details here, please refer to the previous section.

Build settings

We will now set up the project to build for Windows UWP holographics:

1. First, be sure to save the scene (**File | Save Scenes**) and project (**File | Save Project**). If prompted for a scene name choose what you want, such as `PurpleFinch`.

2. Go into **File | Build Settings** and make sure the scene is the only one listed in **Scenes In Build** (press **Add Open Scenes**).

3. In **Build Settings Platform**, make sure **Windows Store** is the target platform (select **Windows Store** and press **Switch Platform**).

4. Choose **SDK: Universal 10**, **UWP Build Type: D3D**, and check the **Unity C# Projects** checkbox.

5. Adjust quality settings **Edit | Project Settings | Quality** , choose **Fastest** default level for Windows Store platform column.

6. Now go to **Player Settings** and look at the **Inspector** on the right.

7. Under **Publishing Settings**, in the **Capabilities** pane, ensure all the following are checked:
   - Internet Client
   - Pictures Library
   - Music Library
   - Videos Library
   - Web Cam
   - Microphone
   - Spatial Perception

8. Under **Other Settings** check the **Virtual Reality Supported** checkbox, and ensure **Windows Holographic** (or Mixed Reality) is present in the list of SDKs.

9. Again, **Save Scene** and **Save Project**.

Building and running

Let's now build and run the app on the HoloLens.

Press **Build** to begin building. We recommend you create a new folder in your project root named `Build` and specify the file or subfolder name under that, as needed. This will generate a Visual Studio project.

Open the project in Visual Studio (double-click the `.sln` file in the build):

1. Set the **Solution Configuration** to **Release**, **Platform** to **x86** and **Target** to emulator or remote device (as explained in `Chapter 3`, *Building Your App*).

2. Set the **Device** to your target device (for example, HoloLens Emulator or physical device).

Please refer to the HoloLens section of Chapter 3, *Building Your App*, for information on using Unity Editor with a physical HoloLens device versus using HoloLens emulator provided by Microsoft.

Building with ARToolkit

Each of the platform variations in this chapter have been using the Vuforia VR toolkit. If you prefer the free open source ARToolkit you can implement the project using the following steps.

In this section, we will use open source ARToolkit in Unity on a Window 10 development machine and targeting an Android device. This is mostly a step-by-step walk-through. If you want a better explanation please refer back to the previous corresponding section and the ARToolkit section in Chapter 2, *Setting Up Your System*.

Setting up the project

Let's jump right in:

1. Create a new 3D project in Unity, named BusinessCardART.
2. Import the ARToolkit asset package (for example, ARUnity5-5.3.2.unitypackage) using **Assets | Import Package | Custom Package....**

Create the AR Controller object.

1. Add an empty object using **GameObject | Create Empty** named AR Controller.
2. Click **Add Component** and add **ARController** to it.
3. Make sure the component script's **Video Options' Layer** attribute is set to **AR Background** (we're referring to the **Video Options Layer** not the object **Layer** at top of the **Inspector**). If necessary create the required layers first, see Chapter 2, *Setting Up Your System*, for instructions.

Create the AR Root object.

1. Add an empty object using **GameObject | Create Empty** named Root.
2. Click **Add Component** and add **AR Origin** to it.
3. Set the object's **Layer** to **AR Background 2** at the top of the **Inspector**.

Add an AR Camera.

1. In **Hierarchy**, move the existing **Main Camera** to be a child of **Root**.
2. Click **Add Component** and add **ARCamera** to it.
3. Reset the camera's transform, using the **Transform | gear icon | Reset.**
4. Set the camera's **Culling Mask** to **AR Background 2** (select **Nothing** then **AR Background 2** to set it).
5. Save your work: **File | Save Scene As** and **File | Save Project.**

At this point you can test it by pressing **Play** and you should see the video feed in the **Game** pane.

Preparing the image target

First import the business card image into your project (for example, drag and drop it into your Project **Assets** folder).

When you installed ARToolkit in Chapter 2, *Setting Up Your System*, we downloaded the Unity asset package. We also downloaded Additional Unity Tools (as a ZIP file) and installed them in a Programs folder (or Applications folder) or somewhere you can find them now. We are going to use the genTextData program, a command-line tool.

ARToolkit offers several types of targets including images (which they refer to as natural feature tracking, or NFT), and then they have square markers, kind of like QR codes, which are black and white markers that have a significant border around them. For this project, we're using the NFT.

Basically, we want to run the genTextData command giving the image file as an argument.

On Windows, you can take the following steps:

1. Using File Explorer, open the folder containing the image file (in our case, PurpleFinchCard.jpg). Actually, you may want to copy the image into a separate working directory as we will be generating additional data files to go with it.
2. Using another File Explorer window, navigate to your installed ARToolkit tools. On Windows this might be C:\Program Files (x86)\ARToolKit5\bin, and open the bin directory.

3. Find the application named `genTextData`.
4. Launch the Windows Command Prompt (right-click **Start | Command Prompt**). (On Mac, open a Terminal window).
5. Drag the **genTextData** program from the `bin` to the terminal.
6. Press the spacebar.
7. Then drag the image file from its folder to the terminal.

Isn't Window's nice to take care of all that typing for you?! Press *Enter* to run the command.

Next you are requested to provide the levels of extraction, or image resolutions, for feature tracking. In ARToolkit you specify a maximum and minimum resolution. The level of extraction are the in-between resolutions.

Resolution is in terms of dots per inch (DPI). Our original `PurpleFinchCard.jpg` image is *1796 x 1024* pixels, and the physical card is 3.5 inches by 2 inches. So, the max resolution we can match against is 512 DPI. Regardless of how much resolution is in the device camera at runtime, the matching can't be more accurate than the target image. But if the runtime camera is moved away from the card, we want to try and match against less pixels. As shown in the following list, the program suggests a min and max image resolution of 65.597 and 2399.000; we will use the min 66 and max 512:

1. **Select extraction level for tracking features**: Choose the default, 2.
2. **Select extraction level for initializing features**: Choose the default, 1.
3. **Enter the minimum image resolution**: Enter 66.
4. **Enter the maximum image resolution**: Enter 512.

It then generates the dataset for the image tracking. The data is crunched and data files are generated (`.fset`, `.fset3`, `.iset`) in the same directory as the given image.

A terminal session for `genTexData.exe` is shown in the following screenshot:

```
02 - Command Prompt                                                    —    □    ×

D:\Users\Jonathan>D:\Programs\ARToolKit5\bin\genTexData.exe "D:\Users\Jonathan\Google Drive\ARBook\Chapter4\PurpleFinchC
ard.jpg"
Select extraction level for tracking features, 0(few) <--> 4(many), [default=2]:
MAX_THRESH  = 0.900000
MIN_THRESH  = 0.550000
SD_THRESH   = 8.000000
Select extraction level for initializing features, 0(few) <--> 3(many), [default=1]:
SURF_FEATURE = 100
Reading JPEG file...
  Done.
JPEG image 'D:\Users\Jonathan\Google Drive\ARBook\Chapter4\PurpleFinchCard.jpg' is 1796x1024.
Enter the minimum image resolution (DPI, in range [65.597, 2399.000]): 66
Enter the maximum image resolution (DPI, in range [66.000, 2399.000]): 512
Image DPI (1): 66.000000
Image DPI (2): 83.154793
Image DPI (3): 104.768478
Image DPI (4): 132.000015
Image DPI (5): 166.309601
Image DPI (6): 209.536972
Image DPI (7): 264.000061
Image DPI (8): 332.619232
Image DPI (9): 419.073975
Image DPI (10): 512.000000
Generating ImageSet...
  (Source image xsize=1796, ysize=1024, channels=3, dpi=2399.0).
  Done.
Saving to D:\Users\Jonathan\Google Drive\ARBook\Chapter4\PurpleFinchCard.iset...
  Done.
Generating FeatureList...
Start for 512.000000 dpi image.
        ImageSize =    83877[pixel]
Extracted features =    3096[pixel]
 Filtered features =    1681[pixel]
218/ 219.
  Done.
Max feature = 68
  1: (185,151) : 0.250407 min=0.274215 max=0.614951, sd=33.176723
  2: (219,152) : 0.253570 min=0.269172 max=0.568804, sd=27.033638
  3: (152,151) : 0.265410 min=0.369168 max=0.666367, sd=41.039131
  4: ( 37,134) : 0.349427 min=0.392059 max=0.714481, sd=52.963791
  5: (118,148) : 0.358640 min=0.365833 max=0.744160, sd=40.400841
  6: ( 74,145) : 0.378788 min=0.446032 max=0.729821, sd=45.130894
  7: ( 74, 65) : 0.764950 min=0.690885 max=0.943973, sd=58.858269
  8: (107, 55) : 0.790948 min=0.551629 max=0.948884, sd=42.896301
  9: ( 92, 99) : 0.791797 min=0.747554 max=0.921094, sd=74.369072
 10: ( 49, 98) : 0.836599 min=0.695498 max=0.900353, sd=70.365387
-------------------------------------------------------------------
Start for 419.073975 dpi image.
        ImageSize =    56027[pixel]
Extracted features =    2282[pixel]
 Filtered features =    1124[pixel]
178/ 179.
  Done.
```

Now in Unity, import the image data into the Project `Assets/StreamingAssets` folder. The easy way to do this is select the files from your `Explorer` (Find) window and drag them directly into Unity. You can (and should) omit the original JPG file.

All the files in your `StreamingAssets` folder will be built into your final app. Delete any unused files, including the original image used to generate the target data, and any sample images that might have been imported with your samples package.

Adding the image target

Back in Unity, we will now tell our scene about the business card image target to use. We identify it in the project using tags. We'll tag our target `PurpleFinch`:

1. In **Hierarchy**, the **Main Camera** should be a child of **Root**. Select **Main Camera**.
2. Using **Add Component**, choose **ARMarker** to add the component to camera.
3. For **Target Tag** enter the name `PurpleFinch`.
4. Set its **Type** to `NFT`.
5. For **NFT dataset name** set the same name of our datafiles (which are now in `StreamingAssets`). Ours is named `PurpleFinchCard`.

Assuming it finds the dataset, you will see confirmation messages in the editor **Console** window, and the component will show the UID of the found marker, as shown in the following screenshot:

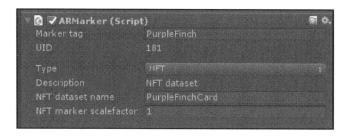

Now we add it to the scene as a tracked object.

1. Add an empty object as a child of **Root**. A quick way is to right-click **Root** and choose **Create Empty.**
2. Rename it `PurpleFinch Target`.
3. Using **Add Component** choose **AR Tracked Object** to add the component to it.
4. It asks for a **Marker Tag**, give it the same tag name we entered earlier (`PurpleFinch`).
5. When the tag is recognized the **Marker UID** will be shown in the component pane.

The resulting AR Tracked Object component values are shown in the following screenshot:

Adding objects

We now can add the drone to the project. First import the model into the project:

1. Import the **SimpleDrone** package using **Assets | Import Package | Custom Package...**.
2. Now we add the drone into the scene. Make it a child of the **PurpleFinch Target** target object.
3. Drag the **SimpleDrone** prefab into the **Hierarchy**, and make it a child of **PurpleFinch Target**.
4. Select the drone and set the scene gizmo to **Scale**, or enter the **Transform Scale** to (0.001, 0.001, 0.001) and move it resting on the center of the card, **Position** (0.01, 0.005, 0).

Scaling in ARToolkit is a bit different than Vuforia. In Vuforia we could set the target size in real-world units, thus the business card is scaled to 0.09.

By default, ARToolkit assumes the target is vertical, as if it's hanging on a wall. Vuforia defaults with the target laying flat, like it's on a table. To lay our target flat and keep the drone upright:

1. Set the Root's **Transform X Rotation** to 90 degrees.
2. Set the **SimpleDrone's Transform X Rotation** to −90 degrees.
3. One last thing, double-check that the objects under **Root** are all on the **AR background 2** layer. Select **Root** and in **Inspector** set its layer again, Unity will prompt you to change all its children's layers also. Do it.

The resulting **Scene** view for ARToolkit version of our project should now look similar to this:

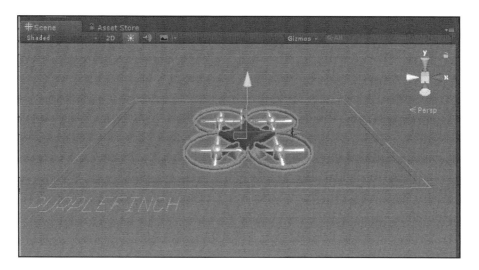

You should also add the animations to make the drone fly. We won't repeat the details here, please refer to the previous section.

Building and running

We can now build and run the app on our target device-- an Android phone. Follow these steps. If you want more detail and explanation, please refer back to the relevant sections of Chapter 3, *Building Your App*:

1. First, be sure to save the scene (**File | Save Scenes**) and project (**File | Save Project**).
2. In **Build Settings** (**File | Build Settings**) make sure the scene is the only one listed in **Scenes In Build** (press **Add Open Scenes**).
3. In **Build Settings Platform**, make sure **Android** is the target platform (select **Android** and press **Switch Platform**).
4. Now go to **Player Settings** (press **Player Settings** in **Build Settings**, or main menu **Edit | Project Settings | Player**) and look at the **Inspector** on the right for the **Settings for Android**.

5. Under **Other Settings**, the **Package Name** must be set to a unique identifier, in the format `com.Company.ProductName` such as `com.PurpleFinch.BusinessCard`.

6. For **Minimum API Level**, select **Android 5.1 Lollipop** (API level 22 or whichever is the current minimum for ARToolkit).

7. Once more save the project.

Now make sure your phone is connected via USB and unlocked. Then press **Build And Run**. As mentioned in Chapter 3, *Building Your App*, we recommend you make a folder named `Build` and save your executable build files there. We can name it `BusinessCard.apk`.

There you go! Whether you choose to use Vuforia or ARToolkit, whether you target Android or iOS, you can impress your business clients with an augmented business card!

Summary

In this chapter, we built our first real augmented reality application, a practical (and fun!) example of a business use case. Using a business card as an image target, we augmented it with a business-related object. In this case it was a drone photography business and the app shows a drone flying around. You can use your own ideas for your own business.

Our first step was to decide the requirements and make a plan. We selected a target image, a computer graphic, and the target platforms. We then chose Windows 10, Unity, and Vuforia for the project and a target of an Android phone. At the end of the chapter, we stepped through the whole project again for iOS, HoloLens, and ARToolkit.

To build the project we set up a new project with Vuforia SDK, including license key, AR camera, and image target data. Then we added the drone object to the scene so it appears when the target image is recognized. Finally, we showed how to use Unity's animator features to build and control animation clips.

Along the way, we discussed what makes a good image target, including a wide border, a detailed non-repetitive pattern, and good contrast. We also talked about scale including units of measure, visual perception of 2D and 3D space, virtual coordinates, and target marker scale for AR.

In the next chapter, we will consider a different application of AR-- science education. We will get to build a model of the solar system that will hover in your living room! In the process, we will introduce you to Unity C# programming and go into detail on using texture maps, along with a lot more AR fun.

5

AR Solar System

Education is an important application of augmented reality. Children of all ages love astronomy and studying the planets of our solar system. So, for this project, we're going to build an educational AR app that will let you explore the solar system and view the planets in the comfort of your living room.

In this chapter, we are going to build a model of the solar system, including the earth, moon, sun, and the other eight planets (yes, Pluto still counts!). We will use actual NASA data to set up the size and texture of each heavenly body. We will animate the planet's spin and orbit using C# programming.

We'll use the primary AR technique of using coded markers to implement the project. We'll print cards with AR markers you can use to interactively explore celestial bodies. We will also show you how to make a markerless version of the project for devices that support spatial mapping.

In this chapter, you will learn the following topics:

- Building a hierarchy of the solar system with orbiting planets and an earth-moon system with the moon orbiting the earth
- Adding texture maps to objects to make realistic-looking planets
- Adding light to the scene and showing both the day and night sides of the earth
- Writing C# scripts for planet spin and orbits
- Using custom markers to control what is visible in the augmented scene
- Creating markerless AR projects for devices that support spatial mapping

In the interest of clarity, this chapter will first walk you through the entire project, as if developing with Vuforia for Android devices. At the end of the chapter, we will walk through the steps for other development targets, including ARToolkit as an alternative to Vuforia. For markerless implementation, you can consider using Apple ARKit for iOS, Google ARCore for Android, and MixedRealityToolkit for HoloLens.

 Refer to the GitHub repository for this book, for completed projects for each platform, at `https://github.com/ARUnityBook/`.

Alright, let's blast off, rocket man!

The project plan

Before we begin implementing the project, it will help if we first define what we're going to do, identify the assets we will use, and make a plan.

The goal of this project is to show a model of the solar system that illustrates the relative position, size, and rotation speeds of the nine planets.

User experience

Users should be able to open our solar system app and see a model of the sun, earth, moon, and the other eight planets rotating as expected. Each body should look reasonably realistic using texture images from NASA and should be scaled proportionally, keeping in mind the diameter, spin rate (day), and orbit (year). The planets will orbit the sun and be illuminated by it.

Using custom cards for each planet, the user will be able to point their camera at a card to zoom in on that specific planet. The user should also be able to watch the bodies move in fast or slow motion. Finally, the app should play background music while it runs.

Because the actual scale of the solar system is so huge, we can take some liberty in terms of compressing distances and sizes so it all fits together for illustration purposes.

AR targets

Our goal is to demonstrate the use of custom markers, as they might appear on trading cards or on the pages of a children's book. Each marker has a different code, such as bar code, that the app will identify for each different planet. Using coded targets is easier and more efficient than photographic image (also known as *natural feature*) tracking.

For this project, we will use markers built from standard examples provided with the Vuforia and ARToolkit packages. We will provide a simple example of such cards in the files provided by the publisher for this book. See `PlanetMarkerCards.pdf` for Vuforia-compatible markers and `PlanetMarkerCardsARTK.pdf` for the AR Toolkit ones in the `Files` folder.

Graphic assets

Each of the heavenly bodies will be spheres with equirectangular textures mapped onto their surface. I recommend you download the texture images now. These files are included with the downloads for this book--`SolarSystemTextures.zip`--which contains individual texture files, named `mercury.png`, `venus.png`, and so on. The source of most of these images is `http://www.solarsystemscope.com` (Pluto's is `https://celestiaproject.net/` and the source of Saturn rings is `http://alpha-element.deviantart.com/art/Stock-Image-Saturn-Rings-393767006`). For example, `earth.png` looks like this:

We also have a chance to throw some real science into our project. The following NASA table shows the actual distance, size, rotation, and orbit values of each of the planets (`https://nssdc.gsfc.nasa.gov/planetary/factsheet/index.html`):

Planetary Fact Sheet - Metric

	MERCURY	VENUS	EARTH	MOON	MARS	JUPITER	SATURN	URANUS	NEPTUNE	PLUTO
Mass (10^{24}kg)	0.330	4.87	5.97	0.073	0.642	1898	568	86.8	102	0.0146
Diameter (km)	4879	12,104	12,756	3475	6792	142,984	120,536	51,118	49,528	2370
Density (kg/m^3)	5427	5243	5514	3340	3933	1326	687	1271	1638	2095
Gravity (m/s^2)	3.7	8.9	9.8	1.6	3.7	23.1	9.0	8.7	11.0	0.7
Escape Velocity (km/s)	4.3	10.4	11.2	2.4	5.0	59.5	35.5	21.3	23.5	1.3
Rotation Period (hours)	1407.6	-5832.5	23.9	655.7	24.6	9.9	10.7	-17.2	16.1	-153.3
Length of Day (hours)	4222.6	2802.0	24.0	708.7	24.7	9.9	10.7	17.2	16.1	153.3
Distance from Sun (10^6 km)	57.9	108.2	149.6	0.384*	227.9	778.6	1433.5	2872.5	4495.1	5906.4
Perihelion (10^6 km)	46.0	107.5	147.1	0.363*	206.6	740.5	1352.6	2741.3	4444.5	4436.8
Aphelion (10^6 km)	69.8	108.9	152.1	0.406*	249.2	816.6	1514.5	3003.6	4545.7	7375.9
Orbital Period (days)	88.0	224.7	365.2	27.3	687.0	4331	10,747	30,589	59,800	90,560
Orbital Velocity (km/s)	47.4	35.0	29.8	1.0	24.1	13.1	9.7	6.8	5.4	4.7
Orbital Inclination (degrees)	7.0	3.4	0.0	5.1	1.9	1.3	2.5	0.8	1.8	17.2
Orbital Eccentricity	0.205	0.007	0.017	0.055	0.094	0.049	0.057	0.046	0.011	0.244
Obliquity to Orbit (degrees)	0.01	177.4	23.4	6.7	25.2	3.1	26.7	97.8	28.3	122.5
Mean Temperature (C)	167	464	15	-20	-65	-110	-140	-195	-200	-225
Surface Pressure (bars)	0	92	1	0	0.01	Unknown*	Unknown*	Unknown*	Unknown*	0.00001
Number of Moons	0	0	1	0	2	67	62	27	14	5
Ring System?	No	No	No	No	No	Yes	Yes	Yes	Yes	No
Global Magnetic Field?	Yes	No	Yes	No	No	Yes	Yes	Yes	Yes	Unknown
	MERCURY	VENUS	EARTH	MOON	MARS	JUPITER	SATURN	URANUS	NEPTUNE	PLUTO

The data values we use in our project will be proportional to the earth values, as given at `https://nssdc.gsfc.nasa.gov/planetary/factsheet/planet_table_ratio.html`. So, when our earth sphere is scaled at 1 unit, the other planets will be relative to the diameter of the earth.

Actual sizes and distances between planets are astronomical! We will need to adjust the real scale to make this model practical. For example, the diameter of the sun is about 109 times the size of the earth, so in this project, we will depict it as 1x the size of the earth. In the scale we're using--where one Unity unit is one earth diameter, which is about one inch on the target marker--the earth-sun distance would be 11,726 inches or almost 1,000 feet (300 meters) in the real world. Pluto would be over 7 miles (11 km) from our target marker! That's a long way to walk to see the whole model. So, when we get to positioning the planets in our model, we'll decide to compress space and time for illustration purposes.

Target device and development tools

Having defined the project's objective, we should also know which development platform, version of Unity, AR toolkit, and target device(s) we're using. This chapter includes instructions for the following combinations:

Target AR Platform	AR SDK	Development Platform
Android	Vuforia	Windows 10
iOS	Vuforia	OS X
HoloLens	Vuforia	Windows 10
Android	ARToolkit	Windows 10

At the end of the chapter, we will also introduce a markerless version of the project that uses spatial mapping to determine the solar system's location in the real world, rather than recognizable target markers, for the following platforms:

Target AR Platform	AR SDK	Development Platform
iOS	Apple ARKit	OS X
HoloLens	MixedRealityToolkit	Windows 10

 Refer to the GitHub repository (`https://github.com/ARUnityBook/`) for this book for completed projects for each platform, including Google ARCore for Android.

Setting up the project

Let's begin the implementation by setting up a new project in Unity and getting it ready for AR. This may be familiar by now, so we'll go through the steps quickly (even more abbreviated than the previous chapter). If you require more information, refer to the relevant topics in Chapter 2, *Setting Up Your System*, and Chapter 3, *Building Your App*.

Creating our initial project

Use the following steps to create a new AR project in Unity. You will need to have downloaded the Vuforia packages first (refer to Chapter 2, *Setting Up Your System*). Refer to the following steps to do this:

1. Open Unity and create a new 3D project. Name it something like SolarSystem.
2. Go to **Assets | Import Package | Custom Package...** to import vuforia-unity-xxxx.
3. Go to **Assets | Import Package | Custom Package...** to import VuforiaSamples-xxxx.
4. Browse to Vuforia Dev Portal (https://developer.vuforia.com/targetmanager/licenseManager/licenseListing) and choose or create a license key. Copy the license key to your clipboard.
5. Back in Unity, go to **Vuforia | Configuration** and paste the license key to **App License Key**.
6. Review the other configuration settings, including the current **Webcam Camera Device**.

Setting up the scene and folders

Next, replace the default **Main Camera** object with Vuforia's **ARCamera** prefab:

1. Delete the **Main Camera** object from **Hierarchy**.
2. Locate the **ARCamera** prefab in the Project Assets/Vuforia/Prefabs folder and select and drag it to the **Hierarchy**.
3. Use **Add Component** to add a **Camera Settings** component to **ARCamera**.
4. Save the scene as SolarSystem (**File | Save Scene As**) and save the project (**File | Save Project**).

For this walkthrough, we are going to target Android devices. We can do some basic settings now. This way, you can periodically carry out a build and run to see your progress on the actual device throughout the project:

1. Go to **File | Build Settings**.
2. Set **Switch Platform** to **Android**.
3. Also, add the curret scene and press **Add Open Scenes.**
4. Choose **Player Settings**, then set your **Identification Package** name (com.Company.Product) and **Minimum API Level** (Android 5.1).
5. Save the scene, then save the project.

At this point, if you press the **Play** button in the Unity editor, you should see the video feed from the webcam. This will allow you to debug AR applications inside the Unity editor.

It's useful if we now create some empty folders in the project's Assets folder which we will use soon:

1. In the **Project** window, select the top-level Assets/ folder.
2. Create a new folder in Assets/, named SolarSystem.
3. Within Assets/SolarSystem/, create three more new folders: Textures, Scripts, and Materials.

The resulting project's Assets folders are shown in the following screenshot:

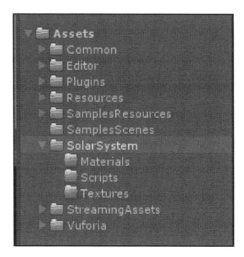

Using a marker target

We need a physical target image while developing this project. Choose a target image and print it out. We will talk more about customizing AR targets later in this chapter. Choose one of the follow to print:

- You can use `VuMark00` as provided with the samples package. Print a copy of `VuMark00.pdf`, found in `Assets/Editor/Vuforia/ForPrint/Vuforia-VuMark-Instances-00-99.zip` (unzip the file into another folder outside the project directory).
- Alternatively, use the marker sheet provided with the downloadable files for this book. The filename is `PlanetMarkerCards.pdf`. Print it and cut out the first one: **SOLAR SYSTEM** (this is the `VuMark00` marker).

The following is one of the markers:

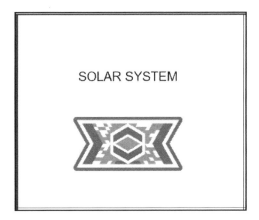

In Unity, follow these steps:

1. Activate the database. Go to **Vuforia** | **Configuration**, check the **Load Vuforia Database** checkbox, and then its **Activate** checkbox.
2. Drag the `Vuforia/Prefabs/VuMark` prefab to **Hierarchy** (reset its **Transform**, if necessary).
3. In **Inspector**, under **Vu Mark Behavior**, set **Database** to **Vuforia**.
4. Check **Enable extended tracking**.

The **Vu Mark Behavior** component settings are shown in the following screenshot:

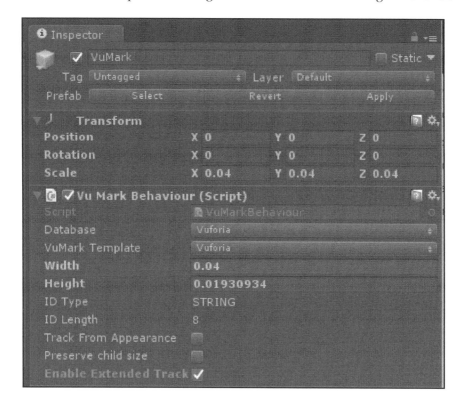

Creating a SolarSystem container

Now we should create an empty game object that is a child of **VuMark** and that will be the container parent of all the heavenly bodies of our solar system. For this, perform the following steps:

1. Select **VuMark** in **Hierarchy**, right-click on **Create Empty** and name it `SolarSystem`.
2. Verify that it is a child of **VuMark**.

If you press **Play** in the editor now, you will be able to see the video feed from your webcam. But it will not do anything in response to detecting the target marker.

3. Add a **Sphere** child of **SolarSystem** (select **SolarSystem** and right-click on **Sphere** under **3D Object**). Make sure the sphere's **Transform** is reset (**Transform | gear icon | Reset**).

4. Hover your mouse over the **Scene** window and press *F* to find and zoom to the object (or double-click on the **SolarSystem** object in **Hierarchy**).

5. Select **SolarSystem** from **Hierarchy** again, then position it above the target, such as (0, 0.75, 0).

6. Save the scene and the project.

7. Press **Play** now and point the webcam to the target. You should see the sphere.

The current scene hierarchy is shown in the following screenshot:

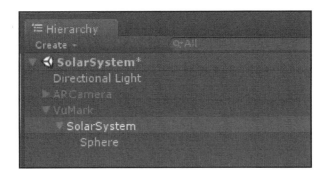

It should look something like this in the **Scene** window:

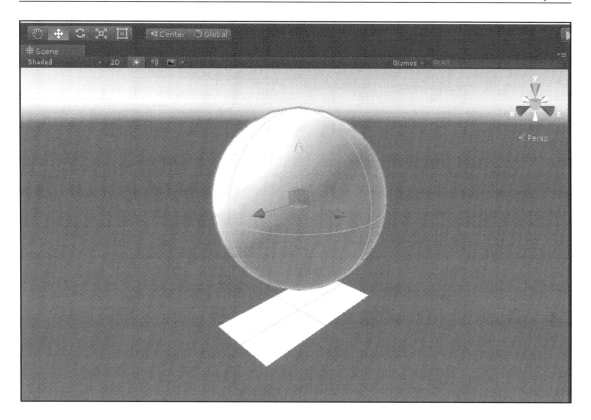

Building the earth

According to the Bible, in the beginning, the earth was unformed and void. But in Unity, it starts as an untextured sphere. 3D objects in Unity, such as spheres, cubes, or arbitrarily shaped meshes, are rendered by default using an untextured default material.

Materials define the details of how the surface of an object should look, usually using texture images. A texture is an image that is mapped onto the surface of an object as if it were painted or was a wallpaper. This is referred to as the *Albedo* texture or surface reflection. Advanced materials can use other textures to simulate additional surface detail, bumps, rust, metals, and other physical characteristics.

Suppose a sphere had a surface texture like this:

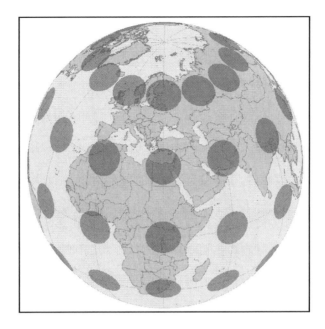

The texture unwrapped from the sphere and flattened into a 2D image is called an **equirectangular projection**, as shown in the following figure, much like you would find in the maps of the world (see https://en.wikipedia.org/wiki/Equirectangular_projection). This type of projection is also commonly used in 360-degree virtual reality images:

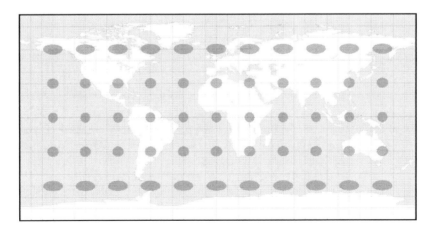

Creating an earth

To create an earth in Unity, refer to the following steps:

1. If you do not have a **Sphere** child of **SolarSystem**, create one now (in **Hierarchy**, right-click on **SolarSystem**, then go to **3D Object | Sphere**). Rename it `Earth`.
2. Ensure it is a child of **SolarSystem**.
3. If necessary, reset its **Transform** (**Transform | gear icon | Reset**).
4. Remove its **Collider** (**Sphere Collider | gear icon | Remove Component**).

A **collider** is a component that defines the shape of an object for the purpose of detecting physical collisions. It is invisible and is typically a simpler geometry than the object itself, since physics calculations can become computationally very expensive. We are not using Unity physics in this project so our planets do not need colliders.

Now we can apply the texture.

5. Import `earth.png` into the project's `Assets/SolarSystem/Textures/` folder (you can do this easily by dragging and dropping them from your operating system file explorer (finder) to the Unity **Project** window).
6. Now, drag the earth texture from `Assets/SolarSystem/Textures/` onto the **Earth** object (either in the **Scene**, **Hierarchy**, or **Inspector** window).

If you browse to the project's `Assets/SolarSystem/Materials` folder, you will discover that Unity has automatically created a new material, with the same name as the texture, with your texture set as its **Albedo** (surface texture image).

7. Open its material (in the earth's **Inspector** or directly in `Assets`).
8. Uncheck **Specular Highlights**, then uncheck **Reflections**.

We will keep our earth scaled at 1 unit. We can scale other planets in proportion to this.

If you want to adjust the size or position of the earth relative to the target, use the parent `SolarSystem` object and keep the earth scaled at 1 and centered at (0,0,0) for now.

Save the scene, save the project, and press **Play**, then point your camera to the target marker and see the globe. The following is a screen capture of my **Game** window with the project running, recognized by the marker and displaying our `Earth` object:

Rotating the earth

In the previous chapter, we implemented an animation using the Unity graph editors for animator states and animation curves. This time, we will do it using C# scripting.

Earth rotates once a day! (You knew that.) That is about 15 degrees per hour (*360/24*). If we wanted to go for realism, it might be a little boring to have to watch our model spin at that rate (and when we add the sun, we'd have to wait for a year to watch the animation of a complete orbit). Instead, let's rotate all the way in 24 seconds. That's one game second per real hour.

We'll write a quick script to spin the globe. If you're new to programming, just follow along and then read the introduction to programming in the next section:

1. In **Hierarchy**, select **Earth**, then in **Inspector** (you may need to scroll it down), press **Add Component**, **New Script** (**C-Sharp**). Name it `Spin` and press **Create and Add.**

   The **Spin** script now appears as a component in the earth's **Inspector**, as shown in the following screenshot:

2. Double-click on the Spin script to open it in your editor.

 Depending on how you install Unity, the default editor for program scripts may be either MonoDevelop or Visual Studio. Either is fine. Unity creates an empty script from a default template.

   Edit the file so it looks like this:

```
File: Spin.cs
using System.Collections;
using System.Collections.Generic;
using UnityEngine;

public class Spin : MonoBehaviour {
    public float gametimePerDay = 24.0f;

    void Update () {
        float deltaAngle = (360.0f / gametimePerDay) * Time.deltaTime;
        transform.Rotate(0f, deltaAngle, 0f);
    }
}
```

We declared a variable named `gametimePerDay` with a value of `24` (a **float** is a number with decimal points versus an integer). Each time the game updates the display, it will rotate the current object by `deltaAngle` degrees around the *y*-axis (vertical axis). The deltaAngle attribute is the number of degrees to rotate per game second (*360 / gametimePerDay*) times the current frame time (*Time.deltaTime*).

3. After making the edits, save the file.

4. Back in Unity, press **Play** and point the camera to your marker to watch the globe rotate.

 If the script has any errors, Unity will report these to you in the **Console** window. Be sure to have the **Console** window visible (**Window | Console**) so you can know whether you have made any typos or other mistakes while writing your script.

5. Now, for a little bit of cleanup, in the **Project** window, drag the **Spin** script from `Assets/` to the `Assets/SolarSystem/Scripts` folder.

6. Save the scene and the project.

Adding audio

This is getting pretty exciting! We now have a spinning world to augment our reality. Let's add some juice by playing some background music while it spins.

Choose an MP3 file of your choice. We decided to use a free version of Laurie London singing *He's got the whole world in his hands* (`http://www.bulkmp3.co/song/Laurie-London-He-S-Got-The-Whole-World-In-His-Hands-1958.html`). The file is included with the downloads for this book. Alternatively, maybe you'd prefer a choice of classical music, or David Bowie's Starman:

1. In the **Project** window, create a folder named `Assets/Audio` and import (drag and drop) the MP3 file into it.

2. In **Hierarchy**, create an empty object at root and name it `BackgroundMusic` (reset its **Transform**, if necessary).

3. Go to **Add Component | Audio | Audio Source**.

4. Now, drag the MP3 audio clip from the **Project** window to the **AudioClip** slot of Audio Source.

5. Check **Play on Awake** and **Loop** because we want it to start playing when the app loads and loop back to the beginning after it plays through.

OK! Press **Play** and enjoy your app. Then, save the scene and the project. The **Audio Source** component we just defined is shown in the following screenshot:

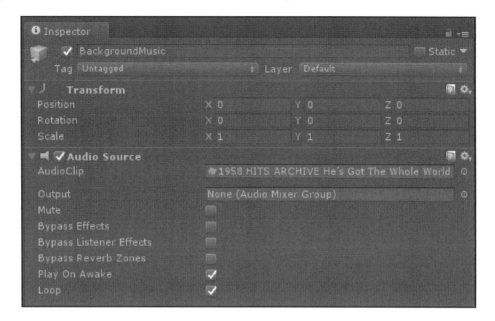

If the music gets annoying, you can disable audio in the editor's **Play** mode in the **Game** window using **Mute Audio**. Alternatively, you can temporarily disable it altogether by unchecking the **BackgroundMusic** object (upper-left corner of **Inspector**) or disable its **Audio Source** component (just remember to turn it back on before you build).

Lighting the scene

Our goal is to make a solar system, not just a spinning globe. That means we need to illuminate the planet from the side as if it were receiving sunlight. We will do this by replacing the default scene lighting with point light.

First, remove the default lighting:

1. In **Hierarchy**, delete **Directional Light**.
2. Next, go to the **Lighting** panel. If it's not enabled, go to **Window** | **Lighting** | **Settings** and drag its tab next to **Inspector**.

3. In **Lighting** , on its **Scene** tab in the **Environmental Lighting** section, set **Source** to Color and **Ambient Color** to black (000).

4. Also, in the **Environmental Reflections** group, set **Intensity Multiplier** to 0.

This looks pretty dark.

Adding sunlight

Unity provides a variety of different types of light sources for your scenes. For the sunlight, we are going to use point light since it radiates in all directions:

1. In **Hierarchy**, go to **Create | Light | Point Light** and name it Sunlight (you may need to go and click on the **Inspector** tab to expose that panel now).

2. Move it as a child of **SolarSystem**, reset its **Transform**, and move it away from the center, say, (-5, 0, 0).

3. Set its range to 10, 000 (something really big).

4. Set **Mode** to **Realtime**.

5. Set its **Intensity** to 1.3 (adjust so it looks good).

6. Set **Shadow Type** to **Soft Shadows**.

 Remember, you can rotate your view in the **Scene** panel using the right-mouse button and move the view using the middle-mouse button.

Now play the scene and decide if you like it. Then, save the scene and the project.

Night texture

Something's not quite right. Our earth looks uninhabited. Unlike other planets in our solar system (to my knowledge), only earth has city lights that are visible from space on the night side of the planet. We have another texture of earth at night, called earth_night.png, that we can add to the **Earth** material. We will make this texture an emission, meaning it will produce its own light (which city lights would do on the dark side of the planet):

1. Import earth_night.png into the Project Assets/SolarSystem/Textures folder, if not already.

2. Select the **Earth** material. In **Hierarchy**, select **Earth**, and in **Inspector**, unfold its material (or navigate to Assets/SolarSystem/Materials/earth).

3. Check the **Emission** checkbox.
4. Drag the **earth_night** texture onto the square chip next to **Emission Color.**
5. Dial down the emission level (far right of **Emission Color**) to something like 0.5.
6. Save the scene and the project and click on **Play.**

I don't know whether you can see in the following screenshot, but the day side the planet is lit by the sunlight, and the back shows city lights' emission. Cool!

Building an earth-moon system

Let's add the moon and animate it to orbit the earth. We will organize this in the hierarchy under a new container object that we'll call Earth-Moon. This way, we can keep the earth and the moon together so later we can move them as a unit (a celestial pair) when they orbit around the sun.

You may wonder why not just make the moon a child object of the earth so they'll move together around the sun? Well, the earth also spins its day-night cycle, and we don't want the moon to inherit that angular rotation, so its orbit is separate.

Creating the container object

First, let's create the Earth-Moon container:

1. In **Hierarchy**, create a new empty object under **SolarSystem**, named Earth-Moon and reset its **Transform**.
2. Move **Earth** as a child of **Earth-Moon**.
3. Set their positions as follows: **SolarSystem** (0, 0.75, 0), **Earth-Moon** (0, 0, 0), and **Earth** (0, 0, 0).

The resulting hierarchy is shown in the following screenshot:

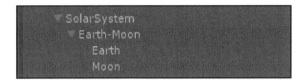

Creating the moon

Next, we can create a Moon object from **sphere**. We'll hide the earth temporarily while we work on the moon:

1. Temporarily hide the **earth** by unchecking the enable checkbox in the upper-left corner of its **Inspector**.
2. Under **Earth-Moon**, create **3D Object | Sphere** and rename it as Moon.
3. Delete its **Sphere Collider** component (**Sphere Collider | gear icon | Remove Component**).
4. Import moon.png into SolarSystem/Textures, if not already done.
5. Drag **moon** onto the **moon** in the scene (or **Hierarchy**).
6. Open its material (in the Earth's **Inspector** or directly in Assets) and uncheck **Specular Highlights** and **Reflections**.

   The **Moon** sphere is presently scaled at (1,1,1), which is the same size as our earth. We need to scale it to be proportionally smaller. According to our NASA data, the moon is 27 percent the size of the earth.

7. In **Hierarchy**, select **Moon**, and in **Inspector**, change **Transform Scale** to (0.27, 0.27, 0.27).

Positioning the moon

Now, we will position the moon relative to the earth. To assist, let's change our scene to the top-down orthographic view:

1. In the **Scene** window, use the view gizmo in the upper-right corner to give a top view (click on the *y*-axis arrow).
2. Click on the box in the center of the gizmo for *orthographic.*

The **Scene** window should look something like this:

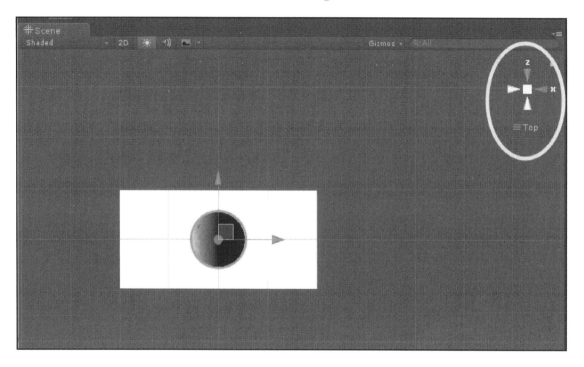

The moon is 3,84,400 km from the earth. The diameter of the earth is 12,756 km. As per our units, one Unity unit equals the earth's diameter. So, if we position the moon accurately proportional to the sizes of the bodies, it is 30.13 units from the earth:

3. Set the Moon's **Transform Position** to (30.13, 0, 0).
4. Enable **Earth** by selecting it in **Hierarchy** and rechecking its enable box in **Inspector**.
5. Zoom out so both are visible.

At this point, your **Scene** window may look like this, with a tiny earth and an even smaller moon:

Whoa! That's a huge distance. We have to zoom out to get both in view. The earth and the moon look so small. This might be accurate, but it's not great for visualization.

Let's just eyeball it and compress the size of space to about 5 percent of the actual distance, where 30.15/20 is about 1.5:

6. Set **Transform Position** to (1.5, 0, 0).

This looks better for our purposes, as shown in the following screenshot:

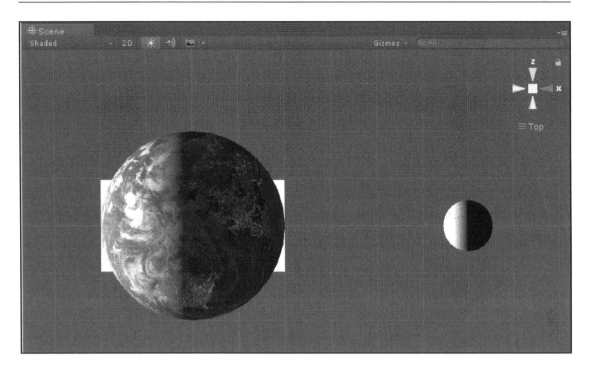

A quick introduction to Unity C# programming

Unity does a lot of things: it manages objects, renders them, animates them, calculates physics, and more. Unity itself is a program. The internal Unity code is accessible by you, the game developer, through the Unity point-and-click Editor interface we've already been using. Within the Unity Editor, scripts are manifested as configurable components. But, it's also more directly accessible by you through the Unity scripting API.

API, or application programming interface, simply refers to published software functions that you can access from your own scripts. Unity's API is very rich and nicely designed. That's one reason people have written amazing plugin add-ons for Unity.

There are many programming languages available. Unity has chosen to support the C# language from Microsoft. Computer languages have a specific syntax that must be obeyed or the computer will not understand your script. In Unity, script errors (and warnings) appear in the **Console** panel of the editor, as well as the bottom footer of the app window.

The default script editor for Unity is an **integrated development environment** (**IDE**) called *MonoDevelop*. You can configure a different editor if you want, such as *VisualStudio*. They have helpful features, such as text formatting, autocompletion, and pop-up help, that understand the Unity documentation. C# scripts are text files, named with a .cs extension.

In a Unity C# script, some of the words and symbols are part of the C# language itself. Some come from the Microsoft .NET Framework, and others are provided by the Unity API. Then, there's the code that you write.

An empty default Unity C# script looks like this:

```
using System.Collections;
using System.Collections.Generic;
using UnityEngine;

public class NewBehaviourScript : MonoBehaviour {

    // Use this for initialization
    void Start () {
    }
    // Update is called once per frame
    void Update () {
    }
}
```

Let's dissect it. The first three lines indicate that this script needs some other stuff to run. The using keyword is C#. The using UnityEngine line says we'll be using the UnityEngine API. The using System.Collections line says we might also use a library of functions named Collections for accessing lists of objects.

C# requires that each line of code ends with a semicolon. Double-slashes (//) indicate comments in the code, and anything from there to the end of that line will be ignored.

This Unity script defines a class named NewBehaviorScript. Classes are like code templates with their own properties (variables) and behaviors (functions). Classes derived from the base class MonoBehaviour are recognized by Unity and used when your game runs. The public class NewBehaviorScript: MonoBehaviour line basically says we are defining a new public class named NewBehaviorScript that inherits all the abilities of the Unity base class MonoBehaviour, including the capability of Start() and Update() functions. The body of our class is enclosed in a pair of curly braces ({}).

When something is *public*, it can be seen by other code outside this specific script file; when it's *private*, it can only be referenced within this file. We want Unity to see our NewBehaviorScript class.

Classes define variables and functions. A *variable* holds data values of a specific type, such as *float*, *int*, *boolean*, *GameObject*, and *Vector3*. *Functions* implement logical step-by-step instructions. Functions can receive *arguments*--variables enclosed in parenthesis--used by its code, and they can return new values when done.

Numeric *float* constants, such as 5.0f, require an f at the end in C# to ensure that the data type is a simple floating-point value and not a double-precision floating-point value.

Once you've written or modified a script in your code editor, save it and then switch to the Unity **Editor** window. Unity will automatically recognize the script has changed and reimport it. If errors are found, it will report them right away, in the **Console** panel.

Unity will automatically call specific named functions if you've defined them. Note that Start() and Update() are two examples of callbacks. Empty versions of these are provided in the default C# script. The datatype in front of a function indicates the type of value returned; Start() and Update() do not return values, so they're *void*.

Each Start() function from all the MonoBehaviour scripts in your game is called before the gameplay begins. It's a good place for data initialization.

At runtime, Unity runs a big loop, repeating over and over as the display needs to be updated in each frame, perhaps 60 times a second. All Update() functions are called at each time slice, or frame, while the game is running. This is where much of the action is.

Unity programs live in the real world and must be able to respond to events, such as user input, network messages, or video feed. Events are processed by event handlers, or callbacks, that you can write in your own code. These functions usually start in this format: On[EventName] (such as OnMouseDown).

This is just a cursory introduction to Unity programming. As we work through our projects in this book, we will explain additional things as they're introduced.

Animating the moon orbit

OK, back to work. With that short explanation of Unity programming, we're better armed to write more code. Let's get the moon moving; it should be orbiting the earth.

Adding the moon orbit

Let's write a script called `Orbit` that rotates one object, the moon, around another object, the earth. We want to be able to specify its orbital period as the number of earth days for one complete orbit. For the moon, that's 27.3 days. And, like our `Spin` script, we'll also provide a scalar that converts earth days into game time seconds as shown ahead:

1. In **Hierarchy**, select **Moon** and **Add Component, New Script (C-Sharp).** Name it `Orbit`, then press **Create and Add.**

2. Double-click on the new script to open it in your code editor.

   Write the `Orbit` class as follows:

```
File: Orbit.cs
using System.Collections;
using System.Collections.Generic;
using UnityEngine;

public class Orbit : MonoBehaviour {
    public Transform aroundBody;
    public float orbitalPeriod = 27.3f; // earth days for one complete
orbit
    public float gametimePerDay = 24f;  // realtime seconds per game earth
day

    void Update () {
        float deltaAngle = (360.0f / (gametimePerDay * orbitalPeriod)) *
Time.deltaTime;
        transform.RotateAround(aroundBody.position, Vector3.up,
deltaAngle);
    }
}
```

This is similar to the `Spin` code. The difference is this time we have another variable, `aroundBody`, which will be the earth's Transform. Then, we call `transform.RotateAround` (instead of `transform.Rotate`) to update the moon's rotation and position as it orbits the `aroundBody` object.

 To learn more about these API functions and many others, visit the Unity Script API documentation at `https://docs.unity3d.com/ScriptReference/Transform.RotateAround.html`.

Save your scripts and go back to Unity; you will see the `Orbit` component now has slots for the public variables, including Around Body.

3. Drag **Earth** from **Hierarchy** to the **Around Body** slot, as shown in the following screenshot:

When you press **Play**, the moon orbits at a slow rate (one second is one hour, so 27 days means it will take about 11 minutes to watch one full orbit). Now, try changing **Gametime Per Day** to 1 or 0.05. It will go faster! Also, change the same parameter in the earth's Spin script to the same value so the motions stay in sync.

You can modify component values while still in **Play** mode. But, when you exit **Play** mode, any values you change while in **Play** will revert to their starting values.

Now, for a little bit of cleanup, perform the following steps:

4. In the **Project** window, move the Orbit script from Assets/ to the Assets/SolarSystem/Scripts folder.
5. Save the scene and the project.

Adding a global timescale

Presently, you might have already noticed that both our scripts, Spin and Orbit, have a gametimePerDay variable that does the same thing--defines the number of game seconds that correspond to an earth hour.

No one writes code without expecting to change it. Programming is a dynamic art as you rethink how to do things, as requirements grow, and problems get fixed. Sometimes, these changes are not necessarily to add a new feature or fix a bug but to make the code cleaner, easier to use, and easier to maintain. This is called **refactoring**, when you change or rewrite parts of a program but do not necessarily change what it does, that is, its behavior.

Let's refactor our code to remove this duplication and put this variable in a master `GameController` object instead:

1. In **Hierarchy**, create an empty game object and name it `GameController`.
2. **Add Component, New Script (C-Sharp)** and name it `MasterControls`, then press **Create and Add.**

Open it for editing, as follows:

```
File: MasterControls.cs
using System.Collections;
using System.Collections.Generic;
using UnityEngine;

public class MasterControls : MonoBehaviour {
    public float gametimePerDay = 0.05f;
}
```

The script sets the default time to `0.05f`, which will run pretty fast, but it will show the earth orbiting the sun once every 18 seconds (*365 * 0.05*).

Now, we will modify both `Orbit.cs` and `Spin.cs` to reference `gametimePerDay` of `MasterControls` rather than their own.

While we're at it, in preparation for adding other planets, we will also modify the `Spin` script so it also takes `rotationRate`. This is its local day in earth days. For earth, it'll be 1.0. For other planets, it can be different:

```
File: Spin.cs
public class Spin : MonoBehaviour {
    public float rotationRate = 1f; // in earth days
    private MasterControls controls;

    void Start() {
        GameObject controller = GameObject.Find("GameController");
        controls = controller.GetComponent<MasterControls>();
    }

    void Update () {
        float deltaAngle = (360.0f / (rotationRate *
controls.gametimePerDay)) * Time.deltaTime;
        transform.Rotate( 0f, deltaAngle, 0f);
    }
}
```

In `Spin.cs`, we added two variables: `rotationRate` (which for the earth is 1.0) and a private `controls` reference to the `MasterControls` component. Then, we added a `Start()` method that will initialize `controls` when the app starts by finding `GameController` in **Hierarchy** and getting its `MasterControls` component so we can reference it in `Update()`. Then, in `Update()`, we used `controls.gametimePerDay` instead of a local one.

Experienced programmers may disapprove of using `GameObject.Find`, as it carries a performance overhead and is error-prone, requiring an object specifically named `GameController`. A better practice would be to use the singleton pattern (see https://unity3d.com/learn/tutorials/projects/2d-roguelike-tutorial/writing-game-manager) or Unity-scriptable objects (see https://unity3d.com/learn/tutorials/modules/beginner/live-training-archive/scriptable-objects).

Next, we will make a similar change to `Orbit.cs` to use *MasterControlsgametimePerDay*, as follows:

```
File: Orbit.cs
using System.Collections;
using System.Collections.Generic;
using UnityEngine;

public class Orbit : MonoBehaviour {
    public Transform aroundBody;
    public float orbitalPeriod = 27.3f; // earth days for one complete orbit
    private MasterControls controls;

    void Start() {
        GameObject controller = GameObject.Find("GameController");
        controls = controller.GetComponent<MasterControls>();
    }

    void Update() {
        float deltaAngle = (360.0f / (orbitalPeriod *
controls.gametimePerDay)) * Time.deltaTime;
        transform.RotateAround(aroundBody.position, Vector3.up,
deltaAngle);
    }
}
```

Save the scripts. Press **Play**. You can change the value of **Gametime Per Day** while it's running to see it change dynamically.

Orbiting the sun

To turn this into a solar system, the earth-moon pair needs to orbit around the sun in the center.

Making the sun the center, not the earth

Presently, we're still setting things up with the earth at the center of our universe. Let's make things right, as advised by Copernicus, and move the earth into an orbital position so the sun can be the center. For this, we recommend that you go back to a top-down view in the **Scene** pane:

1. In the **Scene** window, use the gizmo view in the upper-right corner to give a top view (click on the *y*-axis arrow).
2. Click on the box in the center of the gizmo.
3. Now move **Earth-Move** to **Position X**=5 and move **Sunlight** to the origin.
4. Select **Earth-Moon** in **Hierarchy** and set **Position** to (5, 0, 0).
5. Select **Sunlight** in **Hierarchy** and reset **Position** to (0,0,0).

Creating the sun

Creating the sun is a lot like making the earth and moon spheres, with one exception though. Since the sunlight source will be inside the sun (at 0,0,0 origin), its surface won't get illuminated. Instead, we'll make the sun material an emission:

1. Import `sun.png` into `Assets/SolarSystem/Texture`.
2. Create a **Sphere** object named `Sun`, which will be a child of **SolarSystem**.
3. Delete its **Sphere Collider.**
4. Drag the **Sun** texture onto the **Sun** object.
5. Unfold its material and uncheck **Specular Highlights** and **Reflections.**
6. Check **Emission.**
7. Drag the sun texture onto the **Emission Color** chip.
8. Move **Sunlight** so it becomes a child of the **Sun.**

The following is the resulting **Scene** view:

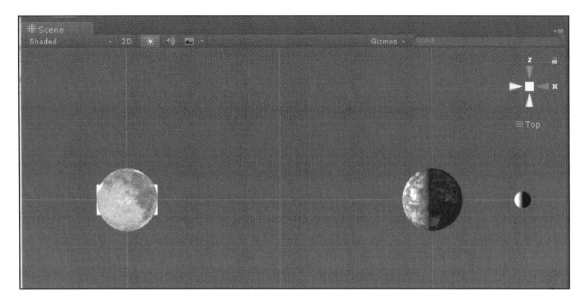

The following is the resulting **Hierarchy**:

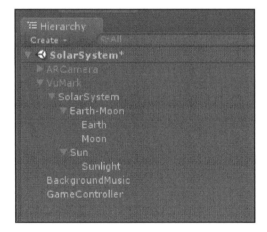

Also, here is the sun material that we made:

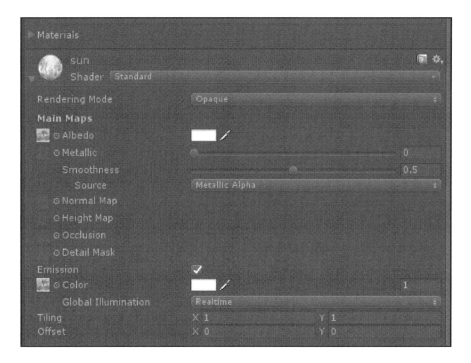

In reality, the sun is about 109 times the size of the earth. It is not practical to show the actual relative size of the sun in this project, so we will keep its size at 1 unit for now. Alternatively, we can try something bigger but not ginormous; however, this could be an interesting extension to this project--to provide a mode that illustrates real-life relative scales and distances of the bodies in our solar system.

The earth orbiting around the sun

We can reuse the `Orbit` script we wrote for the moon for the earth's orbit around the sun. Of course, where the earth goes, our moon goes too, so we're actually orbiting the earth-moon object:

1. Select the **Earth-Moon** object from **Hierarchy**.
2. **Add Component | Scripts | Orbit.**
3. Drag the **Sun** object from **Hierarchy** onto the **Around Body** slot.
4. Set **Orbital Period** to `365.25` (days in a year).
5. Save the scene and the project, then press **Play**.

Try changing **Gametime Per Day** of `GameController` between `24` and `0.05`.

Tilt the earth's axis

Oh! One more thing, before we forget. Earth has seasons because our planet's axis of rotation is tilted at an angle of 23.4 degrees, relative to our orbital plane (the plane of earth's orbit around the sun).

Now that we've defined a parent `Earth-Moon` object, we can also tilt the earth without affecting the position of this whole celestial pair system:

1. Select **Earth** and change its **Transform Rotation** to (0, 0, `23.4`).
2. If you use the rotate gizmo in the **Scene** view, be sure to set it to **Local** (not **Global**).
3. Make sure **Transform Position** is still (0,0,0).
4. Save the scene and the project.

The following screenshot shows our **Scene** view with the sun, tilted earth, and orbiting moon:

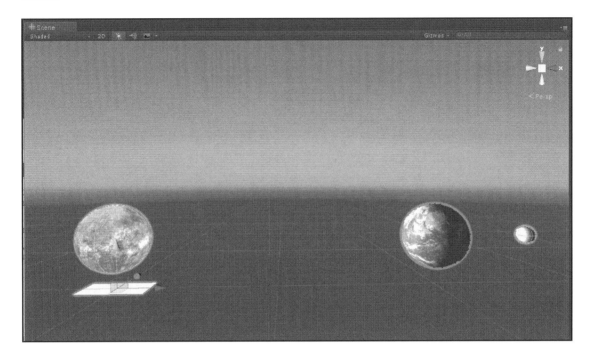

Adding the other planets

The following table shows the data of each of the planets, in values relative to the earth (source:
`https://nssdc.gsfc.nasa.gov/planetary/factsheet/planet_table_ratio.html`). For example, you can see that Mercury is 0.38 smaller than Earth, and Jupiter is 11.21 times bigger than Earth. Mercury takes 58.8 days to make one rotation that Earth does in 24 hours, yet makes its way around the sun in just 87.7 earth days.

	Relative diameter	Relative distance from Sun	Rotation (Earth days)	Orbit (Earth days)
Mercury	0.38	0.39	58.8	87.7
Venus	0.95	0.74	-244	226.5
Earth	1	1	1	365.25
Moon	0.27		0	27.4
Mars	0.53	1.55	1.0	686.67
Jupiter	11.21	5.29	0.42	4,346
Saturn	9.45	9.7	0.45	10,592
Uranus	4.01	19.5	-0.72	32,032
Neptune	3.88	30.6	0.67	59,791
Pluto	0.19	40.2	6.41	90,545

We will accurately scale the planets relative to the earth's size.

You can try to adjust their positions to be in line with the real distance from the sun. But as mentioned at the top of this chapter (as we saw with the earth and the moon), these distances are literally astronomical! I recommend you just make them evenly spaced out for the purposes of this project so you can see all the planets on your AR device without walking around and keep the planets scaled big enough to observe and enjoy.

You can use the actual rotation (day) and orbit (year) values for each planet. This will be in Unity's *earth days*, which will be relative to the earth. However, since the outer planets' years are so long, they may not appear to move at all in our model. So, you can perhaps use 1/10th for those or even 1/100 for the really slow ones. Tweak any other value as per your desired effect. The following are the values we used in our version of the project. Your mileage may vary:

	Scale	Position X	Spin Rotation	Orbital Period
Mercury	0.38	1.4	58.8	87.7
Venus	0.95	3	-244	226.5
Earth	1	5.7	1	365.25
Moon	0.27	1.5	n/a	27.3
Mars	0.53	8.7	1.0	686
Jupiter	11.21	17	0.42	434 *
Saturn	9.45	36	0.45	1059 *
Uranus	4.01	50	-0.72	320 **
Neptune	3.88	58	0.67	597 **
Pluto	0.19	66	6.41	905 **

Please note that the values in the above table which we have chosen to use in our simulation are accurate in scale and spin rotation, the orbit rate is accurate or scaled as indicated, and the position values (distance from the sun) is completely fudged. (* Orbit rate 10% actual), (** Orbit rate 1% actual).

Creating the planets with textures

The steps for creating the other eight planets are much like what we followed earlier in the project.

Repeat the following steps for each planet:

1. With **SolarSystem** selected in **Hierarchy**, right-click on **3D Object | Sphere.**
2. Name the planet, reset its **Transform**, and delete its **Collider**.
3. Scale the planet to the size suggested in the preceding table.
4. Position it (*x*-axis) in a reasonably spaced manner between its neighbors.
5. If not imported already, import the planet's `.png` texture file into `Assets/SolarSystem/Textures`.
6. Drag the texture onto the planet sphere.
7. On the material, disable **Specular Highlights** and **Reflections**.
8. Add a `Spin` component and set its rotation rate as suggested in the table.
9. Add an `Orbit` component and set the orbital period to the number of earth days, as suggested in the table.
10. Drag **Sun** onto the **Around Body** slot.

It might be quicker to duplicate an existing planet object (*Ctrl+D*), attach its material, and set its scale and orbital period.

The following screenshot shows all our planets defined and lined up neatly in the **Scene** window:

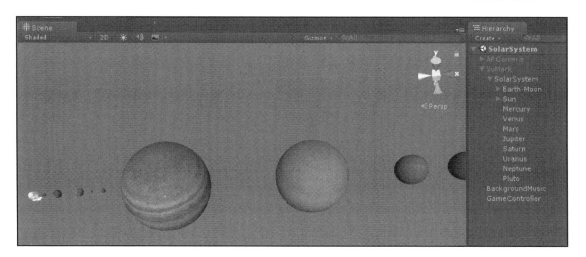

Isn't that a sight to behold?

When working in the **Scene** view, you may want to disable the scene lighting by unclicking the **Scene Lighting** toggle in its toolbar, especially for the outer planets that may appear in the shadow of Jupiter.

When ready to test, press **Play** (remember, you might need to set **Gametime Per Day** on GameController to 0.05 to see all the orbits in faster action).

One more thing to note: if you want to change the model scale as a whole and keep the proportions you've set up, scale the **SolarSystem** container object in **Hierarchy**, rather than the individual objects.

Adding rings to Saturn

Saturn's rings have a diameter of about 282,000 km and are about 2.35 times the diameter of Saturn, the planet (282,000 / 120,000). We have a texture, saturn_rings.png, that we can render on a flat plane to display as rings. In Unity, a 1x-sized plane actually measures 10 units across. So, we will set the plane's **Scale** to 0.235.

For the rings to have transparency, we can change **Rendering Mode** to **Cutout**. This will use the alpha channel of the image as a threshold to determine whether that pixel of the texture is displayed or not. The shader lets you choose the **Alpha Cutoff** value as shown ahead:

1. In **Hierarchy**, right-click on **Saturn**, then **3D Object | Plane**.
2. Choose **Transform Reset**, then scale to (0.235, 0.235, 0.235).
3. Import saturn_rings.png into SolarSystem/Textures and drag saturn_rings onto the SaturnRings object.
4. Open its material, then uncheck **Specular Highlights** and **Reflections.**
5. Change **Rendering Mode** to **Cutout**.
6. Adjust **Alpha Cutoff** to something like 0.3.

The resulting settings are shown in the following screenshot. Now, we have Saturn rings.

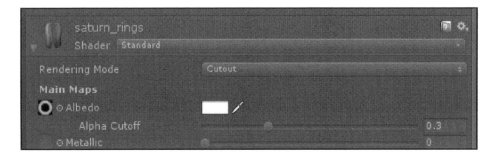

However, if you have an issue, if you look at them from underneath (pan or rotate the view in the **Scene** window), you'll see that they disappear. This is because the plane is only rendered on its front-facing side (this is an optimization in computer graphics, called *back-face culling*, which determines whether a polygon of a graphical object is visible). To resolve the issue, we could write a custom shader that does not perform back-face culling. Instead, we will duplicate our rings and flip them over for the underside.

7. Right-click on **SaturnRings** and select **Duplicate** (or *Ctrl+D*).
8. Set its **Transform Rotation** to **X** = 180.

Saturn with its double-sided rings is shown in the following screenshot:

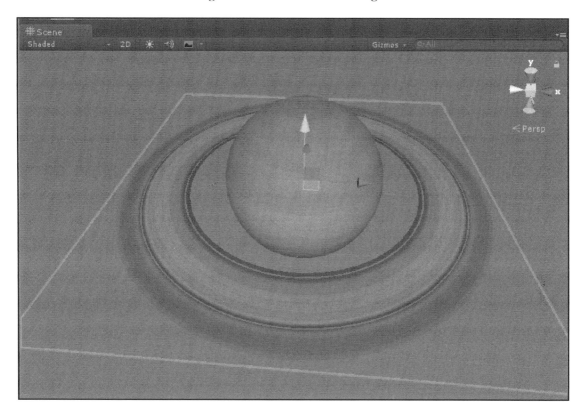

Note that our rings rotate with the planet. If you want to correct this, you could make a `SaturnAndRings` parent and move the rings so they are no longer a direct child of the planet, similar to what we did for earth-moon.

Switching views

When **SolarSystem** is at position (0, 0), the sun is centered at our marker. When **SolarSystem** is at position (-5, 0), the earth is on the marker. In this way, we can recenter our view by switching between bodies in the center using the object's **Transform** position relative to the **SolarSystem** parent.

Let's write a script for this. We'll attach it as a component to **GameController**:

1. In **GameController**, add **Component** | **New Script** and name it `PlanetView`.

Open the script and edit it as follows:

```
File: PlaneView.cs
public class PlanetView : MonoBehaviour {
    public Transform solarSystem;
    public Transform planet;
    void Update () {
        Vector3 position = solarSystem.localPosition;
        if (planet != null) {
            // move solar system so planet is in the center
            position.x = -planet.localPosition.x *
solarSystem.localScale.x;
            position.z = -planet.localPosition.z *
solarSystem.localScale.x;
        } else {
            // center solar system on the sun
            position.x = 0f;
            position.z = 0f;
        }
        solarSystem.localPosition = position;
    }
}
```

Note that we could also scale the position offset by `solarSystem.localScale`. This is not an issue while **SolarSystem** is scaled to `1.0`, but if you resize it, this will be required:

2. Drag the **SolarSystem** object onto the **Solar System** slot of **GameController**.
3. Drag the **Earth-Moon** object onto the **Planet** slot.
4. Click on **Play** in the editor.

5. Now the sun appears to rotate around the earth. We can dynamically change it while running the app in the editor. While in **Play** mode, drag the **Sun** object onto the **Planet** slot, replacing **Earth-Moon**.

Now the sun is in the center again and the earth rotates around it

The following **Scene** view shows the earth is now at the **ImageTarget** origin, while the other bodies are positioned relative to it:

6. Now, for a little bit of cleanup, in the **Project** window, move the script from `Assets/` to the `Assets/SolarSystem/Scripts` folder

Using VuMark targets (Vuforia)

We are now ready to wire up our application with real-world targets. Our objective is to give the user *cards* for each of the planets. When they point their camera at one of the cards, they should see the solar system from the point of view of that planet. And, of course, we have a solar system card that puts the sun at the center.

VuMark is Vuforia's system for generating coded markers. Vuforia comes with a set of example VuMarks, encoded for values from 0 through 99, part of the Vuforia Samples package. They (once imported into your Unity project) can be found in `Assets/Editor/Vuforia/ForPrint/Vuforia-VuMark-Instances-00-99.zip`, which contains versions in SVG, PNG, and PDF formats.

As mentioned at the top of this chapter, we have provided a PDF file with example cards using the VuMark examples for this project, as illustrated in the following figure. Each card has a separate VuMark marker that embeds a 2D bar code representing the numbers 0 through 9. Some of the marker cards are shown as follows:

SOLAR SYSTEM

MERCURY

Diameter: 4879 km

Distance from Sun: 57.9 million km

Length of day: 4222.6 hours

Length of year: 88.0 days

VENUS

Diameter: 12,104 km

Distance from Sun: 108.2 million km

Length of day: 2802.0 hours

Length of year: 224.7 days

EARTH

Diameter: 12,756 km

Distance from Sun: 149.6 million km

Length of day: 24 hours

Length of year: 365.25 days

MARS

Diameter: 6792 km

Distance from Sun: 227.9 million km

Length of day: 24.7 hours

Length of year: 687.0 days

JUPITER

Diameter: 142,984 km

Distance from Sun: 778.6 million km

Length of day: 9.9 hours

Length of year: 4331 days

The objective is when our app sees a marker with value 0, it should show the sun at the center; the marker will be 1 for Mercury, 2 for Venus, all the way up to 9 for Pluto. See the file included with this book, `PlanetMarkerCards.pdf`, with printable cards of 3.33 by 4 inches (Avery 5524 sheet layout). When you print the markers, be sure to cut them into separate cards; our app can only recognize one target at a time.

We are not going to do this here, but Vuforia offers the ability to design your own custom VuMarks (and we'll see later that AR Toolkit has a similar utility for their bar code markers). It requires Adobe Illustrator; they provide design templates. For more information, see the following articles:

- Introduction to the VuMark video at
  `https://www.youtube.com/watch?v=kHP9JzY8uiE`
- Design of a VuMark in Adobe Illustrator at
  `https://library.vuforia.com/articles/Solution/Designing-a-VuMark-in-Adobe-Illustrator`
- VuMark Design Guide at
  `https://library.vuforia.com/articles/Training/VuMark-Design-Guide`

Associating markers with planets

To associate markers with planet views, we need to write our own marker handler script. We will build this script incrementally, so it's easy to see what is going on.

First, we'll write in the code to register our callback function to VuMark Manager. This is a standard pattern in Unity C# for handling events:

1. In **Hierarchy**, select **GameController** and go to **Add Component | New Script**; name it `PlanetMarkerHandler`.

   Open the script in your editor and write it as follows:

```
File: PlanetMarkerHandler.cs
using System.Collections;
using System.Collections.Generic;
using UnityEngine;
using Vuforia;

public class PlanetMarkerHandler : MonoBehaviour {
    private VuMarkManager mVuMarkManager;

    void Start () {
        // register callbacks to VuMark Manager
```

```
        mVuMarkManager =
TrackerManager.Instance.GetStateManager().GetVuMarkManager();
        mVuMarkManager.RegisterVuMarkDetectedCallback(OnVuMarkDetected);
    }

    public void OnVuMarkDetected(VuMarkTarget target) {
        Debug.Log("New VuMark: " + target.InstanceId.StringValue);
    }
}
```

We included the line `using Vuforia` to get access to their SDK, including `VuMarkerManager`. We then registered our callback function, `OnVuMarkDetected`, with `TrackerManager`. The callback, for now, just prints to the debug console the name (*StringValue*) of the marker it finds when one is detected.

2. Save the script and press **Play** in Unity. Show the camera to different marks, and the console will print the mark ID it finds.

To open the console, go to **Window | Console** and dock it in the Unity editor.

The target ID is a string (text) that we obtained using `target.InstanceId.StringValue` in the VuMark00 format. We need it as an integer. So we will now write a little helper function, `markIdToInt`, to convert it from a string to an integer (it finds the substring starting at position 6 and takes the next two characters, for example, `00`) and print that to the console instead. Change the script as follows:

```
public void OnVuMarkDetected(VuMarkTarget target) {
    int id = markIdToInt(target.InstanceId.StringValue);
    Debug.Log("New VuMark: " + id);
}

private int markIdToInt(string str) {
    return int.Parse(str.Substring(6, 2));
}
```

Now we will give the handler a list of planetary bodies. The list is indexed from 0 through 9.

Add this line to the top of the `PlanetMarkerHandler` class (inside curly braces):

```
public class PlanetMarkerHandler : MonoBehaviour {
    public List<Transform> bodies = new List<Transform>();
```

3. Go to Unity and do the following:
    1. You will see a list of planetary bodies is now available in the **Planet Marker Handler** component. Give it size 10.
    2. Then, drag each of the objects from **Hierarchy** to the corresponding slots, starting with **Sun** for 0, **Mercury** for 1, and so on through **Pluto**. As before, be sure to use **Earth-Moon** for the earth system.

Your **Planet Market Handler** component should now look like this:

Back in the code, all we need to do is set the **Planet** value of the **Planet View** component to the one identified by the VuMark marker. The completed script looks like this:

```
File: PlanetMarkerHandler.cs
public class PlanetMarkerHandler : MonoBehaviour {
    public List<Transform> bodies = new List<Transform>();
    private VuMarkManager mVuMarkManager;
    private PlanetView planetView;

    void Start () {
        // get the Planet View component
        planetView = GetComponent<PlanetView>();

        // register callbacks to VuMark Manager
        mVuMarkManager =
TrackerManager.Instance.GetStateManager().GetVuMarkManager();
        mVuMarkManager.RegisterVuMarkDetectedCallback(OnVuMarkDetected);
```

```
    }

    public void OnVuMarkDetected(VuMarkTarget target) {
        int id = markIdToInt(target.InstanceId.StringValue);
        Debug.Log("Changing view: " + bodies[id].name);
        planetView.planet = bodies[id];
    }

    private int markIdToInt(string str) {
        return int.Parse(str.Substring(6, 2));
    }
}
```

The new code gets the integer ID by calling `markIdToInt` on the instance ID. It then looks up the corresponding object in our list and assigns it to `planetView.planet`, thereby switching which planet is now in the center of our view in the app.

When you show your camera to different markers, you will see different planets.

Adding a master speed rate UI

One last feature I'd really like to have. When **Gametime Per Day** of `GameController` is set to `0.1`, the planet orbits are dynamically animated, nice and fast. But that's too fast to see the planet surfaces. When **Gametime Per Day** is slowed down, say, to `24`, we can see the planet texture more clearly, but the orbits are barely noticeable. Let's provide a button to let users toggle between these speeds. Remember, this value is the number of game seconds per earth hour. So, 24 will show one earth day in 24 seconds; 0.05 will show one earth year in about 18 seconds. It should start out fast, and when you press the button, everything slows down, hence, inspect `GameController` and ensure **Gametime Per Day** is set to `0.05`.

Creating a UI canvas and button

In Unity, **user interface (UI)** buttons reside on a canvas. Create a canvas:

1. In **Hierarchy**, select **Create | UI | Canvas**.
2. Select **Canvas** and change **UI Scale Mode** to **Constant Physical Size**.

   By default, the **Canvas UI Scale Mode** is set to **Constant Pixel Size**. This is an issue since mobile devices can have many different screen sizes and density (DPI), and your buttons will get smaller or bigger depending on the screen size. We will change it to **Constant Physical Size**.

You can then arrange your UI on the canvas as you desire. Create and position a button in the lower right-hand corner of the screen.

3. With the **Canvas** selected, right-click on **UI | Button.**

The button is easily previewed in the **Game** window. In **Inspector**, note the **Anchor Presets icon** in the upper-left corner of **Rect Transform** for the button.

4. Press the **Anchor Presets** icon to open the presets dialog box.

At this point, you can set the anchor with a mouse click or set both the anchor and pivot using *shift*+click. Or, you can set the anchor and pivot and position using *Alt*+*Shift*+click the mouse. We will do that:

5. Press *Alt*+Shift on the keyboard and then click on the icon on the **Bottom-Right** corner:

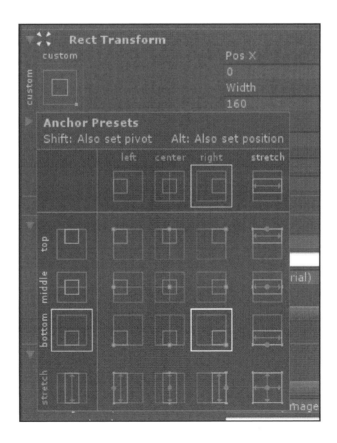

Our button should now be in the lower right corner in the Game view too.

6. In **Hierarchy**, unfold **Button** and select **Text**. Change **Text** to say `Slow`, as shown in the following screenshot:

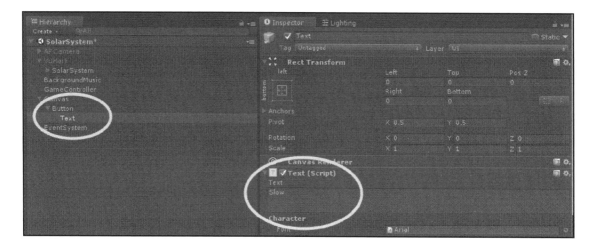

Gametime event handlers

Now we can implement the behavior when the user clicks down the mouse and releases it. Very simply, we'll set `gameTimePerDay` to `24f` and `0.5f`, respectively. We'll add these functions to `MasterControls.cs`. Open that script and add two functions, namely `SlowTime()` and `ResetTime()`, like this:

```
File: MasterControls.cs
using UnityEngine;

public class MasterControls : MonoBehaviour {
    public float gametimePerDay = 0.05f;

    public void SlowTime() {
        gametimePerDay = 24f;
    }

    public void ResetTime() {
        gametimePerDay = 0.05f;
    }
}
```

The `SlowTime()` function will change `gametimePerDay`, so the animation is slow. Likewise, `ResetTime()` will speed it back up.

Trigger input events

We can now tell the button to call our event handlers when events occur:

1. On the **Button**, go to **Add Component** | **Event** | **Event Trigger**.
2. Press **Add New Event Type** | **PointerDown**.
3. In the **Pointer Down** list, press the plus icon, then drag **GameController** from **Hierarchy** onto the **Object** slot.
4. Now in the function list (presently says `No Function`), select **MasterControls** | **SlowTime()**.

   Repeat this for a **PointerUp** event:

5. Press **Add New Event Type** | **PointerUp**.
6. Press the plus icon, then drag **GameController** onto the **Object** slot.
7. Now in the function list, select **MasterControls** | **ResetTime()**.

Event triggers should look as follows:

Save the scene and the project and click on **Play**. Now when you press the **Button**, time slows down and you can see the pretty planets and stuff!

That's it! If it's working, you did a fantastic job.

Be sure to test your app thoroughly. Use each of the marker targets and check they move your view to the given planet. Use the **Slow** button to verify it modifies the play rate. Test it both in Unity Editor and on your target device(s).

Building and running

In this section, we'll quickly step through the process of building the project for Android, iOS, and HoloLens devices. And, we'll see how to build it using AR Toolkit, instead of Vuforia.

Exporting the SolarSystem package

If you are considering building for more than one platform, you may want to save **SolarSystem** as a prefab and then export it as a Unity package to reuse in a different project:

1. In **Hierarchy**, select the **SolarSystem** object and drag it onto the project window's `Assets/SolarSystem/Prefabs` folder.
2. Right-click on the `SolarSystem` folder and select **Export Package...**.
3. Uncheck **Include Dependencies**.
4. Uncheck the `PlanetMarkerHandler.cs` script since it specifically has Vuforia dependencies.
5. Export it.

Now if you create a new project or scene, such as for HoloLens or AR Toolkit, you can drag the entire **SolarSystem** prefab into that scene.

Building for Android devices – Vuforia

Well, this is a short section. We have already set up the project for Android and Vuforia in the beginning of the chapter. You should be able to just do this: **Build And Run**. The following is an image of the completed project running on an Android phone:

Building for iOS devices – Vuforia

Using Unity and Vuforia for iOS requires developing on a Mac. Other than that, the project is nearly identical. Briefly,this is what you'll need to do:

1. In **Build Settings**, select **iOS** as the target platform**.**
2. When you use **Build And Run**, it will open Xcode to complete the build.

Refer to the iOS steps detailed in Chapter 3, *Building Your App*, and/or Chapter 4, *Augmented Business Cards* (the Building for iOS devices section), for specifics and troubleshooting.

If you want to try and build a markerless version of the project for iOS, see the *Building and running – iOS with ARKit* section.

Building for HoloLens – Vuforia

To build this project for HoloLens using the VuMark targets is not very different from the project we have built throughout the chapter. HoloLens-specific settings are the same that we've seen in previous chapters. Here is a summary of this:

1. Set up the HoloLens Camera. In **Hierarchy**, create **GameObject | Camera** and rename it `HoloLensCamera`.

2. Set **Clear Flags** to **Solid Color** and set **Background** to black (0,0,0).

3. Bind the camera to Vuforia. Go to **Vuforia | Configuration**, set **Select Eyewear Type** to **Optical See-Through**, and set **See Through Config** to **HoloLens**.

4. In **Hierarchy**, select the **AR Camera** object and drag **HoloLensCamera** to the **Central Anchor Point** slot in the **Vuforia Behavior** component.

5. Build the settings. Select **Windows Store** as **Target Platform,** choose **SDK: Universal 10, UWP Build Type: D3D**, and check the **Unity C# Projects** checkbox.

6. In quality settings, choose the **Fastest** default level for the Windows Store platform.

In Player settings, do the following:

1. Go to **Publishing Settings**. In **Capabilities**, ensure all the following are checked: **Internet client, Pictures library, Music library, Videos library, Webcam, Microphone, Spatial perception.**

2. For **Other Settings**, check **Virtual Reality Supported** and ensure **Windows MixedReality** is present in the list of SDKs.

3. Set up a build and open the project in Visual Studio. Then, set **Solution Configuration** to **Release**, **Platform** to **x86**, and **Target** to the emulator or remote device (as explained in `Chapter 3`, *Building Your App*).

That should do it.

If you want to try and build a markerless version of the project for HoloLens, see the *Building and running – HoloLens with MixedRealityToolkit* section.

Building and running ARTookit

So far, we have built this project using the Vuforia AR SDK. Like in previous chapters, we also want to show there are alternatives, including the open source ARToolkit SDK.

In this section, we will rebuild the project using AR Toolkit and its own 2D bar code target marker system. We will assume you have built the **SolarSystem** prefab as described previously so we can just drag it into the scene when we need it.

ARToolkit markers

ARToolkit supports a variety of marker types, including what they call *Square Tracking* markers. As the name implies, they are square with thick solid borders and a recognizable pattern in the center. The pattern can be a custom design. Or, it can be a 2D bar code. In this project, we will use Square Tracking targets with 2D bar code markers.

To learn more about AR Toolkit markers, see their documentation, including the following:

- Creating and training traditional Template Square markers at
  `https://archive.artoolkit.org/documentation/doku.php?id=3_Marker_Train ing:marker_training`
- Using 2D bar code markers at
  `https://archive.artoolkit.org/documentation/doku.php?id=3_Marker_Train ing:marker_barcode#Examples`

You can generate 2D bar code markers using an online tool from AR Toolworks. For example, for this project, we generated code for the ID values 0 through 9, as follows:

1. Go to `https://archive.artoolkit.org/documentation/doku.php?id=3_Marker_ Training:marker_training`.
2. Select **Generate a range of markers from code**, enter 0 and 9 for the range.
3. Click on the download link to get `AR_MATRIX_CODE_3x3_0-9.zip`.
4. Unzip the file.

This produces 2D bar code images, named `00.png`, `01.png`, through `09.png`. We then paste the markers into a Word template to make the solar system planet cards, as shown in the following figure, and save it to a PDF file; see the `PlanetMarkerCardsARTK.pdf` file included with the file downloads for this book.

SOLAR SYSTEM

MERCURY

Diameter: 4879 km

Distance from Sun: 57.9 million km

Length of day: 4222.6 hours

Length of year: 88.0 days

VENUS

Diameter: 12,104 km

Distance from Sun: 108.2 million km

Length of day: 2802.0 hours

Length of year: 224.7 days

EARTH

Diameter: 12,756 km

Distance from Sun: 149.6 million km

Length of day: 24 hours

Length of year: 365.25 days

Building the project for AR Toolkit

Let's begin building the project with AR Toolkit. We will assume you have a **SolarSystem** prefab as described previously. If not, you must have exported it into a Unity package; use **Assets | Import Package | Custom Package** to import `SolarSystem.unitypackage` now. Also, import the AR Toolkit package:

1. Import the `ARToolkit` asset package (for example, `ARUnity5.unitypackage`).
2. Create an **AR Controller**. In **Hierarchy**, create an empty object named `ARController`.
3. Go to **Add Component | ARController** and verify the **AR Background** layer is set in **Video Options.**

   When we created our bar code markers (in the previous section), we made them **AR_MATRIX_CODE_3x3** types. So, in **Square Tracking Options** of **ARController**, perform the following:

4. Set **Pattern Detection Mode** to AR_MATRIX_CODE_DETECTION.
5. Set **Matrix Code Type** to AR_MATRIX_CODE_3x3.

   The current Square Tracking Options now look like this:

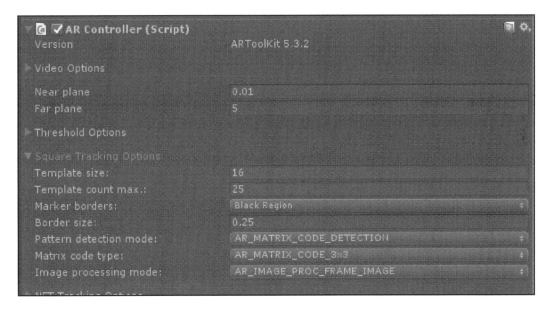

6. Create a root object in **Hierarchy**:
    1. In **Hierarchy**, create an empty object named `Root`.
    2. **Add Component | AROrigin.**
    3. Set the **Layer** object to **AR Background 2**.
    4. Set its **Transform Rotation X** axis to `90` so the marker lays flat rather than upright.

7. Create an AR Camera by following these steps:
    1. Move **Main Camera** to the child of **Root** and reset its **Transform**.
    2. **Add Component | ARCamera.**
    3. Set **Culling Mask** to **AR Background 2**.

8. Add an AR Marker. We will tag our markers with a name and ID so it's easy to remember. The first one will be tagged solarsystem0, corresponding to the bar code ID 0 as shown ahead:
    1. On **ARController**, do this: **Add Component | AR Marker.**
    2. Set **Marker Tag** to **solarsystem0**, **Type** to Square **Barcode**, and **Barcode ID** to 0.

9. Now add the solar-system-tracked object:
    1. As a child of **Root**, create an empty object named `SolarSystem0`.
    2. **Add Component | AR Tracked Object** and set **Marker tag** to **solarsystem0**.
    3. Drag the `Assets/SolarSystem/Prefabs/SolarSystem` prefab as a child of **SolarSystem0**.
    4. Set the **SolarSystem Transform** as follows: **Position**: 0, 0, 0, **Rotation**: `-90`, 0, 0, and **Scale**: `0.04, 0.04, 0.04`.
    5. Select **Root** and (again) set **Layer AR background 2**. Then say OK to **Yes, change children**, which now includes **SolarSystem**.

As we saw in the previous chapter, scaling in ARToolkit is a bit different than Vuforia. Our square marker is in real-life units, about one inch or 0.04 meters. Thus, if we want our earth to be about the width of the marker, we can scale to 0.04.

The following screenshot shows the current Layer and **Transform** settings for the **SolarSystem** object:

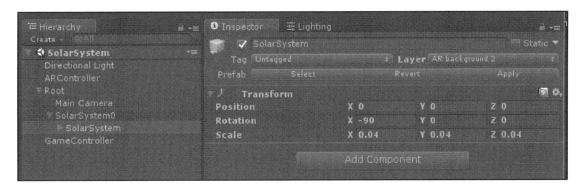

10. Now we need to complete the scene with a **GameController**, with **MasterControls** for the animation:

    1. In **Hierarchy**, create an empty object named GameController.

    2. **Add Component | Master Controls.**

Let's not forget to set the environmental lighting like we did earlier in the chapter

11. Go to the **Lighting** panel (**Window | Lighting | Lighting Settings**).
12. Set **Environment Lighting Source** to **Color** and **Ambient Color** to black.
13. Also, in the **Environmental Reflections** group, set **Intensity Multiplier** to 0.

OK! Save the scene and the project. Then click on **Play**!

Using 2D bar code targets (AR Toolkit)

Now let's enable the local planet views for each of our barcode markers. In the Vuforia version of the project, we did this with a script. With ARToolkit, we will use a more brute-force method.

Perform the following steps for each of the planets. We'll start with Earth-Moon:

1. On **ARController**, add a new **ARMarker** component (or copy/paste the existing one as new).
2. Change **Marker Tag** to the planet + ID, such as earth3.
3. Change **Barcode Id** to the same number: 3.

4. Under **Root**, duplicate the **SolarSystem0** object (*Ctrl+D*) and rename it like the tag: `Earth3`.

5. On **AR Tracked Object**, set **Marker tag** as previously: `earth3`.

6. Unfold **Earth3** to see its copy of **SolarSystem**; unfold that too, then drag the **Earth-Moon** object onto the **Planet** slot in **Planet View**.

In the following screenshot, you can see in the **Hierarchy** we now have an **Earth3** object with its own copy of **SolarSystem**, whose **PlaneView** component uses **Earth-Moon**. So, when this is active in the scene, we'll see an earth-centric view of the solar system, as follows:

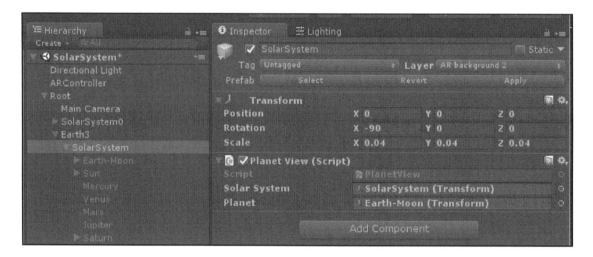

Now when you run the app and show the bar code marker cards to the camera, our view of the solar system will shift to the center of the corresponding planet.

To get this to work, we also need to modify the `PlanetView.cs` script to account for the axis rotation used here, as follows:

```
// move solar system so planet is in the center
position.x = -planet.localPosition.x * solarSystem.localScale.x;
position.z = planet.localPosition.z * solarSystem.localScale.z;
```

There are a few other things we did in the preceding project, including the introduction of the **Slow** button to change the time scale. We also added background music. Go ahead and add these to your AR Toolkit version of the project now.

Markerless building and running

An early premise of this project was to use markers to trigger the solar system AR graphics at the target location and use the bar code on the markers to select the planet or sun-centric view. There is an alternative markerless approach to AR, one that Microsoft coined as *holographics*.

With holographics, or anchor-based AR, the viewing device is able to scan your environment and map its 3D space. When you add an AR graphic to the scene, it is anchored at a specific 3D location. It uses its sensors to scan and model the 3D space.

This type of AR scene does not use target recognition. Target images and markers are not needed, nor are they usually supported in the toolkits. Therefore, we do not need to use Vuforia at all. We will do our iOS implementation using Apple ARKit and our HoloLens implementation using MixedRealityToolkit for Unity from Microsoft.

We used markers to select which planet to view in the center of the scene; the user experience will be different here. For a handheld smartphone or tablet device, we can use the touch screen for user input. For a wearable smartglasses device, we can use gaze and click or the hand gesture input. For the present chapter, we will keep this basic.

Building and running iOS with ARKit

Earlier, we built the project on iOS using Vuforia for marker recognition. The Apple ARKit for iOS does not do target recognition; instead, it uses spatial mapping to locate where to place virtual objects in the space. For that, we do not need to use Vuforia at all.

The scene **Hierarchy** we are going to build now is shown in the following screenshot. You can refer to this as we work through the scene:

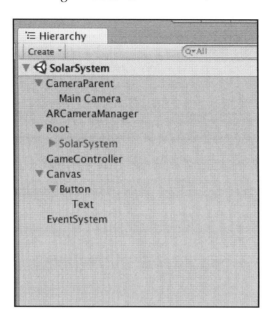

Setting up a generic ARKit scene

To get started, we'll create a new Unity project, import the ARKit, and then import the `SolarSystem` package with the prefab that we exported previously. We are going to build the scene from scratch rather than modify one of the examples (as we did in the previous chapter). Then, we'll recreate a bit of the user interface we made previously. Follow these steps to do this:

1. Create a new Unity 3D project, named `SolarSystem-arkit`.
2. From **Window | Asset Store**, download and import the `Apple ARKit` package.
3. Create a new scene (**File | New Scene**) and then save the scene as `SolarSystem`.
4. Let's remove the ambient lighting in the scene:
   1. Open the lighting tab and go to **Window | Lighting | Settings**.
   2. Set **Skybox Material** to none (using the doughnut icon to the right of the parameter).
   3. Set Environment Lighting **Source** to **Color**.
   4. Set Lightmapping Settings **Indirect Resolution** to 1.

5. Now we set up the camera with AR components and create `ARCameraManager`, as follows:
   1. In the **Hierarchy** root, create an empty object named `CameraParent`; reset its **Transform** if necessary (**Transform | gear-icon | Reset**).
   2. Drag **Main Camera** so it is a child of **CameraParent**, and reset its **Transform** too.
   3. With **Main Camera** selected, **Add Component | Unity AR Video**.
   4. For its **Clear Material** slot, click on the doughnut icon and select **YUVMaterial**.
   5. Add this component: **Unity AR Camera Near Far**.
   6. In the **Hierarchy** root, create an empty object named ARCameraManager.
   7. Add this component: **Unity AR Camera Manager**.
   8. Drag **Main Camera** onto its **Camera** slot.

That's it for the generic ARKit scene setup. Next, we can add our project objects.

Adding SolarSystem

SolarSystem will be parented by a root or anchor object. It is this anchor that will be positioned in the real world to place the solar system. Let's place **SolarSystem** about 3 meters in front of you when you first launch the app:

1. In the **Hierarchy** root, create an empty object named `Root` and reset its **Transform**.
2. Then, set its position Z to -3.
3. Drag the **SolarSystem** prefab from the `Assets/SolarSystem/Prefabs/` folder as a child object of **Root**.
4. Set its transform position to $(0, 0, 0)$ and scale to $(0.03, 0.03, 0.03)$.

   The scale of 0.03 looks good to us; you may decide to choose other values if you want.

5. For our scene, the sun will provide illumination, so we can delete directional light from the scene if present.

You can go ahead and build and run the app now to see how it looks. It will open Xcode to complete the build. Refer to the iOS steps detailed in `Chapter 3`, *Building Your App*, and/or `Chapter 4`, *Augmented Business Cards* (the Building for iOS devices section) for specifics and troubleshooting.

You should see the planets about 3 meters in front of the device, but they're not moving. If you recall from our previous implementation of the Gametime variable (see the Adding a master speed rate UI section), to animate their orbits (and we do), we need to create a `GameController` object.

6. In the **Hierarchy** root, create an empty object named `GameController`.
7. Find the `MasterControls` script (in the `Assets/SolarSystem/Scripts/` folder) and drag it as a component to **GameController**.

Now build and run again and the planets will be animated, at full speed.

Placing SolarSystem in the real world

The next thing we'll do is let you regenerate the anchor position of the solar system. The plan is when you touch the screen of your iPhone or iPad device, the app calculates a likely position you are indicating in real-world 3D coordinates. We'll move the root position there. We will do this with a script named SolarSystemHitHandler:

1. In your `Scripts` folder, create a new C# script named `SolarSystemHitHandler`.
2. Drag it to the **SolarSystem** object as a component.
3. Then, open the script for editing as follows:

```
File: SolarSystemHitHandler.cs
using System.Collections;
using System.Collections.Generic;
using UnityEngine;
using UnityEngine.EventSystems;
using UnityEngine.XR.iOS;
public class SolarSystemHitHandler : MonoBehaviour {
  public Transform anchor;
  void Update () {
    List<ARHitTestResult> hitResults;
    ARPoint point;
    if (Input.touchCount > 0 && anchor != null) {
      var touch = Input.GetTouch(0);
      if
(!EventSystem.current.IsPointerOverGameObject(Input.GetTouch(0).fingerId)
```

```
&& touch.phase == TouchPhase.Began) {
        Vector3 screenPosition =
Camera.main.ScreenToViewportPoint(touch.position);
        point.x = screenPosition.x;
        point.y = screenPosition.y;
        hitResults =
UnityARSessionNativeInterface.GetARSessionNativeInterface().HitTest( point,
            ARHitTestResultType.ARHitTestResultTypeExistingPlaneUsingExtent);
        if (hitResults.Count == 0) {
            hitResults =
UnityARSessionNativeInterface.GetARSessionNativeInterface().HitTest( point,
                ARHitTestResultType.ARHitTestResultTypeHorizontalPlane);
        }
        if (hitResults.Count == 0) {
            hitResults =
UnityARSessionNativeInterface.GetARSessionNativeInterface().HitTest( point,
                ARHitTestResultType.ARHitTestResultTypeFeaturePoint);
        }
        if (hitResults.Count > 0) {
            anchor.position = UnityARMatrixOps.GetPosition(
hitResults[0].worldTransform);
            anchor.rotation = UnityARMatrixOps.GetRotation(
hitResults[0].worldTransform);
        }
      }
    }
  }
}
```

We declare a `public Transform anchor`, which we'll assign to the Root parent of SolarSystem.

The body of the script is the `Update()` function, which simply looks for a screen touch from the user (`Input.GetTouch()`). If it's not a UI button, press (*if* `(!EventSystem.current.IsPointerOverGameObject(Input.GetTouch(0)` `.fingerId)`), then it tries to determine the corresponding 3D real-world point.

As ARKit scans your room, it catalogs a variety of planes. When we map the screen point to world space (using the `ScreenToViewportPoint` function), we should test it against each kind of plane, in order of logical significance, namely:

- `ARHitTestResultTypeExistingPlaneUsingExtent`: A plane in the foreground that was detected up to its edges but not beyond it.
- `ARHitTestResultTypeHorizontalPlane`: A horizontal plane, such as a tabletop or floor.

- `ARHitTestResultTypeFeaturePoint`: Any other continuous surface.

For the full list of possible hit test result types, see `https://developer.apple.com/documentation/arkit/arhittestresulttype?language=objc`.

If and when a hit is found, the ARKit Unity helper function, `UnityARMatrixOps`, is called to do the math of transforming the point to a 3D real-world anchor point. And the anchor (root) object's transform position is moved there, placing **SolarSystem** in a new position.

4. Save the script, then back in Unity, drag the **Root** object from **Hierarchy** to the **Anchor** slot of the component.

Go ahead and build and run. After the app launches, use the device camera to scan your room for a few seconds, then touch the screen to place the solar system when you want to see it.

UI for animation speed

For the last step of this project's ARKit implementation, we'll go ahead and add a screen button to slow down the planet orbits, like we did previously in the Adding a master speed rate UI section. We'll list the same steps here; please refer to the earlier section for details:

1. In **Hierarchy**, select **Create | UI | Canvas**.
2. Select **Canvas** and change **UI Scale Mode** to **Constant Physical Size**.
3. With the **Canvas** selected, right-click on **UI | Button.**
4. Press the **Anchor Presets** icon to open the presets dialog box.
5. Press *Alt+Shift* on the keyboard, then click on the **Bottom-Right** corner icon.
6. In **Hierarchy**, unfold **Button** and select **Text**. Change **Text** to say `Slow`.
7. On the **Button**, go to **Add Component | Event | Event Trigger.**
8. Press **Add New Event Type | PointerDown**, and in the **Pointer Down** list, press the plus icon.
9. Drag **GameController** from **Hierarchy** to the **Object** slot. And, in the function list, select **MasterControls | SlowTime().**

10. Again, for a PointerUp event, press **Add New Event Type | PointerUp**, then the plus icon.

11. Drag **GameController** to the **Object** slot, and in the function list, select **MasterControls | ResetTime().**

One more time, build and run. We now have a **Slow** button. When you press this button, the planets slow down, such as the earth day in 24 seconds versus a year in 18 seconds in the default fast mode.

Hurray! This is cool!

Building and running HoloLens with MixedRealityToolkit

Using marker targets for this project is not necessary for wearable AR devices, such as HoloLens, but you can; earlier, we did build and run the app on HoloLens using Vuforia for marker recognition. Instead, we could use spatial mapping to locate where to place virtual objects in space. For that, we do not need to use Vuforia at all. We will see this HoloLens implementation using MixedRealityToolkit for Unity from Microsoft.

In the handheld version of our project, we provided a screen-space button to toggle the game time speed. We also provided separate AR markers on cards to let the user center their view on a specific planet. For HoloLens, we'll simplify this. We will provide a single selection to alternate (toggle) between a fast-rotating full solar system view and a slowed-down zoom of the earth. Fortunately, we can use much of the code we wrote earlier with just one additional script.

Creating the scene

To get started, we'll create a new Unity project, import the toolkit, and then import the `SolarSystem` package with the prefab that we exported previously. Using MixedRealityToolkit provides some convenient shortcuts as prefabs and provided scripts:

1. Create a new Unity 3D project, named `SolarSystem-holo`.

2. Import the **MixedRealityToolkit** plugin for the Unity package (if you haven't downloaded it yet, you can find it at `https://github.com/Microsoft/MixedRealityToolkit-Unity`).

3. Conveniently, go to **MixedReality | Configure | Apply HoloLens Scene Settings** (or the mixed reality equivalents) and accept. This sets the camera settings for you.

4. Save the scene and give it a name, such as `solarsystem`.

5. Choose **MixedReality | Configure | Apply HoloLens Project Settings** and accept. This sets the build settings for you.

6. Choose **MixedReality | Configure | Apply HoloLens Capability Settings** and accept. This sets the player settings for you.

7. Reset the camera transform so its position is (0,0,0).

8. Delete the default *Directional Light* option from the scene.

9. In the **Lighting** window tab, delete **Skybox Material** and set **Ambient Color** to black.

10. Lest we forget, in **Build Settings**, set **Add Open Scenes** as the build scene.

11. Save the scene and the project.

Personally, for this project, I prefer to set the camera's near-clipping plane closer, such as 0.3, but I prefer to leave a little ambient light in the Lighting settings (for example, RGB 0.25, 0.25, or 0.25) so you can still see a bit of the far side of each planet.

You can test the scene on your HoloLens device by connecting it to Unity (open **Window | Holographic** and **Connect**) and pressing **Play**.

Then, deploy a test build to the device. Select **Build**, open in Visual Studio, set **Release**, **x86**, and **Remote Machine** (or emulator) and go to **Debug | Start without Debugging**.

Adding user selection of scale and time

To handle input events, we will first add a few components to the scene, including a Unity Event System, a HoloToolkit Input Manager, and a cursor. To do this, perform the following steps:

1. Go to **GameObject | UI | Event System** to add it to the scene **Hierarchy**.

2. From Project `Assets/HoloToolkit/Input/Prefabs`, drag **InputManager** into the **Hierarchy**.

3. From Project `Assets/HoloToolkit/Input/Prefabs/Cursors`, drag **BasicCursor** into the **Hierarchy**.

Note that you have options to modify the look and behavior of the cursor. For the cursor to work properly, it needs to *collide* with the objects in the scene. Presently, we have not added colliders to individual planets; we could do that now. Instead, we will add one big spherical collider for the entire solar system to go to the earth view. Add a collider to the sun to go back to the solar system view (if later, you decide to enhance this project and allow clicking on individual planets, then each should be given their own collider).

4. Select **SolarSystem** from **Hierarchy**, then **Add Component | Physics | Sphere Collider.**
5. Adjust the radius of the collider to something like 60 so that it covers the extent of the solar system, including Pluto but not further.
6. Select **Sun** from **Hierarchy**, then **Add Component | Physics | Sphere Collider.**

Note that if you click on the **Edit Collider** icon in the **Sphere Collider** component, you can see (and modify) the boundary lines, in the **Scene** window, shown with green lines. We need it spherical and centered on the Sun. Since the planets are orbiting, they can be all around it. The **Scene** window with Sphere Collider is shown in the following screenshot:

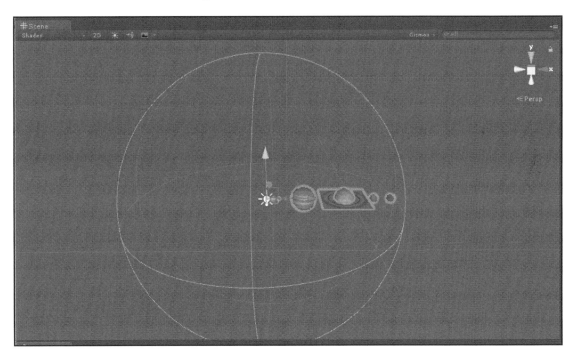

Next, let's write a script to handle Select events. For starters, it will just print a message to the **Console**:

7. In **Hierarchy**, select **SolarSystem** and create a new C# script; name it ViewToggler.

8. Open the script for editing and write it as follows:

```
File: ViewToggler.cs
using UnityEngine;
using HoloToolkit.Unity.InputModule;

public class ViewToggler : MonoBehaviour, IInputClickHandler {

    public void OnInputClicked(InputClickedEventData eventData) {
        Debug.Log("CLICKED");
    }
}
```

Now when you run and look at the solar system, the cursor should change its shape (fatter), indicating it's ready for input. When you use the *Select* gesture, the word CLICKED will print in the console (the log message will appear if you're using the Unity Holographic editor emulation; otherwise, you can test it on the device and see the cursor change but not necessarily see the log message).

We're ready to really implement the function. As mentioned, when the user selects the scene, it will switch between the initial view scale with the sun in the center and reset **Gametime Per Day** to 0.05. You can then change to earth in the center, at 10x scale and slowed down to 24 Gametime (one second equals one earth hour).

The code will reference another component script we wrote earlier, PlanetView, which modifies the position offset of the solar system so the planet of interest is at the center:

9. With **GameController** selected in **Hierarchy**, **Add Component | PlanetView**.

10. Drag the **SolarSystem** object from **Hierarchy** to the component's **Solar System** slot.

Leave the Planet slot empty as this will get populated only when we're in the earth zoom view. Here's the code:

```
File: ViewToggler.cs
public class ViewToggler : MonoBehaviour, IInputClickHandler {
    public Transform earth;
```

```
    public float earthScaleFactor = 10f;

    private bool earthView = false; // T=zoom into earth, F=full solar
system
    private MasterControls controls;
    private PlanetView view;
    private Vector3 startScale;

    private void Start() {
        GameObject controller = GameObject.Find("GameController");
        controls = controller.GetComponent<MasterControls>();
        view = controller.GetComponent<PlanetView>();
        startScale = view.solarSystem.localScale;
    }

    public void OnInputClicked(InputClickedEventData eventData) {
        Debug.Log("CLICKED");
        if (earthView == true) {
            // switch to solar system view
            controls.ResetTime();
            view.planet = null;
            earthView = false;
            view.solarSystem.localScale = startScale;
        } else {
            // switch to earth view
            controls.SlowTime();
            view.planet = earth;
            earthView = true;
            view.solarSystem.localScale = startScale * earthScaleFactor;
        }
    }
}
```

Reading the code, you can see we defined public variables for the earth object transform and a size scale factor for that view. We also declared four private variables to hold the current state of the view, including a Boolean earthView, when True we are on the Earth view and when False we are on the SolarSystem view.

In the Start() method, we get a reference to GameController in the scene and get its MasterControls and PlanetView components so we can reference their current values. Note startScale is assumed to be the default **SolarSystem** transform scale.

When a click is detected, `OnInputClicked` is called (this is part of the HoloToolkit input system). It is here we modify the time (`controls.Reset()`/`SlowTime()`), Solar System center (null/earth), and scale (startScale vs 10x).

11. Now all we need to do is drag the **Earth-Moon** object from **Hierarchy** to the reference slot on the **ViewToggler** component.
12. Save your work and give it a try!

At this point, you may want to further improve your project by letting the user position and resize the solar system in the real-world space. We encourage you to explore this further. HoloToolkit makes this pretty straightforward. Check out the Holograms 211 tutorials at `https://developer.microsoft.com/en-us/windows/mixed-reality/holo grams_211`.

Summary

In this chapter, we built a science project, a lot like I did when I was 8 years old; however, instead of wires and styrofoam balls, we made our solar system for augmented reality. Here, virtual objects interact with the real world using special cards we made with coded markers, one for each planet view. This idea could be extended, instead of cards, to pages in a book or labels on products.

Our first step was to make the earth, using an equirectangular texture of the earth's surface to build the material mapped to a sphere. Then, we added a second texture for the night side of the globe. Similarly, we built all the nine planets, the moon, and the sun. Each body was scaled and rotated accurately based on NASA data, but we compressed space and time for distance and orbits in some cases. The sun provides the light source.

We also learned to program in C# for Unity, writing short scripts to spin and orbit the planets, move the center viewpoint, and change the time scale in response to user input button presses. Along the way, we also explored ways to structure our project files, build object hierarchies, and set up a master controller for global parameters.

We also took the time and space to provide instructions for building the project for a plethora of devices and platforms (seven in all). We used the Vuforia toolkit to build for Android, iOS, and HoloLens. We refactored the project to use the open source ARToolkit too for Android and iOS. Then, we considered how to rework the project for markerless augmented reality platforms, including Apple ARKit and Microsoft HoloLens' MixedRealityToolkit.

In the next chapter, we will consider an educational application again, but instead of a simulation, it'll be more like a tutorial or guided instructions-- we will write an app that will help you change the tire on your car! In the process, we will go deeper into Unity's UI (user interface) components and screen space and input events and learn how to sequence the user experience.

6

How to Change a Flat Tire

An important emerging application of Augmented Reality is professional and industrial training, including equipment maintenance and how-to manuals. Over the years, traditional paper documents have given way to digital multimedia. First came DVDs, then web-based online docs, and then dedicated mobile apps. The next step will be the adaptation of more interactive and immersive media using AR.

In this chapter, we show you how to build an app that guides someone in changing a flat tire on their car, using step-by-step instructions. Labels and explanations will be superimposed on the real-world objects. You just click **Next** through the steps.

For this project, we will start with an existing web-based tutorial from wikiHow, *How to Change a Tire*, convert it to a regular mobile app, and then augment it with Augmented Reality features. This mimics similar real-world business situations.

We will also use this as an opportunity to introduce important programming patterns which Unity developers favor. These patterns, including abstract classes, inheritance, event observers, and serialized data, will make your code cleaner, more flexible, and, in the long run, easier to maintain. If you're new to programming, just follow along. If you are an experienced developer, you may appreciate that we're taking the examples up a notch.

This project is split across two chapters. In this chapter, we will build a conventional non-AR version of the app. The next chapter will convert the project to AR. In this chapter, you will learn about the following:

- Software design patterns
- Screen space UI (user interface), layout, and scrolling
- Importing data from CSV files
- Refactoring your app to use Unity events and class inheritance
- Using images, video clips, and video player

Our implementation targets Android mobile devices, but does not require them. If you prefer to develop for standalone (PC or Mac) desktop, that will work too.

The project plan

Before we begin implementing the project, it helps to first define what we're going to do, identify the assets we will use, and make a plan.

Project objective

The goal of the app is to provide a step-by-step tutorial on how to change a tire, which can be used on the spot when someone needs it most -- you've got a flat tire!

Rather than inventing our own content from scratch, we will start with the *wikiHow* article, *How to Change a Tire*, which can be found at http://www.wikihow.com/Change-a-Tire (under Creative Commons license). We are using it to illustrate how one might use Augmented Reality for How-to type instruction manuals. A screen capture of the *wikiHow* article page is shown ahead:

To be honest, it was pure luck and fortuitous that we found this *wikiHow* article with annotated images and videos. When we first decided on this subject for the chapter, we assumed we would write all the instructions ourselves. Then we discovered the *wikiHow* article. Even better, the images and videos have been marked up, which fits very well and is in line with the objectives of our project -- demonstrating the value of annotating real-world imagery. Moving this concept to live AR helps make the point that this is a natural next step for content presentation.

The content will be imported into the project from a Google spreadsheet. This, too, is a realistic scenario where one person or team may be developing and maintaining the application code, while others may be responsible for writing and editing the content.

User experience

What does the user see? How does the user interact? What are the user's goals and how does the app help achieve those goals? When designing an application, it is critical to think about the user experience, not just the technical implementation challenges.

Basic mobile version

The first iteration of the project will be a simplistic mobile app. Open the app to see the title screen. There will be **Next** and **Previous** buttons to step through the instructions. Each step will display a title, body text, and an image or video, if included. A screenshot of the finished mobile version is depicted ahead:

AR mobile version

The AR mobile version of the app will add Augmented Reality to the mix. It will have the same sequence of steps, but you can see them in Augmented Reality, with the ability to point your camera at the flat tire while the app instructs by annotating the real world for you.

In capture mode (when the user tells the app what tire to annotate), the user will see a circle graphic on the screen, as shown ahead, and is asked to point the camera at the tire so it fills the circle end-to-end. Then press **Capture** to capture the user-defined AR target. Following is a concept photo of how the app might be used:

Then the view will be annotated by the graphic relevant to the current step. For example, step 3 will show how to block the good tires with bricks, and step 6 will illustrate how to loosen the lug nuts.

Markerless version

With holographic or anchor-based AR, the viewing device is able to scan your environment and map its 3D space. When you add an AR graphic to the scene, it is anchored at a specific 3D location. It uses its sensors to scan and model the 3D space.

This type of AR scene does not use target recognition. Target images and markers are not needed, nor are they usually supported in the toolkits. Therefore, we do not need to use Vuforia at all. We will do our iOS implementation using Apple ARKit, Android version using Google ARCore, and our HoloLens implementation using the MixedRealityToolkit for Unity from Microsoft. For this, there is no need for screen space UI at all. All of the content and navigation elements will be in the AR world space.

AR targets

The AR target will be a user-defined image captured at runtime. With Vuforia, a *user-defined target* means you can define the AR target at runtime using the device's camera, and then the app will register and recognize that image for displaying the associated virtual objects. It makes sense in this project because it would be impossible to provide a predefined database of target images since every automobile is different, in different conditions, and situated in unique environments.

The image-quality requirements for user-defined targets are similar to those for natural feature targets. You want them to be rich in detail, in good contrast, and with no repetitive patterns. But we do not need to worry about ease of availability because our user can capture the target at runtime. We will provide a user interface that lets the user capture a target, but will show a notification if the target does not meet the minimum detail and pattern quality criteria.

If your AR toolkit does not support user-defined targets, or if for another reason it is not practical, you can fall back to printed marker targets like we used in Chapter 5, *AR Solar System*. By this we mean that, instead of using the dynamic image capture feature of Vuforia, you can print out a predetermined image or marker, tape it to your tire's hubcap, and develop the app to recognize that target for the AR graphics.

Graphic assets and data

Take a closer look at the wikiHow article and consider the various elements that make up each instructional step. We found that each instruction may include the following data:

- Step number (integer, required)
- Title (string, required)
- Text (string, required)
- Image (PNG or JPG, optional)
- Video (MP4, optional)
- AR graphic (unity prefab, optional)

We have prepared a Google sheet with data populated from the wikiHow article, http://tinyurl.com/ChangeTireAR. It contains rows for each instructional step, and columns for each data field, as shown ahead:

	Step	Title	Text	Image	Video	Graphic
1						
2		0 How to Change a Tire	Have you ever been stuck on the side of the road with a flat tire? Do you want to be able to change a tire without having to ask for help? Fortunately, changing a tire is a pretty simple task, provided you're prepared and willing to exert a little effort.			
3		1 Find a flat, stable and safe place to change your tire.	You should have a solid, level surface that will restrict the car from rolling. If you are near a road, park as far from traffic as possible and turn on your emergency flashers (hazard lights). Avoid soft ground and hills.	step1		
4		2 Apply the parking brake and put car into "Park" position.	If you have a standard transmission, put your vehicle in first or reverse.		step2-video	
5		3 Block other tires	Place a heavy object (e.g., rock, concrete, spare wheel, etc.) in front of the front and back tires.		step3-video	

The step number starts at 0 (for the introductory start screen), then includes 1 through 14, exactly mimicking the wikiHow article that contains 14 steps. The title and text are borrowed directly from the web page. We then have three optional columns:

- If the step includes an image (PNG or JPG), we put the base name there
- If the step includes a video (MP4), we put the base name there
- If the step includes a Unity prefab, we put the prefab name there

As we will see, we will expect the image and video files to be in an Assets Resources directory for your project, to be built into the production files when we build. Alternatively, we could provide the URL of the asset directly on the *wikiHow* website and let our app load it from there at runtime. We decided not to implement that in this project to keep things a little simpler, and avoid the chance that *wikiHow* itself could break our book chapter by changing things after we publish. But it's an easy change in this project, and you get the idea, so you can make similar decisions that are relevant to your own projects.

This app could be refactored to be completely independent of the content, making it a more general mobile and AR instruction manual app, using downloadable content. Unity provides the ability to dynamically add assets to your application at runtime, using AssetBundles. Just about anything can be included such as models, textures, sounds, or animations. Even the instructions, CSV data file, and your graphic prefabs could be updated or replaced over the internet with the careful architecting of your app. See `https://docs.unity3d.com/Manual/AssetBundlesIntro.html`

In Google sheets, you can export the data as follows:

1. Go to **File** | **Download As** | **Comma Separated Files**.
2. Rename it `instructionsCSV.csv` to be consistent with the instructions given later in this chapter.

We have also included copies of the CSV file, images, and videos in the file package included with this book.

We will go through building the graphic annotations used in the AR views in the next chapter, as we get to it. And these graphics will reside in your project assets as prefabs.

Software design patterns

Software design patterns are not hard-and-fast programming rules, but are general, reusable solutions to commonly occurring problems in software design. Over the years, people have identified such patterns and given them names. The details often vary depending on the context and who you are talking to. Having design patterns helps avoid *re-inventing the wheel* in each project and choosing solutions to problems that have been visited before. It also provides a vocabulary for us to talk about how to implement our projects.

To learn more about software design patterns, we recommend these books:
Head First Design Patterns: A Brain Friendly Guide, Freeman et al.--a popular, practical, less formal approach to learning design patterns (2004)
Patterns of Enterprise Application Architecture, Martin Fowler--the classic book from an object-oriented design pioneer (2002)
Design Patterns: Elements of Reusable Object-Oriented Software, Gamma et al.--the original book on design patterns by "the gang of four" designers (1994)

Before we begin the project, let's talk about some software design patterns that we are going to use. These include the following:

- Model-view-controller
- Object encapsulation
- Class inheritance
- Event observer pattern

In this project, we use a **Model-View-Controller** (**MVC**) architecture. **Model** is your data, **view** is the screen layout, and **controller** manages the events from the user, making sure the screen is updated with the correct data. See the illustration ahead:

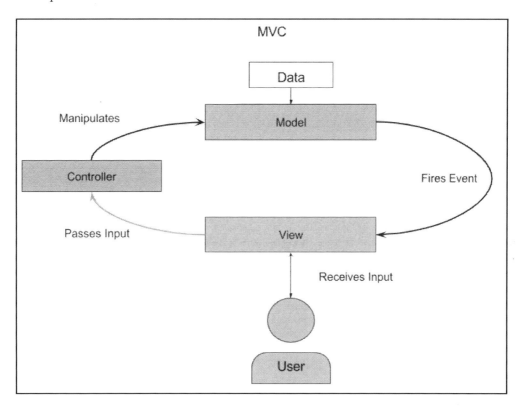

The **view** is independent of the content data. Think of it as a layout template. The view is handed some data (**model**) to show on the screen. In this app, the instructional steps that explain how to change a tire are the data. Then, a **controller** ties it all together, keeping track of which step the user is currently viewing, and responds to user input to navigate between steps.

We will create an `Instruction Model` class that parses the instructions data, loaded from an external database file, into C# objects that we can use. It will implement a simple **object-oriented programming** (**OOP**) interface using C# classes. The data will come from an external spreadsheet CSV file. There will be a public function, `GetInstructionStep()`, that returns the data for a specific record of data, which we'll name `InstructionStep`.

A characteristic of OOP is that objects keep their data as private as possible, limiting access by other parts of the system through its public functions interface. This is referred to as **encapsulation**, as illustrated ahead:

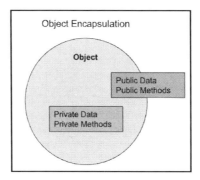

We will also create an `Instructions Controller` that manages the UI and the current state of the application. It makes sure the UI is displaying the correct information. It will provide functions, `NextStep()` (called by the **Next** button) and `PreviousStep()` (called by the **Previous** button).

The controller will also handle an `OnInstructionsUpdate` event, which forwards events to the Title, Body Text, Image, and Video UI elements that are listening and respond by adding the data to the screen. Using this event-driven pattern will provide a clean way to ensure the UI is updated any time the user presses the **Next** or **Previous** buttons. This *event-observer* design pattern, which we have used often in Unity projects, is as illustrated ahead.

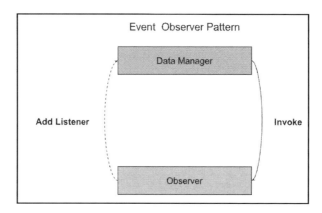

As you probably realize, in object-oriented programming we talk a lot about *classes* and *objects*. **Classes** define the properties and functions of a type of object. And **objects** are specific instances. A `Dog` class says any dog has four legs and barks. An instance of `Dog` may be named `Spot` and belongs to you. A `Dog` is a kind of `Mammal` (for example, derived from the `Mammal` class). If mammals nurse their young, `Dog` inherits the property of *nursing their young* from `Mammal`.

In Unity, your scripts usually inherit from a base class provided by Unity itself, called `MonoBehaviour`. These scripts get all the `MonoBehaviour` goodness that Unity provides, including the `Start()` and `Update()` methods that you can define, and are called from the engine. In our project, we will also create a base class, `InstructionElement`, and then develop new classes that inherit from it. The class `inheritance` of `InstructionElement` and its subclasses are illustrated ahead:

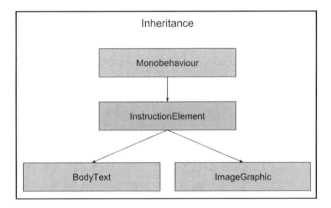

We will talk about these design patterns later in the chapter as we use them in the code. But, first, let's build a user interface. OK, let's go!

Setting up the project

This first version of the project will be a mobile app that simply lets you step through the instructions for changing a tire. Unlike the projects in the previous chapters, the first iteration of this project will not use AR. So, the Unity project setup is quite simple.

1. Open Unity and create a new 3D project, and name it something like `How to Change a Tire`.
2. Save the empty scene and name it `Main`.

Set the project for your target platform. We will assume Android for purposes of our discussion.

1. Go to build settings via **File | Build Settings.**
2. **Switch Platform** to **Android**.
3. Add the current scene and press **Add Open Scenes.**
4. Choose **Player settings...**, then set your **Identification Package** name (`com.Company.Product`) and **Minimum API Level** (Android 5.1).

If you are developing for iOS or Windows UWP instead, set the platform accordingly.

At this point in the project we are not developing for AR, so you should not set the AR or **Virtual Reality Supported** settings, assumed previously in the book, until the next chapter when we modify the project for AR.

It's useful now to create some empty folders in the Project Assets that we will use soon.

1. In the **Project** window, select the top-level `Assets/` folder.
2. Create a new folder in `Assets/` named `HowToChangeATire`.
3. Within `Assets/HowToChangeATire`, create four more new folders, `Resources`, `Scenes`, `Scripts`, `Textures`, as shown ahead:

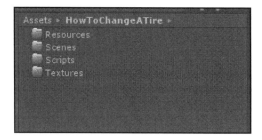

4. Tidy up by moving the main scene file into the new `Scenes` folder.
5. Save your work (save scene, then save project).

OK, now we can get started building our first scene.

Creating the UI (view)

The **user interface** (**UI**) will consist of a navigation bar at the top of the screen and content filling the rest of the screen. We will call these *Nav Panel* and *Content Panel*, respectively, and define them as children of a full screen *Instruction Canvas*.

While developing our screen space UI, it will be useful to be working with a 2D view of the scene. That will allow you to see the UI as you create it.

1. Change the **Scene** view from 3D to 2D.
2. Have both the **Scene** window and **Game** window visible.

The following image shows the **Scene** window in 2D mode, with the 2D selection button pressed:

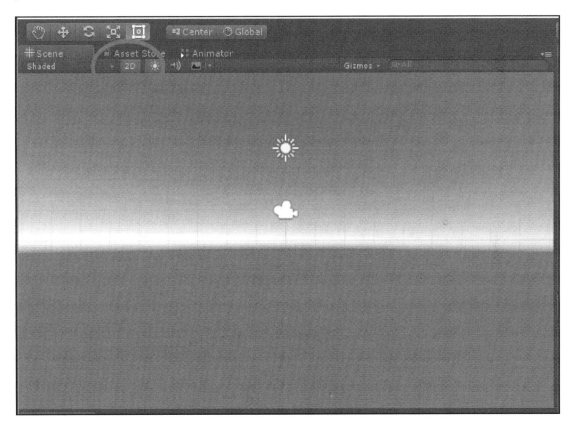

Creating an Instruction Canvas

To begin, we first create a new Canvas.

1. In **Hierarchy**, select **Create | UI | Canvas** and name it `Main Canvas`.
2. Double-click the **Canvas** (in **Hierarchy**) so it fits the current view.

   We want to make sure we're editing a canvas that matches the screen size.

3. In the **Game** view, change the resolution to one of the preset resolutions (not Free Aspect), such as 480 x 800, which is a mobile portrait shape.

The current **Scene** view and **Game** view are empty, but shaped for the device-screen canvas, shown ahead:

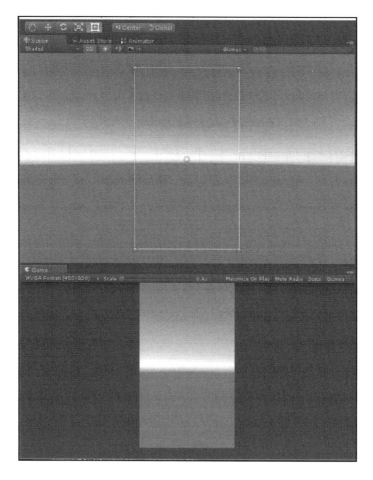

You may now zoom up the canvas, and we can begin planning the UI.

When the app runs, we want the canvas to remain in screen space and it should respond to the screen size correctly. Use the resolution that we have in our **Game** window. Use the following settings in the **Main Canvas**:

1. In **Inspector**, set **Render Mode** to **Screen Space - Overlay**.
2. Set **UI Scale Mode to Scale With Screen Size**.
3. Set **Reference Resolution** to 480 x 800.

The **Main Canvas** in **Inspector** is shown ahead:

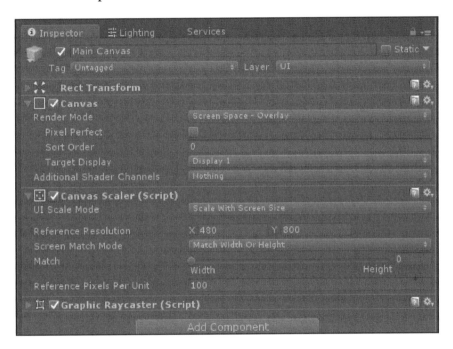

Note that creating the Canvas also automatically creates an Event System, which is necessary for any UI elements, such as buttons, to receive and respond to user-input events.

Creating a Nav Panel

Create a navigation panel under the `Main Canvas` that will be 50 units high and positioned at the top of the screen. It is going to contain a step number and the **Next/Previous** navigation buttons.

1. In **Hierarchy**, select `Main Canvas`, right click to create a **UI | Panel**, and name it `Nav Panel`.
2. Set its **Height** to `50`.
3. Set the **Anchor Presets** point to **top/stretch**.
4. In **Rect Transform**, set the **Height** of the panel to `50`.
5. Then, in **Anchor Presets** again, use *Alt*+click on **Top/Stretch** again to position the panel at its anchor point, at the top of the Canvas.

The Nav Panel's Anchor Presets settings now look like this in **Inspector**:

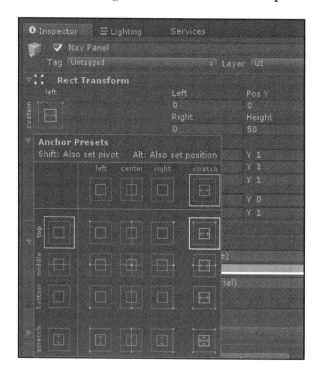

To stylize the application bar, remove the **Source Image** of the Nav Panel and set the color to a pleasant, opaque hue such as teal, as follows:

1. Set its **Source Image** to none
2. Set its **Color** to RGBA (74, 182, 208, 255) or #4AB6D0FF

The panel will have **Previous** and **Next** buttons on the left and right, respectively, and a title in the middle. First the step text:

1. In **Hierarchy**, select **Nav Panel**, right-click, and add a **UI | Text**.
2. Name it Step Text.
3. Set its **Paragraph Alignment** to be **Middle/Center**.
4. Set its **Color** to white (#FFFFFFFF).
5. Set **Font Size** to 25.
6. Ensure the **Anchor Presets** point is **Middle/Center** and press *Alt*+click to make it jump to **Middle/Center**, if it's not already positioned there.
7. Set its **Text** string to Step #.

The Nav Panel's child **Step Text** settings are shown ahead:

Now we will make the buttons. The **Previous** button will be on the left and show a left arrow:

1. With **Nav Panel** selected, right-click and select **UI | Button.**
2. Name it Previous Button.
3. Change the **Rect Transform Width** to 50.
4. Set the **Anchor Presets** point to **Middle/Left,** and then *Alt*+click to move it there.
5. Set its **Source Image** to **None** and **Color: Alpha** to 0.
6. In the (child) **Text** of the button, set the **Text** to < (less-than symbol), **Font Size** to 25, **Style** to **Bold,** and **Color** to White (#FFFFFFFF).

The **Next** button will be on the right and show a right arrow:

1. Duplicate the button, rename it `Next Button`, set the **Anchor Presets** point to the other side, and change the **Text** to >.
2. Set **Font Size** to 25.

The following screenshot shows the resulting **Nav Panel** in the **Scene** and its object **Hierarchy**:

At this point, we suggest you save your work (save scene and save project).

Creating a Content panel

As a child of the `Main Canvas`, create a new panel named `Content` with a solid white background, we will give it a vertical layout, where any child UI elements are arranged in a stack from the top of the panel and expand down.

1. In **Hierarchy**, select **Main Canvas** and right-click to create **UI | Panel** and name it `Content`.
2. Set the **Anchor Presets** to **Top/Stretch**, then *Shift*+Click to set its **Pivot** point also at the top, and, finally, *Alt*+click to position it there.
3. Set its **Height** to 750.
4. Set its **Pos Y** to -50 to leave room for the Nav bar.

5. Stylize the panel as transparent.

6. Set its **Source Image** to none (using the *doughnut* icon, or press *Delete*).

7. Set its **Color** to white and **Alpha** to 255 so it is opaque white (#FFFFFFFF).

Its **Inspector** settings are shown ahead:

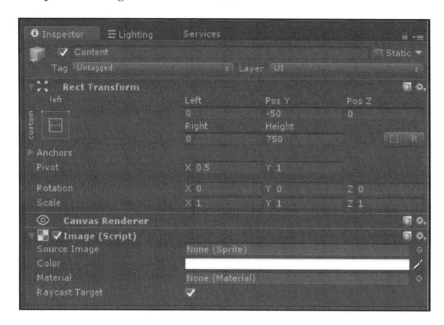

Now we will add a **Vertical Layout Group**, and we want to make sure that it force-expands the width but not height. But leave padding at the top to make room for our title bar (50 pixels).

8. **Add Component | Layout | Vertical Layout Group**.

9. Set **Child Alignment** to **Upper Center**.

10. Select **Width** and **Height** in **Control Child Size**.

11. Uncheck both **Width** and **Height** in **Child Force Expand**.

12. Unfold the **Padding,** and set **Left** and **Right** to 10, **Top** to 20, **Bottom** to 10, and **Spacing** to 20.

The **Vertical Layout Group** component settings in **Inspector** are as shown ahead:

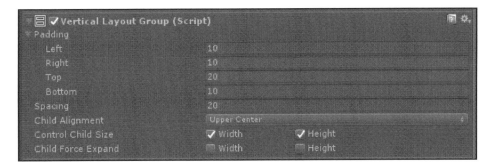

Adding a title text element

Now create a text element for the instruction's title:

1. With **Content Panel** selected, add **UI | Text**.
2. Rename it `Title Text`.
3. Set **Font Style** to **Bold** and **Font Size** to 25.
4. Set its **Text** string to `Title text`.

Adding a body text element

Now we will create another text element for our body text:

1. With **Content Panel** selected, add **UI | Text**.
2. Rename it `Body Text`.
3. Set **Font Size** to 25.
4. Set its **Text** string to say, `Instruction text paragraphs`.
5. Save your work (save scene and save project).

So now we have a full-screen Instruction canvas that contains a navigation panel and an instruction panel. The instruction panel has sub-panels for the title and body text. Later, we will add other optional sub-panels for images and videos. Your layout and full **Hierarchy** should now look as follows:

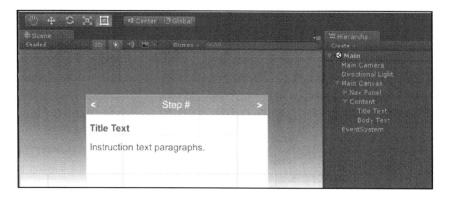

Creating an Instructions Controller

We're now going to create a controller object and script for our project. This first implementation will be relatively simplistic. It will grow and improve later in the chapter. In Unity, perform the following:

1. In the **Project** window, create a **C# Script** in your scripts folder (`Assets/HowToChangeATire/Scripts/`) and name it `InstructionsController`.
2. In **Hierarchy**, select **Create Empty** object.
3. Rename it `Game Controller`.
4. Drag the `InstructionsController` script into **Inspector**, adding it as a component.

Save the scene and then open the script for editing. Like most Unity scripts, this class will be derived from `MonoBehaviour`. We write a couple of functions required to update the UI based on user input. Open `InstructionsController.cs` for editing and write the following:

```
File: InstructionsController.cs
using System.Collections;
using System.Collections.Generic;
using UnityEngine;
```

```
using UnityEngine.UI;

public class InstructionsController : MonoBehaviour {
    public Text stepText;

    private int currentStep;

    void Start () {
        currentStep = 0;
        CurrentInstructionUpdate();
    }

    public void NextStep() {
        currentStep++;
        CurrentInstructionUpdate();
    }

    public void PreviousStep() {
        currentStep--;
        CurrentInstructionUpdate();
    }

    private void CurrentInstructionUpdate() {
        stepText.text = "Step: " + currentStep;
    }
}
```

Note, at the top of the file, we add `using UnityEngine.UI;` so the Unity UI components will be recognized, including the `Text` reference.

The script is going to update the title text with the current step number. It knows which text element to change because we declare a `public Text stepText`. Later, we'll populate that in the **Inspector**.

In this script, we keep track of the `currentStep`, which is an integer that is initialized to `0` in `Start()`, incremented by one in `NextStep()`, and decremented by one in `PreviousStep()`. Any time the step number changes, we call `CurrentInstructionUpdate()` to update the text on the screen.

Save the script file.

Wiring up the controller with the UI

Returning to Unity, we need to tell the component about our Step Text UI element.

1. Select **Game Controller** in **Hierarchy**.
2. Locate the **Step Text** object (`Main Canvas/ Nav Panel/ Step Text`) and drag it onto the **Step Text** slot of the **Instructions Controller**.

If you press **Play** in Unity now, the nav bar text should read **Step 0** (instead of **Step #**).

Now let's wire up the buttons to our controller:

1. In **Hierarchy**, select the **Next Button** (`Instruction Canvas/ Nav Panel/ Next Button`).
2. In **Inspector**, press + in **On Click()** to add a new click event response.
3. Drag the **Game Controller** onto the empty object slot.
4. In its function select list, locate and select the **NextStep()** function, as shown ahead:

5. Following similar steps for the **Previous Button**, add a click event response, drag **Game Controller**, and select **PreviousStep()**.

Save your work and press **Play**. Now when you click the **Next** and **Previous** buttons (in the **Game** window not the **Scene** one!), the step text is updated with the counter value! Simple, yet satisfying. The title and body text don't update yet, we'll work on that next.

Also notice that if you keep pressing **Previous**, the step number can go negative. We'll fix that too.

Creating an instruction data model

Now that we have a UI and a controller, we're ready to round out our MVC architecture and define the data model. We will first define an `InstructionStep` class that represents the data for one of the instructions steps. Then we'll define an `InstructionModel`, which has the list of steps used in the app.

InstructionStep class

We'll get started by creating a new C# script named `InstructionStep`, which will basically be a data structure or container for a row of data from our spreadsheet (in CSV format), including fields the for title, body text, image, and video.

1. In the Project `Assets/HowToChangeATire/Scripts` folder, right-click and create a new **C# Script** and name it `InstructionStep`.
2. Open it for editing.

When Unity creates a new script it uses a default template for a typical object class derived from `MonoBehaviour`. We want this to be just a simple object and do not want it to be a `MonoBehaviour` (and do not need the `Start/Update` functions).

```
File: InstructionStep.cs
using System.Collections;
using System.Collections.Generic;
using UnityEngine;

public class InstructionStep {
    public string Name;
    public string Title;
    public string BodyText;
}
```

Now we will define a constructor for this class. A **constructor** is a public method with the same name as the class itself, which initializes the property values of a new instance of the class. This constructor will receive the list of value strings as its argument and assign the value to the corresponding properties. Add the following code to your class:

```
private const int NameColumn = 0;
 private const int TitleColumn = 1;
private const int BodyColumn = 2;

public InstructionStep(List<string> values) {
    foreach (string item in values) {
```

```
        if (values.IndexOf(item) == NameColumn) {
            Name = item;
        }
        if (values.IndexOf(item) == TitleColumn) {
            Title = item;
        }
        if (values.IndexOf(item) == BodyColumn) {
            BodyText = item;
        }
    }
}
```

The constructor will expect a list of string values where the first element is the step number (index 0), the second is the title (index 1), and the third is the body text (index 2). Not coincidentally, this is also how the columns are set up in our CSV data and spreadsheet. There may be additional elements of the array, but we'll ignore them for now.

That's it, for now. Save the file. Later we'll add fields for image and video file names.

InstructionModel class

The InstructionModel contains a list of instructions. We defined the InstructionStep class previously, and now we define the InstructionModel class with our list of instructions. The app will then grab instructions one at a time from the model as the user steps through the instructions. At first, we'll just hardcode some example data. Soon, we'll load the data from the external CSV file instead.

Create the script now:

1. In Project Assets/ChangeTire/Scripts, right-click and create a new **C# Script**.
2. Name it InstructionModel.
3. Open it for editing.

Like InstructionSteps, the InstructionModel does not inherit from MonoBehaviour. For now, its only property is a list of steps:

```
using System.Collections;
using System.Collections.Generic;
using UnityEngine;

public class InstructionModel {
    [SerializeField]
    private List<InstructionStep> steps = new List<InstructionStep>();
```

```
    public void LoadData() {
        steps.Add(new InstructionStep(new List<string> { "0", "Hello
World!", "Intro body text." }));
        steps.Add(new InstructionStep(new List<string> { "1", "This is the
first step", "Body text of first step" }));
        steps.Add(new InstructionStep(new List<string> { "2", "This is the
second step", "Body text of second step" }));
    }
}
```

We've also written a `public LoadData()` function that builds a list of steps. Eventually, we'll actually load this data from an external file, but to get started we are just calling our `InstructionStep` constructor directly with a hardcoded list of strings. We define three steps, numbered 0 through 2.

Keeping with our object-oriented practices, the steps list is private and we provide a getter method, `GetInstructionStep()`, to obtain a specific `InstructionStep` from the list. It checks the requested index to ensure it is valid.

```
    public InstructionStep GetInstructionStep(int index) {
        if (index < 0 || index >= steps.Count)
            return null;
        return steps[index];
    }

    public int GetCount() {
        return steps.Count;
    }
```

We also add a function, `GetCount`, to get the number of steps presently in the list.

 If you want to expose the *steps* list in **Inspector** for debugging, there's no need to change it from `private` to `public`. Use `[SerializeField]` instead. Declaring a variable as `public` means you expect other code to modify its value, which should be used judiciously, if at all. `[SerializeField]` tells Unity to expose it in the **Editor Inspector**, but does not violate object oriented principles.

Save your file.

Connecting the model with the controller and UI

Let's see this in action before populating our list with real data. We just need to make a few changes to the `InstructionsController` script. Namely, the controller will be responsible for telling the model to load its data, get the current instruction step, and display it on the screen.

At the top of the class, we will add variables for the `titleText` and `bodyText` UI objects. These will be populated using the **Inspector**. We also have a `currentInstructionModel` variable.

```
File: InstructionsController.cs
public class InstructionsController : MonoBehaviour {
    public Text stepText;
    public Text titleText;
    public Text bodyText;

    private int currentStep;
    private InstructionModel currentInstructionModel = new
InstructionModel();
```

`MonoBehaviour` allows us to define an `Awake()` function, which will be run at the very beginning of initialization of our app, before any of the `Start()` functions are called. In the `Awake()` function, add a call to tell the model to load its data:

```
void Awake() {
    currentInstructionModel.LoadData();
}
```

And then `CurrentInstructionUpdate()` can do its thing with the current step data:

```
private void CurrentInstructionUpdate() {
    InstructionStep step =
currentInstructionModel.GetInstructionStep(currentStep);
    stepText.text = "Step " + currentStep;
    titleText.text = step.Title;
    bodyText.text = step.BodyText;
}
```

Finally, we should check the boundary conditions of the `currentStep` value since we know it can't go below 0, or be greater than or equal to the size of the steps list:

```
public void NextStep() {
    if (currentStep < currentInstructionModel.GetCount() - 1) {
        currentStep++;
        CurrentInstructionUpdate();
    }
}

public void PreviousStep() {
    if (currentStep > 0) {
        currentStep--;
        CurrentInstructionUpdate();
    }
}
```

Save the files.

Back in Unity, don't forget to populate the Instruction Controller's **Title Text** and **Body Text** slots with your UI elements. The resulting **Instructions Controller** component is shown ahead:

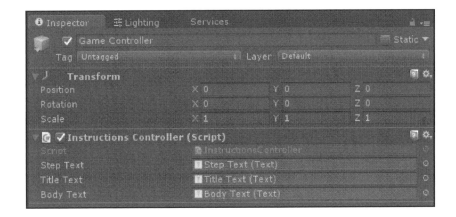

Now when you press **Play** in Unity, you can step forward and back through our mock instructions, within the limits of 0 to 2, as shown ahead:

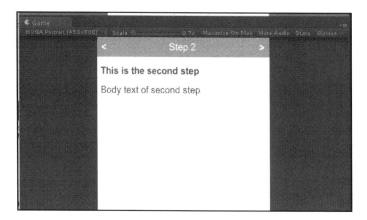

Loading data from a CSV file

The next thing to do is tell `InstructionModel` to read its data from an external CSV file.

If you recall, we decided to compose our content using a spreadsheet, and then export it into a **comma-separated values** (**CSV**) file. We will read this data into the app at runtime. If you're using the one provided with the book, the filename is `instructionsCSV.csv`.

Import the CSV file as an asset into your project. Since we are going to load it from our scripts at runtime, it needs to be put into a specially named folder, `Resources`, anywhere within `Assets`.

Drag the CSV file from your file system into the Project `Assets/HowToChangeATire/Resources` folder in Unity (or use main menu **Assets | Import New Asset**).

In the `InstructionModel` script, we will read the file, taking one line at a time, and then parse each line, using the comma separators, into an array of strings. We can then populate our steps list with these values.

We found some open source code that does the CSV parsing, located at `https://github.com/frozax/fgCSVReader`. It takes into account some of the trickier situations, such as value strings, that may themselves contain commas. Just save a copy of the `fgCSVReader.cs` file (`https://raw.githubusercontent.com/frozax/fgCSVReader/master/fgCSVReader.cs`) into your `Scripts` folder. (A copy is also included with the download files for this book, just in case the GitHub version disappears).

1. Import the `instructionsCSV.csv` file.
2. Import the `fgCSVReader.cs` script.

Open the `InstructionModel.cs` file for editing and add the helper function required by `fgCSVReader`, called `csvReader`, as follows:

```
private void csvReader(int line_index, List<string> line) {
    if (line_index == 0)
        return;
    steps.Add(new InstructionStep(line));
}
```

As specified in the `fgCSVReader` documentation, we provide a private delegate function that gets called for each line, receiving the line index and list of strings. It instantiates a new `InstructionStep` and adds it to the list. We skip the first row, as it contains the column header labels, not actual data.

Now replace our mock `LoadData()` function with one that uses `fgCSVReader` and loads the data from the external CSV file, as follows:

```
public void LoadData() {
    steps.Clear();
    TextAsset text_asset =
(TextAsset)Resources.Load("instructionsCSV");
    fgCSVReader.LoadFromString(text_asset.text, new
fgCSVReader.ReadLineDelegate(csvReader));
}
```

The Unity `Resources.Load()` function will find the file named `instructionsCSV` in any sub-folder within `Assets` named `Resources` and load the entire file into the variable `text_asset`. It will then parse it using `fgCSVReader.LoadFromString`, passing it the text and using our `csvReader` function as the `ReadLineDelegate` it requires.

The built-in `steps.Clear()` call will empty the *steps* list before loading the data, in case it is not presently empty, to prevent duplicates from being created.

Save your work and in Unity press **Play**. We should have a pretty real app going now! It should look something like this:

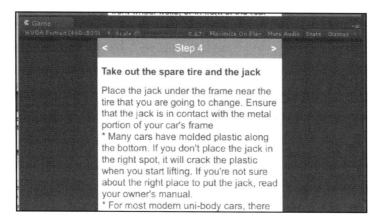

Abstracting UI elements

We still need to add the image and video content. We could go ahead and add them into our current software design, but we're starting to see a pattern emerge in how we've set things up, and it might make sense to refactor our code, abstracting out some of the common elements.

 Refactoring in software development means reworking parts of your code to make it cleaner, more maintainable, and more extendable without modifying the behavior or features.

In this case, we're going to refactor how the controller updates the screen by abstracting out our UI elements. If you noticed, each time we add a new UI element to the view or the model, we need to modify and add it to the controller. It would be cleaner if the controller could just broadcast the fact that there's new data, and the UI elements, listening for such events, could go ahead and update themselves on the screen.

So, we're going to make our own little event system, called `InstructionEvent`, using `UnityEvent`.

Adding InstructionEvent to the controller

The first step in refactoring our code to use events and listeners is to define a UnityEvent called InstructionEvent. Open InstructionsController.cs and add the following:

```
File: InstructionsController.cs
using UnityEngine.Events;

public class InstructionEvent : UnityEvent<InstructionStep> { }

public class InstructionsController : MonoBehaviour {
    public InstructionEvent OnInstructionUpdate = new InstructionEvent();

...
```

As you can see, we also declare a public InstructionEvent named OnInstructionUpdate, which is what all our UIs will be listening to, so we can ensure they update correctly.

Refactoring InstructionsController

Since we are going to an event-listener model, the controller no longer needs to directly know which UI elements to update each time the user steps through the instructions data. Delete the declarations for stepText, titleText and bodyText.

Then we can replace CurrentInstructionUpdate() with the following, much simpler, code that invokes our event by calling OnInstructionUpdate.Invoke():

```
    private void CurrentInstructionUpdate() {
        InstructionStep step =
  currentInstructionModel.GetInstructionStep(currentStep);
        OnInstructionUpdate.Invoke(step);
    }
```

Now, whenever the controller wants to update the screen, it invokes our OnInstructionUpdate event.

Defining InstructionElement

To help organize our code in a clean object-oriented structure, we will define UI elements which will all inherit from an InstructionElement class. This will be the base class. Therefore, we should label the class as abstract. This means that new instances of InstructionElement cannot be created directly, only one of its subclasses.

We shall also require that each subclass of InstructionElement must provide its own implementation of an InstructionUpdate function, which gets the instruction-step data it can use to update its specific UI element. So, in our abstract class, we also declare an abstract function for InstructionUpdate:

1. In Unity, in the Assets/HowToChangeATire/Scripts/ folder create a subfolder named UIElements.
2. Create a new script named InstructionElement.

Open it for editing, as follows:

```
File: InstructionElement.cs
using System.Collections;
using System.Collections.Generic;
using UnityEngine;

public abstract class InstructionElement : MonoBehaviour {
    protected abstract void InstructionUpdate(InstructionStep step);
}
```

This will ensure that all the classes that inherit from InstructionElement will be required to have a function called InstructionUpdate. This is important because, in the Awake() function, we will look for the instance of our InstructionsController.

Now in Awake(), we register the InstructionUpdate function as a listener to OnInsturctionUpdate of the InstructionsController. We can write that as a one-liner, as follows:

```
    void Awake() {
FindObjectOfType<InstructionsController>().OnInstructionUpdate.AddListener(
InstructionUpdate);
    }
```

This will ensure that all our sub-classes now will get an event call when the instruction steps are updated.

We are using the `FindObjectOfType` function to find the instance of our controller. This is a slow function, and could be replaced with a public field or the singleton pattern. This option was simply the easiest to implement for new developers.

Now we can start creating our other UI elements:

1. In the `Scripts/UIElements/` folder, create three new C# scripts named:
   - `StepText`
   - `TitleText`
   - `BodyText`

   Starting with `StepText` first, instead of inheriting from `MonoBehaviour`, it will inherit from `InstructionElement`. Open it for editing. First load the Unity UI definitions:

```
using UnityEngine.UI;
```

   We are going to declare this class, a subclass of `IntructionElement`, then remove the empty `Start()` and `Update()` functions:

```
public class StepText : InstructionElement {
  }
```

2. In your editor, you'll see a *red squiggly* on the class name and see an Intellisense *yellow lamp*
3. Click the lamp and choose **Implement Abstract Class**

Now we can implement the function, and declare `using UnityEngine.UI;` at the top so we can reference the `Text` component. And, since we know we are going to be using `Text`, we can go ahead and declare that the `Text` component is required. Now we can easily get the `Text` component and set its text value to the `step.Title`. Here's the code:

```
File: StepText.cs
using UnityEngine;
using UnityEngine.UI;

[RequireComponent(typeof(Text))]
public class StepText : InstructionElement {
    protected override void InstructionUpdate(InstructionStep step) {
        GetComponent<Text>().text = "Step: " + step.Name;
    }
}
```

The title and body ones are similar, referencing `step.Title` and `step.BodyText`, as follows:

```
File: TitleText.cs
using UnityEngine;
using UnityEngine.UI;

[RequireComponent(typeof(Text))]
public class TitleText : InstructionElement {
    protected override void InstructionUpdate(InstructionStep step) {
        GetComponent<Text>().text = step.Title;
    }
}

File: BodyText.cs
using UnityEngine;
using UnityEngine.UI;

[RequireComponent(typeof(Text))]
public class BodyText : InstructionElement {
    protected override void InstructionUpdate(InstructionStep step) {
        GetComponent<Text>().text = step.BodyText;
    }
}
```

Be sure to save your files in the editor.

Linking up the UI elements in Unity

Now back to Unity; we can assign the UI element components we just created to the elements in our hierarchy.

1. In **Hierarchy**, select the **Main Canvas/Content/Title Text**.
2. Drag the **TitleText** script onto its **Inspector**.
3. In **Hierarchy**, select the **Main Canvas/Content/Body Text**.
4. Drag the **InstructionText** script onto its **Inspector**.
5. In **Hierarchy**, select the **Main Canvas/Nav Panel/Step Text**.
6. Drag the **StepText** script onto its **Inspector**.

Save the scene and the project. Press **Play** in Unity. When you press **Next** and **Previous**, it should behave exactly as it did before. Only now we know that under the hood the code is so much cooler, and extendable.

Now, not only is our code much cleaner and more modular, it's also easier to add new content elements. Let's go ahead, and add images and videos.

Adding image content

Given our `InstructionElement` events, to add images to the instructions requires updates to the UI and the data model, but not the controller.

Adding an image to the instruction Content panel

First let's add an image to the **Content** panel. Actually, we will add a Unity UI `Raw Image`, since the element named `Image` is reserved for sprites.

1. In **Hierarchy**, locate the **Content panel** (under **Main Canvas**), right-click, and select **UI | Raw Image.**
2. Rename it `Image Graphic`.
3. Select **Add Component | Layout Element.**
4. Select **Preferred Width**: `395`.
5. Select **Preferred Height**: `250`.
6. Position it in the **Hierarchy** between **Title Text** and **Body Text**.

The image ahead shows the now current **Hierarchy**, along with the **Scene** view of the Canvas:

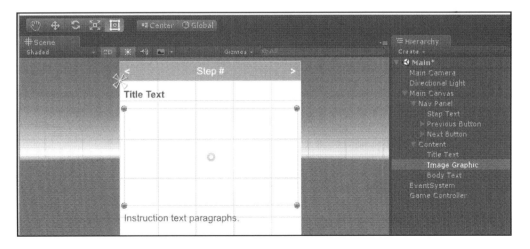

Adding image data to the InstructionStep model

From our CSV data, images will be referenced by name. The app will look in the Resources folder for the files. We could use an image URL instead (and that is provided as another column in the CSV data), but, just in case wikiHow changes its article we don't want that to break this book.

The image name is the fourth column in your database (index 3). We can capture it when the file is loaded.

To InstructionStep.cs, add the following:

```
public string ImageName;
private const int ImageColumn = 3;
```

And then add this to the InstructionStep constructor function:

```
if (values.IndexOf(item) == ImageColumn) {
    ImageName = item;
}
```

Now we create a UI element component. In your Scripts/UIElements/ folder, create a C# script named ImageGraphic and write the following:

```
File: ImageGraphic.cs
using UnityEngine;
using UnityEngine.UI;

[RequireComponent(typeof(RawImage))]
public class ImageGraphic : InstructionElement {
    protected override void InstructionUpdate(InstructionStep step) {
        if (!string.IsNullOrEmpty(step.ImageName)) {
            GetComponent<LayoutElement>().enabled = true;
            GetComponent<RawImage>().texture =
Resources.Load(step.ImageName) as Texture;
        } else {
            GetComponent<RawImage>().texture = null;
            GetComponent<LayoutElement>().enabled = false;
        }
        Canvas.ForceUpdateCanvases();
    }
}
```

The script is very similar to the ones we wrote for title, body, and step text. The difference is what we do inside the `InstructionUpdate` function for an image. If the current step includes an image, we load it as a texture. If not, we clear any image textures that may already be in the UI. We also enable or disable the `LayoutElement` component to show or hide it as necessary.

Afterwards, we call `ForceUpdateCanvases` on the canvas to ensure Unity takes the changes right away, in the current frame.

Save the file and add the `ImageGraphic` script to the **Image Graphic UI** object in **Hierarchy**.

In **Hierarchy**, select the **Image Graphic** (`Instruction Canvas/ Instruction Panel/ Content Panel/ Image Graphic`) and drag the **ImageGraphic** script into **Inspector**.

OK, now we can import the image files.

Importing the image files into your project

We expect the image files to be in your Project Assets. If you haven't imported them yet, do so now. Presently, only steps 1 and 14 of our data reference images (`step1.jpg` and `step14.jpg`). (The other steps reference videos, which we'll add next.) The following screenshot shows the Project `Resources` folder with the imported images and videos for this project:

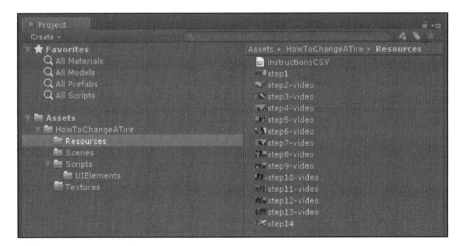

Press **Play** and, as you step through the instructions, ones that include images will be included on that screen. The following screenshot shows step 1 now with an image included:

Adding video content

Adding video content is very similar to adding images. Instead of an image texture, we can use Unity's `MovieTextures`, with one extra step to add the Unity `VideoPlayer`.

Adding video to the instruction content panel

First, let's add another **Raw Image** to the **Content panel** (child of **Main Canvas**) that we'll use as a `MovieTexture`.

1. In **Hierarchy**, right-click **Content panel** and select **UI | Raw Image**.
2. Rename it `Video Graphic`.
3. Select **Add Component | Layout Element**, and select **Preferred Height**: `360`.
4. Position it in the **Hierarchy** between **Title Text** and **Body Text**.

We found a height of `360` works for our layout.

Adding video player and render texture

To render videos in Unity we can use a `MovieTexture` in conjunction with the `VideoPlayer` component.

1. In the `Assets/HowToChangeATire/Textures/` folder, create a **Render Texture**.
2. Name it `Video Render Texture`; we can leave its default settings.

Now for the video player:

1. In **Hierarchy**, create **Video | Video Player.**
2. Check **Loop** and uncheck **Play On Awake.**
3. Select **Aspect Ratio: Fit Vertically**.

And link to the texture:

1. Drag the **VideoRenderTexture** onto the **Target Texture** slot.
2. In **Hierarchy**, select the **Video Graphic UI** object.
3. Drag the **VideoRenderTexture** onto its **Raw ImageTexture** slot.

Adding video data to the InstructionStep model

Videos will be referenced by name in the CSV data. The app will look in the `Resources` folder for the files. As with images, we could use the video URL instead.

The video name is the fifth column in your database (index 3). We can capture it when the file is loaded.

To `InstructionStep.cs`, add the following:

```
    public string VideoName;
```
And,
```
    private const int VideoColumn = 4;
```
And then add to the InstructionStep constructor function,
```
            if (values.IndexOf(item) == VideoColumn) {
                VideoName = item;
            }
```

Now we create a UI element component. In your `Scripts/UIElements/` folder, create a C# script named `VideoGraphic` and write it as follows:

```
File: VideoGraphic.cs
using UnityEngine;
using UnityEngine.UI;
using UnityEngine.Video;

[RequireComponent(typeof(RawImage))]
public class VideoGraphic : InstructionElement {
    public VideoPlayer videoPlayer;

    protected override void InstructionUpdate(InstructionStep step) {
        if (!string.IsNullOrEmpty(step.VideoName)) {
            GetComponent<LayoutElement>().enabled = true;
            videoPlayer.clip = Resources.Load(step.VideoName) as VideoClip;

            GetComponent<RawImage>().SetNativeSize();
            videoPlayer.Play();

        } else {
            videoPlayer.Stop();
            GetComponent<LayoutElement>().enabled = false;

        }
    }
}
```

This time we specify we're using the `UnityEngine.Video` components. We also declare a public variable for the video player.

In `InstructionUpdate`, if the current step includes a video, we load it as a `VideoClip` and start to play it. If not, we stop any video that may presently be playing and disable the `LayoutElement` component to hide the layout. The `SetNativeSize` adjusts the image size to make it pixel perfect.

Save the file and add the **VideoGraphic** script to the **Video Graphic UI** object in **Hierarchy**.

1. In **Hierarchy**, select the **Video Graphic** (`Main Canvas/ Content/ Video Graphic`) and drag the **VideoGraphic** script into **Inspector**.
2. Drag the **Video Player** from **Hierarchy** onto the Video Graphic's **Video Player** slot.

Woo hoot! Press **Play** and, as you step through the instructions, steps that include videos will be played on that screen.

There it is! We have an instruction manual app with text, images, and video, built with Unity.

Adding a scroll view

Some of the instructions may have relatively long body text, and now, with the addition of image or video graphics, it becomes obvious that not all our content may fit on the screen. When you try the app in landscape orientations, it's even more obvious. We need to scroll the content when it overflows the panel.

In the Unity UI, scrolling is implemented using a special scrolling panel:

1. Under **Main Canvas**, select **UI | Scroll View** and name it `Content Scroll View`.
2. Set its **Anchor Presets** to **Stretch/Stretch**, and *Alt*+click on the same to reset its position.
3. Make room for the nav bar by setting **Top** to `50`.
4. Uncheck **Horizontal** (keep **Vertical**) scrolling.
5. Set its **Source Image** to `none` and **Color** to opaque white (#FFFFFFFF).

The other options can be left as the default values. But note that the **Scroll Rect** has a reference to its child **Viewport**.

When you unfold the **Content Scroll View** in **Hierarchy**, you can see it has a **Content** slot populated with its grandchild **Content**. Instead of re-creating our **Content panel**, we will just move it into the **Viewport** and rewire the scroll view.

1. Delete the **Content** under **Viewport**.
2. Drag the **Content** from **Main Canvas** into **Viewport**.
3. Set its **Anchor Presets** to **Top/Stretch**, and *Alt*+click on the same to reset it.
4. On **Control Scroll View**, drag the **Content** object onto its **Content** slot.

Now we can use a **Content Size Fitter** on the **Content panel**:

1. With **Content panel** selected, **Add Component | Content Size Fitter**.
2. Leave **Horizontal Fit** set to **Unconstrained**.
3. Set **Vertical Fit** to **Preferred Size**.

Shown ahead is the final scene **Hierarchy** after all of this:

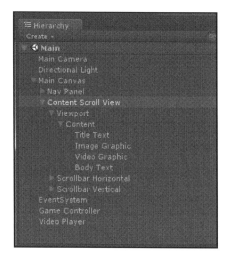

Press **Play** and, when you get to a step with a lot of content, the vertical scroll bars will let you scroll through it all, as shown ahead:

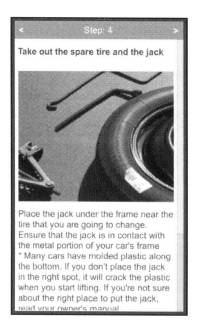

Throughout this chapter we have tested our app in the Unity Editor. Hopefully, you also periodically did **Build and Run** to deploy it onto your mobile device, and test it there.

Summary

In this chapter, we created a real app that provides a step-by-step, how-to guide for changing a flat tire. We did not build Augmented Reality features into it yet, but we covered a lot of ground, including introducing some great features in Unity, powerful software design patterns, and practical procedures such as importing external data from a database. All very important stuff for developing Augmented Reality apps too.

First, we defined our project requirements to take an existing web-based instruction manual and convert it into a mobile app, with the intent of adding AR capability (in the next chapter). We also introduced a number of software design patterns that professional developers commonly use, not only in Unity applications, and then got a chance to use them ourselves throughout the chapter. These include model-view-controller (MVC), event listeners, and object inheritance.

For the implementation, we started by building the user interface (view) using Unity's UI system, and constructing a functional hierarchy of canvas, panels, and UI elements. We explored Unity's tools for layouts of these elements.

Then we wrote our data model classes that manage the instruction content, including loading the data from an external CSV file. Then, we wrote a game controller that manages the state of the app and ensured the data is displayed on the screen. As the project progressed, we added content, including body text, images, and videos.

Along the way, we refactored the code to use Unity events and abstract object classes. We showed how this improves the architecture and facilitates extending the system with more content types.

In the next chapter, we will extend the project by adding AR content and taking it from 2D to 3D. It will take advantage of all the groundwork we did here in part one, so we can focus on the AR capabilities as we build up the application.

7
Augmenting the Instruction Manual

It took a bit of work, but in the previous chapter we built a solid app that guides someone through the instructional steps of how to change a flat tire. How can we make it even better? Using augmented reality, of course!

In this project, we are thinking of AR as just another media type you can add to enhance learning materials, and make them more effective, immersive, and engaging. While in some augmented reality apps, the AR is the central feature and *raison d'etre* of the app, not so here. We started with text, images, and video content. And now we will add AR, too.

In this chapter, you will learn about:

- Designing user experiences for adding AR to existing 2D mobile apps
- Using user-defined AR targets
- Handling poor tracking events
- Adding world space UI to AR scenes
- Using spatial anchors (with ARKit)
- User interface for Hololens

Our implementation started using just Unity for the mobile app, and now we'll add Vuforia and mobile AR. Then, we'll show you how to make it work with Apple's ARKit instead. Lastly, we will adapt the project to work with HoloLens using MixedRealityToolkit.

 Please refer to the the GitHub repository for this book for completed projects for each platform (`https://github.com/ARUnityBook/`), including Google ARCore for Android.

For this project, you will need a Unity package we have prepared, named `ChangeATire-ARGraphics.unity`. Download this file from the publisher's site.

If you plan to implement this for HoloLens or ARKit, you can skip to that topic at the end of this chapter.

If you want to follow along and implement both Vuforia and markerless versions, please make a copy of the project as shown in `Chapter 6`, *How to Change a Flat Tire*. Or, if you use version control, such as Git, then tag or branch the current commit state of the project. The HoloLens, ARKit, and ARCore implementations will assume the same starting point as at the beginning of the chapter.

Setting up the project for AR with Vuforia

We will assume you have the project built from the previous chapter, `Chapter 6`, *How to Change a Flat Tire*. If not, you can download it with the files provided with this book. That will be the starting point for this chapter.

The initial scene **Hierarchy** should look like this:

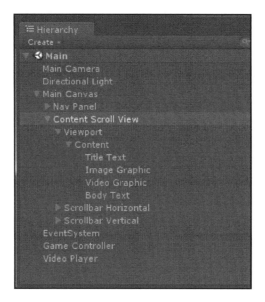

We have a **Main Canvas** that contains a **Nav Panel** and **Content** panel (within a **Scroll View Viewport**). The **Nav Panel** has buttons for next and previous steps through the instructions data. The **Content** panel has elements for title, body text, image, and video content. The **Game Controller** has an **InstructionsController** component that manages the state of the application. In the `Assets/HowToChangeATire/Scripts/` folder, we have our `InstructionModel` and `InstructionStep` classes. The following screenshot shows the **Project** window with the project **Scripts** files:

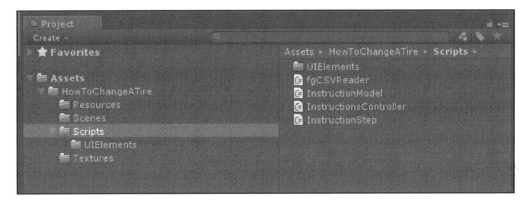

And in the `UIElements/` folder, we have scripts for each content type, as shown in the following screenshot:

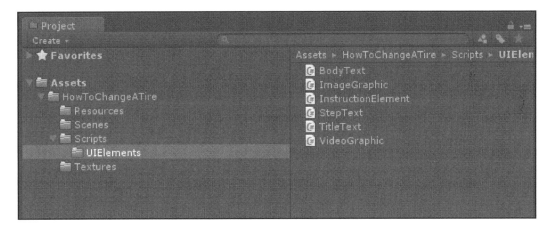

Let's begin by setting up the Unity project for AR with the Vuforia toolkit. This may be familiar to you by now, so we'll go through the steps quickly. If you require more detail, please refer to the relevant sections in Chapters 2, *Setting Up Your System* and Chapter 3, *Building Your App*:

1. Choose **Assets | Import Package | Custom Package...** to import vuforia-unity-xxxx.

2. Choose **Assets | Import Package | Custom Package...** to import VuforiaSamples-xxxx.

3. Browse to the Vuforia Dev Portal (https://developer.vuforia.com/targetmanager/licenseManager/licenseListing) and choose or create a license key. Copy the license key to your clipboard.

4. Back in Unity, choose main menu **Vuforia | Configuration**, and paste it into **App License Key.**

Now we will modify the scene as needed for AR. You may choose to do a **File | Save Scene As** so the AR one is separate from the non-AR. We will call our scene Main-AR (in your HowToChangeATire/Scenes/ folder). It would be a good idea to now go into **File | Build Settings...** and make this scene the only **Scenes to Build** for the next time you build for your mobile device.

Then:

1. Delete the **Main Camera** object from the **Hierarchy**.

2. Locate the **ARCamera** prefab in the Project Assets/Vuforia/Prefabs folder, select, and drag it into the **Hierarchy** list.

3. Use **Add Component** to add the **Camera Settings** component to **ARCamera**.

4. Save the scene and save the project.

   Although we replaced the camera, the app should still work as it did with the default camera. Press **Play** and verify.

   One more thing to make sure things are set up OK. If you disable the content panel you should see the camera video feed instead.

5. In **Hierarchy**, disable the **Main Canvas' Content Scroll View** object (by un-checking its enabled checkbox in the upper left of **Inspector**).

Press **Play**. You should see the video feed in the UI, such as the following view of a wall in my room:

Good. Now re-enable the **Content Scroll View** and we can get started.

Switching between AR Mode

The first thing we'll do is provide an easy way for users to toggle views of the app between conventional 2D views to a 3D AR view by adding an **AR Mode** button on the bottom of the screen. We have decided a 50 pixel height, to be consistent with the nav bar at top.

Make room for it on the bottom by shortening the **Content Scroll View**:

1. In **Hierarchy**, select the **Content Scroll View** (under **Main Canvas**).
2. On its **Rect Transform**, set **Bottom** to 50.
3. Now to add a new button to the **Main Canvas;** select it, go to **UI | Button,** and rename it AR Button.
4. Set **Height** to 50.

5. For **Anchor Presets**, set **Bottom/Stretch** and then also *Alt*+click the same to move it into position.

6. Set **Source Image** to **none** and **Color** the same as the **Nav Panel**: 74, 182, 208, 255 (#4AB6D0FF).

The following screenshot shows us setting the **Anchor Presets** for the AR Button:

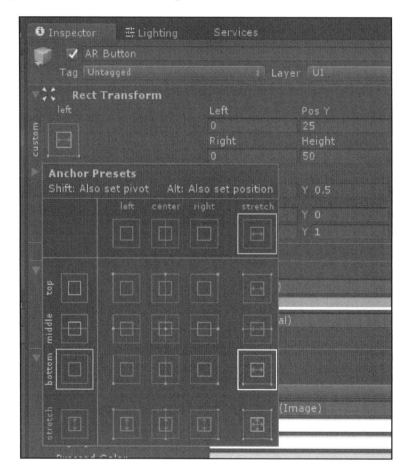

Next, edit its child text with the following values:

1. **Text**: AR Mode.
2. **Font Size**: 25.
3. **Color**: White (#FFFFFFFF).

The new button should look something like this on the bottom of the screen:

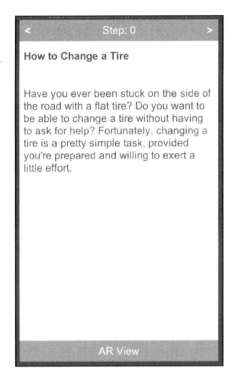

As we did a few moments ago to verify the AR Camera video feed, when one presses the AR View button we want to hide the 2D content. Edit the `InstructionsController.cs` script to provide a `ToggleAr()` function.

First, we declare we're using Vuforia:

```
using vuforia;
```

And then define a public variable for the Content panel; we named it `StandardContent`. Add a private variable to track the current mode:

```
public GameObject standardContent;
private bool arMode;
```

The we add the code to toggle the AR mode; at this point we're just hiding or showing the 2D panel:

```
public void ToggleAr() {
    arMode = !arMode;
    if (arMode) {
```

```
            TurnOnArMode();
      } else {
            TurnOffArMode();
      }
}

void TurnOnArMode() {
      standardContent.SetActive(false);
}

void TurnOffArMode() {
      standardContent.SetActive(true);
}
```

Save your changes. Then continue in Unity as follows:

1. Select **Game Controller** and drag the **Content Scroll View** object onto the **Standard Content** slot.
2. Select the **AR Button** and add the **OnClick** event.
3. Press the + in the **OnClick** list.
4. Drag the **Game Controller** to the **Object** slot, and then choose the function `InstructionsController.ToggleAr()`.

When you press **Play** you can toggle between the 2D content and the video feed on the screen.

Using user-defined targets

Unlike pre-existing images or encoded targets, user-defined targets are images captured at runtime that the software will recognize and use as the trigger for rendering virtual AR content.

As we prepare to begin working in 3D, change the **Scene** view from 2D to 3D.

In the **Scene** window, uncheck **2D** in its icon toolbar, because we want to start working in 3D now, as shown in the following screenshot:

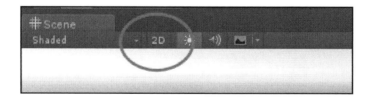

Adding a user-defined target builder

Let's add the **UserDefinedTargetBuilder** to our project now:

1. Drag the **UserDefinedTargetBuilder** prefab from the `Vuforia/Prefabs/` folder into **Hierarchy**.
2. Check **Start Scanning Automatically**.

For now, we are telling the target builder to start scanning automatically. This is useful at this point in our development.

But really, we want to control the scanning to occur only while in AR mode. We can add this to the **InstructionsController** script as follows:

```
File: InstructionsController.cs
    public UserDefinedTargetBuildingBehaviour UserDefinedTargetBuilder;
    ...

    void TurnOnArMode() {
        UserDefinedTargetBuilder.StartScanning();
        StandardContent.SetActive(false);
    }

    void TurnOffArMode() {
        UserDefinedTargetBuilder.StopScanning();
        StandardContent.SetActive(true);
    }
```

Then in Unity:

1. Drag **UserDefinedTargetBuilder** onto the Game Controller's **User Defined Target Builder** slot.

The following screenshot shows the **Instructions Controller** component now:

Adding an image target

Now let's add an **ImageTarget** prefab:

1. From Project `Assets/Vuforia/Prefabs`, drag the **ImageTarget** prefab into the **Hierarchy**.
2. Rename it `User Defined Target`.
3. Set its **Type** to **User Defined**.
4. Set the **Target Name** to something relevant; we will use `Tire`.
5. Check **Enable Extended Tracking.**

You can see the setting now in the **Inspector**:

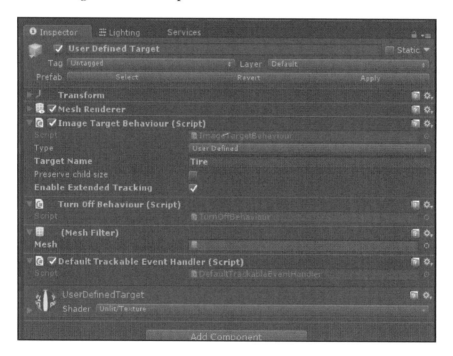

Let's add a simple graphic as a temporary placeholder, a cube, which will appear when our target is recognized.

1. In **Hierarchy**, double-click the **User Defined Target** to put it in the middle of our **Scene** view.
2. Right-click **User Defined Target** and select **3D Object | Cube.**

3. Shrink it down to something like **Scale**(0.1, 0.1, 0.1) and move it up to **Position Y** = 0.1, as shown in the following screenshot.

4. Save the scene.

The **Scene** view now shows the cube positioned relative to the **User Defined Target**, as follows:

Adding a capture button

The app needs to provide users with a way to say *here, use this view of the real world as my image target*, which Vuforia can then recognize and activate the AR content. For this we'll add a prompt and a capture button. The various prompt UI elements will be enclosed in an **AR Prompt** panel. Let's create that first:

1. Select **Main Canvas** in **Hierarchy**.
2. Create **UI | Panel**.
3. Name it AR Prompt.

It will have no background at all, since we need to show a video feed. We can remove its **Image component** entirely.

In the **gear-icon** for the **Image component**, select **Remove Component.**

Meanwhile, the work we're composing now will be seen by the user when in *VR Mode*, so you can manually disable the **Content Scroll View** panel now, temporarily.

Now add the big fat capture button:

1. With **AR Prompt** selected, create **UI | Button** and name it `Capture Target Button`.
2. Set its **Height** to `100`.
3. Set **Anchor Presets** to **Bottom/Stretch**, and then *Alt*+click to position it there.
4. Adjust its **Pos Y** position to `100` to leave room for the **AR View button**.
5. Set **Source Image** to **none**. We picked a darker green **Color**: #004C5EFF.

Its **Rect Transform** looks like this:

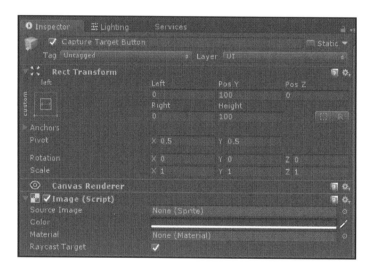

For its child Text object:

1. Set **Text** to `Capture Target`.
2. Set **Size** to `25`.
3. **Color**: white.

OK, we're getting there.

Wire capture button to UDT capture event

To enable **user defined target** (UDT) events, we need to add Vuforia's **UDT Event Handler** component to the **UserDefinedTargetBuilder**:

1. With **UserDefinedTargetBuilder** selected in **Hierarchy**, **Add Component UDT Event Handler**.
2. Drag the **UserDefinedTarget** from **Hierarchy** onto the **Image Target Template** slot.

Now we can tell the button that **OnClick** events should call the `BuildNewTarget()` function:

1. In the **Capture Target Button's Inspector**, press the + on **OnClick()**.
2. Drag the **UserDefinedTargetBuilder** onto the **Object** slot.
3. And set the function to **BuildNewTarget().**

The following screenshot shows the **Capture Button OnClick** setup for the **UDT Event Handler**:

Save your work. Now when you press **Play**, point your webcam at a target and press **Capture**. Whenever the camera sees and recognizes that camera view, it will render the AR content. For now, it's the cube.

In the following screenshot, I am testing the app with a toy truck on my desk (a real car wouldn't fit in my office). I captured its tire as the target.

Now let's try it with the AR View too:

1. Re-enable the **Content Scroll View** object.

   You'll notice that the **Capture Target** button is still visible.

2. Move the **AR Prompt** panel up in the **Hierarchy** so it's just under the **Nav Panel**, as shown in the following screenshot:

Now press **Play**. Then press **AR View** and press **Capture Target**. Voila!

You might want to disable **Content Scroll View** again as we proceed.

 More experienced developers can open the **UDTEventHandler** script (click the gear on the component and choose **Edit Script**) to peruse the script, read through it, and understand fully what's going on.

Adding visual helpers to the AR Prompt

Our plan is for the user to capture an image of his flat tire and then register augmented graphics to the captured image target. We are not so advanced as to have **artificial intelligence (AI)** image recognition (sorry, that's beyond the scope of this book), so we're going to rely a little bit on our user to choose a capture that's approximately the right position and size for our illustrations. Therefore, we need to provide some visual helpers to guide the user.

Adding a cursor

First we will add a small cursor to the middle of the screen, to indicate where the center of the car's tire is:

1. In **Hierarchy**, select **AR Prompt** and create **UI | Image**; name it `Center Cursor`.
2. Set its **Source Image** sprite (by clicking the little doughnut icon) to `Knob`.
3. Change its **Scale** to `0.2, 0.2, 0.2`.

If you press **Play**, I think you'll agree that's helpful.

Adding a registration target

The cursor helps guide the position of the capture. We also need something to guide the size. A circle will do.

We have created a Unity package with graphics we can use. This package also includes arrow graphics and other prefabs that will be used later in the project. If you haven't already, please download the file `ChangeATire-ARGraphics.unity` from the publisher's site for this book.

1. From the main menu, select **Assets | Import Package | Custom Package...**, find the `ChangeATire-ARGraphics` package, and import it.

   The package includes a `circle.png` sprite that we can use now.

2. On **AR Prompt**, create a **UI | Image**, and name it `AR Prompt Idle`.
3. Set its **Source Image** to `Circle`.
4. Set its **Width** and **Height** to `400, 400`.

We can leave everything else as the default settings; we want it just centered on the screen.

We'll provide some on-screen instructions to the user. Position it beneath the circle.

1. On **AR Prompt**, create **UI | Text** and name it `AR Prompt Text`.
2. **Text**: `Align outline to tire, then press Capture Target`.
3. **Anchor Presets** to **Middle/Stretch.**
4. **Font Style: Bold.**
5. **Align**: Center, Middle.
6. **Horizontal Overflow**: Overflow.
7. **Pos Y**: `-220`.

Save your work. Then press **Play**. The following screenshot shows how our AR Mode screen looks, with a small dot cursor in the middle, a circle image for guiding the image registration, and a text prompt (perhaps too small to read on this book's page):

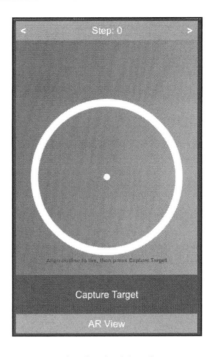

At this point the **AR Canvas** in **Hierarchy** looks like this:

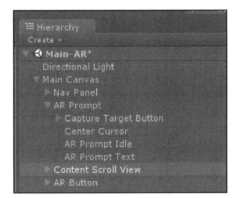

Removing the AR prompt during tracking

It is really great having the graphics on the screen to assist the user while capturing a target. But once it's captured, we want to hide the prompts and display only the annotation graphics instead. If the camera loses tracking, we can restore the UI so the user has the option to recapture.

To do this, we need a script that disables Canvas elements. Unfortunately, presently the Vuforia components are only implemented to disable object renderers, and it does not support canvases. So, we will write our own, and we will make it generic enough to work with any GameObjects. We can do this in a script, using the Vuforia Trackable Events that will be attached to the UserDefinedTarget object.

To begin, in your Scripts folder, create a C# script named TrackableObjectVisiblity, and open it for editing. The full script is as follows:

```
File: TrackableObjectVisiblity.cs
using System;
using System.Collections;
using System.Collections.Generic;
using UnityEngine;
using UnityEngine.Events;
using Vuforia;

[RequireComponent(typeof(TrackableBehaviour))]
public class TrackableObjectVisibility : MonoBehaviour,
ITrackableEventHandler {

    public UnityEvent OnTargetFound;
    public UnityEvent OnTargetLost;

    private TrackableBehaviour trackableBehaviour;

    void Start() {
        trackableBehaviour = GetComponent<TrackableBehaviour>();
        trackableBehaviour.RegisterTrackableEventHandler(this);
    }

    public void OnTrackableStateChanged(TrackableBehaviour.Status
previousStatus, TrackableBehaviour.Status newStatus) {

        if (newStatus == TrackableBehaviour.Status.DETECTED || newStatus ==
TrackableBehaviour.Status.TRACKED || newStatus ==
TrackableBehaviour.Status.EXTENDED_TRACKED) {
            OnTargetFound.Invoke();
        } else {
            OnTargetLost.Invoke();
        }
    }

}
```

At the top, we first declare that we will be using definitions from UnityEngine.Events and from Vuforia.

The script references the `TrackableBehaviour` component of the `UserDefinedTarget` so we require it up front.

Then we declare the class to implement the `ITrackableEventHandler` interface. If you use the Intellisense (light bulb), the editor will insert a prototype for the `OnTrackableStateChanged` function.

We add two public UnityEvent variables, `OnTargetFound` and `OnTargetLost`, which will let us declare in the Editor what object functions to call when the trackable events occur.

In the `Start()` function, we initialize the `trackableBehavior` and register this class as an event handler.

Then in `OnTrackableStateChanged`, we invoke either `OnTargetFound` or `OnTargetLost`. Vuforia provides a number of different tracking statuses. We don't need such a level of detail, as ours is a binary decision, tracking or not, and considers, `DETECTED`, `TRACKED`, and `EXTENDED_TRACKED` to all be tracking.

For more information on the Vuforia `TrackableBehavior` class and tracking statuses, see the documentation at `https://library.vuforia.com/content/vuforia-library/en/reference/unity/classVuforia_1_1TrackableBehaviour.html`

Save the script, go back to Unity, and attach the script to **User Define Target**, as follows:

1. Select **UserDefinedTarget** in **Hierarchy**.
2. Drag the **TrackableObjectVisibility** script as a component.

Now we can add the event handlers. For **On Target Found()**:

1. Press the + to add to the list.
2. Drag the **AR Prompt** panel to the **Object** slot.
3. For function, choose **GameObject.SetActive.**
4. Leave the checkbox unchecked.

Similarly, for **On Target Lost()**:

1. Press the + to add to the list.
2. Drag the **AR Prompt** panel to the **Object** slot.
3. For function, choose **GameObject.SetActive.**
4. This time check the checkbox.

The **Trackable Object Visibility** panel should look like this:

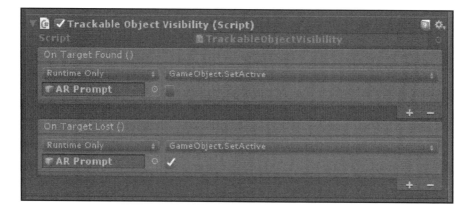

Now when you press **Play**, you will see the circle and capture button. Then when you capture and track, and the cube appears, the UI hides. If you move the camera too fast or otherwise lose tracking, the cube goes away and the capture UI reappears. Woot!

We will use this script again later when we integrate a world space version of the instruction canvas into the AR experience. But first, let's add one more feature.

Preventing poor tracking

We've mentioned several times in this book that image targets, whether they be natural feature textures or user-captured images, should meet certain criteria in order to be effective recognizable targets. Characteristics include being rich in detail, having good contrast, and including no repetitive patterns. As developers, if we provide the targets to our users, we can make sure these requirements are met. With user-defined targets captured at runtime, it could be more of a problem.

Fortunately, Vuforia provides a feature that checks the viability of the video feed as a potential target. And we can listen in on these events to provide feedback to the user.

For this project, when the app is scanning and ready for the user to capture a target, we display a white circle along with the **Capture** button. What we'll do is show a red circle instead when the video feed is low quality for a target. Let's add that now:

1. In **Hierarchy**, duplicate the **AR Prompt Idle** object (**right-click | Duplicate**).
2. Rename it AR Prompt Error.
3. Set its **Color** to red (#FF0000FF).

Add some help text:

1. Create a child text, **UI | Text.**
2. **Anchor Presets**: **Stretch/Stretch**, and *Alt*+click to center it.
3. **Paragraph Alignment:** Middle, Center**.**
4. Set its **Text** to say `Target needs more detail.`

Now we need to tie this in with the Vuforia event.

The Vuforia user-defined target behavior will use Unity events to signal when the current device camera view would be an acceptable target image or not. We can use these events (`UserDefinedTargetEvent` interface) as feedback to our users when the app is ready to capture a potential target image.

We can provide the `UserDefinedTargetBuilder` as a way to reference our `AR Prompt Error` by attaching the `Quality Dialog` component to it. This component is intended for a dialog box that might say **The image has little detail, please try another**, but we're going to use graphic feedback to the user instead of text.

1. On the **AR Prompt Error** object, **Add Component | Quality Dialog.**

   Now the `UserDefinedTarget` will automatically enable this object if there is an error with the image that was captured.

   To dismiss the red circle, we have to do that ourselves.

2. On **UserDefinedTarget**, add another event handler for **On Target Found()** by pressing +.
3. Drag the **UserDefineTargetBuilder** to the **Object** slot.
4. For the function, choose **UDTEventHandler | CloseQualityDialog().**

The **Trackable Object Visibility** component dialog event settings will now look like this:

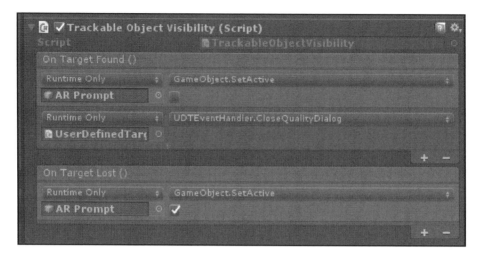

Save your work.

Now when you press **Play**, if you try to capture a poor target (like a blank wall), you'll see the red circle instead of the white one. When you press **Capture** on an acceptable target, then the AR content will appear.

Very good.

So just to recap, so far in the project:

- We added an **AR Mode** button to the 2D UI that toggles the user to an AR view.
- When AR mode is enabled, we hid the **Main Canvas' Content Scroll View** and started scanning for AR targets.
- Behind the scroll view is the **AR Prompt** panel that contains a **Capture Target** button, a small cursor in the middle of the screen, and a white circle to guide the user to fit the view of his automobile tire in its circumference.
- When the target is captured, the **AR Prompt** panel is disabled and the AR graphics are displayed. If the user tries to capture a poor target, we use the Vuforia Quality Dialog event to turn the prompt circle red.

Now it's time to use this AR mode to present graphic content to the user.

Integrating augmented content

Augmented content for our instruction manual will assume the car tire is captured at the correct position and size on the screen (fortunately, we provided prompt graphics to guide the user). We can make some assumptions about the size and placement of our annotation graphics in the world space scene.

The graphics content will be represented as Unity Prefab objects in our project's `Assets Resources` folder. This way, they can be loaded and instantiated at runtime. When the user selects an instruction step in the app, we display the title, text, image, or video that belongs to that step. The CSV data also includes the name of a prefab object to use in AR mode.

When someone designs an instruction manual like this, they will (obviously) identify the instructional steps and write the title and body text. They will prepare the images or video graphics. Now, with AR, they'll also need to prepare a 3D graphic. We created the 3D annotation graphics and animations for you and saved them as prefabs. These are included in `ChangeATire-ARGraphics.unitypackage`, which you should have imported into the project earlier (it also includes the circle sprites we used for AR Prompt). If not, please import the package now.

The package also includes arrow graphics, a **CarJack** model, and other useful assets. In its `Resources` folder are the prefabs referenced by the steps. The project `Assets` are shown in the following screenshot:

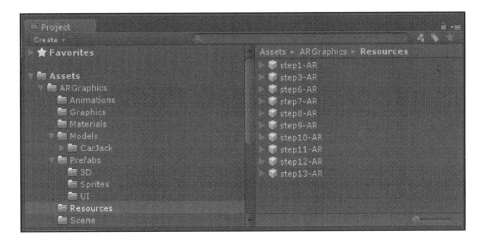

Reading the AR graphic instructions

In `Chapter 6`, *How to Change a Flat Tire*, we implemented an `InstructionModel` class that maintains the data list of instructions for how to change a tire. The data is read from our CSV data file. `InstructionModel` calls `InstructionStep` to extract data from each row of the file. We expect the AR prefab name to be the fifth column in your database. We can grab it when the file is loaded.

To `InstructionStep.cs`, add a new variable:

```
public string ARPrefabName;
private const int ARColumn = 5;
```

Then add this to the `InstructionStep` constructor function:

```
if (values.IndexOf(item) == ARColumn) {
    ARPrefabName = item;
}
```

Next, add its UI element.

Creating AR UI elements

In the previous chapter, we also implemented an `InstructionElement` abstract class that we subclass for each of the content types: title, body, image, and video. We will now make a similar one for the AR graphic content.

Technically, the graphic is not a *UI* one because it's going to be displayed in 3D world space, not 2D screen space like the other instruction content. But it fits nicely with our architecture design because we can load it from CSV like other content, and can broadcast its updates like other UI content when the user changes steps.

In your `Scripts/UIElements/` folder, create a C# script named `ARGraphic` and write it as follows:

```
File: ARGraphic.cs
using UnityEngine;

public class ARGraphic : InstructionElement {
    private GameObject currentGraphic;

    protected override void InstructionUpdate(InstructionStep step) {
        Debug.Log("ARGraphic:" + step.ARPrefabName);
```

```
        // clear current graphic
        if (currentGraphic != null) {
            Destroy(currentGraphic);
            currentGraphic = null;
        }

        // load step's graphic
        if (!string.IsNullOrEmpty(step.ARPrefabName)) {
            currentGraphic = Instantiate(Resources.Load(step.ARPrefabName,
    typeof(GameObject))) as GameObject;
        }
    }
}
```

Save your files.

Displaying the augmented graphic

The final step in integrating the AR graphic is to show it in the augmented view, instead of the stand-in cube object:

1. In **Hierarchy**, select **UserDefinedTarget** and **Create Empty** object.
2. Rename it Augmented Instructions.
3. If necessary, reset its **Transform (gear-icon | Reset)**.

Now simply add the **ARGraphic** script as a component:

1. Drag **ARGraphic** to **Augmented Instructions** as a component.
2. We no longer need the cube, so we can delete the **Cube** object under **User Defined Target**.

That's it! When you press **Play**, press **Next** to go through the steps, press **AR View** and capture your tire, then the associated AR graphic will be displayed (if there is one in the data) to augment the real-world view. An example for step six of the instructions is shown as follows:

Making the augmented graphics

We provided the prefab annotation graphics to you (in the `ChangeATire-ARGraphics.unitypackage`). We should take a quick look at how they were created.

The general idea was to provide graphics that somewhat mimic the annotations used in the video graphics for the original *How To Change A Tire* article on the wikiHow site (`http://www.wikihow.com/Change-a-Tire`).

One approach is to create a new scene in our Unity project that will be used to compose the graphics:

1. From the main menu, select **File | New Scene**.
2. Then **File | Save Scene As**; name it Composition.
3. In **Hierarchy**, **Create Empty**, and name it Compose.
4. Ensure its **Transform** is reset.

We will create a canvas with the circle on it, like the one we used in the actual scene. But this one will be in World Space, and will have to be scaled for world space coordinates.

1. With **Compose** selected, create **UI | Canvas.**
2. Set its **Render Mode** to **World Space.**
3. As we did in Chapter 6, *How to Change a Flat Tire*, set its **Width** and **Height** to 480, 800.
4. Set **Rotation** to 90, 0, 0, so it's flat on a top-down view, like in AR.
5. Set **Scale** to 0.00135, 0.00135, 0.00135.

The seemingly magic numbers for the scale are to set the 480 x 800 canvas in world space. We don't want it 480 meters wide!

On the canvas, we can show the circle:

1. With Canvas selected, create **UI | Image.**
2. For **Source Image**, use the doughnut icon to select **circle**.
3. In **Rect Transform**, set **Width** and **Height** to 400, 400 as we did in the main scene.

Now the scene view has a world space composition area we can use for making the AR graphic, shown as follows, with the *step6-AR* prefab also added to **Compose**:

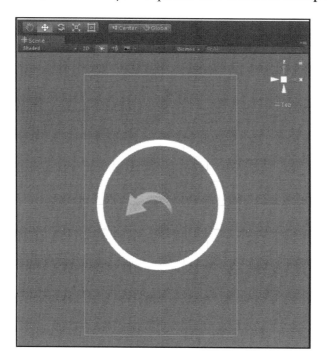

For even more accurate rendition and registration of the graphics, you could add a backdrop image similar to what you expect the user to capture. Or, use Vuforia's built-in **User Defined Target** default image, as follows:

1. With **Compose** selected, create **3D | Quad** and name it UDT.
2. Set **Rotation** to 90, 0, 0 to align with the other world space objects.
3. Find the Vuforia UserDefinedTarget material (in Assets/Vuforia/Materials/) and drag it to the **UDT**.

Your **Scene** view now looks like this when composed against the UDT image:

Now that we have a composition layout area, we can work on the graphics.

To review an existing graphic, drag one of the prefabs into the hierarchy.

This graphic has an animation on it. When you press **Play**, you can also preview the animated graphic.

If you modified the prefab and want to save your changes, select **Apply** in its **Inspector**. The following screenshot is included to indicate where you can find the **Apply** button:

Some of the graphics use Unity's built-in 3D primitive objects. The *step1-ar*, for example, is made of three cubes, as shown here in a perspective view:

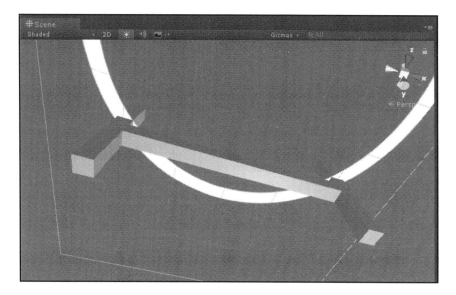

Noting that the number of the annotations requires a stylized arrow graphic, we found something that works on the Pixabay image sharing site (https://pixabay.com/).

For example, the animated graphic for step six shows a green arrow rotating counter-clockwise to indicate the direction for loosening the lug nuts on the tire. The following explanation is just a walkthrough of the existing *step6-AR* graphic and animation; you are not expected to make any changes.

The arrow graphic used is named curved_arrow (located in Assets/ARGraphics/Graphics/curved_arrow.png). This was imported into Unity as a **Sprite** texture, as shown in the following screenshot:

The step6-AR has a **CurvedArrow** that includes the curved arrow sprite image and a **CurvedArrow2D Animator Controller**. You can inspect it on your own, as follows:

We went into detail in Chapter 4, *Augmented Business Cards*, about using the animation editor for making animation clips in Unity. It is driven by an **Animator** graph with a single animation clip. Both the **Animator** and **Animation** windows are shown in the following screenshot:

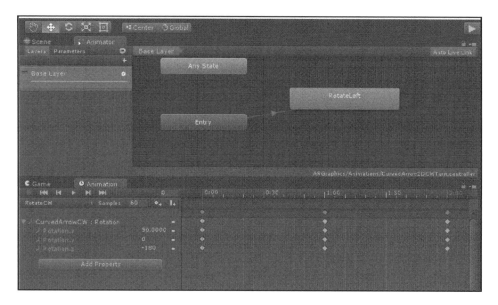

When done, we saved each of our graphics as prefabs to the `ARGraphics/Resources/` folder. And then we exported the whole `ARGraphics/` folder as a Unity package, using main menu **Assets | Export...**

Before continuing with the project, save this scene and then reload the *Main-AR* scene.

Including the instructions panel in AR

Our *How To Change A Tire* app seems completely done. But in user testing, we found that users didn't like having to toggle back and forth between AR Mode and non-AR 2D mode to see the text instructions. We have decided to show the 2D instruction panel in world space also while in AR. Let's name it `AR Canvas` and scale and position it in the scene as follows:

1. In **Hierarchy** root, **Create | UI | Canvas** and name it `AR Canvas`.
2. Set its **Render Mode** to **World Space.**
3. Set **Width** and **Height** to `100, 100`.
4. **Rotation**: `90, 0, 0`, so it's flat on a top-down view, like in AR.
5. **Scale** from pixel layout space to world space; we like `0.004, 0.004, 0.004` (or try other values, such as `0.001`).
6. Position it a bit out of the way, at **Pos X, Pos Y, Pos Z**: `0.0, 0.0, 0.1`.
7. **Dynamic Pixels Per Unit**: `2` to make the text a little crisper.

Now, we want to show basically the same content panel that we already built in the **Main Canvas**. The easiest thing to do is duplicate it and move the copy into the **AR Canvas**.

1. In **Hierarchy,** in `Main Canvas / Content Scroll View / Viewport /` select the **Content** object.
2. Duplicate it (**right-click Duplicate**).
3. Drag that copy into **AR Canvas**, as a child.
4. Rename it `AR Content`.

We just moved it from a screen space canvas to a world space one. We need to clean up its **Rect Transform**:

- **Scale**: 0.2, 0.2, 0.2 (or try other values, such as 1.0)
- **Rotation**: 0, 0, 0
- **Anchor Presets: Bottom/Stretch**, and then *Alt*+click to position it
- **And the parameters, Left**: -218.5, **Pos Y**: 56, **Pos Z**: 0

These numbers work for me. You can tweak them as needed.

Now, when you press **Play** and go into **AR Mode** after you've captured a target, the AR content will display as registered with the tire, and the instructions panel will also show in the scene, as shown in the following screenshot. It even includes any images or video!

When you toggle back to 2D view, the screen space instructions are viewed. When toggling again to AR Mode, the instructions panel is still shown, but in world space. When you go to a next or previous step, both the 2D and world space panel content gets updated simultaneously.

At this point you may really appreciate our UI Element design, where we made each content type's `InstructionUpdate` a registered event. We didn't have to do any extra coding to ensure that the duplicated UI elements were updated with the text and media data. It happened automatically, because the updated events are broadcast to everyone that is listening.

Congratulations! This completes our project.

Using ARKit for spatial anchoring

On iOS, we have the option to use Apple ARKit for spatial anchoring, for devices that support this technology. In this section, we will implement the project on iOS using ARKit. We will not use Vuforia at all, rather, we will modify the project version completed in Chapter 6, *How to Change a Flat Tire* (also where this chapter started at the beginning), and develop it into an AR-only app using the Unity ARKit plugin.

This version will behave very similarly to the Vuforia one, but we do not need to use image targets (user defined or otherwise). We can skip those previous steps that handle capturing and tracking the user defined target, and replace them with a simple button to let the user set the AR graphic position.

We've listed all the steps to build the project as follows, even when identical to the ones shown earlier in the chapter. This time, for expediency, we'll only list them without a lot of explanation and screen captures. Please review the previous corresponding topics if necessary.

As before, we'll have two modes: regular 2D screen view and AR view mode. There will be an **AR Mode** button to toggle between the views. The non-AR view is the one we built in the previous chapter. The **AR mode** will hide the 2D content, show the device's video feed, and add 3D graphics to it.

When in AR mode, there will be another mode: *anchor mode,* activated by pressing the **Set position** button. When setting the position, we'll display an AR prompt--a circle--to assist the user with registering the AR graphic with the automobile tire in real life. The buttons and modes are shown in the following table:

	2D mode	AR mode	Anchor mode
AR Mode button (`ARButton` object)	Turn on AR mode	Turn off AR mode	Turn off AR mode
Set Position button (`AnchorButton` object)	disabled	Turn on Anchor mode	disabled
Press screen prompt with circle (`ARPrompt` object)	disabled	disabled	Sets position and Turn off Anchor mode

To give you a heads up with what we're going to build, the following screenshot shows the screen space UI we will have when we are done (all the elements are visible; at runtime specific elements will show only for specific modes):

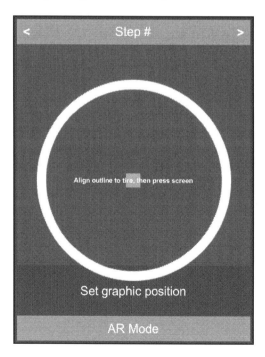

And the following screenshot shows the scene **Hierarchy** we will have when we are done:

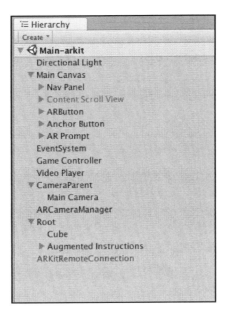

Let's get started!

Setting up the project for ARKit

We decided to give this version of the project a different name, How to Change a Tire-ARKit. Open the project in Unity and import the ARKit plugin via the Asset Store:

1. With the old *Main* scene open, select **File | Save Scene As**, and name it Main-ARKit.
2. Select **File | Build Settings** and replace **Main** with **Main-ARKit** in the **Scenes To Build.**
3. Switch platforms to **iOS**. We will let the toolkit set the other configurations.
4. From **Window | Asset Store**, **Download** and **Import** the **Apple ARKit** package.
5. Accept the option to let it **Override Project Settings**.

Let's remove the ambient lighting in the scene:

1. Open the **Lighting** tab; **Window | Lighting | Settings**.
2. Set **Skybox Material** to none (using the doughnut icon to the right of the parameter).
3. Set **Environment Lighting Source** to **Color**.
4. Set **Lightmapping Settings Indirect Resolution** to 1.

Now we set up the camera with AR components and create the ARCameraManager, as follows:

1. In the **Hierarchy** root, **Create Empty** named CameraParent, and reset its **Transform** if necessary (**Transform | gear-icon | Reset**).
2. Drag the **Main Camera** so it is a child of **CameraParent**, and reset its **Transform** too.
3. With **Main Camera** selected, **Add Component Unity AR Video**.
4. For its **Clear Material** slot, click the doughnut icon and select **YUVMaterial**.
5. **Add Component Unity AR Camera Near Far**.
6. In the **Hierarchy** root, **Create Empty** named ARCameraManager.
7. **Add Component Unity AR Camera Manager**.
8. Drag the **Main Camera** to its **Camera** slot.

That's it for the generic ARKit scene setup.

Preparing the scene

Our AR graphics will be parented by a **Root** game object and then positioned when the **AR Prompt** detects a screen touch. We can add **Root** now. We'll start with a temporary **Cube** as our content, then add the real graphics next:

1. Temporarily disable the **Main Canvas' Content Scroll View** panel in **Hierarchy**.
2. In **Hierarchy**, **Create Empty** named Root, reset its **Transform**, and set its **Position Z** = 2.
3. Create **3D | Cube**, and set its **Transform Scale** to 0.1, 0.1, 0.1.

    At this point we can import the ChangeATire-ARGraphics package we have provided with the files for this chapter of the book.

4. Choose **Assets | Import Package | Custom Package...** to import the package.

Next, we can continue to build our project.

Modifying the InstructionsController

The `InstructionsController` will handle the AR and anchor modes for the app. Now we'll edit the `InstructionsController` script (component of **Game Controller** in the scene). Open the script for editing and change it as follows:

```
File: InstructionsController.cs
```

At the top of the class, add the following public and private variables:

```
public GameObject standardContent;
private bool arMode;

public GameObject anchorButton;
public GameObject arPrompt;
private bool anchorMode;
```

Add the following methods to toggle the AR mode:

```
public void ToggleAr() {
    arMode = !arMode;
    if (arMode) {
        TurnOnArMode();
    } else {
        TurnOffArMode();
    }
}

void TurnOnArMode() {
    standardContent.SetActive(false);

    TurnOffAnchorMode();
}

void TurnOffArMode() {
    standardContent.SetActive(true);

    anchorButton.SetActive(false);
    arPrompt.SetActive(false);
}
```

Lastly, add the following methods to toggle the set-position anchor mode:

```
public void ToggleAnchor() {
    anchorMode = !anchorMode;
    if (anchorMode) {
        TurnOnAnchorMode();
    } else {
        TurnOffAnchorMode();
    }
}

void TurnOnAnchorMode() {
    anchorButton.SetActive(false);
    arPrompt.SetActive(true);
}

void TurnOffAnchorMode() {
    anchorButton.SetActive(true);
    arPrompt.SetActive(false);
}
```

The script exposes the public methods `ToggleAr()` and `ToggleAnchor()` that will be wired to screen buttons for switching modes and showing/hiding UI elements on the screen.

Save your changes.

Adding the AR mode button

Earlier in this chapter there was a section called *Switching between AR Mode*. We will implement the same thing here. We will make room at the bottom of the screen and add a button that reads **AR Mode** as follows:

1. In **Hierarchy**, select the **Content Scroll View** (under **Main Canvas**).
2. On its **Rect Transform**, set **Bottom** to 50.
3. With **Main Canvas** selected, go to **UI | Button** and rename it AR Button.
4. Set **Height** to 50.
5. For **Anchor Presets**, set **Bottom/Stretch**, and then also *Alt*+click the same to move it into position.
6. Set **Source Image** to **none** and **Color** the same as the **Nav Panel**: 74, 182, 208, 255 (#4AB6D0FF).
7. Edit its child text object; **Text**: AR Mode, **Font Size**: 25, **Color**: white (#FFFFFFFF).

Very well. We can now wire up the button and test it.

1. Select **Game Controller** and drag the **Content Scroll View** object to the **Standard Content** slot.
2. Drag the **Anchor** button to the **Anchor Button** slot.
3. And drag the **AR Prompt** to the **AR Prompt** slot.
4. Select the **AR** Button, and add the **OnClick** event.
5. Press the + in the **OnClick** list.
6. Drag the **Game Controller** to the **Object** slot, and then choose the function **InstructionsController.ToggleAr()**.

When you press **Play** you can try the **AR Mode** button to toggle back and forth between the 2D content and the video feed on the screen.

Adding the anchor mode button

Next, add the button that lets the user set the graphics position:

1. At the **Hierarchy** root, create **UI | Button** and name it Anchor Button.
2. Set its **Height** to 100.
3. Set **Anchor Presets** to **Bottom/Stretch**, then *Alt*+click to position it there.
4. Adjust its **Pos Y** position to 100 to leave room for the **AR Mode** button.
5. Set **Source Image** to none; we picked a darker green **Color**: #004C5EFF.
6. For its child Text object, set **Text** to Set graphic position, **Font Size**: 25, **Color**: white.

Now to wire up the Anchor button:

1. Select the **Anchor Button** and add the **OnClick** event.
2. Press the + in the **OnClick** list.
3. Drag the **Game Controller** to the **Object** slot, then choose the function **InstructionsController.ToggleAnchor()**.

If you press **Play** now, you can get into Anchor mode, but cannot get out because there's more to do. We need to respond to the user's screen touch to change the **AR Root** object position.

Adding the AR prompt

We can add the AR prompt as follows:

1. With **Main Canvas** selected in **Hierarchy**, create **UI | Panel** and name it AR Prompt.
2. In the **gear icon** for the image component, select **Remove Component**.
3. On **AR Prompt**, create **UI | Image** and name it AR Prompt Idle.
4. Set its **Source Image** to Circle.
5. Set its **Width** and **Height** to 400, 400.
6. On **AR Prompt**, create **UI | Text** and name it AR Prompt Text.
7. Set its **Text** string to Align outline to tire, then press screen.
8. Set its **Anchor Presets** to **Middle/Stretch**, **Font Style: Bold**, **Align**: Center, Middle, and **Horizontal Overflow: Overflow**.

We're prompting the user to touch the screen. We need a script to handle that.

1. Create a new C# script named ARHitHandler.
2. Add it as a component to **AR Prompt**.

Then open the file for editing, as follows:

```
File: ARHitHandler.cs
using System.Collections;
 using System.Collections.Generic;
 using UnityEngine;
 using UnityEngine.EventSystems;
 using UnityEngine.XR.iOS;

public class ARHitHandler : MonoBehaviour {
    public Transform anchor;
    public InstructionsController controller;

    void Update () {
        List<ARHitTestResult> hitResults;
        ARPoint point;
        float scale;

        if (Input.touchCount > 0 && anchor != null) {

            var touch = Input.GetTouch(0);
            if (touch.phase == TouchPhase.Began) {
                Vector2 center = new Vector2(Screen.width/2,
```

```
Screen.height/2);
                    Vector3 screenPosition =
Camera.main.ScreenToViewportPoint(center);
                    point.x = screenPosition.x;
                    point.y = screenPosition.y;
                    Vector2 edge = new Vector2(Screen.width, Screen.height/2);
                    Vector3 screenEdge =
Camera.main.ScreenToViewportPoint(edge);
                    scale = screenPosition.x - screenEdge.x;

                    hitResults =
UnityARSessionNativeInterface.GetARSessionNativeInterface().HitTest( point,
ARHitTestResultType.ARHitTestResultTypeExistingPlaneUsingExtent);
                    if (hitResults.Count == 0) {
                        hitResults =
UnityARSessionNativeInterface.GetARSessionNativeInterface().HitTest( point,
ARHitTestResultType.ARHitTestResultTypeHorizontalPlane);
                    }
                    if (hitResults.Count == 0) {
                        hitResults =
UnityARSessionNativeInterface.GetARSessionNativeInterface().HitTest( point,
ARHitTestResultType.ARHitTestResultTypeFeaturePoint);
                    }

                    if (hitResults.Count > 0) {
                        anchor.position = UnityARMatrixOps.GetPosition(
hitResults[0].worldTransform);
                        anchor.rotation = UnityARMatrixOps.GetRotation(
hitResults[0].worldTransform);
                        anchor.scale = new Vector3(scale, scale, scale);
                    }
                }
            }
        }
    }
```

This script is very similar to the `SolarSystemHitHandler.cs` we wrote in `Chapter 5`, *AR Solar System*. Please refer to that chapter for an explanation of the `UnityARSessionNativeInterface` usage code.

The primary difference is we do not use the exact screen touch point to determine where to place the root anchor. Rather, when the user touches anywhere on the screen, we use the center of the screen (width/2, height/2), which is also the center of the circle.

We also use the size of the circle on the screen (approximated to the right edge of the screen) to determine the scale of the graphics in 3D, using the distance between the world coordinate of the center and the world coordinate of the edge.

We've added a public variable to the `InstructionsController`, so after the root is repositioned, we toggle off the Anchor mode.

Using a screen space prompt may not be the best approach for registering AR graphics to a real-world tire when you have spatial anchoring technology. You may want to consider and try other solutions, such as:

- Do not use the circle prompt at all, just a small cursor that's positioned on the spatial map surface so you can identify the position, including 3D depth, before clicking, and assume the size of the graphics in a real-world scale.
- Use a world space canvas or a 3D graphic for the circle prompt. In that case, you might modify ARHitHandler to update the prompt graphic on every frame update while in anchor mode. This will allow the user to preview the graphic extents relative to the real world in real-time.
- Allow the user to interactively edit the graphic position, scale, and rotation after it is placed. This is a more involved UI, but it gives the most flexibility. See `Chapter 8`, *Room Decoration with AR*, for implementation ideas.

Adding AR graphic content

The final step is to enable the augmented instruction graphic in the scene. These are the same steps we did previously for Vuforia, but assuming this is a new project we should make changes here. For a more detailed explanation, please read through the integrating augmented content section in this chapter.

To `InstructionStep.cs`, add a new variable:

```
public string ARPrefabName;
private const int ARColumn = 5;
```

Then add this to the `InstructionStep` constructor function:

```
if (values.IndexOf(item) == ARColumn) {
    ARPrefabName = item;
}
```

Create an `ARGraphic.cs` script to handle the UIElement events. In your `Scripts/UIElements/` folder, create a C# script named `ARGraphic` and write it as follows:

```
File: ARGraphic.cs
using UnityEngine;

public class ARGraphic : InstructionElement {
    private GameObject currentGraphic;

    protected override void InstructionUpdate(InstructionStep step) {
        Debug.Log("ARGraphic:" + step.ARPrefabName);

        // clear current graphic
        if (currentGraphic != null) {
            Destroy(currentGraphic);
            currentGraphic = null;
        }

        // load step's graphic
        if (!string.IsNullOrEmpty(step.ARPrefabName)) {
            Object data = Resources.Load(step.ARPrefabName,
typeof(GameObject));
            currentGraphic = Instantiate(data, transform ) as GameObject;
        }
    }
}
```

We need to make sure the instantiated prefab is a child of this (Augmented Instruction) object.

Save your files.

The final step in integrating the AR graphic is to show it in the augmented view:

1. In **Hierarchy**, **Create Empty** object as a child of **Root**, and name it `Augmented Instructions`.
2. Reset its **Transform.**
3. Add the `ARGraphic` script as a component.

We need to make some **Transform** adjustments:

1. **Scale**: `0.1, 0.1, 0.1`.
2. **Rotation**: `-90, 0, 0`.

Save the scene.

Now when you **Play**, try the following:

- Navigate to an instruction step that contains 3D graphics
- Press the **AR Mode** button to toggle into AR Mode
- Press **Set Position** to give the device a chance to scan your room
- Point the camera at the object you want to anchor the graphics to (your flat tire)
- The AR graphics will be displayed on the flat tire
- You can toggle back and forth between the 2D content and the 3D AR content
- As you navigate to other instruction steps, those AR graphics will be positioned at the same anchor points in the real world

There it is!

Building for Android using Google ARCore
Please refer to the the GitHub repository for this book for the implementation notes and code about using Google ARCore for Android: `https://github.com/ARUnityBook/`. The principles are very similar to ARKit, but the Unity SDK and components are different.

In the next section, we will adapt the project to work with wearable AR devices such as the Microsoft HoloLens.

A Holographic instruction manual

In this section, we will implement the project on Microsoft HoloLens. We will not use Vuforia at all, rather we will modify the project version completed in Chapter 6, *How to Change a Flat Tire* (also where this chapter started at the beginning), and develop it into an AR-only app using the Microsoft MixedRealityToolkit SDK.

How does this version of the project differ from the mobile AR implementation using Vuforia and ARKit? In the mobile AR version, the app starts up like a normal screen space 2D mobile app. An **AR Mode** button lets you switch to the AR view, which lets you see 3D graphics that augment a real-world video feed. The HoloLens version will be entirely in 3D; there is no mode toggle. And there is no need for target image recognition. Instead, we will create a hologram with the instructions, including 3D augmented graphics, along with text, images, and video.

For this chapter, we are going to use as many drag and drop components as we can to keep the steps short and simple. In the next chapter, we are going to dive into the Microsoft MixedReality SDK for HoloLens in more detail and explanation.

Let's get started.

Setting up the project for HoloLens

We decided to name this version of the project `How to Change a Tire - Holo`. Open the project in Unity, and set it up for HoloLens development using the HoloToolkit:

1. With the old *Main* scene open, select **File** | **Save Scene As** and name it `Main-Holo`.

2. Select **File** | **Build Settings** and replace **Main** with **Main-Holo** in the **Scenes To Build.**

3. Switch platforms to the **Windows Store**. We will let the toolkit set the other configurations.

4. Import the `MixedRealityToolkit` package (if you haven't downloaded it yet, you can find it at `https://github.com/Microsoft/MixedRealityToolkit-Unity`).

 Note that the following Unity Editor menu item names may have changed in your version of the toolkit.

5. Choose main menu **Mixed Reality** | **Configure** | **Apply HoloLens Scene Settings** and accept all the settings. This sets the Camera Settings for you.

6. Save the scene.

7. Choose main menu **Mixed Reality** | **Configure** | **Apply HoloLens Project Settings** and accept all the settings. This sets the **Build Settings** for you, and restarts Unity.

8. Choose main menu **Mixed Reality** | **Configure** | **Apply HoloLens Capability Settings** and accept all the settings. This sets the **Player Settings** for you.

9. Save the scene and save the project.

Also, import the `ARGraphics` package. We have created a Unity package with graphics we can use. This package includes arrow graphics and other prefabs used in the augmented instruction content. If you haven't already, please download the file `ChangeATire-ARGraphics.unity` from the publisher's site for this book.

From main menu, select **Assets | Import Package | Custom Package...**, find the `ChangeATire-ARGraphics` package, and import it.

The project is now ready to port the content to AR.

World space content canvas

The first step will be to change the **Main Canvas** content from screen space to world space. And in the process, let's set up an object hierarchy, which will be convenient for placing them in space.

We will define an **Origin** at the top of the **Hierarchy**, with a child **Hologram** that contains all our instructional content that should stay together. Then when the user places the content, they'll move the **Hologram** relative to the **Origin**:

1. In **Hierarchy**, **Create Empty** object, and name it `Origin`.
2. Reset its **Transform (gear-icon | Reset)**.
3. With **Origin** selected, **Create Empty** child object, and name it `Hologram`.
4. Reset its **Transform** too.
5. Set the initial Hologram **Position** to 0, 0, 2 so it's right in front of the user, 2 meters away.

Now we can work on the **Main Canvas**. With **Main Canvas** selected in **Hierarchy**:

1. Change its **Render Mode** to **World Space.**
2. Set its **Rect Transform Position** to 0, 0, 0.
3. Set its **Width** and **Height** to 480, 800.
4. **Scale**: 0.0004, 0.0004, 0.0004. As we've seen before, the scale of Unity UI objects in world space requires tiny numbers because it correlates to the size of pixels in meters.
5. Set its **Dynamic Pixels Per Unit** to 2, to make it a little crisper.

Now move the **Main Canvas** in the **Hologram**.

1. In **Hierarchy**, drag the **Main Canvas** so it's a child of **Hologram**.
2. Set its **Rect Transform Position** to 0, 0, 0.

Save the scene and try it in the HoloLens. You should see the first page of our in view.

As usual, you can use the **Holographic Emulation** window to configure Unity to use your physical HoloLens device in *Remote to Device* mode and the Holographic Remoting app in your device. See Chapter 3, *Building Your App* or the Windows Mixed Reality site for documentation. Or **Build and Run** the app on the HoloLens via Visual Studio, also described in Chapter 3, *Building Your App*.

Enabling the next and previous buttons

In order to interact with the **Next** and **Previous** button on our canvas, we need to handle the HoloLens' standard *Select* gesture as a click, much the same as a mouse click or smartphone screen tap on the Unity UI buttons. We can do this by adding the prefab Input Manager to the scene, and then adding an Input Module component to the existing UI EventSystem:

1. From the Project Assets / HoloToolkit / Input / Prefabs folder, drag the **InputManager** into the **Hierarchy**.
2. From the Project Assets / HoloToolkit / Input / Prefabs / Cursor folder, drag the **CursorWithFeedback** into the **Hierarchy**.
3. In **Hierarchy**, with **EventSystem** selected, **Add Component HoloLens Input Module**.
4. Disable the **Standalone Input Module**, as it won't be needed and we do not want it to interfere with the HoloLens one.

Save the scene and try it in HoloLens. You should now see a cursor following your gaze. And (if you're precise) you might be able to select the **Next** and **Previous** buttons to step through the instructions.

You'll probably discover that finding and selecting small things with head movements and your gaze is not nearly as precise as using a mouse or touchscreen. We need to make our buttons bigger.

1. Within the **Hierarchy**, select the **Previous Button** (under Main Canvas / Nav Panel).
2. Change its **Scale** to 3.5, 3.5, 3.5 to make it larger.
3. Set **Pos Y** to 90, so it's above the **content** panel.
4. Set **Source Image** to **UISprite**.
5. **Color**: # 4AB6D0FF.
6. Also set its **Highlighted Color** to something else, such as yellow (#F1FF00FF), to give the user additional visual feedback when they can select the button.

Follow the same steps for the **Next Button**. Now, when you **Play**, it should be easier to navigate through the instruction steps, as follows:

 For more information on the HoloLensInputModule for Unity and how it translates tap and navigation gestures into emulated mouse input, see `https://docs.unity3d.com/ScriptReference/EventSystems.HoloLensIn putModule.html`.

Adding an AR prompt

Much like we did earlier in the mobile AR version of the project, we are going to provide an AR prompt for the user to center the hologram and permit us to register our 3D instruction graphics on the car's flat tire.

Let's make this prompt the center of our view. Move the main canvas over a bit, and add a circle graphic:

1. Modify the **Main Canvas Position** to `-0.25, 0, 0`. Later, you can further adjust this and even add a little rotation along the *y* axis.
2. In the project's `Assets/ARGraphics/Prefabs/Sprites` folder, drag the **Circle2D** prefab so it's an immediate child of **Hologram** (sibling of **Main Canvas**).
3. Rename it `Circle Prompt`.
4. Set its **Scale** to `0.06, 0.06, 0.06`.

Your scene now looks like this:

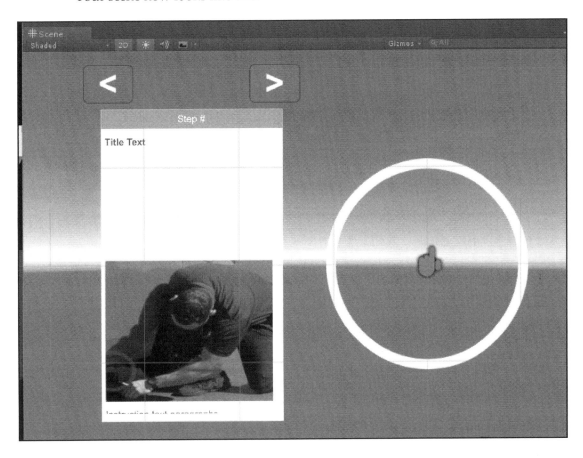

While we're here, add a `Box Collider` to the circle graphic, as we'll need it next to select it for moving and placing the hologram in the world.

5. With **Circle Prompt** selected, **Add Component** `Box Collider`.

The **Inspector** for the **Circle Prompt** is shown in the following screenshot:

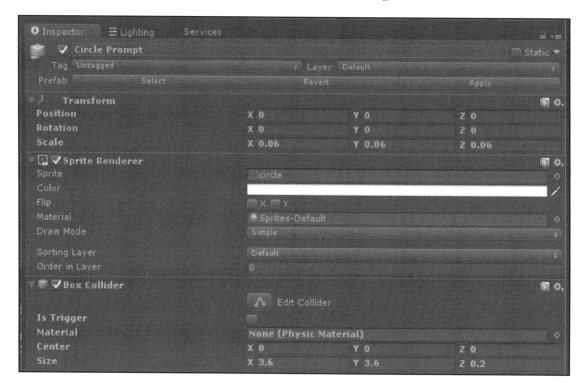

Placement of the hologram

The user will be able to place the hologram in the real world. We expect they will use the prompt to circumscribe the tire. And then we can display the instruction graphics registered to the tire.

To place the hologram, the user will click on it using the *select* gesture while gazing at the **Circle Prompt**. Then, moving their head to gaze at a new location, the hologram will follow the gaze until another *select* is detected. That will be the new position of the hologram.

Placing objects in the real world uses HoloLens Spatial Mapping. The device is always scanning the environment, taking depth readings, and constructing a 3D mesh of all surfaces. To place the hologram in the space, the user will gaze at the desired location. We will cast a ray (draw a straight line) from the user's gaze and determine where it intersects with the Spatial Map mesh. This 3D point will be the location we move the hologram to.

There's a bit of math involved in accomplishing this, but Unity provides all the functions we need:

1. Find the **SpatialMapping** prefab in Project `Assets/Holotoolkit/SpatialMapping/Prefabs`, and drag it to the **Hierarchy**.
2. In your `HowToChangeATire/Scripts` folder, create a new C# script named `TapToPlaceInstructions`.
3. In **Hierarchy**, select **Circle Prompt**.
4. Drag the **new script** component to the **Circle Prompt**.
5. Double-click the script to open it for editing.

 Note that the HoloToolkit namespace is pending to be renamed to MixedRealityToolkit at the time of publishing this book. By the time you read this, you may need to use the updated namespace.

The full script is shown as follows. Enter the following code into your script:

```
File: TapToPlaceInstructions.cs
using UnityEngine;
using HoloToolkit.Unity.InputModule;
using HoloToolkit.Unity.SpatialMapping;

public class TapToPlaceInstructions : MonoBehaviour, IInputClickHandler {
    public SpatialMappingManager spatialMapping;
    public bool placing;

    public void OnInputClicked(InputClickedEventData eventData) {
        placing = !placing;

        spatialMapping.DrawVisualMeshes = placing;
    }

    void Start() {
        spatialMapping.DrawVisualMeshes = placing;
    }

    void Update() {
        if (placing) {
            Vector3 headPosition = Camera.main.transform.position;
            Vector3 gazeDirection = Camera.main.transform.forward;
            int layerMask = 1 << spatialMapping.PhysicsLayer;
            RaycastHit hitInfo;
            if (Physics.Raycast(headPosition, gazeDirection, out hitInfo,
```

```
30.0f, layerMask)) {
                this.transform.parent.position = hitInfo.point;
                Quaternion toQuat = Camera.main.transform.localRotation;
                toQuat.x = 0;
                toQuat.z = 0;
                this.transform.parent.rotation = toQuat;
        }
    }
  }
}
```

At the top of the script, we declare that we will be using the HoloToolkit (MixedRealityToolkit) Input Module and Spatial Mapping APIs.

The `TapToPlaceInstructions` class will implement an interface for `IInputClickHandler`, the event system for the Input Module. When the user does a *select* gesture while gazing at the current object (Circle Prompt), the `OnInputClicked` method will get called.

We declare two variables for the class. `spatialMapping` is a reference to the `spatialMapping` object in the scene, so we can turn the spatial map mesh visibility on and off. `placing` is a Boolean that keeps track of when we're in the middle of placing the object.

So, when the user clicks on the circle, `OnInputClicked` is called, and `placing` is enabled, then we turn on the meshes. When not placing, the meshes are turned off. Rather than writing `if placing then DrawVisualMeshes = true else DrawVisualMeshes = false`, we use a coding shortcut and simply use the `placing` Boolean value to set the `DrawVisualMeshes` value itself.

`placing` is a public variable, and it can be set in the Unity editor. If we choose to start the app with placing turned on (to force the user to begin placing the hologram first thing), we want to draw the meshes in `Start()` also.

While `placing` on each `Update()`, we cast a ray from the head position (camera position) in the gaze direction (camera forward vector) and see if and where it intersects the spatial mesh. We limit the ray cast to 30 meters.

How does `Physics.Raycast` know we're looking for a spatial mesh intersection and not anything else in the scene? If you go back to Unity and click the **SpatialMapping** object, you'll see its (default) **Physics Layer** is set to 31. The `Raycast` will only look for objects on layer 31 (the `Raycast` function requires a binary layer *mask* which we generate by binary-shifting the value 1 over 31 positions with the instruction *1 << 31*).

If we get an intersection hit point, we set the Hologram's position to that point. (**Hologram** is the parent of **Circle Prompt** in **Hierarchy**.) We also rotate the hologram, like a billboard, so it's always facing you.

When the user *selects* again, the placing mode is disabled, and wherever the hologram was last positioned is where it stays.

1. Save the script.
2. Drag the **SpatialMapping** object from **Hierarchy** to the **Spatial Mapping** slot on the **Tap To Place Instructions** component.
3. Check the **Placing** checkbox.

And try it in the HoloLens. When you're placing the circle, the spatial map mesh will be drawn. As you move your gaze, the hologram moves around your room, as follows:

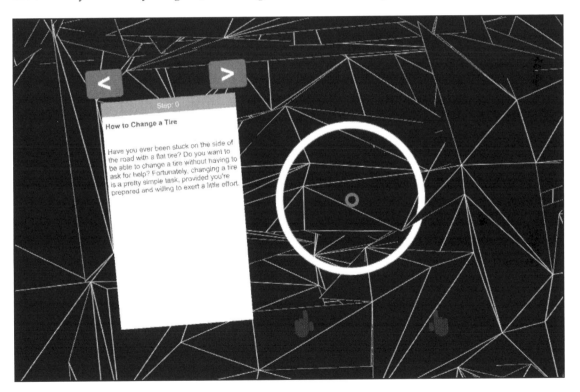

When you click again, it is done, the mesh is hidden, and the instructions hologram is now in its new position.

Adding AR graphics content

The final step is to enable the augmented instruction graphic in the scene. These are the same steps we did for mobile VR, but assuming this is a new project, we have to make the changes here. For a more detailed explanation, please read through the integrating augmented content section in this chapter.

Tell `InstructionStep` to read the AR prefab data from the CSV file.

To `InstructionStep.cs`, add a new variable:

```
public string ARPrefabName;
private const int ARColumn = 5;
```

Then add this to the `InstructionStep` constructor function:

```
if (values.IndexOf(item) == ARColumn) {
    ARPrefabName = item;
}
```

Create an ARGraphic.cs script to handle the UIElement events. In your `Scripts/UIElements/` folder, create a C# script named `ARGraphic` and write it as follows:

```
File: ARGraphic.cs
using UnityEngine;

public class ARGraphic : InstructionElement {
    private GameObject currentGraphic;

    protected override void InstructionUpdate(InstructionStep step) {
        Debug.Log("ARGraphic:" + step.ARPrefabName);

        // clear current graphic
        if (currentGraphic != null) {
            Destroy(currentGraphic);
            currentGraphic = null;
        }

        // load step's graphic
        if (!string.IsNullOrEmpty(step.ARPrefabName)) {
            Object data = Resources.Load(step.ARPrefabName,
    typeof(GameObject));
            currentGraphic = Instantiate(data, transform ) as GameObject;
        }
    }
}
```

We need to make sure the instantiated prefab is a child of this (Augmented Instruction) object.

Save your files.

The final step in integrating the AR graphic is to show it in the augmented view.

1. In **Hierarchy**, **Create Empty** object as a child of **Hologram**, and name it `Augmented Instructions`.
2. Reset its **Transform**.
3. Add the **ARGraphic** script as a component.

Because the original graphics were designed for the mobile version of the app, we need to make some Transform adjustments.

1. **Scale**: `0.5, 0.5, 0.5`.
2. **Rotation**: `-90, 0, 0`.
3. **Position**: `0.025, 0.025, 0`.

Save the scene.

Now, when you play and navigate to an instruction step that contains 3D graphics, it will be displayed on the flat tire, along with the 2D instruction content. The following is a depiction of the mixed reality view of our app with my toy truck on my desk:

Summary

For this chapter, we started with the 2D instruction manual project developed in `Chapter 6`, *How to Change a Flat Tire*, and extended it to include augmented reality graphics as a new media type. After preparing the project to use the Vuforia SDK, we first implemented a screen button to toggle **AR Mode**. The AR Model hides the 2D content panel and allows the camera video feed to show.

We set up the project to capture **User Defined Targets**. We added an **AR Prompt** panel with a cursor, circle registration guide, and a **Capture** button. When the button is pressed, the app uses the current view as the AR target and displays the AR content on it. We used Vuforia's Trackable Events to know when to hide **AR Prompt** or to show a red circle as an error prompt if the capture target is of poor quality.

With the AR mode and user-defined targets, we then integrated 3D annotations into the instruction manual. The graphics are prefabs we imported into the project, and one may be instantiated when the user navigates to a step in the instruction manual. We also reviewed how these prefabs can be created, edited, and exported. Lastly, we also brought a copy of the 2D instructions (text, images, and video) into the AR view so that the user does not need to toggle back and forth between 2D and AR modes.

We also showed another way to implement the AR mode on iOS mobile devices using Apple ARKit. Instead of registering the AR graphics in the real world using image targets, we enabled the ARKit's spatial anchors to determine a real-world 3D location. A similar approach can be used on Android using Google ARCore (see our GitHub repository for details).

The chapter also showed how to implement the project for the Microsoft HoloLens wearable AR device. In this version, everything is in world-space coordinates. We created a single hologram that includes the 2D instruction content canvas, the navigation buttons, and the 3D AR graphics. We added an input module so that the *select* gesture can control UI buttons and scroll bar. Then, we added Spatial Mapping for tap to place the hologram in real space.

In the next chapter, we will explore the spatial mapping in even more detail. In that project, we'll virtually decorate your room with framed photos and take a new approach. The chapters starts with a HoloLens implementation and then shows a version for mobile AR.

8
Room Decoration with AR

A common use case of augmented reality (and virtual reality too) is the visualization of models that belong in the real world but aren't there yet. For architects, these may be called preconstruction renderings. For interior designers, they are called visual presentations. Virtual reality is useful when you need to transport the user to this other space virtually. Augmented reality is useful when the user is already in the space and you want to show them something different, to augment the environment.

In addition to design, this also applies to marketing and sales. Ikea and Wayfair, for example, are furniture retailers who offer AR-enabled mobile apps that let you visualize potential furniture purchases, placed in your home where you might want them.

In this chapter, we will build an AR app that lets you decorate your room with personalized framed photos. You'll be able to select a frame from a shopping catalog, then pick from a gallery of photos and place the framed photos on the walls of your room.

For this project, we will mix things up a bit compared with other projects in the book. We start with a Microsoft HoloLens implementation first, since this is a more natural application of wearable see-through AR. Then we will port it to iOS and ARKit. Then we will port it to Android and older iOS devices using Vuforia.

We will learn how AR devices scan your room and create a spatial map mesh. We will then learn how to use this mesh model in augmented reality. The project also shows you how to build 3D user interfaces, including button tools, modal tools, and menus.

In this chapter, you will learn more about the following:

- Building a 3D user interface and elements from scratch
- Understanding spatial mapping for AR
- Using the Microsoft Mixed Reality Toolkit InputManager and Unity GestureRecognizer

- Additional software design patterns, including action-command, inheritance, and input events
- More about using ARKit and Vuforia

 Please refer to the the GitHub repository for this book for completed projects for each platform `https://github.com/ARUnityBook/`. At the time of writing, Google ARCore SDK does not support vertical plane surfaces (only horizontal ones), which inhibits its usability for this project.

The project plan

Imagine an app from a photo frame retailer that lets you choose a frame from their catalog and visualize it, along with your own photos, on the walls of your room. In our demo version of this concept, you are presented with three types of frames and a collection of photos. You can edit the framed photos. Throughout the project we will use the following terminology:

- **Frame** - A photo frame
- **Image** - A photo
- **Picture** - A framed image (frame and image object)

User experience

The app lets you create framed photos (pictures) on your walls. To modify a picture, just click it and an edit toolbar will appear with a variety of editing tools. The tools we will include are as follows:

- Move - Reposition the picture along a wall in the room. Select the tool and drag the picture to a new location.
- Scale - Resize the picture in place. Select the tool and drag to enlarge or shrink the picture.
- Image - Choose an image. Clicking the tool opens the image menu, with a scrollable list of images shown. Clicking an image will place it in the picture frame.
- Frame - Choose a frame. Clicking the tool opens the frame menu, with a list of frames shown. Clicking a frame will replace the frame in the picture.
- Done - Finishes editing and removes the toolbar.

- Cancel - Cancels editing, restores the picture properties (position, size, image, frame) to the state they were in before editing began.
- Delete - Deletes the current picture from the scene.
- Add - Creates a new picture in the scene, ready for editing.

You can place any number of pictures on your walls to enjoy.

Graphic assets

For the project, we provide a Unity package with assets you can use, including sample photos and picture frames. We also provide a `SimpleIcons` package with **prefab** buttons. As explained later in the chapter, you're welcome to use our assets, or create your own.

Photos

Our implementation assumes you are using image texture assets already imported into Unity. The project can be easily adapted to grab photos at runtime from your asset resource folder, from your device's photo stream, or over the web. Note that you do not need large, many-megabyte megapixel photos for the app. The `mountains.jpg` image used throughout this chapter is 1280 x 774 (about 5:3 aspect ratio) and 425KB.

Frames

The photo frames provided for the project for this chapter are shown here:

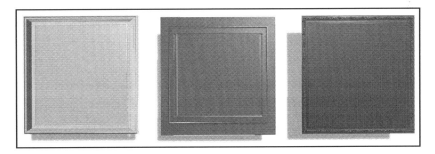

The frames are 3D models, created in Blender. They default to 1 x 1 units square, and we rescale them in Unity for placement in the scene and to fit the images' aspect ratio.

Blender is an open source 3D creation tool for modelling, texturing, animation, and more. We recommend exporting Blender models to FBX format when importing them into Unity. See `https://www.blender.org/` for more information.

User interface elements

For this project, we are going to create several types of the 3D user interface elements commonly used in AR applications, defined as follows:

- Action buttons- Click to trigger one action. This implementation uses an action-command design pattern.
- Manipulation tools - Click and hold to edit an object. This implementation uses an update sequencing design pattern.
- Modal menus - Click to open an option selection menu; click the item in the menu to select it. This implementation uses a modal design pattern.

Each type of UI element is used for different UI activities. We will provide examples of each. For instance, **Delete** is a button tool, **Resize** is a manipulation tool, and **Choose Image** is a modal menu.

And as we will see, each UI element type is implemented with a different software design pattern. The button tool uses an action-command design pattern where clicking (and releasing) once on the button issues a single action; a manipulation tool, such as an object *handle* seen in many graphical editors, is a click-and-drag action, which is implemented using an update sequencing design pattern. Modal menus-implemented using a modal design pattern, where you click a button to open a separate menu-perform one or more actions within that modal menu, closing when the user is done.

Icon buttons

We made some nice Chiclet-style icon button prefabs for use in the toolbar and have provided them with the Unity package for this chapter. We found the icons themselves on the image sharing site Pixabay, created by Raphael Silva (`https://pixabay.com/en/users/raphaelsilva-4702998/`). The icon buttons that we use in the toolbar are shown here:

We created the icon box model itself using Blender. Further, we provide simple animations in the button prefabs that can be played, for example, when the button is clicked. These animations were created directly within Unity.

Setting up the project and scene

To get started, we will create a new Unity project, import the `Asset` packages we will be using, set up our project `Asset` folders, and create a basic scene **Hierarchy** with a default framed image.

Let's get started!

Create a new Unity project

Let's begin implementation by setting up a new project in Unity and getting it ready for AR. The steps here are abridged as it should be familiar to you by now. If you require more detail, please refer to the relevant topics in `Chapter 2`, *Setting Up Your System*, and `Chapter 3`, *Building Your App*:

1. Open Unity and create a 3D project; I named mine `PhotoFrames`.

2. Now is as good a time as any to import the Unity package with the assets for this project. You can download the file `PhotoFramesAssets.unitypackage` from the publisher's website (if you do not have access to the file, we will show you how to create your own substitute assets as needed in this chapter).

   `Images` folders contains the images to show in the app; you can add your own favorites here. `PhotoFrames` contains the frame models and prefabs (simply named `Frame 1`, `Frame 2` and `Frame 3`). The `SimpleIcons` folder contains the icon buttons, including textures, models, animations, and prefabs.

3. Add an `App` folder for stuff we create in the project by navigating to the **Project | Assets** window, and creating a folder named `App` for our application-specific folders.

4. Then, create subfolders named `Materials`, `Prefabs`, `Scenes`, and `Scripts`, as shown here:

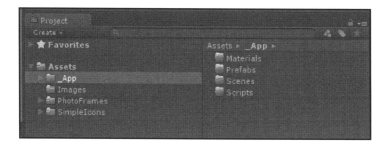

5. Save the scene named `Main` and save the project.

Developing for HoloLens

This implementation of the project will focus on Microsoft HoloLens, using the `MixedRealityToolkit` Unity plugin. As we build the project, we will have the opportunity to explore the toolkit in more depth and with more explanation than in previous chapters:

1. In **File | Build Settings**, first add the scene with **Add Open Scene**.
2. Then **Choose Platform Windows Store**.
3. Import the `MixedRealityToolkit` package (if you haven't downloaded it yet, you can find it at `https://github.com/Microsoft/MixedRealityToolkit-Unity`) using **Assets | Import Package | Custom Package...**.

 Note that the following Unity Editor menu item names may have changed in your version of the toolkit.

4. From the main menu, choose **MixedReality | Configure | Apply HoloLens Project Settings** and reload Unity.
5. From the main menu, choose **MixedReality | Configure | Apply HoloLens Scene Settings** and accept them all.
6. From main menu, choose **MixedReality | Configure | Apply HoloLens Capability Settings** and accept them all.

7. Save the scene and save the project.

 Unlike some of the other projects in this book, we are using MixedRealityToolkit for HoloLens directly. We're not using the Vuforia support for HoloLens. If you want to try the project for both platforms, we recommend that you maintain two separate copies of the project to avoid library conflicts.

8. Add some `MixedRealityToolkit` prefabs to the scene **Hierarchy** for input management, which we'll start using right away in the following way:
    1. From Project `Assets/HoloToolkit/Input/Prefabs`, drag **InputManager** into the **Hierarchy**.
    2. From Project `Assets/HoloToolkit/Input/Prefabs/Cursors`, drag **CursorWithFeedback** into the **Hierarchy**.

Creating default picture

For starters, let's work with just one picture in the scene. We'll name it `DefaultPicture`. `DefaultPicture` will be an object **Hierarchy**. Later, we'll make it a prefab that gets instantiated when the user adds new pictures to the scene.

1. In **Hierarchy**, click **Create Empty** and name it `DefaultPicture`.
2. As a child of **DefaultPicture**, create another **Empty** and name it `FramedImage`.
3. From Project `Assets/PhotoFrames/Prefabs`, drag the **Frame 1** prefab to be a child of **FramedImage**.

If you are not using our frame prefabs, you can make a quick one by creating a cube and creating an appropriately colored material for it, as follows:

1. With **FramedImage** selected, right-click **3D Object | Cube**, and name it `Frame 1`
2. **Scale** the frame to (`1.2, 1.2, 0.02`) **Position** (`0, 0, 0.02`).
3. In the Project `Assets/App/Materials` folder, **Create | Material** and name it `Frame 1`.
4. Give it an interesting color.
5. Drag the **Frame 1** material onto the **Frame 1** object.

4. Add an image. We'll use a quad primitive object with a new *Image* material to hold the `.jpg` texture:
   1. In your Project `Assets/App/Materials` folder, **Create | Material** and name it `Image`.
   2. From the `Assets/Images/` folder, drag the **mountains** texture onto the **Albedo** texture *chip* (left side of the Albedo property).
   3. In **Hierarchy**, with **FramedImage** selected, right-click **3D Object | Quad** and name it `Image`.

5. Drag the **Image** material from the project's `Assets` onto the quad.

   The image appears in the frame, but the frame and image are square. We know that this image is 1280 x 774, or about 1:0.6 aspect ratio.

6. Let's scale the **FramedImage** accordingly (we'll automate this with a script later on) by setting the **FramedImage Transform Scale Y** to `0.6`.

   If you look at the **Game** window right now, it's empty. That is because both the **Main Camera** and the **DefaultPicture** are at the origin, so the camera cannot see it.

7. Let's move the picture out in front of the camera and scale it down a bit as shown ahead (this isn't the Louvre; a one-meter-wide picture is too big for my house!):
   1. Set the **DefaultPicture Transform Position** to 0, 0, `1.6`.
   2. Set its **Scale** to `0.3`, `0.3`, `0.3`.

8. Save the scene.
9. Press **Play** in the Unity Editor to take a look.

As explained in `Chapter 3`, *Building Your App*, you should have your HoloLens set up for development. To use the device from Unity **Play** mode, do the following:

1. Run the **Holographic Remoting player** app on the device (find it in the *bloom* gesture system menu).
2. Then, in Unity, from the main menu, open the **Window | Holographic Emulation**.
3. Choose **Emulation Mode: Remote to Device**, and enter the **Remote Machine IP address** of your HoloLens device (as displayed on its screen).
4. Press **Connect**.

Now you are set up. When you press **Play** in the editor, it will run on your device.

You will see the framed image floating about five feet in front of you, as shown here:

You will also see the cursor, tracked with your head movement. This is the `CursorWithFeedback` cursor controlled using the `InputManager` that we added to the scene. Let's take a closer look at Input Manager and cursors.

About Mixed Reality Toolkit Input Manager

The HoloToolkit Input Manager prefab is an empty (nongraphical) object that includes the components Gaze Manager, Input Manager, and (in a child object) Gestures Input, as well as others. You can open these scripts to read through them and see in detail what they do and how they're implemented.

Gaze Manager

The `GazeManager` provides a useful Unity interface for managing the gaze ray-the user's camera view direction-and its interaction with other objects in the scene. This includes the current *HitInfo* (see `https://docs.unity3d.com/ScriptReference/RaycastHit.html`). `GazeManager` is a singleton class, ensuring that there is only one instance in the scene. In each game update, it gathers the current gaze info and does a physics raycast to see if any objects are at the center of the user's view. It also includes some magic goodness to stabilize the gaze pose for comfort, compensating for the fact that it's tied to your head movement, which may not be as smooth as our visual biology perceives it!

In concert with `GazeManager`, the HoloToolkit provides various cursor prefabs you can include in your project. The `ObjectCursor` component attached to a cursor will make a cursor game object follow the user's gaze. The component has advanced features, such as the ability to position itself at the gaze hit object's distance, *billboard* orienting so that the cursor object always faces the user, and the ability to switch between cursor game objects depending on their state. The `CursorWithFeedback` prefab we use in this project, for example, includes this component.

It is very important for AR comfort and usability to position the cursor on the surface of the object the user is gazing at. Why? Say that you always displayed the cursor at a distance of one meter. If you gaze at an object that is 3 meters away, but the cursor is just 1 meter away, your eyes cannot focus on both at the same time. One will be out of focus, and/or you will experience an *accommodation-convergence* conflict that can be annoying at best and may often cause headaches (see `https://www.wired.com/2015/08/obscure-neuroscience-problem-thats-plaguing-vr/`). MixedRealityToolkit handles this for you by positioning the cursor at the hit point of any object you are looking at.

Input Manager

The HoloToolkit `InputManager` is a singleton responsible for managing input sources and dispatching corresponding events to the various input handlers. Input sources for HoloLens include gestures and voice commands.

MixedRealityToolkit provides a number of different input event handler components, some of which we'll be using in this project. For example, `IInputClickHandler` provides an interface for *click* events, like those generated when the user does a *select* hand gesture (pinching the forefinger and thumb together). The input handlers can be found in the `HoloToolkit/Input/Scripts/InputEvents/` folder, a summary of which is shown ahead.

Mixed Reality Toolkit input events

Handler	Description	Events	Data structure
IFocusable	Reacts to focus enter/exit	`OnFocusEnter` `OnFocusExit`	

IHoldHandler	Reacts to hold gestures	`OnHoldStarted`
		`OnHoldCompleted`
		`OnHoldCanceled`
			Hold EventData

IInputClickHandler	Reacts to simple click input	`OnInputClicked`	InputClicked EventData

IManipulationHandler	Reacts to manipulation gestures	`OnManipulationStarted`
		`OnManipulationUpdated`
		`OnManipulationCompleted`
		`OnManipulationCanceled`
			Manipulation EventData

INavigationHandler	Reacts to navigation gestures	`OnNavigationStarted`
		`OnNavigationUpdated`
		`OnNavigationCompleted`
		`OnNavigationCanceled`
			Navigation EventData

ISourceStateHandler	Reacts to source state changes	`OnSourceDetected` `OnSourceLost`	SourceState EventData
ISpeechHandler	Reacts to speech recognition	`OnSpeechKeyword` `Recognized`	SpeechKeyword Recognized EventData

`InputManager` provides a generic interface to various input sources supported by the HoloLens device. Notably, this includes gestures and speech. The code that implements the gesture input source is `GesturesInput`.

The `GesturesInput` class is a wrapper on top of the Unity built-in `GestureRecognizer` class. `GestureRecognizer` is part of the `UnityEngine.VR.WSA.Input` library, Microsoft's mixed reality Windows Store Apps input SDK. The `GesturesInput` is used by `InputManager` as the gesture input source.

The 3D UI system elements that we build in this project include scripts that illustrate using these input events.

Creating a toolbar framework

The first thing we'll do is create a simplistic toolbar framework that supports editing pictures using the various types of input elements-action buttons, manipulation tools, and modal menus. Our framework will require us to create the following components:

- `PictureController`: A component on the root parent Picture object that maintains the state of the picture editing
- `PictureAction` - A component on buttons and other clickable objects that sends commands to the `PictureController`
- `PictureMenu` - A component on modal menus where users can choose from a list of objects
- `ClickableObject` - A utility component used by the `PictureMenu` to handle selection events

We will implement the first two now. The menu components will be introduced when we get to the Frame and Image selection menus later on.

For the moment, we will implement a simple mechanism. The `PictureController` manages picture updates based on user commands through the UI as the picture is being edited. When you click on a picture in the scene, a toolbar appears. The toolbar will have a **Done** button, which tells the controller to stop editing and closes the toolbar. We'll add more buttons and features later.

Create a toolbar

To begin, create a toolbar object under `DefaultPicture` that will contain our icon buttons. We add one button: the **Done** button:

1. With **DefaultPicture** selected in **Hierarchy**, click **Create Empty** and name it `Toolbar`.
2. Set its **Position** to (0, 0.4, -0.1) so that it's near the top of the picture and a little in front.
3. From `Assets/SimpleIcons/Prefabs/` drag the **DoneButton** prefab into **Hierarchy** as a child of **Toolbar**
4. Set its **Position X** to 0.45, placing it in the upper right of the picture.

If you are not using the `SimpleIcons` package we provided, you can just add a cube with the scale (0.1, 0.1, 0.04), and name it `DoneButton`.

PictureController component

The `PictureController` manages picture editing commands from the UI. Our picture editor can perform various actions on a picture object. These are enumerated in the `PictureComand` enum. We will design it to encapsulate the implementation of the commands and only expose them through a single `Execute()` API function.

1. In your Project `Assets/App/Scripts/` folder, create a C# script named `PictureController`
2. Open it for editing and you will see the following:

```
File: PictureController.cs
using UnityEngine;

public enum PictureCommand { ADD, EDIT, DONE, CANCEL, MOVE, SCALE, DELETE,
IMAGE, FRAME }

public class PictureController : MonoBehaviour {
    public GameObject toolbar;
    void Start() {
        BeginEdit();
    }

    public void Execute(PictureCommand command) {
        switch (command) {
            case PictureCommand.EDIT:
                BeginEdit();
                break;

            case PictureCommand.DONE:
                DoneEdit();
                break;
        }
    }

    private void BeginEdit() {
        toolbar.SetActive(true);
    }

    private void DoneEdit() {
        toolbar.SetActive(false);
    }
}
```

At the top of the file, we declare the `public enum PictureCommand` that is used in this component, as well as the `PictureAction` component that triggers the commands. The `BeginEdit` and `DoneEdit` functions are called via the `Execute` `switch` statement. We also call `BeginEdit` from `Start()` so that a new picture will always start in the editing state.

3. Drag the **PictureController** onto the **DefaultPicture** object in **Hierarchy**.
4. Then drag the **Toolbar** object from **Hierarchy** onto its **Toolbar** slot.

PictureAction component

The **PictureAction** component, which should send an action-command to the `PictureController` when clicked will be added to the object. Create a new C# script in your `Scripts` folder named `PictureAction` and open it for editing. You will see the following:

```
File: PictureAction.cs
using UnityEngine;
using HoloToolkit.Unity.InputModule;

public class PictureAction : MonoBehaviour, IInputClickHandler {
    public PictureCommand command;
    protected PictureController picture;

    void Start() {
        picture = GetComponentInParent<PictureController>();
    }

    public void OnInputClicked(InputClickedEventData eventData) {
        picture.Execute(command);
    }
}
```

The `PictureAction` responds to `OnInputClicked` events. Using a HoloLens, these events are generated when it recognizes the user doing a finger-thumb pinch *select* gesture. The `Start()` function finds the parent `PictureController`. Then, when a user clicks, it simply sends its command to the controller.

Wire up the actions

When the user clicks a picture, they activate it for editing. When the user clicks the **Done** button, it stops editing. Let's wire this up:

1. Add the **PictureAction** component to the **FramedImage** object in **DefaultPicture**.
2. Set its **Command** to **EDIT**.
3. Add the **PictureAction** component to the **DoneButton** object in the **Toolbar**.
4. Set its **Command** to **DONE**.
5. Add a collider which the **FrameImage** needs to receive events from **InputManager** as shown ahead:
    1. When **FramedImage** is selected, **Add Component** then **Box Collider**.
    2. Set the **Center** to (0, 0, 0.05).
    3. Set the **Size** to (1, 1, 0.1).
6. Save your work and press **Play**. When you click the **Done** button, the toolbar should be deactivated and disappear. When you click the picture, the toolbar reappears. The scene with our (one-button) toolbar now looks like this:

Let's start adding some editing capability to our app.

Move tool, with spatial mapping

The first editing feature we'll add to the project is a tool for moving the picture into place on walls in your room. This will take advantage of the HoloLens spatial mapping capability. Let's add it first, then look at spatial mapping in more detail.

The plan is to enable positioning when the user clicks the **Move** button. Clicking again will cancel the **Move** command. Specifically, the **Move** tool will work like this:

- Pressing the button will activate the **Move** manipulation mode. The button will grow enlarged to show it is activated.
- As you move your gaze, the button acts like a *handle* on the picture object. The picture follows your gaze to move to a new position.
- The tool uses spatial mapping to detect vertical surfaces in your environment, which we'll assume to be a wall (you don't want to hang the picture on the floor or ceiling!).
- Clicking the tool one more time deactivates **Move** mode, restores the icon button to its normal size, and leaves the picture in its new position.

This is a type of *update sequencing* design pattern.

Add the Move button and script

First, let's add the `MoveButton` prefab to the toolbar.

1. From `Assets/SimpleIcons/Prefabs/`, drag the **MoveButton** prefab into **Hierarchy** as a child of **Toolbar**.

   If you are not using the `SimpleIcons` package we provided, you can just add a cube with the scale (`0.1, 0.1, 0.04`) and name it `MoveButton`.

2. Now let's write the `MoveTool.cs` script for the button.
3. In your `Scripts` folder, create a new C# script, name it `MoveTool`, and open it for editing.
4. Start to write the script as follows:

```
File: MoveTool.cs
using UnityEngine;
using HoloToolkit.Unity.InputModule;

public class MoveTool : MonoBehaviour, IInputClickHandler {
```

```
    private bool isEditing;
    private Vector3 originaButtonScale;
    private BoxCollider collider;
    private Vector3 originColliderSize;

    void Start() {
        isEditing = false;
        originaButtonScale = transform.localScale;
        collider = GetComponent<BoxCollider>();
        originColliderSize = collider.size;
    }

    public void OnInputClicked(InputClickedEventData eventData) {
        if (!isEditing) {
            BeginEdit();
        } else {
            DoneEdit();
        }
    }

    private void BeginEdit() {
        if (!isEditing) {
            isEditing = true;
            transform.localScale = originaButtonScale * 2.5f;
            collider.size = Vector3.one;
        }
    }

    private void DoneEdit() {
        if (isEditing) {
            isEditing = false;
            transform.localScale = originaButtonScale;
            collider.size = originColliderSize;
        }
    }
}
```

The first thing we do is declare that we're using the
HoloToolkit.Unity.InputModule library, and then specify the
IInputClickHandler interface on the class declaration. The interface expects us
to define an OnInputClicked method.

Clicking the tool will activate it, setting `isEditing` to true. Clicking the tool again will toggle off `isEditing`. Our private `BeginEdit` and `DoneEdit` methods toggle this flag, and for now, it just enlarges the `MoveButton` object when active.

We also modify the box collider while editing. Although we intend to keep the button object in the middle of our gaze while moving the picture to its new position, we want to ensure the second click is received by this tool. Other factors also explain why we would want to have an oversized collider while editing, including the fact that it prevents other toolbar buttons from being clicked; the visual parallax of the camera view direction may make the gaze ray not actually hit the button object, and, potentially, the moved picture could fall behind miscellaneous triangle faces on the mesh and not receive the click event. For these reasons we temporarily set the box collider size to (1, 1, 1).

5. Save the script.
6. Drag the script onto the **MoveButton**.
7. Save the scene.
8. Press **Play**.

When you gaze at the button and do the HoloLens "select" (finger-thumb pinch gesture), the button should enlarge. Click it again and it goes back to normal.

Use Spatial Mapping for positioning

To actually move the picture with the tool and have it attached to the walls, we are going to need the `SpatialMapping` prefab from MixedRealityToolkit. Its *Spatial Mapping Manager* component controls the scanning and display of the room model mesh. The HoloLens uses depth sensing technology in the device to build a 3D geometric mesh of your local environment, what is called a **Room Model**. This mesh is added to your scene as a game object (children of the **SpatialMapping** object), and resides on a separate layer-Layer 31 by default-and it is specified in the physics layer. The **SpatialMapping Inspector** is shown here:

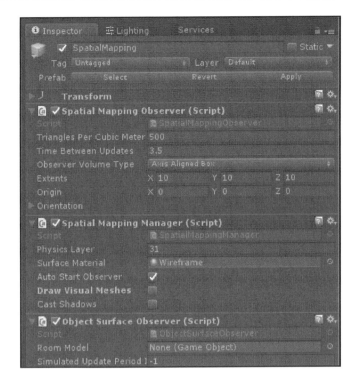

Let's add it now:

1. From Project `Assets/HoloToolkit/SpatialMapping/Prefabs`, drag **SpatialMapping** into **Hierarchy**.

2. In **Inspector**, in the **Spatial Mapping Manager**, uncheck the **Draw Visual Meshes** checkbox.

   If you want, leave **Draw Visual Meshes** checked and **Play** the scene. You will see that the meshes generate in view. We will control the display of the visual mesh with our script, so uncheck it, but leave the **Auto Start Observer** checked so that the device will begin capturing the mesh when the app starts. Let's add that now.

3. Add the following code:

   ```
   using HoloToolkit.Unity.SpatialMapping;
   ```

4. In addition, add the following code:

```
private SpatialMappingManager spatialMapping;

void Start() {
    ...
    spatialMapping = SpatialMappingManager.Instance;
}
private void BeginEdit() {
    if (!isEditing) {
        ...
        spatialMapping.DrawVisualMeshes = true;
    }
}
private void DoneEdit() {
    if (isEditing) {
        ...
        spatialMapping.DrawVisualMeshes = false;
    }
}
```

5. Press **Play** and select the **Move** button; the button enlarges and the spatial mesh is displayed, as shown here (from the **Scene** window view):

Now all we need to do is write the Update() function that positions the picture. It will get the current head position and gaze direction from the camera, find where it hits a wall, and position the picture at that point. It will also rotate the picture to be flat against the wall, using the normal vector of the hit point.

To accomplish this, we need to initialize the tool with a reference to the root picture object and the relative offset of the button with respect to the picture's anchor point. Since the picture object, `DefaultPicture`, has a `PictureController` component, and we know it's the only one in this hierarchy, we can find it with a call to `GetComponentInParent`.

6. At the top of the class, add the following variables:

```
private PictureController picture;
private Vector3 relativeOffset;
private float upNormalThreshold = 0.9f;
```

7. Initialize them in `Start()`:

```
void Start() {
    ...
    picture = GetComponentInParent<PictureController>();
    relativeOffset = transform.position - picture.transform.position;
    relativeOffset.z = - relativeOffset.z;
}
```

8. Then add `Update()` as follows:

```
void Update() {
    if (isEditing) {
        Vector3 headPosition = Camera.main.transform.position;
        Vector3 gazeDirection = Camera.main.transform.forward;
        int layerMask = 1 << spatialMapping.PhysicsLayer;
        RaycastHit hitInfo;
        if (Physics.Raycast(headPosition, gazeDirection, out hitInfo,
30.0f, layerMask)) {
            picture.transform.position = hitInfo.point -
relativeOffset; // keep tool in gaze
            Vector3 surfaceNormal = hitInfo.normal;
            if (Mathf.Abs(surfaceNormal.y) <= (1 - upNormalThreshold))
{
                picture.transform.rotation = Quaternion.LookRotation(-
surfaceNormal, Vector3.up);
            }
        }
    }
}
```

The call to `Physics.Raycast` determines if and where the gaze vector intersects the spatial map (on the `spatialMapping.PhysicsLayer`). The hit point is used to set the picture's transform position. To keep the Move button in the middle of our gaze we set the picture position with a relative offset distance. Then, using the surface normal at the hit point (`hitinfo.normal`), we set the picture transform rotation.

Press **Play** and try it. You may find that the wall mesh sometimes obscures the picture as it moves around. This is because the spatial map's mesh has noise, and some vertices extrude from the true surface normal. We can temporarily compensate by offsetting the `FramedImage` from the DefaultPicture's anchor point by setting the **FramedImage Position Z** to -0.1 to offset it a little from the picture's anchor point.

An even better solution is to use the `SurfacePlane` prefab. Let's see how that would work.

Understanding surface planes

As mentioned previously, the spatial map mesh is a triangle mesh subject to noise in the device's depth sensing and mesh generating technology. But since we're not looking for complex geometric shapes (like furniture or other objects), we can safely apply algorithms to simplify the mesh into surface planes. HoloToolkit includes spatial processing and interpreting components to assist with this.

The key to it is the `SurfaceMeshesToPlanes` component (found in the `Holotoolkit/SpatialMapping/Scripts/SpatialProcessing` folder). Add this component to your **SpatialMapping** object in **Hierarchy**. The component takes a number of parameters, including a `SurfacePlane` prefab that it uses to replace mesh geometry with any planar surfaces it discovers. The `SpatialMapping/Prefabs` folder includes a prefab `SurfacePlane` you can drag onto the component slot. You can also specify which types of planes you're interested in: Wall, Floor, Ceiling, and/or Table. The following are some example settings for a `SurfaceMeshesToPlane` component and a `SurfacePlane` prefab to detect and draw only the walls. The `SurfaceMeshesToPlanes` component is shown here:

As shown here, we've created a new **Wall Material**, named `Wall` to highlight the wall planes that are detected (the material uses a translucent yellow-ish hue). It will be used in the `SurfacePlane` component:

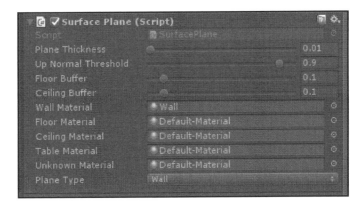

For more information on using these components, see the following:

- Holograms 230 Tutorial:
  `https://developer.microsoft.com/en-us/windows/mixed-reality/holograms_230`
- HoloToolkit Spatial Understanding:
  `https://github.com/Microsoft/MixedRealityHoloToolkit/wiki/HoloToolkit.SpatialUnderstanding`

Scale tool with Gesture Recognizer

The next tool we'll implement is the **Scale** tool that lets you resize the picture. Like the **Move** tool, it uses an *update sequencing* design pattern to implement a modal manipulation tool. However, we'll use a different user scenario, and a different underlying implementation.

The **Scale** tool will work like this:

- Pressing and holding the button using the finger-thumb pinch gesture will activate the scale manipulation mode. The button will grow enlarged to show it is activated.
- As you continue to hold the pinch gesture and move your gaze to the right, the picture object gets bigger. Move your gaze to the left and the picture shrinks.

- Releasing the pinch gesture (unclicking the button) deactivates **Move** mode, restores the button icon to its normal size, and leaves the picture in its new position.

So, this tool provides an example that operates differently than the **Move** tool. With the **Move** tool, you click once (and release) to begin moving, and then click again to stop. This tool will be a click-and-hold operation instead.

Also, we use this example to show a different way of accessing HoloLens input events. In our other UI elements, we use the `InputManager` and, specifically, the `IInputClickHandler` interface to respond to `OnInputClicked` events. For the **Scale** tool, we use the lower level, Unity built-in `GestureRecognizer` class. (See the Unity API manual `https://docs.unity3d.com/ScriptReference/VR.WSA.Input.GestureRecognizer.html`). To use `GestureRecognizer`, you specify which gesture types you want to capture, and then register callback functions to be called when one of those events occurs.

Adding the scale button and script

First, let's add the `ScaleButton` prefab to the toolbar:

1. From `Assets/SimpleIcons/Prefabs/` drag the **ScaleButton** prefab into **Hierarchy** as a child of **Toolbar**.
2. Set its **Transform Position X** to −`0.15`.

    If you are not using the `SimpleIcons` package we provided, you can just add a cube with the scale (`0.1, 0.1, 0.04`), and name it `ScaleButton`.

3. Now let's write the `ScaleTool.cs` script for the button. In your `Scripts` folder, create a new C# script, name it `ScaleTool`, and open it for editing.

    First, we will capture an initial pinch-gesture, much like the `OnInputClicked` we used before, to begin editing. We will also define the completed or cancelled events for when we are done editing.

    1. Start to write the script as follows:

```
File: ScaleTool.cs
using UnityEngine;
using UnityEngine.VR.WSA.Input;
```

```
public class ScaleTool : MonoBehaviour {
    private PictureController picture;
    private Vector3 originaButtonScale;

    private GestureRecognizer scaleRecognizer;
    private bool isEditing;
    void Start() {
        picture = GetComponentInParent<PictureController>();
        originaButtonScale = transform.localScale;

        scaleRecognizer = new GestureRecognizer();
scaleRecognizer.SetRecognizableGestures(GestureSettings.ManipulationTransla
te);

        scaleRecognizer.ManipulationStartedEvent += OnStartedEvent;
        scaleRecognizer.ManipulationUpdatedEvent += OnUpdatedEvent;
        scaleRecognizer.ManipulationCompletedEvent += OnCompletedEvent;
        scaleRecognizer.ManipulationCanceledEvent += OnCanceledEvent;
        scaleRecognizer.StartCapturingGestures();
        isEditing = false;
    }
```

2. The following helper functions are called when the user begins and
   ends the editing mode:

```
private void BeginEdit() {
    transform.localScale = originaButtonScale * 2.5f;
    isEditing = true;
}

private void DoneEdit() {
    transform.localScale = originaButtonScale;
    isEditing = false;
}
```

3. Remove the event handlers (opposite of `Start()`) as a matter of
   housekeeping when this object is destroyed:

```
private void OnDestroy() {
    scaleRecognizer.StopCapturingGestures();
    scaleRecognizer.ManipulationStartedEvent -= OnStartedEvent;
    scaleRecognizer.ManipulationUpdatedEvent -= OnUpdatedEvent;
    scaleRecognizer.ManipulationCompletedEvent -= OnCompletedEvent;
    scaleRecognizer.ManipulationCanceledEvent -= OnCanceledEvent;
}
```

4. Define the event handlers for start, update, complete, and cancel:

```
    private void OnStartedEvent(InteractionSourceKind source, Vector3
position, Ray ray) {
Camera.main.transform.forward);
        if (!isEditing) {
            RaycastHit hitInfo;
            if (Physics.Raycast(Camera.main.transform.position,
Camera.main.transform.forward, out hitInfo)) {
                if (hitInfo.collider.gameObject == gameObject) {
                    BeginEdit();
                }
            }
        }
    }

    private void OnUpdatedEvent(InteractionSourceKind source, Vector3
position, Ray ray) {
    }

    private void OnCompletedEvent(InteractionSourceKind source, Vector3
position, Ray ray) {
        if (isEditing) {
            DoneEdit();
        }
    }

    private void OnCanceledEvent(InteractionSourceKind source, Vector3
position, Ray ray) {
        if (isEditing) {
            DoneEdit();
        }
    }
}
```

In this script, we're using the `UnityEngine.VR.WSA.Input` library. Like the **Move** tool, we keep a variable for the `PictureController` and original button scale, and initialize those in `Start()`.

We also have a `GestureRecognizer` that is initialized in `Start()`, registering our handler functions. Then we tell it to start capturing gestures.

When a pinch gesture is detected, `OnStartedEvent` is called. It checks if the click event pertains to us-that is, we use the camera gaze vector to determine if the user is looking at this object when the event was detected. If so, we will call `BeginEdit()`.

`BeginEdit()` resizes the **Scale** button object. We've also written a corresponding `DoneEdit()` and `OnDestroy()`, which reverses and cleans up the initializations. The `isEditing` flag tracks whether this component has been started, since we don't want to track Manipulation events started elsewhere.

Press **Play** and select the **Scale** button with a pinch gesture. It will enlarge. Release the gesture and it will go back to normal size. Pinch again and move your hand outside of the device's view-it will again go back to normal size, this time because the `OnCanceledEvent` was detected.

Scaling the picture

Now we can scale the picture after each update. We will use a simple hack that ties head movement (gaze direction) to the object scale. Rather than literally casting a ray to determine a size based on gaze hit point, we'll use the head direction angle as a relative scaling factor (much like a pinch gesture is used to scale on a touch screen). By trial and error, we've decided to scale the object by 10% for each degree of head movement.

The object in our **Hierarchy** that is to be scaled is not the root `Picture` object itself, but the `FramedImage` object. The tool needs to know this, and will ask the `PictureController` for a reference to this object. Modify `PictureController` as follows:

```
File: PictureController.cs
    public Transform framedImage;
```

Then populate the framedImage slot:

Then drag the **FramedImage** object from **Hierarchy** into the DefaultPicture's **Picture Controller Framed Image** slot.

Now, back in `ScaleTool.cs`, we will capture the starting gaze direction when we begin editing. On each update, calculate the angle from this starting gaze direction to the current gaze direction. We also capture the starting picture scale for our calculation of the new scale. Add these variables to the top of the class:

```
File: ScaleTool.cs
    private Vector3 startGazeDirection;
    private Vector3 startScale;
```

Initialize them in `BeginEdit()`:

```
private void BeginEdit() {
    startGazeDirection = Camera.main.transform.forward;
    startScale = picture.framedImage.transform.localScale;

    transform.localScale = originaButtonScale * 2.5f;
    isEditing = true;
}
```

Lastly, write `OnUpdatedEvent` to modify the scale in proportion to the delta head angle:

```
private void OnUpdatedEvent(InteractionSourceKind source, Vector3
position, Ray ray) {
    if (isEditing) {
        float angle = AngleSigned(startGazeDirection,
Camera.main.transform.forward, Vector3.up);
        float scale = 1.0f + angle * 0.1f;
        if (scale > 0.1f) {
            picture.framedImage.transform.localScale = startScale *
scale;
        }
    }
}

// Determine the signed angle between two vectors, with normal 'n' as
the rotation axis
private float AngleSigned(Vector3 v1, Vector3 v2, Vector3 n) {
    return Mathf.Atan2(
        Vector3.Dot(n, Vector3.Cross(v1, v2)),
        Vector3.Dot(v1, v2)) * Mathf.Rad2Deg;
}
```

Note that we've added a helper function, `AngleSigned`, that does the angle calculation for us (*Google is your friend* if you're not a math wizard; that's how we found this code). We also prevent the user from scaling the picture to zero or a negative value.

That's it! Press **Play**, select the **Scale** tool, hold the pinch gesture, move your head to scale, release the pinch gesture. Tada!! A augmented reality capture of me scaling an image is shown here:

We purposely are not scaling the toolbar with the picture so it remains a usable size. But at this point you could consider moving the toolbar position so that it's still aligned with the (new) top of the picture frame. We'll leave that exercise up to you.

Supporting Cancel

What if you move or scale or otherwise change the picture and don't like it? The toolbar has a **Done** button; we should add a **Cancel** button. **Cancel** will reset the picture parameters to the values it had before this editing session started. This will be handed in the `PictureController` component.

Presently, the attributes of the picture we've been editing are **FramedImage Transform**. In Unity, you need to save them as three separate values for position, rotation, and scale. We will save the starting transform values when we begin editing, and restore them if we cancel editing.

At the top of the class, add the following to `PictureController`:

```
File: PictureController.cs
    private Vector3 startPosition;
    private Vector3 startScale;
    private Quaternion startRotation;
```

Then add these helper functions:

```
private void SavePictureProperties() {
    startPosition = transform.localPosition;
    startScale = transform.localScale;
    startRotation = transform.localRotation;
}

private void RestorePictureProperties() {
    transform.localPosition = startPosition;
    transform.localScale = startScale;
    transform.localRotation = startRotation;
}
```

Call the `SavePictureProperties` from `BeginEdit`:

```
private void BeginEdit() {
    SavePictureProperties();
    toolbar.SetActive(true);
}
```

Add a new function, `CancelEdit`:

```
private void CancelEdit() {
    RestorePictureProperties();
    toolbar.SetActive(false);
}
```

In the `Execute` function, add a case for CANCEL as follows:

```
case PictureCommand.CANCEL:
    CancelEdit();
    break;
```

Save the `PictureController.cs` script.

Go back to Unity. Add the **CancelButton** and set up its `PictureTool` as follows:

1. From `Assets/SimpleIcons/Prefabs/` drag the **CancelButton** prefab into the **Hierarchy** as a child of **Toolbar**.
2. Set its **Position X** to `0.3`.
3. Add the **PictureAction** component to the **DoneButton** object in the **Toolbar**.
4. Set its **Command** to **CANCEL**.

Try it out. Press **Play**, modify the picture, then press **Cancel** in the toolbar. The picture should return to its pre-edit version.

Abstract selection menu UI

The next feature we want to add is the ability to choose different frames and photo images for your pictures. For this, we'll develop a menu element using a *modal* design pattern. When a menu is activated, the user is presented with a set of choices. When a choice is selected, the choice is applied and the menu closes. It is modal because the menu remains active until the user has made his or her choice.

We will begin by writing an abstract `PictureMenu` class that implements the basic functionality of a menu. Then we'll use it for selecting the frames and images of the picture.

In our framework, a menu will be enabled by making it active in the Unity scene (using `SetActive`). When an object is activated, Unity will call `OnEnable()`, which we can use to begin using the menu. The abstract `PictureMenu` class expects the following methods in the derived classes:

- `InitMenu`: Initialization code; called from `Start()`
- *BeginEdit*: When the menu is opened; called from `OnEnable()`
- `ObjectClicked`: When a menu item is selected; called when a clickable object event is triggered
- *DoneEdit*: When a menu is done; should be called from `ObjectClicked` as appropriate

The menu items will have a `ClickableObject` component. When the object is clicked, it will invoke a `OnClickableObjectclicked` event, passing the game object selected, which the menu handles in its `ObjectClicked` function. So first let's implement that:

1. Create a new C# script in your `Scripts` folder named `ClickableObject` and open it for editing:

```
File: ClickableObject.cs
using UnityEngine;
using UnityEngine.Events;
using HoloToolkit.Unity.InputModule;

public class ClickableObjectEvent : UnityEvent<GameObject> { }

public class ClickableObject : MonoBehaviour, IInputClickHandler {
    public ClickableObjectEvent OnClickableObjectClicked = new
ClickableObjectEvent();

    public void OnInputClicked(InputClickedEventData eventData) {
```

```
        OnClickableObjectClicked.Invoke(gameObject);
    }
}
```

The script declares a `ClickableObjectEvent` as a `UnityEvent`. Using the toolkit `InputManager`, when the current object is clicked, `OnInputClicked` will invoke the `OnClickableObjectClicked` event that the menu will get.

It is important to note that any objects using the `IInputClickHandler` (or any `InputManager` events, for that matter) must have a collider for the `InputManager` and `GazeManager` to detect what object is selected. You can see now why we need to make sure any clickable menu items have a collider.

Now we can write the PictureMenu class.

2. Create a new C# script in your `Scripts` folder named `PictureMenu` and open it for editing:

```
File: PictureMenu.cs
using UnityEngine;

public abstract class PictureMenu : MonoBehaviour {
    public ClickableObject[] clickableObjects;

    protected PictureController picture;
    protected GameObject toolbar;

    void Start() {
        SubscribeClickableObjects();
        InitMenu();
    }

    void OnEnable() {
        Debug.Log("PictureMenu: OnEnable");
        picture = GetComponentInParent<PictureController>();
        picture.toolbar.SetActive(false);
        BeginEdit();
    }

    public abstract void InitMenu();
    public abstract void BeginEdit();
    public abstract void ObjectClicked(GameObject clickedGameObject);

    public void DoneEdit() {
        Debug.Log("PictureMenu: DoneEdit");
        picture.toolbar.SetActive(true);
        gameObject.SetActive(false);
```

```
    }

    public void SubscribeClickableObjects() {
        for (int i = 0; i < clickableObjects.Length; i++) {
clickableObjects[i].OnClickableObjectClicked.AddListener(ObjectClicked);
        }
    }

}
```

As already explained, the `PictureMenu` maintains a list of clickable menu items (`ClickableObjects`) and subscribes them to the `ObjectClicked` function. We will use this class next as we implement a frame selection menu.

Adding the frame menu

Our **Frame** menu will present a list of three picture frames. When the user chooses one, it will replace the current frame used in the picture. It will work like this;

- User selects the **Frame** button from the toolbar, which opens (displays) the **Frame** menu
- User selects one of the frames from the list of clickable frame objects
- The menu tells the `PictureController` to set the selected frame in the picture
- The `Frame` menu is closed (hidden)

The menu will call `SetFrame` in `PictureController`. This function will replace the current frame object in `FramedImage` with the selected one. How does it know which child object of `FramedImage` is the frame (and not the image)? There are a number of ways to implement this, using tags or layers, for example. We will take the approach of parenting the `FramedImage` frame with a new object named `FrameSpawn`:

1. In **Hierarchy**, under **FramedImage**, click **Create Empty** and name it `FrameSpawn`.
2. Move the **Frame 1** object in **FramedImage** as a child of **FrameSpawn**.

The **FramedImage** in **Hierarchy** now looks like this:

Now let's write the `PictureController` code that will be called from the menu when the user selects a new frame.

SetFrame in PictureController

The `PictureController` will expose a method `SetFrame()` that takes a frame game object as a parameter. It will delete the existing frame in the `FramedImage` and spawn (add) the selected one instead. Make the following additions to the `PictureController.cs` script.

At the top of the class, add a variable for the frame spawn:

```
File: PictureController.cs
    private Renderer imageRenderer;
```

Initialize this in `Start()`. We already have a reference to the `framedImage`, so it's safe to just find its child **Image**:

```
void Start() {
    ...
    Transform image = framedImage.Find("Image");
    imageRenderer = image.gameObject.GetComponent<Renderer>();
```

Now we can write the public function `SetFrame` as follows:

```
public void SetFrame(GameObject frameGameObject) {
    GameObject currentFrame = GetCurrentFrame();
    if (currentFrame != null)
        Destroy(currentFrame);

    GameObject newFrame = Instantiate(frameGameObject, frameSpawn);
    newFrame.transform.localPosition = Vector3.zero;
    newFrame.transform.localEulerAngles = Vector3.zero;
    newFrame.transform.localScale = Vector3.one;
}

private GameObject GetCurrentFrame() {
    Transform currentFrame = frameSpawn.GetChild(0);
    if (currentFrame != null) {
        return currentFrame.gameObject;
    }
    return null;
}
```

We also added a helper function to get the current frame as the first (and only) child of **FrameSpawn**. SetFrame gets the current frame and deletes it. Then it creates a new frame based on the one selected from the menu and resets its transform.

The next step is to build the menu itself.

The FrameMenu object and component

The FrameMenu object is an empty game object container that will have its selected option objects as children.

1. In **Hierarchy**, under **DefaultPicture**, click **Create Empty** game object and name it FrameMenu.
2. Set its **Position** (0, -0.5, -0.1) so it's at the bottom of the picture and a little in the front.
3. Now we write the FrameMenu script component. In your Scripts folder, create a C# script named FrameMenu and open it for editing:

```
File: FrameMenu.cs
using UnityEngine;

public class FrameMenu : PictureMenu {

    public override void InitMenu() {
    }
    public override void BeginEdit() {
    }

    public override void ObjectClicked(GameObject clickedGameObject) {
        GameObject frame =
clickedGameObject.transform.GetChild(0).gameObject;
        picture.SetFrame(frame);
        DoneEdit(); // close menu when one pic is picked
    }
}
```

The FrameMenu class is derived from PictureMenu, which we wrote earlier. It doesn't do much. The InitMenu and BeginEdit functions do nothing. The ObjectClicked gets the frame game object and passes it to the controller SetFrame. Then the menu is closed by calling DoneEdit.

Frame options objects

Next, we add the menu selection options as child objects of the `FrameMenu` and make them clickable.

Earlier in the chapter, you may have installed the `PhotoFrames` assets with the chapter's Unity package. If not, you can go ahead and create a couple more, the same way that you created the first one back in the recipe *Create default picture* in the *Setting up the project and scene* section. For example, you may create a cube, scale it to (1.2, 1.2, 0.02), with the **Position** set to (0, 0, 0.02), and create and assign it a colored **Material**. Save them as prefabs named `Frame 1`, `Frame 2`, and `Frame 3`.

Because the menu options are clickable, receiving input events, they must have colliders. We'll handle this by parenting the actual frame prefabs with the menu item objects named `Frame A`, `Frame B`, and `Frame C`.

Follow these steps to create the menu game objects:

1. With **FrameMenu** selected in the **Hierarchy**, click **Create Empty**, and name it `Frame A`.
2. From the Project `Assets/PhotoFrames/Prefabs/` folder, drag the **Frame 1** prefab as a child of **Frame A**.
3. Make sure **Frame A** is still selected and set its **Scale** to (0.25, 0.25, 0.25).
4. Set its **Position X** to −0.35.
5. Add the **ClickableObject** component to it.

Repeat the preceding steps for `Frame B` (Frame 2) and `Frame C` (Frame 3). Position them horizontally at **X** 0.0 and 0.35, respectively.

Now populate the `FrameMenu` component with the frame objects we just created:

1. Select **FrameMenu** in the **Hierarchy**.
2. Enter 3 for **Clickable Objects Size**.
3. Drag each of its child **Frame** objects into the corresponding **Clickable Object Element** slot in the **FrameMenu** component, as shown here:

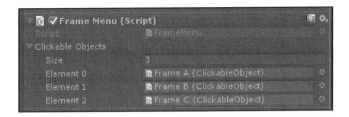

We now have a `FrameMenu`, with clickable child frames for the user to pick. The scene now looks like this:

Let's try it out.

1. Save your files and the current scene.
2. Press **Play**.

You should see the **Frames** menu. Select one of the frames and it will replace the current frame in the picture.

Activating the frame menu

The **Frame** menu should not be visible until the user activates it. We can add this command to the `PictureController` and activate it from the toolbar. Add the FRAME command to `PictureController` script, as follows:

```
File: PictureController.cs
```

At the top of the `PictureController` class add a public variable for the `frameMenu` as follows:

```
public GameObject frameMenu;
```

In its `Execute()` function's switch statement, add:

```
case PictureCommand.FRAME:
    OpenFrameMenu();
    break;
```

Then add the action function:

```
private void OpenFrameMenu() {
    frameMenu.SetActive(true);
}
```

Save the file. Now go back to Unity:

1. Drag the **FrameMenu** into the **FrameMenu** slot of the **Picture Controller**.
2. In the **Hierarchy**, disable the **FrameMenu** object (uncheck the upper-left box in its **Inspector**).
3. We can now add a Frame button to the Toolbar. From the Project `Assets/SimpleIcons/Prefabs` folder, drag the **FrameButton** prefab in the **Hierarchy** as a child of **Toolbar**.
4. Set its **Position X** to −0.45 so it's over on the left side.
5. Add the **PictureAction** script component to the button.
6. Set its **Command** to **FRAME**.

The final hierarchy at this point looks like this:

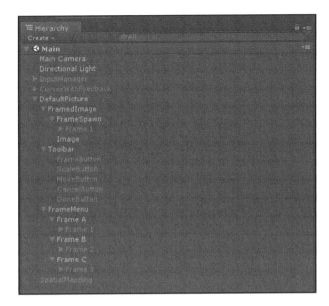

Support for Cancel in PictureController

The PictureController saves the state of a picture when you begin to edit. If you decide to cancel editing, the picture reverts to the original, so if the user has changed the frame during editing, we need to revert the frame too. Let's make these changes now:

```
File: PictureController.cs
```

Add a variable for the startFrame to the top of the class:

```
private GameObject startFrame;
```

Add this to SavePictureProperties:

```
startFrame = Instantiate(GetCurrentFrame());
startFrame.SetActive(false);
```

Then use it in RestorePictureProperties, which is called by CancelEdit:

```
startFrame.SetActive(true);
SetFrame(startFrame);
```

Note that we've instantiated a new game object, and it should be cleaned up when we exit editing and it's no longer needed. Add the follow code to both `DoneEdit` and `CancelEdit`:

```
Destroy(startFrame);
```

Now when you change the frame but press **Cancel**, the original frame is restored, along with any other properties you have edited.

Adding the Image menu

We also want the user to select from a menu of images to fill the frame. The **Image** menu will be very similar to the **Frame** menu, but we will make it a scrolling list so there can be more options than are visible in the menu.

SetImage in PictureController

The `PictureController` will expose a method, `SetImage()`, that takes a game object as a parameter using a texture that should be in the picture. And while you're at it, also add the `IMAGE` command to activate the menu from the toolbar, and handle saving the initial texture to **Cancel**, as we just did for **Frames**.

Make the following additions to the `PictureController.cs` script:

```
File: PictureController.cs
```

At the top of the class, add a public variable for the `imageMenu` and a private variable for the image renderer:

```
public GameObject imageMenu;
private Texture startTexture;
private Renderer imageRenderer;
```

In the `Start()` function, initialize the `imageRenderer`:

```
Transform image = framedImage.Find("Image");
imageRenderer = image.gameObject.GetComponent<Renderer>();
```

In the `Execute()` function, add a case for the `IMAGE` command:

```
case PictureCommand.IMAGE:
    OpenImageMenu();
    break;
```

Then add the corresponding function to open the menu:

```
private void OpenImageMenu() {
    imageMenu.SetActive(true);
}
```

Then add the public `SetTexture` function, which sets the picture **Image** texture based on the current menu selection:

```
public void SetTexture(Texture texture) {
    imageRenderer.material.mainTexture = texture;
}
```

Add the following line to `SavePictureProperties` for when we cancel the edit:

```
startTexture = imageRenderer.material.mainTexture;
```

Then add this line to `RestorePictureProperties`:

```
imageRenderer.material.mainTexture = startTexture;
```

The next step is to build the menu itself.

The ImageMenu object and component

Like `FrameMenu`, the `ImageMenu` is an empty game object container that will have its select option objects as children.

1. In **Hierarchy**, under **DefaultPicture**, click **Create Empty** game object and name it `ImageMenu`.
2. Set its **Position** (`0`, `−0.5`, `−0.1`) so it's at the bottom of the picture and a little in front.
3. Now we write the `ImageMenu` script component. In your `Scripts` folder, create a C# script named `ImageMenu` and open it for editing.

The `ImageMenu` script is like the `FrameMenu` one, but a little more complicated since we're adding scrolling. There will be scroll buttons for next and previous. The three menu items show three of all the possible images in the list. As you scroll, the menu item objects themselves are not replaced; however, their textures will be reassigned.

As you know, the abstract `PictureMenu` class maintains a list of `ClickableObjects`. These will be image container objects. In addition, this menu needs two more clickable objects, for the **Next** and **Previous** buttons. Also, it will maintain a list of all the image textures to pick from. Let's write the `ImageMenu` script now and describe it as follows:

```
File: ImageMenu.cs
using UnityEngine;

public class ImageMenu : PictureMenu {

    public Texture[] ImageTextures;
    [SerializeField]
    private ClickableObject nextButton;
    [SerializeField]
    private ClickableObject previousButton;

    //The items per page is calculated by the number of images shown at
start.
    private int indexOffset;

    public override void InitMenu() {
        base.SubscribeClickableObjects();
previousButton.OnClickableObjectClicked.AddListener(ScrollPrevious);
        nextButton.OnClickableObjectClicked.AddListener(ScrollNext);
    }

    public override void BeginEdit() {
        UpdateImages();
    }

    public override void ObjectClicked(GameObject clickedGameObject) {
        Texture texture =
clickedGameObject.GetComponent<Renderer>().material.mainTexture;
        picture.SetTexture(texture);
        DoneEdit(); // close ImageMenu when one pic is picked
    }

    private void UpdateImages() {
        for (int i = 0; i < clickableObjects.Length; i++) {
            //Sets the texture for the images based on index
clickableObjects[i].GetComponent<Renderer>().material.mainTexture =
ImageTextures[i + indexOffset];
        }
    }

And we add the scroll functions,
    public void ScrollNext(Object eventData) {
```

```
                    if ((indexOffset + clickableObjects.Length) < ImageTextures.Length)
        {
                indexOffset++;
            }
            UpdateImages();
        }

    public void ScrollPrevious(Object eventData) {
        if ((indexOffset - 1) >= 0) {
            indexOffset--;
        }
        UpdateImages();
    }
}
```

Walking through the code, the `ImageMenu` class is derived from `PictureMenu`. We declare a public variable for the list of `ImageTextures`, and add `nextButton` and `previousButton` clickable objects. There's also a private integer that keeps track of the scroll position in the list (`indexOffset`).

The `InitMenu` override function makes sure all the clickable objects are subscribed, including the menu items maintained in the parent `PictureMenu` class and our new scroll buttons.

We have an `UpdateImages` function that reassigns the textures to the menu option objects, starting at the current `indexOffset`. The `ScrollNext` and `ScrollPrevious` functions, called for the **Next** and **Previous** buttons, will increment or decrement the `indexOffset`.

When a menu option is clicked, we grab its **Texture** and pass it to the `PictureController`. Then we're done, so we hide the menu.

Image options objects

Next, we add the menu selection options as child objects of the `ImageMenu` and make them clickable. Follow these steps to create the menu game objects:

1. With **ImageMenu** selected in the **Hierarchy**, create **3D Object | Cube** and name it `Image A`.
2. Set its **Scale** to (0.25, 0.25, 0.02).
3. Set its **Rotation** to (0, 0, 180) (so the images are not upside down).
4. Set its **Position X** to −0.28.

5. Duplicate the objects twice, renaming them `Image B` and `Image C`, and setting the **Position X** to `0.0` and `0.28`.

6. From the `Assets/SimpleIcons/Prefabs` folder, drag the **LeftArrowButton** prefab into the **ImageMenu** hierarchy and set its **Position X** to `−0.5`.

7. From the `Assets/SimpleIcons/Prefabs` folder, drag the **RightArrowButton** prefab into the **ImageMenu** hierarchy and set its **Position X** to `0.5`.

8. Select all five of the objects just created in the **Hierarchy** and drag the **ClickableObject** script component into them.

Now populate the `ImageMenu` component with the frame objects we just created:

1. Select **ImageMenu** in the **Hierarchy**.
2. Enter 3 for **Clickable Objects Size.**
3. Drag each of its child **Frame** objects into the corresponding **Clickable Object Element** slot in the **Image Menu** component.
4. Identify which images you want to include in the menu, set the **Image Textures Size** to reveal its list, and drag each image texture (for example, from `Assets/Images/`) into each of the **Element** slots.

A populated `ImageMenu` component is shown here:

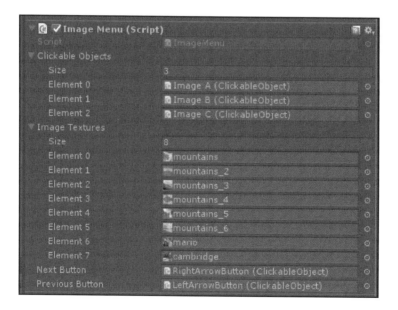

We now have an `ImageMenu` with clickable child frames for the user to pick. The scene now looks like the following. The image option object's textures don't get assigned until runtime:

Let's try it out.

Save your files and the current scene. Press **Play**. You should see the **Image** menu. Select one of the images and it will replace the current image in the picture.

Activating the Image menu

The **Image** menu should not be visible until the user activates it. We can add this command to the `PictureController` and activate it from the toolbar. We already added the `IMAGE` command to the `PictureController` script, so all we need to do is add the button to the toolbar:

1. Drag the **ImageMenu** into the **Image Menu slot** of the **Picture Controller**.
2. In the **Hierarchy**, disable the **ImageMenu** object (uncheck the button in the upper-left of its **Inspector**).
3. We can now add an Image button to the toolbar. From the Project `Assets/SimpleIcons/Prefabs` folder, drag the **ImageButton** prefab in the **Hierarchy** as a child of **Toolbar**.
4. Set its **Position X** to −0.3.
5. Add the **PictureAction** script component to the button.
6. Set its **Command** to **IMAGE**.

Adjusting for Image aspect ratio

You probably noticed that some of your pictures appear squished, especially if they are in a portrait orientation, since our `FramedImage` is shown at a fixed size and aspect ratio. What we really would like is for the frame and image to adjust themselves depending on the dimensions of the image.

When Unity imports a texture, its pre-processes it by default for GPU rendering as an object material texture, which includes resizing it to a square power of two (for example, *1024 x 1024, 2048 x 2048,*and so on). If you adapt your project to read images at runtime, for example, from the `Resources` directory, the device's photo stream, or over the web, then you will have access to the image file's metadata header that includes its pixel width and height. In lieu of that, since we're using imported textures, we can change the **Advanced** import settings for the images we're using:

1. From your `Assets Images` folder (that is, `Assets/Images/`) select an image texture.
2. In **Inspector**, under **Advanced**, change **Non Power of 2** to **None**.
3. Press **Apply**.

Repeat this for each image in the project. Note that this also decompresses the image, so what might start out as a 400k `.jpg` file becomes a 3 MB, 24-bit image in the project, so be cautious of the width and height of the source images you choose to use.

In `PictureController.cs`, add the following helper function, which returns a normalized scale of a texture. The larger dimension will be `1.0` and the smaller one will be a fraction. For example, an image that is 1024w x 768h will get a scale of (`1.0, 0.75`). It also maintains the current relative scale of the picture using the Z scale value, since that's not changed by our aspect ratio calculation, but will be changed by the **Scale** tool!

```
private Vector3 TextureToScale(Vector3 startScale, Texture texture) {
    Vector3 scale = Vector3.one * startScale.z;
    if (texture.width > texture.height) {
        scale.y *= (texture.height * 1.0f) / texture.width;
    } else {
        scale.x *= (texture.width * 1.0f) / texture.height;
    }
    return scale;
}
```

Now add a call to it in `SetTexture`:

```
public void SetTexture(Texture texture) {
    imageRenderer.material.mainTexture = texture;
    framedImage.transform.localScale =
TextureToScale(framedImage.transform.localScale, texture);
}
```

Press **Play**, and select an image with a different aspect ratio from the current one. The picture, including its frame, will resize to match its shape. If you use the Scale tool to resize the whole picture, then choose another image; its shape will be adjusted, but the overall scale will be correct.

Adding and deleting framed pictures

There's just a couple more features to add to the project. So far, we've been working with only a single picture. We want to add many pictures to decorate the walls! Fortunately, our `DefaultPicture` object is very self-contained, with its toolbar and menus and all. So one approach is to save the `DefaultPicture` as a prefab and then instantiate new copies of it for each new image we add to the scene.

The plan is to add **Add** and **Delete** buttons to the toolbar. Clicking **Add** will create a new picture in the scene. Clicking **Delete** will remove the current picture from the scene.

Let's set that up now.

Add and Delete in the Toolbar

We'll first add the **Add** and **Delete** buttons to the toolbar:

1. From the Project `Assets/SimpleIcons/Prefabs` folder, drag the **DeleteButton** prefab to the **Hierarchy** as a child of **Toolbar**.
2. Set its **Position X** to `0.15`.
3. Add the **PictureAction** script component to the button.
4. Set its **Command** to **DELETE**.
5. From the Project `Assets/SimpleIcons/Prefabs` folder, drag the **AddButton** prefab in the **Hierarchy** as a child of **Toolbar**.
6. Set its **Position X** to `0.65` so it's a little off to the side.

7. Add the **PictureAction** script component to the button.
8. Set its **Command** to **ADD**.

The completed toolbar now looks like this:

GameController

We've written one controller for the app, PictureController, which manages a picture. We could add a CreateNewPicture function there, but what if the scene is empty and there is no PictureController? What component function gets called to add a new picture to the scene? Let's create a separate GameController to support creating new pictures.

There should only be one GameController in our scene, so we make it a singleton. The *singleton* pattern ensures there will never be more than one instance of a class. In Unity and C#, we can implement singletons. In your Scripts folder, create a new C# script and name it GameController:

```
File: GameController
using UnityEngine;

public class GameController : MonoBehaviour {

    public static GameController instance;

    void Awake() {
        if (instance == null) {
            instance = this;
        } else {
            Destroy(gameObject);
        }
    }

}
```

Now we'll add a `CreateNewPicture` function to `GameController` to spawn a new instance of the default picture. We'll place the new picture in front of the user's current gaze, a fixed distance away. Add the following code to the class:

```
public GameObject defaultPictureObject;
public float spawnDistance = 2.0f;
public void CreateNewPicture() {
    Vector3 headPosition = Camera.main.transform.position;
    Vector3 gazeDirection = Camera.main.transform.forward;
    Vector3 position = headPosition + gazeDirection * spawnDistance;

    Quaternion orientation = Camera.main.transform.localRotation;
    orientation.x = 0;
    orientation.z = 0;
    GameObject newPicture = Instantiate(defaultPictureObject, position,
orientation);
    newPicture.tag = "Picture";
}
```

The `GameController` references the `DefaultPicture` prefab to spawn, instantiates it, and tags it as a *Picture* so we can find them later. Let's now add it to the scene:

1. In **Hierarchy**, click **Create Empty** game object at the root of the scene, named `GameController`.
2. Add the **GameController** component script to it.
3. Drag the **DefaultPicture** from the **Hierarchy** into your Project `AssetsApp/Prefabs/` folder.
4. Drag the **DefaultPicture** prefab from the `Assets` folder onto the **Default Picture Object** slot.

Next, we support **Add** and **Delete** in the **PictureController**.

 Reminder: Now that the `DefaultPicture` is a prefab, if you make changes to it or any of its child objects in **Hierarchy**, you must remember to press **Prefab Apply** to save those changes to the prefab version.

Add and Delete Commands in PictureController

In the `PictureController` script, add the following code to the `Execute()` function:

```
File: PictureController.cs
            case PictureCommand.ADD:
                AddPicture();
                break;

            case PictureCommand.DELETE:
                DeletePicture();
                break;
```

Write the corresponding implementations of the commands:

```
    private void AddPicture() {
        DoneEdit();
        GameController.instance.CreateNewPicture();
    }

    private void DeletePicture() {
        Destroy(gameObject);
    }
```

`AddPicture` will close the current picture editing and create a new picture via `GameController`. `DeletePicture` will delete the current game object.

Let's try it out. Save your work and press **Play**. Use the toolbar's **Add** button to create a new picture, move it into place, and create another. Use the **Delete** button to delete a picture.

Delete all the pictures in your scene. Now what? We could put an **Add** button in front of you, or some other mechanism for creating new pictures, apart from a current picture's toolbar. Instead, we'll always make sure there's at least one picture in the scene, with its toolbar.

Handling empty scenes

If you delete all the pictures from the scene, we'll respawn a new one, so there's always at least one present. One way to detect the presence of pictures is to use tags. Let's add a *Picture* tag to our project and assign it to the `DefaultPicture`. Then we can see when all pictures are deleted, and we will know when to respawn one:

1. In Unity, with **DefaultPicture** selected, click the **Tag** list and choose **Add Tag**.
2. Press the + to add a new tag and name it `Picture`.

3. Now, back in the DefaultPicture's **Inspector**, use the **Tag** list again and select
   Picture,
4. Press **Apply** to save the prefab,

Now we can add the following code to `GameController`:

```
File: GameController.cs
    private int delay = 1;

    void Update() {
        if (delay == 0 &&
GameObject.FindGameObjectsWithTag("Picture").Length == 0) {
            CreateNewPicture();
        }
        if (++delay > 30) delay = 0;
    }
```

On each game update, we check how many Pictures are in the scene, and if there are none,
we call `CreateNewPicture`. We've added a 30-frame delay for a better user experience.

UI feedback

Before we're done, let's add a little juice to the user experience. We have a feedback cursor
that lets you know what you're gazing at, and the cursor changes shape when the device
recognizes your hand in view. But we do not have feedback when a button or clickable
object is clicked. Let's add an audio feedback and some animation.

Click audio feedback

For the audio, find an audio clip you'd like to use when something is clicked. We include
one named `FingerPressed` with our chapter `Assets` package. Rather than adding it with
an `AudioSource` to every button and clickable object, we'll centralize the sound and add it
to the `GameController`, along with a `PlayClickFeedback()` function:

1. Select the **GameController** in **Hierarchy** and **Add Component Audio Source**.
2. Find your audio clip, such as at
   `Assets/SimpleIcons/Sounds/FingerPressed`, and drag it into the
   AudioClip slot on the **Audio Source** component.
3. Uncheck **Play On Awake**.
4. Leave the **Spatial Blend** at **2D** so it's not affected by the user's head position.

Now edit the `GameController` script:

```
File: GameController.cs
    private AudioSource clickSound;

    void Start() {
        clickSound = GetComponent<AudioSource>();
    }
    public void PlayClickFeedback() {
        if (clickSound != null) {
            clickSound.Play();
        }
    }
```

We can now add the following line of code to the `OnInputClicked` method in both the `PictureAction` and `ClickableObject` scripts:

```
            GameController.instance.PlayClickFeedback();
```

When you press **Play** and click on something, you should hear the feedback.

Click animation feedback

The **SimpleIcons** button prefabs had a simple animation attached that will swing the button as if the toolbar were suspended in space with a rod. You can open the animation asset if you want to look into how it was made. All we need to do is trigger it with a *Click* command.

However, it doesn't work to just play the animation when clicked, because most of our buttons immediately hide the toolbar. So we'll add a second's delay before actually executing its action.

Open `PictureAction.cs` and change it to read like the following:

```
File: PictureAction.cs
using UnityEngine;
using HoloToolkit.Unity.InputModule;

public class PictureAction : MonoBehaviour, IInputClickHandler {
    public PictureCommand command;
    protected PictureController picture;
    protected Animator animator;

    void Start() {
        picture = GetComponentInParent<PictureController>();
```

```
        animator = GetComponent<Animator>();
    }

    public void OnInputClicked(InputClickedEventData eventData) {
        if (animator != null) {
            animator.SetTrigger("Click");
        }
        GameController.instance.PlayClickFeedback();
        Invoke("DoExecute", 1);
    }

    void DoExecute() {
        picture.Execute(command);
    }
}
```

Now, when you click a button in the toolbar, it will swing and beep!

The following is a mixed reality capture of the wonderful photo-wall adorning my office, built with our app:

Building for iOS with ARKit

Although we made this project for Microsoft HoloLens devices, that certainly is not a requirement. In this section, we will adapt the project for mobile devices using the Apple ARKit.

As we now know, the HoloLens device includes a depth sensing camera that estimates the distance of each pixel in view and stitches together a mesh, or spatial map, of the environment. Similar technologies are also available in Google Tango and Intel RealSense. New smartphones are emerging with these sensors built in, and that will make it easier to implement projects such as this using mobile phone devices rather than the expensive HoloLens HMD.

Apple introduced ARKit for iOS 11 to solve this problem without the need for special depth-sensing hardware in the mobile device. It uses regular camera and AI software to scan the environment and infer depth information based on parallax and other spatial cues, and then track the device's movement using its built-in motion sensors.

For iOS devices that support Apple ARKit, you can build the app using the Unity ARKit plugin, available on the Asset Store. Like the HoloLens, ARKit scans the room and provides a spatial map we can use to detect surfaces in the environment. Unlike HoloLens, which uses gaze-based input for UI and spatial positioning, we can use standard Unity screen touch events.

If you have been following along and have already built the HoloLens version of the project, we strongly suggest you save your work and copy the entire project directory tree for the ARKit version. There are incompatibilities between the SDK, and we're going to strip out HoloLens-specific components in this process.

Create a full backup of your HoloLens version of this project before beginning this ARKit version.

If you are starting from scratch, begin a new project with ARKit and then jump back to the beginning of this chapter to implement all the objects and components, substituting the changes that we will shortly describe. But for expediency, this section will assume that the `DefaultPicture` is already built and saved as a prefab.

Set up project and scene for ARKit

We decided to give this version of the project a different name, `PhotoFrames-ARKit`. Open the project in Unity, and import the ARKit plug in via the Asset Store:

1. With the old **Main** scene open, select **File | Save Scene As** and name it `Main-ARKit`.
2. Select **File | Build Settings** and replace **Main** with **Main-ARKit** in the **Scenes To Build**.
3. **Switch Platforms** to **iOS**. We will let the toolkit set the other configurations.
4. From **Window | Asset Store**, **Download** and **Import** the Apple ARKit package.
5. Accept the option to let it **Override Project Settings**.

The following steps build the ARKit scene components from scratch. Alternatively, you could use one of the ARKit example scenes, such as the basic UnityARKitScene, and remove objects we are not using.

Now we set up the camera with AR components and create the `ARCameraManager` as follows:

1. In **Hierarchy** root, click **Create Empty** named `CameraParent`; reset its **Transform** if necessary (**Transform | gear-icon | Reset**).
2. Drag the **Main Camera** so that it is a child of **CameraParent** and reset its **Transform** too.
3. With **Main Camera** selected, **Add Component Unity AR Video**.
4. For its **Clear Material** slot, click the doughnut icon and select **YUVMaterial**.
5. Then select **Add Component Unity AR Camera Near Far**.
6. In **Hierarchy** root, click **Create Empty** named `ARCameraManager`.
7. Click **Add Component** and name it **Unity AR Camera Manager**.
8. Drag the **Main Camera** onto its **Camera** slot.

For this project, we will let ARKit adjust the ambient lighting of the scene to match the lighting of the real-world environment, as follows:

1. In **Hierarchy**, **Create | Light | Directional Light**.
2. Set its **Mode** to **Mixed**.
3. Click **Add Component** and name it **Unity AR Ambient**.

Lastly, we're going to ARKit to generate the planes for positioning our photos on the walls, so let's add the component now:

1. In **Hierarchy**, click **Create Empty** and name it `Generate Planes`.
2. **Add the Component** and name it **Unity AR Generate Plane**.
3. For the **Plane Prefab**, (using the doughnut icon) select **debugPlanePrefab** as the plane object.

That's it for the generic ARKit scene setup.

Next, we can continue to build our project.

If this is a new scene, we need to add the `GameController`, as follows:

1. In **Hierarchy**, click **Create Empty** object and name it `GameController`.
2. Add the **GameController** script as a component.
3. Then drag the prefab **DefaultPicture** from your `Prefabs` folder onto the **Default Picture Object** slot.

It may be prudent to double check the `DefaultPicture` prefab. Drag it into the scene hierarchy and inspect its children. For example, ensure the **Picture Controller** component references the required objects, and the **Picture Action** component (on `FramedImage` and each of the **Toolbar** tools) is set to the correct **Command**. When done, press **Apply** to save any changes back to the prefab, and then disable or delete the object from the hierarchy.

Use touch events instead of hand gestures

The only effort in adapting the project for ARKit is that, instead of the HoloLens `InputManager` and `GestureRecogizer`, we are going to use standard Unity mouse events that also map mobile screen touches.

PictureAction

Open the `PictureAction.cs` script and modify it to use mouse events so that it reads as follows:

```
File: PictureAction.cs
using UnityEngine;
```

```
public class PictureAction : MonoBehaviour {
    public PictureCommand command;

    protected PictureController picture;
    protected Animator animator;

    void Start() {
        picture = GetComponentInParent<PictureController>();
        animator = GetComponent<Animator>();
    }

    void OnMouseDown() {
        if (animator != null) {
            animator.SetTrigger("Click");
        }
        GameController.instance.PlayClickFeedback();
        Invoke("DoExecute", 1);
    }

    void DoExecute() {
        picture.Execute(command);
    }
}
```

ClickableObjects

Open the ClickableObjects.cs script and modify it to use mouse events so that it reads as follows:

```
File: ClickableObjects.cs
using UnityEngine;
using UnityEngine.Events;

public class ClickableObjectEvent : UnityEvent<GameObject> { }

public class ClickableObject : MonoBehaviour {

    public ClickableObjectEvent OnClickableObjectClicked = new
ClickableObjectEvent();

    void OnMouseDown() {
        GameController.instance.PlayClickFeedback();
        OnClickableObjectClicked.Invoke(gameObject);
    }
}
```

If you press **Build And Run** now, much of the UI should work correctly! We need to make further changes to the **Move** and **Scale** tools.

ScaleTool

The `ScaleTool` we wrote for HoloLens doubled as a teaching example of the `GestureRecognizer`, and thus made things more complicated than they should be. For the mobile version, we'll just rewrite the script so it's much more similar to the `MoveTool` one. Here is the whole thing:

```
File: ScaleTool.cs
using UnityEngine;

public class ScaleTool : MonoBehaviour {
    private PictureController picture;
    private bool isEditing = false;
    private Vector3 originaButtonScale;

    //Used to calculate the mouse position
    private Vector3 startPosition = Vector3.zero;
    private Vector3 currentPosition = Vector3.zero;
    private Vector3 initialScale = Vector3.zero;

    void Start() {
        picture = GetComponentInParent<PictureController>();
        originaButtonScale = transform.localScale;
    }

    void Update() {
        if (isEditing) {
            currentPosition = Input.mousePosition;
            float difference = (currentPosition - startPosition).magnitude;
            //Scaling down is possible by dragging your mouse to the left.
            int direction = currentPosition.x > startPosition.x ? 1 : -1;
            float scaleFactor = 1 + (difference / Screen.width) *
direction;
            if (scaleFactor > 0.1f) {
                picture.transform.localScale = initialScale * scaleFactor;
            }
        }
        if (!Input.GetMouseButton(0)) {
            DoneEdit();
        }
    }

    private void OnMouseDown() {
```

```
            if (!isEditing) {
                BeginEdit();
            }
        }

    public void BeginEdit() {
        if (!isEditing) {
            isEditing = true;

            transform.localScale = originaButtonScale * 2.5f;
            startPosition = Input.mousePosition;
            initialScale = picture.transform.localScale;
        }
    }

    private void OnMouseUp() {
        if (isEditing) {
            DoneEdit();
        }
    }

    public void DoneEdit() {
        if (isEditing) {
            isEditing = false;
            transform.localScale = originaButtonScale;
        }
    }
}
```

Now we just need to change the `MoveTool` script.

MoveTool

The `MoveTool` will be the only script that requires ARKit-specific calls. In the Mixed Reality Toolkit, we cast a ray from the camera into the scene and looked for a hit point where it intersects with the spatial map of the environment. For ARKit, we do something similar, but instead of using Unity physics to do the calculation, we use the underlying ARKit SDK directly (from C#):

1. Open the `MoveTool.cs` script and modify it to use mouse events.
2. Remove all references to HoloToolkit and `spatialMapping`.

Then replace the `Update()` function as follows:

```
File: MoveTool.cs
    void Update() {
        List<ARHitTestResult> hitResults;
        ARPoint point;

        if (isEditing) {
            Vector3 screenPosition =
Camera.main.ScreenToViewportPoint(Input.mousePosition);
            point.x = screenPosition.x;
            point.y = screenPosition.y;

            hitResults =
UnityARSessionNativeInterface.GetARSessionNativeInterface().HitTest( point,
ARHitTestResultType.ARHitTestResultTypeExistingPlaneUsingExtent);

            if (hitResults.Count == 0) {
                hitResults =
UnityARSessionNativeInterface.GetARSessionNativeInterface().HitTest( point,
                    ARHitTestResultType.ARHitTestResultTypeVerticalPlane);
            }
            if (hitResults.Count == 0) {
                hitResults =
UnityARSessionNativeInterface.GetARSessionNativeInterface().HitTest( point,
                    ARHitTestResultType.ARHitTestResultTypeFeaturePoint);
            }

            if (hitResults.Count > 0) {
                picture.transform.position = UnityARMatrixOps.GetPosition(
hitResults[0].worldTransform);
                picture.transform.rotation = UnityARMatrixOps.GetRotation(
hitResults[0].worldTransform);
            }
        }
        if (!Input.GetMouseButton(0)) {
            DoneEdit();
        }
    }
```

We've seen similar code before, in the `SolarSystemHitHandler.cs` script we wrote in Chapter 5, *AR Solar System*, and the `ARHitHandler.cs` script in Chapter 7, *Augmenting the Instruction Manual*, where we call the ARKIT *Hit Test* looking for a world space position based on the position of the screen touch. In this case, we first look for any existing object in the foreground (`ARHitTestResultTypeExistingPlaneUsingExtent`), then allow any vertical plane (`ARHitTestResultTypeVerticalPlane`), and if that fails, try to guess a plane based on a feature point (`ARHitTestResultTypeFeaturePoint`). Feel free to play with these options to see which ones work best for you and in which order of priority.

Then replace the input handler with mouse (touch screen) versions:

```
private void OnMouseDown() {
    if (!isEditing) {
        BeginEdit();
    }
}

private void OnMouseUp() {
    if (isEditing) {
        DoneEdit();
    }
}
```

Save the script. Now, when you run the app and press the **Move** tool, it will drag the picture with your touch until you let up.

That's it! **Build And Run** the app for your device. The following is a photo of my family room wall with one real-life picture augmented with two additional virtual ones on the iPad with ARKit:

Building for Android using Google ARCore
Please refer to the the GitHub repository for this book for the implementation notes and code using Google ARCore for Android: `https://github.com/ARUnityBook/`. The principles are very similar to ARKit but the Unity SDK and components are different.

Building for mobile AR with Vuforia

We've shown how to build the project for Microsoft HoloLens wearable AR devices and mobile iOS devices that support ARKit. But this is a limited market, as there are many more mobile devices that run Android, as well as Apple devices that do not support ARKit. In this section, we will adapt the project for mobile devices using the Vuforia toolkit SDK. Unfortunately, these devices are not capable of supporting spatial maps to anchor our AR graphics. Instead, we will use image targets.

A traditional approach used for more than two decades is to print marker images and tape them to the walls. Vuforia and AR Toolkit support the ability to recognize multiple targets concurrently. That is the approach we will take now.

If you have been following along and have already built the HoloLens or ARKit version of the project, we strongly suggest you save your work and copy the entire project directory tree for the Vuforia version. There are incompatibilities between the SDK, and we're going to strip out HoloLens-specific components in this process.

Create a full backup of your HoloLens version of this project before beginning this Vuforia version.

If you are starting from scratch, begin a new project with Vuforia and then jump back to the beginning of this chapter to implement all the objects and components, substituting the changes that we will describe. But for this section, we are going to assume that the `DefaultPicture` is already built and saved as a prefab.

Set up project and scene for Vuforia

Let's begin by setting up the Unity project for AR with the Vuforia toolkit. This may be familiar to you by now, so we'll go through the steps quickly. If you require more detail, please refer to the relevant topics in `Chapter 2`, *Setting Up Your System*, and `Chapter 3`, *Building Your App*:

1. Choose **Assets | Import Package | Custom Package...** to import `vuforia-unity-xxxx`.

2. Choose **Assets | Import Package | Custom Package...** to import `VuforiaSamples-xxxx`.

3. Browse to the Vuforia Dev Portal (`https://developer.vuforia.com/targetmanager/licenseManager/licenseListing`) and choose or create a license key. Copy the license key onto your clipboard.

4. Back in Unity, from the main menu choose **Vuforia | Configuration** and paste into **App License Key**.

5. Delete the **Main Camera** object from the **Hierarchy**.

6. Also delete the MixedRealityToolkit's **InputManager**, **CursorWithFeedback**, and **SpatialMapping** from the **Hierarchy**.

7. Locate the `ARCamera` prefab in the Project `Assets/Vuforia/Prefabs` folder, select, and drag it into the **Hierarchy** list.

8. Use **Add Component** to add the **Camera Settings** component to **ARCamera**.

9. Open **File | Build Settings**, and **Switch Platform** to **Android** and **Add Open Scenes**.

10. In **Player Settings**, set your **Identification Package Name** and **Minimum API Level** (Android 5.1).

11. Save the scene and save the project.

12. When you press **Play** in the Editor, you should see the video feed from your webcam.

Set the image target

Choose an image target for the project. We are using a predefined image, stones, in the StonesAndChips database provided with the Vuforia samples package. Print out a hard copy of this image now if you need to. Let's set up the project to use this image target.

1. Drag the **ImageTarget** prefab from Assets/Vuforia/Prefabs/ into the **Hierarchy**.

2. In **Inspector**, set **Type: Predefined**, **Database**: StonesAndChips, and **Image Target**: stones (or whichever image you prefer to use).

3. Check the **Enable Extended Tracking** checkbox.

4. From the main menu, go to **Vuforia | Configuration**, then check the **Load StonesAndChips Database** checkbox and **Activate**.

5. Save the scene and project.

Add DefaultPicture to the scene

Next, make **DefaultPicture** a child under **ImageTarget**. If it's already in your hierarchy, you can just move it. If not, and you have a prefab in your Prefabs folder, use that. Or, now would be the time to jump up to the beginning of this chapter and implement the DefaultPicture hierarchy objects and scripts.

1. Parent**DefaultPicture** under **ImageTarget**.

2. Reset its **Transform** (use **gear-icon | Reset**).

3. Set its **Rotation X** to 90.

4. We rotate our picture by 90 degrees to align with the way Vuforia targets are on the X-Z plane.

5. Press **Play**, point your camera at the image target, and the **DefaultPicture** should appear, along with the photo image, frame, and toolbar, as shown here, using a target taped to my wall (vuforia-imagetarget.png):

GameController

If this is a new scene, we need to add GameController, as follows:

1. In **Hierarchy**, click **Create Empty** object and name it GameController.
2. Add the **GameController** script as a component.
3. Then drag the prefab **DefaultPicture** from your Prefabs folder into the **Default Picture Object** slot.

   We will spawn new pictures at the target image origin, so modify the CreateNewPicture function as follows:

```
File: GameController.cs
    public Transform imageTarget;

    public void CreateNewPicture() {
        GameObject newPicture = Instantiate(defaultPictureObject,
imageTarget);
    }
```

4. Then in Unity, select**GameController** and drag the **ImageTarget** into its **Image Target** slot.

Use touch events instead of hand gestures

The only effort in adapting the project for Vuforia is, instead of the HoloLens `InputManager` and `GestureRecogizer`, we are going to use standard Unity mouse events (which already map mobile screen touches). We wrote this code for the preceding ARKit version and can re-use it here.

1. For `PictureAction.cs`, use exactly the same script we showed for ARKit.
2. For `ClickableObjects.cs`, use exactly the same script we showed for ARKit.
3. For `ScaleTool.cs`, use exactly the same script we showed for ARKit.

For the `MoveTool`, we must adapt it specifically for Vuforia.

To move our picture along the same plane as the image target, we need to define a large box collider for `ImageTarget` so that input events can be detected on it (in HoloLens, the spatial mesh served a similar purpose). We will put the target on a new *Wall* layer so the **Move** tool does not interfere with other UI inputs:

1. In Unity, select the **Layers** at the top-right of the widow and choose **Edit Layers**.
2. Then unfold the **Layers** list and add one named `Wall`, as shown here:

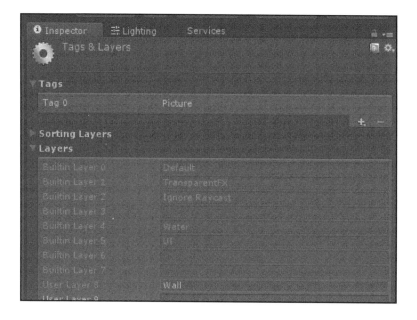

Now, put the `ImageTarget` on the Wall, but not any of its children.

1. In **Hierarchy**, select **ImageTarget**.
2. In **Inspector**, set its **Layer** to **Wall**.
3. When asked **Do you want to set layer to Wall for all child objects as well?**, answer **NO, this object only**.
4. Add a **Box Collider** component to **ImageTarget**.
5. Set its **Size** to (10, 0, 10) making a big plane on X-Z for the mouse events.

Open the `MoveTool.cs` script and modify it to use mouse events and remove all references to `SpatialMapping`, as follows:

```
File: MoveTool.cs
using UnityEngine;

public class MoveTool : MonoBehaviour {
    public LayerMask WallLayerMask;
    ...
    void Start() {
        ...
        relativeOffset = transform.position - picture.transform.position;
        relativeOffset.y = 0f;
    }

    void Update() {
        if (isEditing) {
            Ray ray = Camera.main.ScreenPointToRay(Input.mousePosition);
            RaycastHit hit;
            if (Physics.Raycast(ray, out hit, Mathf.Infinity,
WallLayerMask)) {
                Debug.DrawLine(ray.origin, hit.point);
                picture.transform.position = hit.point - relativeOffset;
            }
        }
        if (!Input.GetMouseButton(0)) {
            DoneEdit();
        }
    }

    private void OnMouseDown() {
        if (!isEditing) {
            BeginEdit();
        }
    }

    private void OnMouseUp() {
```

```
        if (isEditing) {
            DoneEdit();
        }
    }
```

6. Save the script. In Unity, select the **MoveButton** under the toolbar, and in **Inspector**, set its **Move Tool Wall Layer Mask** to **Wall**.

Now, when you press **Play**, the **Move** tool will work, dragging the picture with your touch until you let up.

The following is a photo of the wonderful photo-wall adorning my office, built with the mobile AR version of our app:

Summary

In this chapter, we built an app that is really designed to augment the real world. There are many uses for apps like this, in architecture, design, and retail for example. Our app lets you decorate your walls with framed photos. We developed this project first for HoloLens wearable AR smartglasses, and then we moved it to mobile AR devices using ARKit and Vuforia.

We created an object hierarchy for a picture that includes a frame, an image, a toolbar, and a couple of menus for selecting frames and images. We built a 3D UI framework from scratch that supports toolbars, action buttons, manipulation tools, and modal menus. Then we took a pretty deep dive into the Mixed Reality Toolkit Input Manager and Gaze Recognizer input event systems, as well as the HoloLens spatial mapping room mesh features. Along the way, we used more features of Unity via C# scripts, including tags, audio clips, animations, colliders, and textures.

Then we reworked the project for mobile AR devices. First, we ported to iOS and ARKit. It was a fairly simple process. Most of our implementation architecture was device independent, and we just had to replace the holographic gesture input events with more conventional touch-screen mouse events. Then we ported the project to Android and older iOS devices using Vuforia. In this case, we used image targets to identify walls in lieu of spatial mapping. (And using Google ARCore is similar; see the project at `https://github.com/ARUnityBook/`).

In the next chapter, we look at another dimension of augmented reality-using physics to interact between the virtual and physical environments. In the project, we will build a ball-toss game that will be fun to play!

9
Poke the Ball Game

In the summer of 2016, the Pokémon Go location-based augmented reality game was released for iOS and Android devices. It quickly became a worldwide phenomenon as one of the most popular and profitable mobile apps in 2016. Pokémon Go uses GPS to identify your location and reveal nearby virtual Pokémon characters, superimposed on the live video feed on your screen. You flick a Pokéball towards a Pokémon to capture it.

AR and games are a natural fit for many reasons. Mobile games have been a major driver in the adoption of mobile devices and have become a huge market in itself. Adding AR features to games can be seen as an extension to mobile apps, rather than a new category. We anticipate that, as more devices become AR enabled, including mobile phones and tablets as well as wearable AR smartglasses, games will again be an important driver for adoption and proliferation of these devices.

In this chapter, we will build an AR ball game that uses your coffee table or desk as the ball court stage. Players try to throw balls and make a basket or goal. The app will track the table surface and recognize real physical objects on the desk as obstacles that can occlude (hide) the virtual ball and bounce off.

In this chapter, you will learn about:

- Using Unity physics engine and materials
- Screen space user interaction
- Layered event driven architecture
- Using AR object terrain recognition

This chapter works through the project developing with Vuforia for Android devices, but can be adapted for other development targets, including iOS and HoloLens, without too much rework. Please refer to the the GitHub repository for this book for completed projects for each platform: https://github.com/ARUnityBook/

The game plan

We are going to build an AR ball throwing game that uses any table in your room as a play court. Players will try to make goals by tossing a ball into a basket or goalpost (for consistency, we'll use the word *goal* and *court* throughout the chapter to refer to goal posts or baskets and the play area). The game keeps score. We will implement several different ball games with types of balls, each with different physics properties. The app will recognize objects on your table as obstacles the balls can bounce off.

For implementation we take the following steps:

1. Set up a new Unity AR project.
2. Build a simple game court with goal target and ball.
3. Throw the ball using touch screen input.
4. Detect when the ball hits the goal, cheer, and add points to the player's score.
5. Track all time high scores.
6. Enable Vuforia Smart Terrain so the game really feels like it's on your desk or coffee table.
7. Expand the game by adding alternative ball game courts for basketball, football, and more.

User experience

Before starting the app, the player should have a table surface (coffee table, desk, and so on) cleared but for a few objects to be used as in-game obstacles. An image target will be used to set the position of the goalpost.

When the app starts, the player is instructed to first calibrate the scene, pointing the camera at the target image to initiate the AR. Then the user slowly pulls away so the software can scan the table and recognize the surrounding surfaces and props.

Once calibrated, gameplay may begin. While the screen shows the table with the virtual game court, a new ball appears in the *ready* position. The player then flicks the ball to throw it towards the goalpost. If the ball hits the target, the player gets points. If it misses, points are deducted. The current score is displayed on the screen along with the high score. Sounds fun!

Between rounds, the player can rearrange the court by moving the goal and physical obstacles on the table.

Game components

The ball game is created with the following primary components:

- **GameController** manages the overall game, including the current score. It subscribes to the BallGame's won and lost events, manages the score, and displays game data. As the game supports switching between ball game types, the **GameController** chooses and starts a random game.
- **GameDataManager** saves and restores data for the game. It manages persistent storage of the player progress and high scores.
- The **BallGame** component manages individual ball games. One is attached to each separate ball game. It uses the **ThrowControl** component to determine when the show is done and if the ball hit the goal, and then it invokes a *won* or *lost* event accordingly.
- The **ThrowControl** component is attached to the ball. It reads user input and sets the ball in motion. **ThrowControl** sends events when the ball's starting position is reset and when the ball is thrown.
- **CollisionBehavior** detects when the ball hits the goal collider and sends an event. This component is on the game's goal collider object.
- **AppStateManger** handles the app phases required for Vuforia Smart Terrain, including the initial target recognition, scanning the table surface and props, and running and resetting the game.

The relationship between components and the events passed between them is shown in the following diagram:

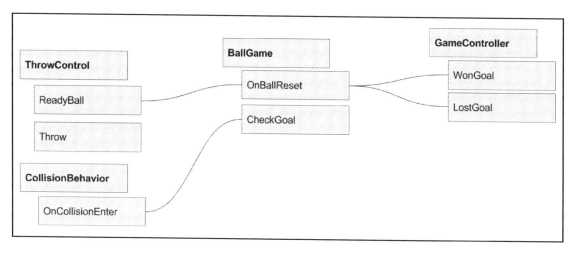

Roughly, the app's messaging follows this flow:

1. To begin a new game, the ball is moved to its starting position by ThrowControl's **ReadyBall**.
2. The ball's **ThrowControl** detects user input and tosses the ball towards the goal (Throw).
3. If the ball collides with the goal, the **CollisionBehavior** component signals the **BallGame** to validate the goal object was actually hit (**CheckGoal**). And **BallGame** remembers that state.
4. We give the ball a chance to bounce around the court, whether or not it hit the goal.
5. After a delay, **ThrowControl** resets the ball via **ReadyBall**.
6. **ReadyBall** also tells the **BallGame** that the ball has reset (**OnBallReset**).
7. At that point, **OnBallReset** notifies the **GameController** whether the previous throw resulted in a won or lost goal, which in turn updates the scoreboard.

An advantage of this architecture is we can have multiple **BallGames** in our app, for example, football, basketball, and so on, but just one **GameController**. **ThrowControl** and **CollisionBehavior** are reusable components that have no dependencies, signally the **BallGame** via events.

We will implement each of these script components as we build up the project. The app state phases for scanning the Smart Terrain is explained in more detail in the augmenting real world objects section.

Setting up the project

Like each of the projects in this book, we will begin with a new empty Unity 3D project. This may be familiar by now, so we'll go through the steps quickly. If you require more detail, please refer to the relevant topics in Chapter 2, *Setting Up Your System*, and Chapter 3, *Building Your App*.

Creating an initial project

Use the following steps to create a new AR project in Unity. You will need to have downloaded the Vuforia packages first (please refer to Chapter 2, *Setting Up Your System*):

1. Open Unity and create a new 3D project; name it something like ARBall.
2. Choose **Assets | Import Package | Custom Package** to import vuforia-unity-xxxx.
3. Choose **Assets | Import Package | Custom Package** to import VuforiaSamples-xxxx.
4. While logged into the Vuforia site, browse to Vuforia Dev Portal (https://developer.vuforia.com/targetmanager/licenseManager/licenseListing) and choose or create a license key. Copy the license key into your clipboard.
5. Back in Unity, choose main menu **Vuforia | Configuration**, and paste it into **App License Key**.
6. Review the other configuration settings, including the current **Webcam Camera Device.**
7. Save the scene (**File | Save Scene As**, name it Main) and save the project (**File | Save Project**).
8. Go to **File | Build Settings**.
9. Add the current scene, press **Add Open Scenes.**

10. **Switch Platform** to **Android**.
11. Choose **Player Settings** and then set your **Identification Package** name (`com.Company.Product`) and **Minimum API Level** (Android 5.1).
12. Save the scene and save the project.

 For this walkthrough, we are going to target Android devices. We can do some basic settings now. This way, you can periodically do a **Build and Run** to see your progress on the actual device throughout the project.

Good, that's the basic project set up.

Setup the scene and folders

Next, we can set up the scene and project folder. First, replace the default **Main Camera** with Vuforia's **ARCamera prefab**:

1. Delete the **Main Camera** object from the **Hierarchy**.
2. Locate the **ARCamera prefab** in the `Project Assets/Vuforia/Prefabs` folder, select and drag it into the **Hierarchy** list.
3. Use **Add Component** to add the *Camera Settings* component to **ARCamera**.
4. Save the scene and project.

At this point, if you press the **Play** button in the Unity editor, you should see the video feed from the webcam camera. This will allow you to debug AR applications inside the Unity editor.

It's useful to now also create some empty folders in the Project Assets that we will use soon.

1. In the **Project** window, select the top-level `Assets/` folder.
2. Create a new folder in `Assets/` named `ARPlayBall`.
3. Within `Assets/ARPlayBall /`, create sub-folders that will be needed as we build up the project, named `Materials`, `PhysicMaterials`, `Prefabs`, `Scenes`, and `Scripts`. Your Project Assets folders should now look like this:

Importing the BallGameArt package

Now is a good time to import the `BallGameArt.unitypackage` assets. This package is provided from the publisher with the download files for this chapter. If you do not have access to these assets, that's OK, we'll suggest how to make substitutes now:

1. Choose **Assets** | **Import Package** | **Custom Package** to import `BallGameArt`.
2. Press **Ok**.

As shown in the following screenshot, the assets are organized in a hierarchy of folders. The package root folder is `BallGameArt`, with sub-folders for each of the ball games provided for the game and other assets. The basketball one, for example, includes FBX models, materials, and textures for the ball, basket with post, and game floor, as follows:

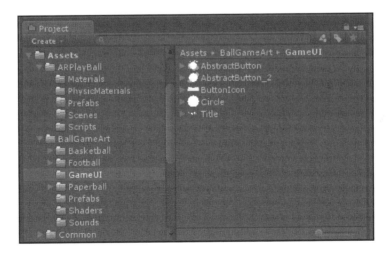

The package also includes a `Prefabs` folder with prefabs for fully constructed ball games for each game type, much like the **Boxball** game we created in this chapter, but without the component script that we will develop in this chapter.

Setting the image target

We want our game court to appear at the image target position in the world. You may choose any image target or marker you prefer. A playing-card sized one, like those used in Chapter 5, *AR Solar System*, might work well.

Choose an image target for the project. We are using a predefined image, stones in the StonesAndChips database provided with the Vuforia samples package. Print out a hardcopy of this image now if you need to. Let's set up the project to use this image target:

1. From the main menu, go to **Vuforia | Configuration** and then check the **LoadStonesAndChips Database** checkbox and **Activate**.
2. Drag the **ImageTarget prefab** from Assets/Vuforia/Prefabs/ into the **Hierarchy**.
3. In **Inspector**, set **Type**: Predefined, **Database**: StonesAndChips, and **Image Target**: stones (or whichever image you prefer to use).
4. Check the **Enable Extended Tracking** checkbox.

We want the target image graphics to remain anchored in 3D space (by default, the objects are anchored to the camera). We do this by setting the **World Center Mode** of the AR camera.

1. With **ARCamera** selected in **Inspector**, set **World Center Mode** to SPECIFIC_TARGET.
2. Then drag the **ImageTarget** onto the **World Center** slot in the camera's **Vuforia Behavior**.

Save the scene and the project. OK, now we can begin building our game.

Boxball game graphics

For our game we need a ball, a goal, and a court floor. The BallGameArt assets (in the package for this chapter available from the publisher) provide a variety of ball game graphics, which we will integrate into the project later. For now, we'll first make a simple set of white-box graphics to use during development. We'll call this game BoxBall.

White box, or **block design**, is a design method used in early stages of game level design, using simple geometric forms. By omitting details that do not affect object behavior and game mechanics, white box design affords us a quick way to focus on more critical aspects of the game and then come back to the visual design later.

Ball game court

Begin building the game assets in **Hierarchy.** Under **ImageTarget** create a root object for our game named `ThrowingGame` and then we'll create ball game graphics under that:

1. In **Hierarchy** with **ImageTarget** selected, create a child empty game object (**Create | Create Empty**), name it `ThrowingGame`.
2. Reset its transform if necessary (**Transform | gear-icon | Reset**) (as you should any time you create an object in a scene so we start with a clean transform).
3. With **ThrowingGame** selected, create an empty game object and name it `BoxballGame`.
4. We're going to put the floor and goal into a `Court` parent object.
5. In **Hierarchy**, with **BoxballGame** selected, create an empty object and name it `Court`.

For the floor plane, make a Unity 3D plane. Recall that Unity Plane objects are default 10 x 10 units, which we'll use as our default court scale also.

1. In **Hierarchy**, with **Court** selected, create a 3D plane (**3D Object | Plane**) and name it `Floor`.
2. In the Project `Assets/ARPlayBall/Materials` folder, create a new Material (**right-click | Material**) and name it `BoxballFloorMaterial`.
3. Set its **Albedo** color to something interesting (we picked a purple #7619FFFF).
4. Drag the new material onto the `Boxball/Floor`.

For the goal, as its name implies, we will make a simple box with a matt-like finish, as follows:

1. In **Hierarchy**, create an empty object as a child of **Court**, name it `Goal`.
2. As a child of **Goal**, create a **3D Cube**, set **Scale** (`2.2`, `0.2`, `0.2`) and **Position** (`0`, `1.5`, `1`).

3. Duplicate the **Cube** three times and set their transforms as follows:
   - **Position**: (0, 1.5, −1), **Rotation**: (0, 0, 0)
   - **Position**: (1, 1.5, 0) **Rotation**: (0, 90, 0)
   - **Position**: (−1, 1.5, 0), **Rotation**: (0, 90, 0)

4. In the Project `Assets/ARPlayBall/Materials` folder, create a new Material, named `BoxballGoalMaterial`.

5. Set its **Albedo** color to something interesting; we picked a green # 0AAB18FF, and adjusted **Metalic**: 0.5 and **Smoothness**: 0.1.

6. Drag the new material onto each of the **Goal** cubes we just created.

Lastly, for the ball, let's make it look like a metallic pinball:

1. In **Hierarchy**, with **BoxballGame** selected, create a 3D Sphere and name it `Ball`.
2. Set its **Scale** to (0.75, 0.75, 0.75) and **Position** to (0, 3, 0).
3. Create a new material named `BoxballBallMaterial`".
4. Set its **Albedo** to # BABABAFF, **Metalic**: 0.8, and **Smoothness**: 0.8.
5. Drag the new material onto the ball.

The scene **Hierarchy** should now contain the following:

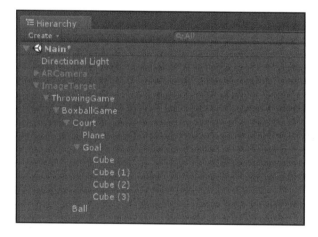

Save the scene. The resulting scene should look something like the following:

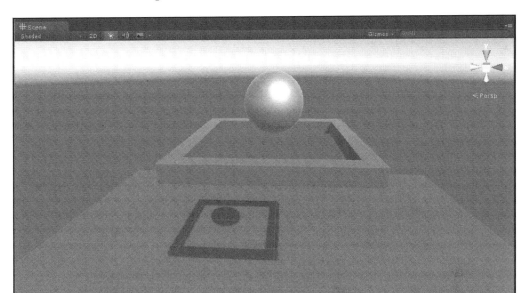

Press **Play** and point your camera at your image target. The game court should appear but it might be excessively over scale.

Scale adjustments

You may expect to adjust the scale of **ThrowingGame** relative to the **ImageTarget**. But if it's too small (for example, hundredths of a meter) that can affect Unity physics calculations in undesirable ways. So instead, we will adjust the **ImageTarget** scale too. We found that an **ImageTarget scale** = 3.0 works well in this project. Modify the object transforms as follows:

1. Select the **ImageTarget** and set its **Scale**: (3, 3, 3).
2. Select **ThrowingGame** and select the scale gizmo in the **Scene** window, then resize it so it fits the way you want relative to the image target, we used **Scale**: (0.06, 0.06, 0.06).

You may also decide to elevate the game court slightly above the image target plane (**Position Y**) so the texture does not bleed through in your **Scene** view. Set its **Position Y** = 0.005.

Now, let's make the ball bounce.

Bouncy balls

In Unity, the physics behavior of an object is defined separately from its shape (mesh) and renderer (material). The Unity physics engine controls the positional and rotational forces that affect the transform of an object, such as gravity, friction, momentum, and collisions with other rigid bodies. The items that play into physics include:

- **Rigidbody** component
- **Collider** component
- Physic material
- Project Physics Manager

So, two things will be needed to make our ball bounce. It must have a **Rigidbody** component, so the Unity physics engine will know to apply forces to it. In particular, we want the ball to respond to gravity. Secondly, we will apply a physic material so the ball not only falls, but then bounces when it hits another object.

To add a **Rigidbody**:

1. Select the **Ball** in **Hierarchy**, and **Add Component | Rigid Body.**
2. Check its **Use Gravity** checkbox.

If you press **Play** now, you will see the ball drop like a brick. It hits the floor and just stops. Let's make it bouncy by applying a physics material (Unity spells it without the "s").

1. In Project `Assets/ARPlayBall/PhysicMaterial`, create a new physic material (right-click **Create | Physic Material**).
2. Name it `BouncyBall`.
3. Set its **Bounciness** to `0.8`.
4. Set the **Bounce Combine** to **Maximum.**
5. Drag the **BouncyBall** physic material onto the Ball's **Sphere Collider's Material** slot, as shown in the following screenshot:

Note that pressing **Play** while **ThrowingGame** is a child of **ImageTarget** may cause the ball to fall infinitely because the Floor plane is not instantiated until the image target is recognized, but Unity begins applying gravity to the ball immediately. We will take care of this in scripting when we throw the ball. For now, to test your bouncy ball, you can move **ThrowingGame** to the root of the **Hierarchy**. Alternatively, you can uncheck **Use Gravity** in the Ball's **Rigidbody**, press **Play**, find the target image so the court is instantiated, then, in the editor, check **Use Gravity** to watch the ball drop and bounce.

Press **Play** now and the ball with bounce, slowly diminishing height, and eventually comes to a stop.

Bounce sound effect

Before moving on, let's add a sound effect when the ball bounces. If you've installed the **BallGameArt** assets, there's a sound effects folder with a sound named bounce. We'll play the clip when the ball collides with anything. Let's script it now and we'll explain colliders more when we add the **GoalCollider** later.

In your Project Assets/ARPlayBall/Scripts folder create a new C# script named PlaySoundOnHit and open it for editing:

```
File: PlaySoundOnHit.cs
using UnityEngine;

[RequireComponent(typeof(AudioSource))]
public class PlaySoundOnHit : MonoBehaviour {

    public AudioClip clip;
    private AudioSource source;

    void Start() {
        source = GetComponent<AudioSource>();
        source.spatialBlend = 1.0f;
        source.playOnAwake = false;
        source.clip = clip;
    }

    void OnCollisionEnter()  //Plays Sound Whenever collision detected
    {
        source.Play();
    }

}
```

Because we include the directive to require an AudioSource component, when we add this script to the ball, Unity will also add an AudioSource component. Let's do this now:

1. Drag the **PlaySoundOnHit** script onto the **Ball** as a component.
2. From the Project Assets/BallGameArt/Sounds folder, drag **Bounce** onto the **Clip** slot.

Bouncy, bouncy, bouncy ball!

Throwing the ball

We can now start building our game mechanics. The first step will be a script to throw the ball. The plan is that, when a new shot is available, the ball will appear at the bottom of your screen. The user taps and flicks the ball on the screen to throw it. This launches the ball into the 3D space and we will detect if the ball collided with the basket goal for a score. The stages of game play are:

- *Ready*: The ball is waiting for player input to play it, disable its Rigid body
- *Holding*: The player is dragging the ball (flick is in process)
- *Throwing*: The ball is travelling with physics

We will track the launch speed and direction of the throw as well as other properties that let us adjust characteristics of the ball and its throw.

Ready ball

To begin, in your Project `Assets/ARPlayBall/Scripts` folder create, a new C# script named `ThrowControl` and open it for editing. First, we'll write the following code that resets the ball to its *ready* state:

```
File: ThrowControl.cs
using UnityEngine;
using UnityEngine.Events;

public class ThrowControl : MonoBehaviour {
    public float ballStartZ = 0.5f;

    public UnityEvent OnReset;

    private Vector3 newBallPosition;
    private Rigidbody _rigidbody;
    private bool isHolding;
    private bool isThrown;
    private bool isInitialized = false;

    void Start() {
        _rigidbody = GetComponent<Rigidbody>();
        ReadyBall();
        isInitialized = true;
    }

    void Update() {
    }
```

```
void ReadyBall() {
    CancelInvoke();

    Vector3 screenPosition = new Vector3(0.5f, 0.1f, ballStartZ);

    transform.position =
Camera.main.ViewportToWorldPoint(screenPosition);

    newBallPosition = transform.position;
    isThrown = isHolding = false;

    _rigidbody.useGravity = false;
    _rigidbody.velocity = Vector3.zero;
    _rigidbody.angularVelocity = Vector3.zero;

    transform.rotation = Quaternion.Euler(0f, 200f, 0f);
    transform.SetParent(Camera.main.transform);

    if (isInitialized)
        OnReset.Invoke();
}
```

In `Start()` we get the ball's `Rigidbody` component and then call `ReadyBall`.

In `ReadyBall`, we position the ball a given distance from the camera, in 3D world coordinates so it appears half visible on the bottom of the screen. This is accomplished using the camera `ViewportToWorldPoint` function given the desired screen position and parent it to the camera. We also disable the ball's rigid body so the ball won't go anywhere right now.

`ReadyBall` also invokes an `OnReset` event, passing along the message to any listeners. Specifically, the `BallGame` component will want to know that the throw is done and ready to go again, so it can update the current score, for example:

1. Save the file.
2. And attach the script as a component of the **Ball**.

Press **Play**. You should see the ball at the bottom of the screen. If you want to adjust the apparent starting size of the ball, adjust its Z distance from the camera value. The following is a live capture of my screen with the ball in ready position and the game court instantiated:

Holding the ball

When the player begins to toss the ball, they'll touch and drag it in a *flick* gesture. We can add that now to the script.

Add the following to the top of the class:

```
private Vector3 inputPositionCurrent;
private Vector2 inputPositionPivot;
private Vector2 inputPositionDifference;

private RaycastHit raycastHit;
```

Add the OnTouch function:

```
void OnTouch() {
    inputPositionCurrent.z = ballStartZ;
    newBallPosition =
Camera.main.ScreenToWorldPoint(inputPositionCurrent);
    transform.localPosition = newBallPosition;
}
```

Update(), on each frame, handles user input. Note that we use the UNITY_EDITOR directive variable to conditionally include code for input via mouse versus input via mobile screen touch:

```
void Update() {
    bool isInputBegan = false;
    bool isInputEnded = false;
#if UNITY_EDITOR
    isInputBegan = Input.GetMouseButtonDown(0);
    isInputEnded = Input.GetMouseButtonUp(0);
    inputPositionCurrent = Input.mousePosition;
#else
    isInputBegan = Input.touchCount == 1 && Input.GetTouch(0).phase ==
TouchPhase.Began;
    isInputEnded = Input.touchCount == 1 && Input.GetTouch(0).phase ==
TouchPhase.Ended;
    isInputLast = Input.touchCount == 1;
    inputPositionCurrent = Input.GetTouch (0).position;
#endif
    if (isHolding)
        OnTouch();

    if (isThrown)
        return;

    if (isInputBegan) {
        if
(Physics.Raycast(Camera.main.ScreenPointToRay(inputPositionCurrent), out
raycastHit, 100f)) {
            if (raycastHit.transform == transform) {
                isHolding = true;
                transform.SetParent(null);
                inputPositionPivot = inputPositionCurrent;
            }
        }
    }

    if (isInputEnded) {
        if (inputPositionPivot.y < inputPositionCurrent.y) {
```

```
                    Throw(inputPositionCurrent);
                }
            }
        }

    void Throw(Vector2 inputPosition) {
    }
```

You can see we've separated the input states between isInputBegan and IsInputEnded. When it's began, we move the ball, mapping from screen coordinates of the input to world coordinates. When input ends, we will call Throw().

Save the script and, when you press **Play**, you can select and drag the ball across the screen.

Throwing the ball

Now, we'll add the throw when you release the ball. First, let's add a couple of public variables to help tune the throwing behavior:

```
public Vector2 sensivity = new Vector2(8f, 100f);
public float speed = 5f;
public float resetBallAfterSeconds = 3f;

private Vector3 direction;
```

And the Throw() function itself as follows:

```
void Throw(Vector2 inputPosition) {
    _rigidbody.constraints = RigidbodyConstraints.None;
    _rigidbody.useGravity = true;

    inputPositionDifference.y = (inputPosition.y -
inputPositionPivot.y) / Screen.height * sensivity.y;

    inputPositionDifference.x = (inputPosition.x -
inputPositionPivot.x) / Screen.width;
    inputPositionDifference.x =
        Mathf.Abs(inputPosition.x - inputPositionPivot.x) /
Screen.width * sensivity.x * inputPositionDifference.x;

    direction = new Vector3(inputPositionDifference.x, 0f, 1f);
    direction = Camera.main.transform.TransformDirection(direction);

    _rigidbody.AddForce((direction + Vector3.up) * speed *
inputPositionDifference.y);
```

```
        isHolding = false;
        isThrown = true;

    if (_rigidbody)
        Invoke("ReadyBall", resetBallAfterSeconds);
}
```

`Throw()` is called when the player untouches the screen to toss the ball. It enables the `Rigidbody`. Then, it figures out a force to apply to the ball based on how far the ball was flicked on the screen (`inputPositionDifference`), direction, and speed.

Press **Play**, toss the ball, and it goes flying into the scene!

Experiment with the ball sensitivity and speed parameters to get the game to work the way you like it. Our settings are shown in the following screenshot:

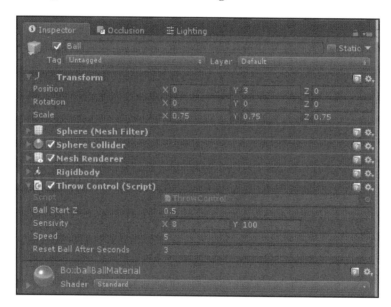

Detecting goals

OK, we can throw the ball. Now, we need to detect if you got a goal and keep score. To detect a goal, we will add a Collider to the goal and handle any collision events from the ball. When you make a goal, you should be congratulated with audio and visual feedback and the points added to your score. First, let's detect whether you've made a goal. In the next section, we'll tackle keeping score.

Goal collider

To detect a goal, we will add a 3D Cube game object with a collider to the basket. It will only be an invisible collider, that is, not rendered as part of the scene. We want collisions to trigger events, which we'll handle in a script:

1. With **BoxballGame** selected in **Hierarchy**, create a new 3D Cube, named
   GoalCollider.
2. Set its **Transform Position** to (0, 2.5, 0) and **Scale** (1.8, 0.05, 1.8).
3. On its **Box Collider** component, check the **Is Trigger** checkbox.
4. Remove its **Mesh Renderer** component (**gear-icon | Remove Component**).
5. The following screenshot shows the scene with **GoalCollider** before its renderer
   is removed:

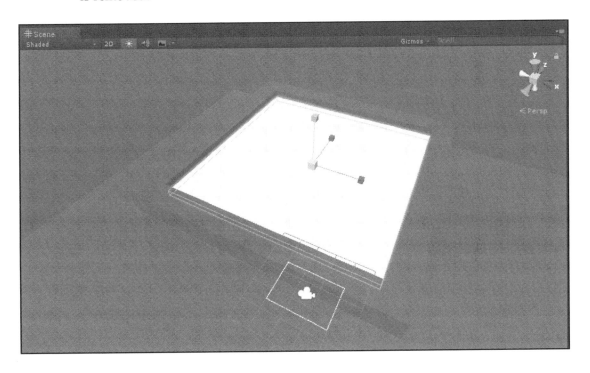

CollisionBehavior component

We will now write a `CollisionBehavior` script to handle the collision events on the goal. In the Project `Assets/ARBallPlay/Scripts/` folder, create a C# script named `CollisionBehavior`. Add the component to the `GoalCollider` object and then open it for editing. The full script is as follows:

```
File: CollisionBehavior.cs
using UnityEngine;
using UnityEngine.Events;

public class GameObjectEvent : UnityEvent<GameObject> {
}

public class CollisionBehavior : MonoBehaviour {
    public GameObjectEvent OnHitGameObject = new GameObjectEvent();
    public UnityEvent OnCollision = new UnityEvent();

    // used to make sure that only one event is called
    private GameObject lastCollision;

    void Awake() {
        //disables the renderer in playmode if it wasn't already
        MeshRenderer targetMeshRenderer = GetComponent<MeshRenderer>();
        if (targetMeshRenderer != null)
            targetMeshRenderer.enabled = false;
    }

    void OnCollisionEnter(Collision collision) {
        if (lastCollision != collision.gameObject) {
            OnHitGameObject.Invoke(collision.gameObject);
            OnCollision.Invoke();
            lastCollision = collision.gameObject;
        }
    }

    //So that the goal can be a trigger
    void OnTriggerEnter(Collider collider) {
        if (lastCollision != collider.gameObject) {
            OnHitGameObject.Invoke(collider.gameObject);
            OnCollision.Invoke();
            lastCollision = collider.gameObject;
        }
    }

    public void ResetCollision() {
        lastCollision = null;
```

```
        }


    void OnDisable() {
        lastCollision = null;
    }
}
```

In `Awake()` we just make sure the `collider` object won't be rendered. We already deleted the `Renderer` component from the object, so this won't do anything here, but just in case the developer forgets to remove or disable the renderer we take care of that.

The script implements handlers for `OnCollisionEnter`, `OnTriggerEnter` and `OnDisable`. It may seem redundant, but it's possible for Unity to trigger either `OnCollisionEnger` or `OnTriggerEnter` events (or both) for the same collision, we will handle both the same.

At the top of the script we define a new `UnityEvent` called `GameObjectEvent`. Our script will invoke the event on collisions so the UI and score keeper can respond to it.

The `OnCollisionEnter` and `OnTriggerEnter` functions are triggered by Unity physics. We check to make sure we don't already know about this goal and then invoke `OnHitGameObject` to notify the UI.

Save the script. Now we can implement the UI.

Goal! feedback

We need to tell the player when they've scored a goal. We can make a UI Canvas to display it with the following steps:

1. With **BoxballGame** selected in the **Hierarchy**, create a new **UI | Canvas**, named `GoalCanvas`.
2. Set its **Render Mode** to **World Space.**
3. For its **Rect Transform**, set **Scale** to (`0.02,0.02,0.02`).
4. And **Anchors**: Min (`0,5, 0.5`), Max (`0.5, 0.5`) and **Pivot** (`0.5,0.5`).
5. Then **Position** (`0, 4, 0`), **Width/Height**: (`100, 50`).
6. Set the **Canvas Scaler Dynamic Pixels Per Unit** to `4`, to give the text some higher resolution.

The **Canvas** gets a child **Panel**, which in turn gets a child **Text** element.

1. Add a child of **GoalCanvas**, create a **UI | Panel**, named `GoalPanel`.
2. Set its **Source Image** to `None` (**doughnut-icon | None**).
3. Set **Color** to white with no transparency (#FFFFFFFF).
4. Add a **UI Outline** component (**Add Component | UI | Effects | Outline**).
5. Set its **Effect Color** to something interesting, we chose Syracuse orange (#CF4515FF).
6. Set the **Effect Distance** to **X**=4, **Y**=-4.
7. Add a child of **GoalPanel** and create a **UI | Text**, named `GoalText`.
8. Set its **Anchor Presets** to **Stretch-Stretch** (anchor-icon in upper left) to center it, and also *Alt*+click **Stretch-Stretch** to set its position (0, 0).
9. Set its **Text** string to `Goal!`.
10. Use **Font Style: Bold, Font Size**: 27, **Alignment**: middle/center, and **Color**: #CF4515FF.
11. The resulting sign looks like this:

By default, the Canvas should be hidden. Then, when the player gets a goal, it is displayed.

1. Select the **GoalCanvas** in **Hierarchy** and disable it in **Inspector**.
2. Select the **GoalCollider** in **Hierarchy**.
3. In its **Inspector**, press the + on the **Collision Behavior** list.
4. Drag the **GoalCanvas** onto the **Object** slot, and select the **GameObject | Set Active** for the function, and check the checkbox, as shown in the following screenshot:

We only want the goal sign to stay up for a few seconds. Then, it should disable itself.

1. In Project `Assets/ARPlayBall/Scripts`, create a new C# script named `TimedDisable`.
2. Drag **TimedDisable** onto **GoalCanvas** as a component.

Now, open the `TimedDisable.cs` script for editing as follows:

```
File: TimedDisable.cs
using UnityEngine;

public class TimedDisable : MonoBehaviour {

    public float time = 4f;

    void OnEnable() {
        Invoke("Disable", time);
    }

    void Disable() {
        gameObject.SetActive(false);
    }
}
```

As its name implies, this script will disable the current game object, **GoalCanvas**, after it's been enabled for a specific length of time, such as four seconds.

Save your work. When you play the game, throw the ball, and make a basket, the *Goal!* sign will appear for a few seconds then disappear and the ball is reset to its starting position. Yes, it's challenging; try moving close to the target while testing the game. The goal will only be registered the first time because the `lastCollision` variable needs to be reset to null between goals. We'll do that in the upcoming `BallGame` script.

Cheers for goals

Before moving on, let's add some cheer! If we add an audio clip (**Audio Source**) to the goal panel and set it to play on awake, we can provide audio feedback in addition to the visual. We have provided a `cheer.mp3` audio file to use:

1. Select **GoalCanvas**.
2. **Add Component | Audio Source.**
3. Drag the **cheer** clip (in `Assets/BallGameArt/Sounds`) onto the **AudioClip** slot.
4. Ensure that **Play on Awake** is checked and **Loop** is not checked.

Now the game is even more exciting!

BallGame component

Now is a good time to add the `BallGame` component to our ball game.

The `BallGame` component is associated with each separate ball game. It uses the `ThrowControl` component to determine when the show is done and if the ball hit the goal. Then, it invokes a `Won` or `Lost` event accordingly.

We'll add a `BallGame` component to our **Boxball** game. When we add more games, such as basketball and football, they'll also have a `BallGame` component:

1. In the Project `Assets/ARBallPlay/Scripts/` folder, create a C# script named `BallGame`.
2. Add the component to the `BoxballGame` object.
3. And then open it for editing.

The full script is as follows:

```
File: BallGame.cs
using UnityEngine;
using UnityEngine.Events;

public class BallGame : MonoBehaviour {
    public ThrowControl BallThrowControl;
    public GameObject CourtGameObject;
    public CollisionBehavior GoalCollisionBehavior;

    public UnityEvent OnGoalWon;
    public UnityEvent OnGoalLost;

    private bool wonGoal;

    void Start() {
        BallThrowControl.OnReset.AddListener(OnBallReset);
        GoalCollisionBehavior.OnHitGameObject.AddListener(CheckGoal);
    }

    void OnBallReset() {
        if (wonGoal) {
            OnGoalWon.Invoke();
        } else {
            OnGoalLost.Invoke();
        }
        //Resets the game
        GoalCollisionBehavior.ResetCollision();
        wonGoal = false;
    }

    void CheckGoal(GameObject hitGameObject) {
        if (hitGameObject == BallThrowControl.gameObject) {
            wonGoal = true;
        }
    }
}
```

The BallGame component reference's the game's ThrowControl in order to determine that the game object in the goal is actually our ball (conceivably, the event could have come from anywhere). If so, we set wonGoal to true.

As explained in the beginning of the chapter, the OnBallReset will invoke an OnGoalWon or OnGoalLost event for the GameController to update the scoreboards. We do this in reset rather than when the goal first detected for effect and to give the ball a chance to bounce around the court.

Save the script. Then do the following steps:

1. Drag the **BallGame** script onto the **BoxballGame** object as a component.
2. Drag the **Ball** object onto the **Ball Throw Control** slot.
3. Drag the **Court** object from **Hierarchy** onto the **Ball** Game component's **Court Game Object** slot.
4. Drag the **GoalCollider** onto the **Goal Collision Behavior** slot.

If you **Play** at this point, the behavior of the game has not changed, but now we're ready to start keeping score.

Keeping score

When you score a goal, it should add to your score. If you miss, points are deducted from your score. Scores are displayed in the UI. We will also keep track of your all-time high score, using persistent storage. First, we'll create a UI for the score board.

Current core UI

The score board will be a canvas child of `ThrowingGame`:

1. With **ThrowingGame** selected in the **Hierarchy**, create a new UI | Canvas, named `GameCanvas`.
2. Set its **Render Mode** to **World Space.**
3. For its **Rect Transform**, set **Scale** to (0.015, 0.015, 0.015).
4. And **Anchors**: Min (0, 5, 0.5), Max (0.5, 0.5) and **Pivot** (0.5, 0.5).
5. Then **Position** (-1, 2.5, 1), **Width/Height**: (100, 100).
6. Set the **Canvas Scaler Dynamic Pixels Per Unit** to 4, to give the text some higher resolution.

The **Canvas** gets a child **Panel**, which in turn gets child **Text** elements:

1. Add a child of **GameCanvas**, create a UI | **Panel**, named `ScorePanel`.
2. Set its **Rect Transform Left**: -40, and **Right**: 40.
3. If you've installed the `BallGame` assets pack, set its **Source Image** to `Circle` (**doughnut-icon | Circle**).
4. And **Color** to Syracuse orange (#D64816FF).

5. Add a **UI Outline** component (**Add Component** I **UI** I **Effects** I **Outline**).

6. Set its **Effect Color** to white (#FFFFFFFF).

7. Set the **Effect Distance** to **X**=2, **Y**=-2 (border width).

Now, add the text elements for the score title and value:

1. Add a child of **ScorePanel** and create a **UI** I **Text**, named ScoreTitle.

2. Set its **Anchor Presets** to **Stretch-Stretch** (anchor-icon in upper left) to center it, and also *Alt*+click **Stretch-Stretch** to set its position (0, 0).

3. **Scale**: (0.75, 0.75, 0.75).

4. Use **Font Style**: **Bold**, **Font Size**: 16, **Alignment**: middle/top, and **Color**: #FFFFFFFF (white).

5. Set its **Text** to Score.

6. Duplicate the **ScoreTitle** and rename it ScoreValue.

7. Change **Font Size**: 35, and **Alignment**: middle/center.

8. Set its **Text** to 0.

The resulting score Canvas now looks like this:

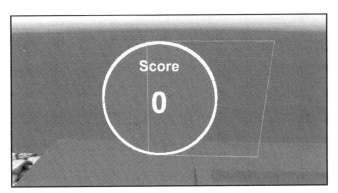

Game controller

The role of the game controller is to keep score and other game-wide features. For now, we'll just keep score. Let's add that as follows:

1. In the root of the **Hierarchy**, create an empty game object, name it GameController.

2. And reset its **Transform**.

3. In the Project `Assetts/ARPlayBall/Scripts/` folder create a new C# script named `GameController` and drag it onto `GameController` as a component.

Open the `GameController` script for editing as follows:

```
File: GameController.cs
using UnityEngine;
using UnityEngine.UI;

public class GameController : MonoBehaviour {
    public int hitPoints = 10;
    public int missPoints = -2;

    public BallGame ballGame;
    public Text scoreDisplay;

    private int playerScore;

    void Start() {
        ballGame.OnGoalWon.AddListener(WonGoal);
        ballGame.OnGoalLost.AddListener(LostGoal);
    }

    void WonGoal() {
        ChangeScore(hitPoints);
    }

    void LostGoal() {
        ChangeScore(missPoints);
    }

    void ChangeScore(int points) {
        playerScore = playerScore + points;
        if (playerScore < 0) playerScore = 0;
        scoreDisplay.text = playerScore.ToString();
    }
}
```

In the `Start` function, we register the `WonGoal` and `LostGoal` functions with the corresponding `BallGame` events, so the controller will update the game scores when the `BallGame` notices a hit or miss. The rest of the code is pretty self-explanatory.

Save the script. Now we just need to tell the game controller where to set the score value. Continue as follows:

1. Drag the **BoxballGame** object from **Hierarchy** onto the **GameController Ball Game** slot.
2. Drag the **ScoreValue** object from **Hierarchy** onto the **GameController Score Display** slot.

When you press **Play** and play the game, the score board is updated each time you make a goal.

Tracking high score

One more thing that would be good to have in our game is tracking the player's high score. For this, we not only need to keep the high score of the current session, but then persist that data so it's preserved for the next time you play.

First, we'll make a UI element to display the current high score. It will be easiest to simply duplicate the **ScorePanel** we just made and modify it:

1. Select the **ScorePanel** in **Hierarchy** and duplicate it (right-click and select the option **Duplicate**).
2. Rename it `HighScorePanel`.
3. Set the **Rect Transform** to **Left**: `-120`, **Top**: `50`, **Right**: `120`, **Bottom**: `-50`.
4. Rename child `ScoreTitle` to `HighScoreTitle`.
5. Change its **Text** to `High Score`.
6. Rename child `ScoreValue` to `HighScoreValue`.
7. Set **Font Style** to **Bold and Italic**, and **Color** to a pale orange (#FF9970FF).

The current high score will be kept in an ordinary C# object class named `PlayerProgress`. We can define that now. In your `Scripts` folder, create a new C# script named `PlayerProgress` and open it for editing:

```
File: PlayerProgress.cs
public class PlayerProgress {
    public int highScore = 0;
}
```

The GameDataManager component is responsible for saving and restoring data for the game. Create another C# script named GameDataManager and open it for editing as follows:

```
File: GameDataManager.cs
using UnityEngine;

public class GameDataManager : MonoBehaviour {

    private PlayerProgress playerProgress;

    public void Awake() {
        LoadPlayerProgress();
    }

    public void SubmitNewPlayerScore(int newScore) {
        if (newScore > playerProgress.highScore) {
            playerProgress.highScore = newScore;
            SavePlayerProgress();
        }
    }

    public int GetHighestPlayerScore() {
        return playerProgress.highScore;
    }

    private void LoadPlayerProgress() {
        playerProgress = new PlayerProgress();

        if (PlayerPrefs.HasKey("highScore")) {
            playerProgress.highScore = PlayerPrefs.GetInt("highScore");
        }
    }

    private void SavePlayerProgress() {
        PlayerPrefs.SetInt("highScore", playerProgress.highScore);
    }
}
```

Player data is saved and restored using Unity's PlayerPrefs API. When the app starts, Awake is called and it loads the current high score. When the game controller updates the current score, SubmitNewPlayerScore should be called to possibly update the high score and save it when it has changed.

For more information on using Unity `PlayerPrefs` see the Unity documentation at
`https://docs.unity3d.com/ScriptReference/PlayerPrefs.html`

Now we just need to modify the `GameController` to display the high score in the UI and check if it has changed:

Add the following code snippet at the top of the class add in `GameController.cs`:

```
public Text highScoreDisplay;
private GameDataManager gameDataManager;
```

In `Start()`, add the following code:

```
gameDataManager = FindObjectOfType<GameDataManager>();
highScoreDisplay.text =
gameDataManager.GetHighestPlayerScore().ToString();
```

Then, at the end of `ChangeScore()` add the following code:

```
gameDataManager.SubmitNewPlayerScore(playerScore);
highScoreDisplay.text =
gameDataManager.GetHighestPlayerScore().ToString();
```

Save the script. Then, in Unity:

1. With **GameController** selected in **Hierarchy**, add the **GameDataManager** script as a component.
2. Drag the **HighScoreValue** object onto the **High Score Display** slot.
3. Save the scene.

Now, when you press **Play** and play the game, the high score is updated when it's the highest score. Exit play mode, then press **Play** again, the high score is restored but the current score is reset to zero.

Congratulations! The game is looking really good so far. The following is a capture of a live play of the current game:

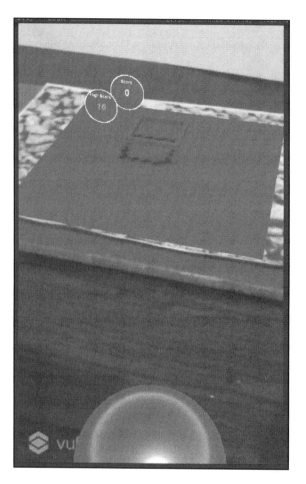

Augmenting real-world objects

You've probably realized that, although we're using AR to position the game objects, the video feed is little more than a background. For example, the ball bounces or rolls on our game court floor, but otherwise isn't realistically interacting with our table top surroundings.

To be a better *augmented reality*, the app needs to see and understand the table top environment. Different AR toolkit SDKs approach this problem differently, if at all. The Vuforia toolkit, for example, provides a feature called *Smart Terrain* that builds a surface mesh from your device's video feed. Similarly (but quite differently), the Microsoft MixedRealityToolkit builds a spatial mesh using its depth sensors and HPU chip and then provides Unity components for surface and smart object understanding. Presently, we will use the Vuforia tools.

About Vuforia Smart Terrain

Smart Terrain is Vuforia's environment reconstruction technique using the video camera on your device and computer vision algorithms in software. The SDK provides a simple authoring workflow and event-driven programming model that may already be familiar to Unity developers. If your device includes a depth-sensing camera, it will use that. For standard device cameras, the internal processing is similar to photogrammetry used in other software for scanning 3D objects as small as a coin or statuette (using a camera and turntable) and as large as an outdoor statue or an entire building (using quadcopter drones). With a small mobile device with just a standard video camera, the capability of Smart Terrain scanning is limited compared with depth-sensing ones, but still quite effective.

The following image, from the Vuforia example *Penguin* app, shows an example 3D mesh generated for a table top stage with detection of prop objects of various shapes and sizes:

For the end user, the SDK requires the staging area be set up with an initialization target and a limited number of prop objects (maximum five). When the app starts, it scans the stage and props to construct the 3D terrain mesh. Then the mesh can be augmented in real time in Unity.

Smart Terrain builds a 3D mesh of the object surfaces in view. When it detects an object in the real world on the table, what they call *props*, a new object is added to your Unity scene. The object added for a prop is defined by a prop template; this defaults to a cube, automatically scaled approximately to the extends of the physical prop detected.

The preceding example image includes the following recognized objects (apologies if you are reading this in black and white):

- A cylindrical can in the center of the table is the target object (Vuforia Object Recognition enabled), outlined with *blue* lines
- A Smart Terrain 3D mesh for the table surface, drawn with *green* lines
- Four props recognized (vase, cup, books, tissue box), represented with 3D cubes and drawn with *cyan* lines
- Once identified at runtime, the mesh and props can be used to occlude your computer graphics. For example, our virtual ball can roll behind one of the props on the table surface and it will be occluded in the AR view. Props can also use colliders to interact with objects and physics.

While the SDK may be *smart*, it is not general purpose, and is relatively low resolution. Also, it is best suited for near-range table top setups that are not dynamically changing, in well-lit stable lighting conditions. Like other image and object targets that can be used in Vuforia based apps, the geometry should have patterns and details characteristics as required for natural feature tracking (NFT image targets) and does not work with reflective or transparent object surfaces. As described in the Vuforia docs:

In general, Smart Terrain has been designed to work with a wide variety of commonly occurring table surfaces found at home and in the office. Ideal stage surfaces are either plain or present a uniform density of feature, and should be visually distinct from near adjoining surfaces.

For more details see
`https://library.vuforia.com/articles/Training/Getting-Started-with-Smart-Terrai`
n. There are some minimum system requirements that you should also check on that page.

We also recommend you look at the Vuforia example *Penguin* app for reference and instruction. We did. It can be found at
`https://library.vuforia.com/articles/Solution/Penguin-Smart-Terrain-Sample`.

User experience and app states

As explained in the Vuforia documentation, there are three phases of a Smart Terrain experience:

- A staging phase, where the user sets up a staging area, adding props and the initialization target
- A scanning phase, where the stage and props use in the setting are captured and reconstructed by the Smart Terrain tracker
- A tracking phase, in which the terrain is augmented in real time by the Unity scene you developed

In order to support the Smart Terrain phases and scanning we'll give the app one of a set of states and coach the player through them to set up the playing area. We will have the following states:

- `OVERLAY_OUTLINE`: During the detection phase, display instructions to the user to *Find Target* with the camera.
- `INIT_ANIMATION`: The animation that is played when the trackable is found the first time - then jump to the `SCANNING` phase.
- `SCANNING`: During the scanning phase, display the wire frame mesh in the scene, and show instructions to the user to **Pull back the device slowly** and display the **Done** button.
- `GAME_RENDERING`: when the user taps **Done**, before the game can be played, hide the wire frame mesh, invoke `OnStartGame`, and jump to the `GAME_PLAY` state.
- `GAME_PLAY`: this is where the user can throw the ball -- Hide the screen instructions, and show the **Reset** button.
- `RESET_ALL`: user taps the **Reset** button, reloads the level - User has pressed the **Reset** button, reload the level and reset the app state.

Keep this in mind when we implement the `AppStateManager` in the following section.

We can now start adding Smart Terrain to our game.

Screen space canvas

To support the app phases for Smart Terrain, we will introduce a screen space canvas that holds the instructions for the user and buttons for stepping through the phases. Let's build that now and then use it next. We will use some graphic sprites provided in the BallGameArt package; if you do not have these assets then just use default UI elements:

1. In the root of your scene **Hierarchy**, create a new **UI | Canvas** and name it ScreenSpaceCanvas.
2. Keep **Render Mode** as **Screen Space - Overlay**, but set **UI Scale Mode** to **Scale With Screen Size** and adjust the **Match** value to 0.5.

Create the title:

1. Under **ScreenSpaceCanvas**, create a child **UI | Panel** named TitlePanel.
2. Set its Anchor Presets to **Top/Stretch, Height**: 72, **Pos Y**: −36 so it stretches across the top of the screen.
3. Then remove its **Image** component (**gear-icon | Remove Component**).
4. As a child of **TitlePanel** create a **UI | Image** named TitleImage.
5. Set its **Source Image** to Title (provided in GameUI folder).
6. **Scale**: (0.15, 0.15, 0.15), **Width**: 1600, **Height**: 560.
7. Add **Component | Outline, Effect Color**: # D64816FF, **Effect Distance**: (10, −10).

Create the instruction panel:

1. Under **ScreenSpaceCanvas**, create a child **UI | Panel** named InstructionPanel.
2. Set its **Anchor Preset** to **Bottom/Stretch**.
3. Set its **Rect Transform Pos Y**: 105, so it rests on the bottom of the screen.
4. For **Source Image** use ButtonIcon, and set its **Color** to # D64816FF.
5. **Add Component | Aspect Ratio Fitter, Aspect Mode: Width Controls Height**, and **Aspect Ratio**: 2.5.
6. **Add Component | Outline, Color**: #FFFFFFFF, **Effect Distance**: (5, −5).

7. **Add Component | Vertical Layout Group**, **Spacing**: 5, **Control Child Size**: Check both **Width** and **Height**, **Child Force Expand**: Check **Width** but *not* Height.

8. For the **Vertical Layout Group Padding**, (you may need to unfold to reveal the slots) use 30, 30, 30, 10.

9. As a child of **InstructionPanel**, create a **UI | Text**, named InstructionTitleText.

10. Set it **Text** string to Instructions, **Font Style**: **Bold**, **Font Size**: 28, **Alignment**: Center/Top, **Color**: #FFFFFFFF.

11. Duplicate the **InstructionTitleText** and rename it InstructionText.

12. Set its **Font Style**: **Normal**, **Font Size**: 20, **Alignment**: Left/Top.

Create the complete button:

1. Under **ScreenSpaceCanvas**, create a child **UI | Button** named CompleteButton.

2. Set its **Anchor Presets** to Bottom/Right, **Scale**: (1.2, 1.2, 1.2), **Pos X,Y**: (-75, 75), **Width/Height**: (98, 98).

3. Set **Source Image**: AbstractButton_2, **Color**: # 513B34FF.

4. Edit its child Text element, **Text**: Complete, **Style**: Bold, **Size**: 12, **Color**: #FFFFFFFF.

Create the restart button:

1. Duplicate the **CompleteButton** and rename it RestartButton.

2. Change the **Image Source Image** to AbstractButton, **Color**: # D64816FF.

3. Change its child **Text** to say Restart.

If you followed along, the resulting screen Canvas should look like this:

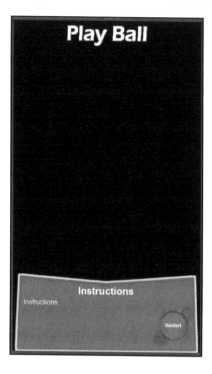

Looking good!

Using Smart Terrain

Presently, we've been using the AR Image Target in Extended Tracking mode. To use Smart Terrain, we will switch it to Smart Terrain instead. Then we will need to coach the user through calibrating the scanning at runtime, using the following steps:

1. With **ImageTarget** selected in **Hierarchy**, in **Inspector**, uncheck the **Enable Extended Tracking.**
2. Check the **Enable Smart Terrain** checkbox.

Checking the Enable Smart Terrain checkbox adds a `SmartTerrain_ImageTarget` prefab to your scene (if not, you can press the **New** button to instantiate a new prefab in the scene).

3. From the main menu select **Vuforia | Configuration**, then in **Inspector** check the **Smart Terrain Tracker | Start Automatically** checkbox, as shown in the following screenshot:

4. Select the **ARCamera** in **Hierarchy** and verify that the **World Center Mode** is **SPECIFIC_TARGET**.
5. Unfold the **SmartTerrain_ImageTarget** in **Hierarchy** and drag its **Primary Surface** object onto the ARCamera's **World Center** slot in **Inspector**, as illustrated in the following screenshot:

Handling tracking events

The default **ImageTarget** prefab that we added to our scene includes a **Default Trackable Event Handler** component. It implements the `ITrackableEventHandler` interface, specifically the `OnTrackingFound`, `OnTrackingLost`, and `OnTrackingChanged` events. We used these events and interface in earlier projects in this book.

For Smart Terrain and our app, we need a different implementation of this interface. Our implementation began with the Penguin example project provided by Vuforia for Smart Terrain. Like all good programmers, don't start coding from scratch when you don't need to! The implementation is slightly different from the `DefaultTrackableEventHandler` class in three ways:

- We provide the option to toggle children components (or not) when tracking is lost and found
- We toggle the **Canvas** component when tracking like other objects
- We send an event when an item is first tracked (to initiate our Smart Terrain)

Let's get started:

1. In the `Scripts` folder create a new C# script named `ImageTrackableEventHandler`.
2. Drag it onto **ImageTarget** as a component.
3. Remove the **Default Trackable Event Handler** component that we're replacing (**gear-icon | Remove Component**).

Open the `ImageTrackableEventHandler` script for editing and begin by defining the class and class variables that are initialized in the `Start()` function, as follows:

```
File: ImageTrackableEventHandler.cs
using UnityEngine;
using UnityEngine.Events;
using Vuforia;

public class ImageTrackableEventHandler : MonoBehaviour,
ITrackableEventHandler {

    public UnityEvent OnImageTrackableFoundFirstTime;
    private bool toggleOnStateChange;

    private TrackableBehaviour mTrackableBehaviour;
    private bool m_TrackableDetectedForFirstTime;

    void Start() {
        mTrackableBehaviour = GetComponent<TrackableBehaviour>();
        if (mTrackableBehaviour) {
            mTrackableBehaviour.RegisterTrackableEventHandler(this);
        }
    }
}
```

Next, add an accessor function to toggle state, which will be used by the UI:

```
    public bool ToggleOnStateChange {
        get { return toggleOnStateChange; }
        set { toggleOnStateChange = value; ToggleComponenets(value); }
    }
```

Now, we implement the `ITrackableEventHandler` interface functions, as follows:

```
    public void OnTrackableStateChanged(
                                    TrackableBehaviour.Status
    previousStatus,
                                    TrackableBehaviour.Status newStatus) {
        if (newStatus == TrackableBehaviour.Status.DETECTED ||
            newStatus == TrackableBehaviour.Status.TRACKED) {
```

```
            OnTrackingFound();
        } else {
            OnTrackingLost();
        }
    }

    private void OnTrackingFound() {
        if (toggleOnStateChange)
            ToggleComponenets(true);
        if (!m_TrackableDetectedForFirstTime) {
            OnImageTrackableFoundFirstTime.Invoke();
            m_TrackableDetectedForFirstTime = true;
        }

        Debug.Log("Trackable " + mTrackableBehaviour.TrackableName + "
found");
    }

    private void OnTrackingLost() {
        if (toggleOnStateChange)
            ToggleComponenets(false);

        transform.position = Vector3.zero;
        transform.rotation = Quaternion.identity;

        Debug.Log("Trackable " + mTrackableBehaviour.TrackableName + "
lost");
    }
```

Finally, the ToggleComponents function reaches all the child renderers, colliders, and canvases:

```
    void ToggleComponents(bool enabled) {
        Renderer[] rendererComponents =
GetComponentsInChildren<Renderer>(true);
        Collider[] colliderComponents =
GetComponentsInChildren<Collider>(true);
        Canvas[] canvasComponents = GetComponentsInChildren<Canvas>(true);
        // Enable rendering:
        foreach (Renderer component in rendererComponents) {
            component.enabled = enabled;
        }

        // Enable colliders:
        foreach (Collider component in colliderComponents) {
            component.enabled = enabled;
        }
```

```
            //Enable Canvases
            foreach (Canvas component in canvasComponents) {
                component.enabled = enabled;
            }
        }
    }
```

Save the script.

App state

Let's define the app states now, as described in the beginning of this section.

Create a new C# script in your `Scripts` folder named `AppStates` and edit it as follows to define an enum of the states:

```
File: AppStates.cs
public enum AppStates {
    OVERLAY_OUTLINE, INIT_ANIMATION, SCANNING, GAME_RENDERING, GAME_PLAY,
RESET_ALL, NONE
}
```

App state manager

We are going to add an `AppStateManager` to the project. Let's begin by making the object and then write the component script:

1. In the root of the **Hierarchy**, create an empty game object, and name it `AppStateManager`.
2. In the `Scripts` folder create a new C# script named `AppStateManager` and drag it onto **AppStateManager** as a component.

Open the `AppStateManager` script for editing, as follows:

```
File: AppStateManager.cs
```

First, we'll declare the appState and a large set of public variables that will be explained as we use them:

```
using UnityEngine;
using UnityEngine.Events;
using UnityEngine.UI;
using Vuforia;
```

```
public class AppStateManager : MonoBehaviour {

    private AppStates appState;
    //Vuforia scripts that are used to get the state of the app. Can be
found using FindObjectOfType<T>();
    public ReconstructionBehaviour reconstructionBehaviour;
    public SurfaceBehaviour surfaceBehaviour;
    public ImageTrackableEventHandler imageTarget;

    ///UI
    public GameObject instructionHolder;
    public Text instructionsText;
    public Button doneButton;
    public Button resetButton;

    //For the game
    public UnityEvent OnStartGame;

    //UI resources for instructions
    public string pointDeviceText;
    public string pullBackText;

}
```

The Start() function will register a listener for when tracking is first detected and set our state to INIT_ANIMATION:

```
    void Start() {
        imageTarget.OnImageTrackableFoundFirstTime.AddListener(
OnImageTrackableFoundFirstTime);
    }

    private void OnImageTrackableFoundFirstTime() {
        appState = AppStates.INIT_ANIMATION;
    }
```

The bulk of our state management is performed in Update(). The update action depends on the current state, where we use a big switch statement. This code directly follows the state definitions specified earlier in this section's *User experience and app states* topic. Begin writing the Update as follows:

```
    void Update() {
        //We declare the bool values here because we want them to be set to
false, unless the state is correct
        //This saves us from setting the values to false in each state.
        bool showDoneButton = false;
        bool showResetButton = false;
```

Now, we begin the big switch statement:

```
switch (appState) {
    //Detection phase
    case AppStates.OVERLAY_OUTLINE:
        instructionsText.text = pointDeviceText;
        surfaceBehaviour.GetComponent<Renderer>().enabled = false;
        break;

    // The animation that is played when the trackable is found for
the first time
    case AppStates.INIT_ANIMATION:
        appState = AppStates.SCANNING;
        break;

    // Scanning phase
    case AppStates.SCANNING:
        ShowWireFrame(true);
        instructionsText.text = pullBackText;
        showDoneButton = true;
        break;

    // When the user taps done. This happens before the game can be
played
    case AppStates.GAME_RENDERING:
        if ((reconstructionBehaviour != null) &&
(reconstructionBehaviour.Reconstruction != null)) {
            ShowWireFrame(false);
            surfaceBehaviour.GetComponent<Renderer>().enabled =
false;
            imageTarget.ToggleOnStateChange = true;
            reconstructionBehaviour.Reconstruction.Stop();
            OnStartGame.Invoke();
            appState = AppStates.GAME_PLAY;
        }
        break;

    //This is where the user can shoot the ball
    case AppStates.GAME_PLAY:
        instructionHolder.gameObject.SetActive(false);
        showResetButton = true;
        break;

    //User taps on [RESET] button - Re-loads the level
    case AppStates.RESET_ALL:
        //Reloads this scene
        UnityEngine.SceneManagement.SceneManager.LoadScene(0);
        appState = AppStates.NONE;
```

```
            break;

        // Just a placeholder state, to make sure that the previous
  state runs for just one frame.
            case AppStates.NONE: break;
        }
```

After the switch statement, we include logic to decide when to display the done or cancel buttons, as follows:

```
        if (doneButton != null &&
            showDoneButton != doneButton.enabled) {
            doneButton.enabled = showDoneButton;
            doneButton.image.enabled = showDoneButton;
            doneButton.gameObject.SetActive(showDoneButton);
        }

        if (resetButton != null &&
            showResetButton != resetButton.enabled) {
            resetButton.enabled = showResetButton;
            resetButton.image.enabled = showResetButton;
            resetButton.gameObject.SetActive(showResetButton);
        }
    }
```

That's the end if the Update function. It calls some helper functions as defined next, as follows:

```
    void ShowWireFrame(bool show) {
        WireframeBehaviour[] wireframeBehaviours =
  FindObjectsOfType<WireframeBehaviour>();
        foreach (WireframeBehaviour wireframeBehaviour in
  wireframeBehaviours) {
            wireframeBehaviour.ShowLines = show;
        }
    }

    //Called by the buttons
    public void TerrainDone() {
        appState = AppStates.GAME_RENDERING;
    }

    public void ResetAll() {
        appState = AppStates.RESET_ALL;
    }
```

I know this is a lot of code and I hope you don't mind following it, let alone typing it into your own app, but when you break it down, each section is just a few lines of code.

The completed code files are included with the downloadable files for the projects in this book from the publisher.

Wiring up the state manager

Back in Unity, we need to populate all the App State Manager variables:

1. With **AppStateManager** selected in **Hierarchy, d**rag the **SmartTerrain_ImageTarget** from **Hierarchy** onto the **Reconstruction Behaviour** slot.
2. Drag the **Primary Surface** (child of **SmartTerrain_ImageTarget**) from **Hierarchy** onto the **Surface Behaviour** slot.
3. Drag the **ImageTarget** from **Hierarchy** onto the **Image Target** slot.
4. Drag the **InstructionPanel** (child of **ScreenSpaceCanvas**) object onto **Instruction Holder.**
5. Drag **InstructionText** (child of **InstructionPanel**) onto the **Instruction Text** slot.
6. Drag the **CompleteButton** onto the **Done Button** slot.
7. Drag the **RestartButton** onto the **Restart Button** slot.
8. For the **Point Device Text**, enter `Find target`.
9. For the **Pull Back Text**, enter `Pull back the device slowly, then press Complete`.

The component should now look like this in the **Inspector**:

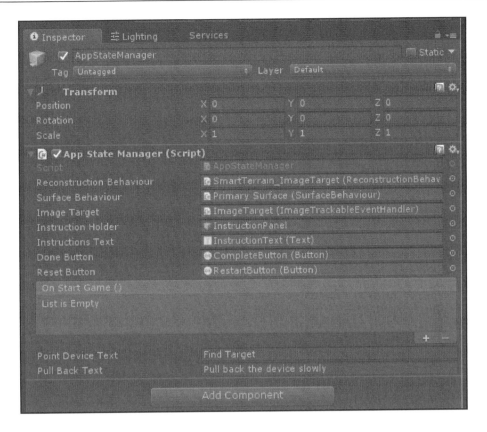

Next, we need to wire up the buttons:

1. Select the **CompleteButton** in **Hierarchy** then, in **Inspector**, add an **OnClick** event by pressing **+**.
2. Drag **AppStateManager** onto the **Object** slot and choose the **AppStateManager** | **TerrainDone** function.
3. For the **RestartButton**, also add to its **OnClick** list, drag the `AppStateManager` object, and choose the **AppStateManager.ResetAll** function.

Save the scene and save the project.

Now, when you press **Play**, you are first prompted to *Find target* and then asked to *Pull back the device slowly* until you press **Completed**. Then you can play the game, or at any point, press **Restart** to reset and start scanning again.

With Smart Terrain implemented, when you throw the ball it will bounce and roll not just on the court floor we created, but the actual table top and props in the real world. How cool is that?

Playing alternative games

We have provided a Unity package with several ball games, including basketball, football, and a paper ball. Each game has assets for goals, court floor, and balls, as shown in the following images:

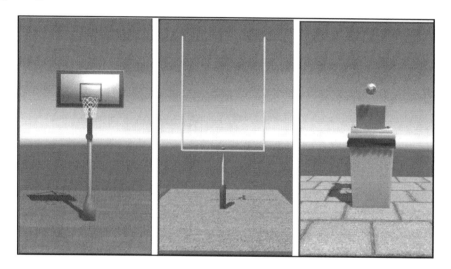

The following are the corresponding ball assets we provide for each ball game type:

We've designed the assets so each court, goal, and ball are together in its own prefab.

Setting up the scene with ball games

Let's add the new ball games to the scene and add the components they need, which we wrote in this chapter.

For each prefab basketball, football, and paperball:

1. From the Project `Assets/BallGameArt/Prefabs` folder, drag the prefab into the **Hierarchy** as a child of `ThrowingGame`.
2. On the ball game object itself, add the `BallGame` script as a component.
3. On its ball object, add the `ThrowControl` script.
4. On its goal object, add the `CollisionBehavior` script.
5. Add to the `OnCollision()` list, drag the **GoalCanvas** to the **Object** slot and set the `GameObject.SetActive` function, and then check the checkbox.
6. On the `GoalCanvas`, add the `TimedDisable` script.
7. On the **GoalCanvas**, add an **AudioSource** component, drag the `Cheer` sound file onto the **AudioClip** slot, and check **Play On Awake.**
8. With the ball game object selected, drag its ball onto the **Ball Throw Control** slot.
9. Drag its court onto the **Court Game Object** slot.
10. Drag its goal onto the **Goal Collision Behavior** slot.

At this point, you should be able to test each of the games individually one at a time, by disabling all the others under **ThrowingGame** except the game you want to play. Then, drag that ball game object onto the GameController's **Ball Game** slot. Try it! Remember, you can adjust the throw control sensitivity and ball speed, as well as the court and goal sizes for each game.

Activating and deactivating games

To automate the activation and deactivation of games we will modify the `BallGame` script to take care of that for its game objects. Edit `BallGame.cs` and add the following functions to enable or disable the ball, court, and goal:

```
File: BallGame.cs
    public void Activate() {
        BallThrowControl.gameObject.SetActive(true);
        CourtGameObject.SetActive(true);
        GoalCollisionBehavior.gameObject.SetActive(true);
    }
```

```
public void Deactivate() {
    BallThrowControl.gameObject.SetActive(false);
    CourtGameObject.SetActive(false);
    GoalCollisionBehavior.gameObject.SetActive(false);
}
```

Controlling which game to play

We can now make the GameController responsible for choosing and switching which games to play. We'll randomly pick a new ball game after each throw.

The GameController will be populated with the list of ball games, subscribe to their events, and then decide to activate or deactivate ones. Modify the script as follows:

```
File: GameController.cs
```

Replace ballGame with a list of ballGames, the current game index, and add a Boolean to ensure we initialize only once:

```
public BallGame[] BallGames;


private int currentGameIndex;
private bool isInitialized;
```

Then, add this code to Start():

```
for (int i = 0; i < BallGames.Length; i++) {
    BallGames[i].OnGoalWon.AddListener(WonGoal);
    BallGames[i].OnGoalLost.AddListener(LostGoal);
    BallGames[i].Deactivate();
}

isInitialized = true;
```

The following helper method will choose and activate a random game:

```
private void SetRandomGame() {
    //clears the last game
    BallGames[currentGameIndex].Deactivate();
    //sets a new game
    currentGameIndex = Random.Range(0, BallGames.Length);
    BallGames[currentGameIndex].Activate();
}
```

Then, the random game gets selected when the app starts and each time the player gets a goal:

```
public void StartGame() {
    SetRandomGame();
}

void WonGoal() {
    ChangeScore(hitPoints);
    SetRandomGame();
}
private void OnEnable() {
    if (isInitialized)
        SetRandomGame();
}
```

Back in Unity, we can now finish wiring up the controller and state manager:

1. Select the **GameController** in **Hierarchy**.
2. Unfold **Ball Games** and set **Size** to 4 (or the number of games you are using).
3. Then populate the list of **Ball Games** from the ball games in the scene **Hierarchy**.
4. Select **AppStateManager**, click + to add to the **OnStartGame** list, drag **GameController** onto the **Object** slot, and select the **GameController.StartGame** function.

There you have it! Our ball game is now a robust app that has multiple level variations.

Play it now. Build and run it for your Android device. You can follow instructions from earlier in the book to also build it for iOS mobile devices. Show it to your friends and family. Have a ball!

Other toolkits

Like each of the other projects in this book, we've been careful to isolate the platform and toolkit specific components from the core game objects and Unity features. If you've been following each of the projects in this book, you've seen the drill and we hope you'll rise to the challenge of trying this project with the other toolkits. Here are some hints:

- User input: The Apple ARKit and Google ARCore can use the same screen touch events as we did here. On HoloLens, you'd replace those with gesture and/or voice commands, in the `ThrowControl` script.

- For interacting with the real-world table top surface and prop objects: With ARKit, be sure to include the Unity Generate Plane component in the scene (see the *UnityARBallz* example scene). For ARCore, utilize the TrackedPlane class in your session (see `https://developers.google.com/ar/reference/unity/class/google-a-r-core/tracked-plane`). For HoloLens, simply include the spatial map in your scene.

Summary

In this chapter, we built a fun AR ball game. Just as mobile games have flourished, the potential opportunity for AR games is equally enormous. In our game, we use the desk or coffee table in front of you as the playing field, set up a ball game, and challenge you to throw balls at the target goal or basket. The game keeps score and lets you switch between multiple ball game levels.

We created a white box design for the first iteration, including a ball court with a floor and a goal. The goal has an invisible collider used to trigger events when the ball makes a hit. We relied on Unity events to bubble up messages from the collision and ball throw to the ball game manager and to the game controller. Each layer remains reasonably isolated from the other layers, allowing the app to be expanded to support multiple games and variations of graphic assets.

The AR started simply using an image target, but then we extended that to use Vuforia's Smart Terrain, which scans the environment to create a mesh of the table surface and physical objects (props). The ball appears to interact with both the virtual and physical worlds.

This concludes our journey and foray into the worlds of augmented reality development with Unity. We dove into details of Unity, various AR SDK (including Vuforia, open source ARToolkit, Apple ARKit, Google ARCore, and Microsoft MixedRealityToolkit for HoloLens) and multiple target platforms, while also exploring higher level concepts, principles, and best practices in AR, software engineering, computer graphics, and user experience design. The future is bright and, as it's been said before, the best way to predict the future is to help invent it!

Index